War Stories

WAR STORIES

*Suffering and Sacrifice in the
Civil War North*

Frances M. Clarke

The University of Chicago Press : Chicago and London

Frances M. Clarke is senior lecturer in the Department of History at the University of Sydney.

The University of Chicago Press, Chicago 60637
The University of Chicago Press, Ltd., London
© 2011 by The University of Chicago
All rights reserved. Published 2011
Printed in the United States of America

20 19 18 17 16 15 14 13 12 11   1 2 3 4 5

ISBN-13: 978-0-226-10862-9 (cloth)
ISBN-10: 0-226-10862-7 (cloth)

Library of Congress Cataloging-in-Publication Data
Clarke, Frances M.
    War stories : suffering and sacrifice in the Civil War North / Frances M. Clarke.
        p.   cm.
    Includes bibliographical references and index.
    ISBN-13: 978-0-226-10862-9 (cloth : alk. paper)
    ISBN-10: 0-226-10862-7 (cloth : alk. paper)
        1. United States—History—Civil War, 1861–1865—Personal narratives. 2. Soldiers'
    writings, American—Northeastern States—History—19th century. 3. Suffering—Social
    aspects—Northeastern States—History—19th century. 4. Sacrifice—Social aspects—
    Northeastern States—History—19th century. I. Title.
    E601.C553 2011
    973.7'8—dc22   2010048794

For my mother, Maureen Clarke

Contents

List of Illustrations : ix
Acknowledgments : xi
Prologue : 1

1 **Suffering in Victorian America** : 8

2 **Heroic Martyrs** : 28

3 **Exceptional Sufferers** : 51

4 **Labors of Love** : 84

5 **Noble Monuments** : 113

6 **Honorable Scars** : 144

Epilogue : 175
Notes : 189
Index : 245

Illustrations

1. Nathaniel Bowditch in his cavalry uniform   33

2. John F. Chase, a Union enlistee   73

3. Donation certificate for Philadelphia's Union Volunteer Refreshment Saloon   79

4. Frontispiece to Frank B. Goodrich's *The Tribute Book*   127

5. First page of Henry H. Chaffee's entry to a left-handed penmanship competition   149

6. First page of Lewis E. Kline's sample of left-handed penmanship   163

7. Alfred D. Whitehouse's entry in a second left-handed penmanship competition   166

Acknowledgments

I'M BOTH THRILLED and relieved that there's finally nothing left to do but thank all the people who've helped to get this book into print. I first began dwelling on the Civil War while studying at Johns Hopkins University under the supervision of two brilliant scholars of nineteenth-century America: Dorothy Ross and Michael Johnson. Along with Harry Marks, Michael Moon, and Larzer Ziff, they pressed me to identify more clearly the object of my study, which at that time was a rather vague notion that Northerners experienced and responded to the Civil War in ways that differed markedly from how participants would experience and react to later conflicts, and that such differences could be attributed to the culture of mid-nineteenth-century America. This may sound like a simple proposition, but trying to pin down the hows and whys turned out to be much like trying to nail jelly to a wall. Without scholars who asked hard questions and gave good advice, I might never have embarked on such a thoroughgoing transformation of my original, messy project.

I will always be tremendously grateful for the opportunity to study in the Hopkins History Department, not least for the lessons I learned while being grilled in Toby Ditz's exceptional writing workshops, or attending seminars run by Ron Walters, Dorothy Ross, and Mike Johnson. The friends I made during these years also had a profound influence on my professional and personal life, especially Nancy Berlage, Dirk Bönker, Carolyn Eastman, Tom

Foster, Michael Henderson, Katherine Hijar, Paul Kramer, Catherine Jones, Cameron Logan, Clare Monagle, Manon Parry, and Rebecca Plant. My friendship with Carolyn and Rebecca, in particular, has been one of the mainstays of my life. They have read and commented on every chapter—sometimes many times over—as well as providing countless memories and crucial intellectual sustenance over the years. I can't possibly thank them enough or find words adequate to express what their friendship has meant to me.

Along the way, I've been indebted to numerous institutions for providing critical financial or research support. Johns Hopkins awarded me a graduate fellowship, a Frederick Jackson Turner Travel Award, and research funding through the Bill and Louis Diamond Fund, which enabled me to complete graduate studies. Fellowships from the Pennsylvania Historical and Museum Commission and the U.S. Army Military History Institute in Carlisle, Pennsylvania, provided the initial time to develop this project, and archivists at both places directed me to material that turned out to be formative. I received additional fellowships from the Gilder Lehrman Institute in New York City, the Massachusetts Historical Society in Boston, and the Filson Historical Society in Louisville, Kentucky—each of which offered a wealth of material and a knowledgeable, supportive staff. In addition, I've gained valuable assistance from archivists at the New York Historical Society, the New York Public Library, the Manuscript Division at the Library of Congress, the National Archives and Records Administration in Washington, D.C., the Library Company of Philadelphia, the Duke University Rare Book, Manuscript, and Special Collections Library, and the Maryland Historical Society Library. In these days of inadequate funding for archives and libraries, I am particularly thankful to the staff who maintain the collections I've used and who have taken the time to answer my questions with patience and expertise (especially Richard Sommers and David Keough at the Military History Institute, James Holmberg at the Filson, and Trevor Plante at NARA).

It was a lucky coincidence that a position opened up in my field at the University of Sydney just as I went on the job market. I've now worked in the history department there for a number of years, but I still pinch myself at my good fortune. Many of our students are amazing, and I'm surrounded by brilliant colleagues. I feel extremely fortunate to have landed in a place with so many Americanists. First, there's the incomparable, indefatigable Stephen Robertson. I have no idea how I would have survived in my first few years without his support and counsel, or the friendship of his partner, Delwyn Elizabeth, and their daughter, Cleo. Then there's Shane White, a font of wisdom on the mysterious workings of the university and a giver of sage advice on everything from publishing and writing to music and African American history. Clare Corbould's dry humor has also helped to keep me sane, and her no-nonsense advice on making an argument clearer or a sentence more elegant has been invaluable. So, too, has Mike McDonnell's many, sometimes maddening questions. I can't imagine a colleague anywhere with more integrity or a better radar for waffling or imprecision. This is a much better book for their input.

I participate in two writing groups at the University of Sydney that have also helped to reshape this project at various points. Stephen Robertson organizes the American Reading Group. Many of its members—including all of my aforementioned American history colleagues, as well as Kate Fullagar, Brendan O'Connell, Blanca Tovias, and Ian Tyrrell—have offered useful questions and advice, for which I am grateful. The Gender History Writing Group has also read and commented on chapters. Its members—Kirsten McKenzie, Cindy McCreery, Penny Russell, and Mike McDonnell—are not only exceptional colleagues and scholars but true friends. I've learned a great deal from reading their work and hearing their comments. Penny has been particularly influential—both as an interlocutor, a mentor, and a friend. My sincere thanks to them all.

Many other people in Australia have enriched my academic and personal life while I finished the seemingly endless job of rewriting chapters. First among them is Glenda Sluga, a wonderful colleague and role model whom I couldn't do without. I've also been fortunate in having friends like Kate Blake and Sarah Gleeson-White in Sydney and Nancy Vaughan, Gwenda Tavan, and Genevieve Tavan-Lawson in Melbourne; they have picked me up and dusted me off when I needed them most, and reminded me what mattered. Without their collective wit and wisdom, my life would be very much impoverished.

I have spent a lot of time during the writing of this book flying back and forth between Australia and the United States. Numerous American friends have opened their homes to me and offered welcome respite from the archives or the blank screen. I'm tremendously grateful to Jane Schultz, one of my favorite Civil War scholars and now a favorite friend as well. I cherish the time I've spent at her home, and look forward to many more hours discussing sources and scholarship, and eating her delicious meals with her and her lovely daughter, Miranda. The Fairchild family also provided me with a home away from home on numerous occasions. Charles Fairchild lived with this project for years, listening patiently to many half-formed ideas and expressions of self-doubts. I am thankful for his support, and for that of the entire Fairchild clan: Lillie, Bill, Sheri, Bob, Keegan, Braden, Lyn, Phil, Stephen, Laura, and David. As I write these acknowledgments, I'm once again at the home of Rebecca Plant and Rand and Samuel Steiger, where I've spent many a joyful visit. When I think of everything that's best in America, it's you guys who come to mind.

For shepherding this book into print, I'd also like to thank my editor, Robert Devens, and his assistant, Anne Summers Goldberg, at the University of Chicago Press. I once had in mind an ideal editor, but Robert has raised the bar. I have many reasons to thank Robert, but foremost among them is his choice of reviewers. The astute remarks from the press's anonymous readers turned out to be vital in shaping my approach to revisions. Most of all, thanks to Stephanie McCurry for her generous support and invaluable comments.

Finally, I appreciate my family's encouragement over the years. Now numbered among them is Amanda Kaladelfos, who came along in the last few months of writing and turned my life around. The next book will be for you, my best beloved. To the rest of my family—my dad, Allan, and his partner, Marj; Kathleen and Steve; Andrew and Cam Van; and my beautiful nieces, Frances and Kathleen—thanks for only infrequently asking "why is your book taking so long?" I've dedicated this work to my mother, Maureen. Thanks for everything, Mum—but especially for the will to get this done.

Prologue

SHORTLY BEFORE the end of the Civil War, a story describing the death of a Union soldier appeared in one of the many hospital newspapers edited by convalescent troops. A chaplain, making his rounds among the sick and maimed, came upon an unfortunate fellow in the final throes of death. Asking if the man was ready to die, the chaplain watched as the soldier raised a trembling hand, motioning for pen and paper. "I am prepared to go to heaven," he wrote, "my trust in Jesus Christ is perfect." Underneath, he scrawled the title of the patriotic tune "Come, rally 'round the flag, boys." As the chaplain read the message aloud, a nearby patient who had lost an arm leapt from his bed and, "waving the mutilated stump in the air, burst forth with the glorious song his dying comrade had suggested." According to the author, the effect of this display was "electric," as a "thousand voices" took up the tune, transforming the place of suffering "with the thunder of melody." When the music ceased, the chaplain turned, "just in time to catch the last faint smile that flickered across the sunburnt face, as the soul was wafted on the strains of that Union music to the throne of liberty."[1] One sufferer's steadfast faith in God and country had irresistibly communicated itself to onlookers, converting anguish into inspiration.

Modern readers are quick to dismiss Civil War stories like this one as hackneyed nonsense. With its pitiable victim so clearly representing the standard ideal of the selfless patriot—his long service indicated by his weatherbeaten face, his uncomplaining agony registered through labored breath and trembling hands, his love of country unshaken till the end—such a tale cannot but strike a discordant note today. We are far more likely now to read war stories in which soldiers are not all God-fearing and courageous, death scenes are far from uplifting, and few men expire gently after turning their eyes heavenward in praise of their cause. Ever since World War I, the paradigmatic ironic or embittered writer who pits the "truth of his own vision against the lie of patriotism" has become the standard for truthful writing about war.[2] Those who question government actions, war's effects, or prewar ideals now command scholarly attention: anything else seems like a willful denial of war's horrors. As one preeminent historian commented some time ago, understanding the Civil War requires us to look only at those historical actors who "held a genuine interest in ideas and a powerful urge to find meaning and coherence in their experience" and to ignore "the many who avoid difficult issues and are content to speak in outdated clichés."[3]

This book starts from a different premise. Instead of assuming that only a few meditated on their surroundings while the rest spoke thoughtlessly, it takes seriously the favored stories that Unionists told about their response to wartime suffering. Some of these stories focused on the impressive character of sufferers themselves, applauding their conduct in the face of sickness or injury. Others described the equally laudable civilian response to suffering, charting the enormous scale of voluntary efforts and noting how Northerners maintained a tight-knit society by strengthening the bonds between men in the army and citizens at home. Invariably, these popular tales centered around figures who will be instantly recognizable to anyone familiar with the period: martyred Union officers, cut down while rallying their men; amputees who maintained their cheerfulness or piety despite agonizing wounds; kindly civilians who tenderly nursed the injured as if they were their own children; or dedicated volunteers working their fingers to the bone sewing uniforms or packing supplies. These stories—sentimental, idealistic, and patriotic—can be found in every collection of wartime poetry, songs, or essays, and in any archive containing Union soldiers' letters or diaries. Insisting that war's carnage could be redeemed, they portrayed suffering not as a physical occurrence affecting a single individual but as an opportunity for religious revelation, a chance to increase civic engagement and social cohesiveness, or a lesson in how to shape a strong character. Today these tales are viewed as mere curiosities that point to the war's Victorian origins. This study instead asks why they continued to be told and retold, no matter how high the death tolls climbed.

The question is worth posing because stories of Northerners' exceptional response to suffering retained their popularity against all odds. The Civil War was one of the largest and most vicious wars the world had ever seen. It killed and maimed hundreds of thousands, touching off mass protests in the North over hated draft laws, rising prices, and battlefield stalemates. Newspapers overflowed with discussions of flawed military leadership, administrative ineptitude, and corruption of every kind. An antiwar press and parts of the Democratic Party consistently denounced the war as brutal and unjust.[4] Meanwhile, the Union war effort underwent a series of changes that transformed both the original goals and strategies of Union commanders and the nature of warfare.[5] Given all this, it is remarkable that people continued telling tales that idealized Northerners' response to suffering.

In focusing on stories that did not appreciably change over the course of the war, and in looking solely at the appeal of these stories to a single group of pro-Union Northerners, this study goes against the grain of much recent writing on the Civil War. Contemporary scholarship tends to examine change over time and to focus on both the Union and the Confederacy. Above all, scholars have concerned themselves with demonstrating the extent to which the Civil War ushered in modernity. Indeed, one of the reasons why this conflict remains so intriguing is that it sits on the cusp of two eras. On one side stands a Victorian culture in which the majority viewed their world through religious and communal frames of reference, still worked the land or engaged in small-scale manufacturing, and retained a fundamental optimism in infinite progress and the likelihood that men of the right character would get ahead. On the other side stands the rise of corporate capitalism and the birth of modern warfare: the former with its army of wage-workers, its endorsement of mass consumption, and its faith in scientific and technological expertise; the latter with its mass slaughter, extended campaigning, and routine targeting of civilian morale. Scholars continue to debate whether this was the first modern war or the last Napoleonic one, querying the extent to which new technologies, military strategies, or modes of social organization signaled a fundamental break with the past.

Even as they contest the nature of these changes, most would agree that the Civil War significantly altered the nation's race relations, economy, political life, and social order.[6] There is far less agreement, however, on how this conflict affected its participants, leading to broader shifts in American culture. On the amorphous question of cultural change or continuity, two conflicting arguments stand out. First, numerous studies portray the Civil War as the catalyst for revising people's understandings of themselves and their place in the world. These studies tend to focus on men and women who wrote about the war's darker side, or who entered the war full of idealism but later came to question received dogmas. Seeking such wartime figures, scholars have found the same small number: writers like Walt Whitman, Ambrose Bierce, Mark Twain, and Emily Dickinson; or elite officers, such as Charles Francis Adams, John W. De Forest, and Oliver Wendell Holmes, to name the most prominent. By eloquently expressing their ambivalence toward war, these well-known commentators have come to hold a privileged place in histories portraying the Civil War as a cultural watershed. In the mid-1960s, historian George Fredrickson published one of the earliest and most influential of these accounts, arguing that wartime experiences prompted Northern elites to exchange their religious convictions and romantic idealism for faith in pragmatism and bureaucratic efficiency. Several decades later, Gerald Linderman advanced similar claims regarding Civil War soldiers, suggesting that the conflict shattered "prewar certainties," especially the belief that God controlled all earthly events. Most recently, Drew Gilpin Faust explored the way death and suffering caused a number of prominent thinkers to move further in the direction of religious skepticism and materialism.[7] Relying on widely recognized writers and intellectuals as representative of broader cultural change, these and other studies suggest that the Civil War generation's confrontation with suffering caused a profound "crisis of belief" that forever altered American culture.[8]

In contrast, those who study mainstream thought—reflected in the writings of common soldiers, lesser-known authors, and the mass of ordinary civilians—suggest that no such abrupt cultural shift was evident by war's end. Critics of the war's literary output, indeed, have long bemoaned this fact, pointing to the failure of wartime writers to produce literature capable of encompassing the conflict's less heroic aspects, its cowardice and terrors, slaughter and disease, social turmoil and inequality.[9] If the guileless sentimentality and unabashed patriotism of most wartime writing distinguish it as a product of its time and place, so too does the widely noted lack of cynicism in Civil War soldiers' letters and diaries. As numerous studies have shown, these men did not, on the whole, follow a trajectory typical of later wars, in which soldiers grew increasingly detached from homefront sentiment and disillusioned with their prewar ideals.[10] They consequently produced nothing even vaguely resembling the mass of embittered, ironic, or brutally realistic war commentary that poured forth from those who fought in twentieth-century conflicts.[11] Nor did the majority emerge from war questioning God's providence.[12] In fact, religious convictions not only remained intact, according to Mark Schantz's new study, they helped to ensure the war's continuance and limit protests over steadily mounting casualties by imagining death as redemptive, holding out the possibility of eternal bliss, and aestheticizing battlefield fatalities. "In the religious world of the Civil War soldiers, and that of the families to which they returned when the war was done, nothing fundamental had changed," agrees historian Stephen Woodworth. "Indeed, one of the most remarkable aspects of the Civil War may be how little it changed, rather than how much. The idea that the Civil War wrought significant changes in the foundation of the American Republic may be the greatest illusion of U.S. history."[13]

Rather than choosing between change and continuity, or trying to determine the precise nature of the war's effects on American culture, I start from the paradox that in the midst of change a great deal remained the same. The majority of Northerners remained optimistic about the potential for progress at war's end. They continued to believe in a loving God who controlled their destinies. They remained convinced that the war had vindicated democratic republicanism and positively remade their society by knitting citizens closer together. And they confidently asserted that their victory resulted not from superior numbers or technology, but from the voluntary participation of virtuous men and women in a divinely ordained cause. The persistence of these beliefs requires explanation, for it was by no means inevitable. A war of this magnitude had the potential to create far greater cultural ruptures than it did. Rather than denying that the war wrought significant changes on American culture, this study seeks to show how people mobilized stories about suffering in response to some of the war's most wrenching transformations. Unlike recent histories that point to the endurance of religious or political frameworks that spanned both regions of the country, it looks at how people told stories for their own specific ends, appropriating and using idealized tales of suffering and sympathy to cope with loss, define personal and national identity, achieve wartime unity, and give meaning to their experiences.[14] Drawing attention to a vociferous British and European debate over America's war, it illuminates the transatlantic context in which these tales gained credence.

In the broadest sense, stories that idealized the Northern response to suffering appealed because they allowed their tellers to contain the conflict's potential impact on some of their most cherished beliefs. The Civil War threatened the foundations of Northern culture in no uncertain terms. At a time when many saw family bonds as the bedrock of the social order and the mainspring of manly character, this conflict removed millions of young men from their homes. It threw them together with others who scorned religion, drank or gambled, swore or stole; it taught them how to kill. During a period in which citizens still viewed standing armies as powerful threats to liberty, the war subsumed the nation's men into rigid hierarchies, sacrificing their most prized attributes of individualism and autonomy to military expediency, in a move that had the potential to bring men home stripped of independence, self-control, and moral virtue. Would they follow the frightening precedents set by Europe and return to become a plague on peaceful society? Equally worrying, the war's burdens obviously fell most heavily on the poor. In an era when middle-class Northerners widely proclaimed their society's classlessness, well-publicized inequalities—especially among soldiers' families—threatened to expose the myth of Northern egalitarianism, unleashing social conflict and atomization on a mass scale. Likewise, at a moment when America stood as one of the world's few democratic republics, an isolated island in a sea of monarchies, European spokesmen attacked the core of Northern nationalism, portraying the Union war effort as evidence of hypocrisy and democratic excess. Most significantly, the sheer scale of the war, with its anonymous deaths and unmarked graves, threatened to make the suffering of countless individuals a pointless waste.

The stories examined herein directly addressed these looming possibilities. The people who created them were not mouthing simplistic platitudes. They were engaged in an effort to take control of wartime carnage, invest it with meaning, and turn it to individual, political, and cultural advantage. For every image of a battle-hardened, cynical soldier, Unionists presented an innocent blue-eyed boy, grateful to have sacrificed life or limb in a noble cause. For every blood-soaked field littered with anonymous corpses, they held up a portrait of volunteers kindly ministering to the wounded. For every suggestion that the war's costs were unevenly distributed, they produced an image of unified volunteers generously giving up time and money to support the Union; for every indication that they were engaged in vicious slaughter, they replied with a depiction of compassionate Northerners engaged in an unparalleled effort to mitigate suffering and civilize warfare. What follows is an attempt to chart what these stories did for their tellers, concentrating not on their truth or falsity, but on the reasons for their enduring appeal.

After exploring the meanings and politics of suffering in mid-nineteenth-century America, this book focuses on five of the North's most popular tales of wartime suffering: stories that depicted Union officers' heroic deaths; those that described the behavior of white enlistees in confronting wounds and sickness; tales focusing on the effects of voluntary efforts on suffering men; those that imagined the beneficial impact of Northern voluntarism on warfare itself; and, finally, some of the most pervasive stories of all: those featuring Union amputees as the conflict's most evident and inspirational victims.

Each of these tales is told from a different perspective, using a range of different sources. There is the story of a single officer, told through the letters, diaries, and memorials that his family collected in the wake of his death.

There are stories of ordinary white sufferers conveyed by those who worked among the wounded, as well as by soldiers themselves in their private writings. There are tales about what voluntarism meant for sufferers as well as what it said about American society, expressed through white Northern volunteers' published and unpublished writings. Finally, there are portrayals of Union amputees, told from the perspective of hundreds of limbless men who narrated their injuries for penmanship competitions staged in the war's immediate aftermath. Comparing these stories to those told in earlier and later conflicts, it is possible to see that what at first glance looks like the trivial and generic utterances common to all wars were, in fact, specific to their time and place and meaningful in precise ways to their tellers.

Placing stories of sufferers side-by-side with those of their caregivers also makes it clear that these disparate tales of suffering shared a similar logic: stories that soldiers told about their suffering required an audience of receptive civilians, just as civilians' stories about their efforts to mitigate suffering only made sense in light of soldiers' responses. Mutually reinforcing and often told together, these tales ultimately transformed what could easily have become a destabilizing reality into an affirmation of Unionism, religious faith, civic cohesion, self-controlled manhood, and American exceptionalism. That was precisely their point.

Within a few decades of the Civil War, Northerners would become much less interested in tales of suffering soldiers and sympathetic civilians. By the turn of the century, an altered economic, political, and religious climate, new medical understandings, and different ways of conceptualizing gender identity and civic participation led both women and men to rewrite their war stories—a shift charted in the epilogue. Emphasizing the equal heroism of white soldiers on both sides of the conflict, these new narratives of war celebrated a sectional reunion that elided the nation's on-going history of racial discrimination, as many scholars point out.[15] But they also did something else that has received little comment: by directing attention toward battlefield participation and bravery, these new war stories made the idealization of suffering, once apparently so sensible and crucial, now seem merely irrelevant and insincere.

1

Suffering in
Victorian America

NOT ALL WARS are the same. When people suffered in the Civil War, they had experiences that were in many ways unique. Bullets continued to pierce skin and bone in later wars, memories of suffering still recurred unbidden, but the way these impacts were felt and understood necessarily changed over time. Pain, and by extension suffering, has never been simply a bodily phenomenon. Suffering exists at once in the body and the mind. It is impossible to separate the physical sensations of pain from the context that makes sense of those sensations. Pain exists "only as we perceive it. Shut down the mind and pain too stops. Change the mind (powerfully enough) and . . . pain too changes."[1] Emerging at the intersection between mind, body, and culture, suffering has been experienced and understood variously in different times and places. It has been used differently as well, as individuals mobilized their culture's specific understandings of suffering for their own particular ends. To comprehend why Northerners responded to suffering in certain ways, or told certain stories about their response to war's carnage, it is thus necessary to start with the range of historically and culturally specific meanings that were given to suffering and sympathy in Victorian America.

People shared an intimate acquaintance with suffering at this time. Women entered the birthing room knowing they had a high likelihood of dying.[2] Parents commonly lost young children, and their offspring regularly stood at the gravesides of brothers and sisters, mothers and fathers. Even as late as 1870, fewer than 10 percent of Americans reached the age of fifteen with both of their parents and all their younger siblings still living. Average life expectancy at mid-century stood at a mere thirty-nine years of age. Rampant diseases like cholera, smallpox, and yellow fever periodically tore through cities and towns, leaving behind thousands, sometimes tens of thousands, of dead. Shocking numbers were killed or maimed at work, left to fend for themselves without the aid of pensions or workplace safety rules. Equally frightening, spiraling cycles of inflation and depression constantly threatened to bring misery down upon the heads of vulnerable wage laborers.[3]

Individuals responded to this abundant suffering in class-specific ways. Privileged Americans are well known for having created an elaborate cult of death in an effort to tame the terrors of the grave. Far from keeping death hidden, they laid out bodies in family parlors and actively monitored the dying to ensure they adhered to prescribed ideals of deathbed behavior. The bereaved did not look for "closure" when funerals ended in the manner of modern Anglo-Europeans. Instead, they continued to hold death close, cherishing physical mementos of the departed in the form of post-mortem photographs, mourning jewelry made from the deceased's hair, or printed eulogies. Creating what historian Mark Schantz calls a "death embracing culture," genteel Americans communed with the dead at spiritualist séances, constructing intricate bereavement rituals, ornate cemeteries, and a literary culture saturated with sentimental death scenes.[4] And they shared class-based understandings of suffering, too, especially a belief that other classes and races were less prone to suffering and less capable of sympathizing with distress.

The fiction of an insensible working class helped to rationalize enormous disparities in suffering among different classes in Victorian America. In poor urban neighborhoods low wages, inadequate diets, and unsanitary living conditions all took their toll, contributing to astronomical rates of disease and mortality.[5] Living hand-to-mouth, wageworkers confronted the constant prospect of job loss and thus the distinct possibility of starvation. Nor could they escape the suffering of others. The poor were daily surrounded by the sights and sounds of pain: the howls of animals being slaughtered in city abattoirs or sliced apart in open butcher shops; the shrieks and groans of the sick in neighboring tenement rooms; the whipping of draft animals on city streets. Refusing to submit passively, sizable numbers of working-class men chose to stare down violence and danger instead. Some did so by consuming newspapers filled with lurid murders; others followed the fictional exploits of heroes who set out to conquer alien lands and peoples or joined in blood sports like bare-knuckle prize-fighting, bear baiting, ratting, or cock-fighting. Continuing a long tradition of reveling in displays of aggression and riotous disorder, these popular urban pastimes implicitly shunned an evolving middle-class embrace of nonviolence and respectability.[6]

Working-class Northerners also had their own ways of confronting death. They did not simply imitate middle-class mourning practices. Most lacked the funds needed to purchase specially designed outfits or ornaments testifying to their grief. They could not cloister themselves for a designated mourning period, send out black-bordered stationery announcing their loss, erect a decorative headstone, or purchase post-mortem photographs of the dead. Such complex and costly expressions of grief were only available to people who had the time, money, and motive enough to engage in them. The death of a poor Northerner was a relatively austere affair: a short church service for the lucky ones, followed by burial in a pine box beneath a grave marked by a simple wooden or stone headboard, and perhaps a day of two of grieving with family and friends before work resumed.[7]

Yet although class differences divided Northerners in terms of the extent of their suffering and responses to bereavement, powerful assumptions about pain and suffering also cut across and blurred class lines. Most important, no matter their station, all nineteenth-century people were born in a prebacteriological era. This simple fact had important ramifications for the way suffering was understood. Most crucially, it meant that physicians could not claim a monopoly over the treatment and comprehension of affliction. Since they were unable to diagnose or cure disease successfully, their professional standing was necessarily limited. Why pay a hefty fee to a physician with dubious healing credentials when one could rely on patent medicines or prayer to have an equally beneficial impact? Tens of thousands of ordinary people asked themselves this question, judging by the increasing volume of homemade remedies and popular elixirs consumed in the first half of the century. Moreover, physicians not only had to compete with itinerant salesmen and traditional treatments, they also had to contend with a growing range of alternative healing therapies and theories—ranging from homeopathy to hydropathy—all of which promised ordinary people the power to manage their own health and well-being. When it came to comprehending suffering, professional medicine was just one voice among a plethora of others.[8]

It was also the case in the prebacteriological era that trained physicians and healers did not necessarily *want* to eradicate suffering, for many viewed pain as a positive sign of medical intervention. For doctors, a patient's visible discomfort proved that they had acted decisively on the body. Until well into the nineteenth century, these external proofs were all that physicians had to go on in gauging the effect of their treatments. Their senses—not stethoscopes, microscopes, or x-rays—were their only guides. Believing that disease was identical to its symptoms—that all illnesses produced exterior signs, without which no illness existed—physicians imagined that removing symptoms cured disease. Judging their treatments solely in terms of their external impact, physicians could at least be sure that painful therapies would always produce "visible and predictable physiological effects."[9]

Moreover, some nineteenth-century physicians believed that pain itself could be medically efficacious. Anesthetics like ether and chloroform had been tested with great fanfare in America by the 1840s. Yet for decades thereafter, doctors refused to dispense pain relief indiscriminately, even during some forms of major surgery. Part of the reason lies in their understanding of the therapeutic and moral value of pain. In drawing the line between life and death, medical men accepted the fact that pain signaled vitality, whereas loss of consciousness tended to augur death. Pain thus seemed critical for well-being and for life itself. "Painful ... sensations all require sound and healthy organs," declared one physician in an American medical journal in 1826. "It is, therefore, our axiom, that the greater the pain, the greater must be our confidence in the power and energy of life."[10] Given this belief that pain was integral to existence, both physicians and laypeople typically thought of suffering as functional in medical treatment. Bodily discomfort offered both patients and their doctors the reassurance that at least something was being done to alleviate symptoms, that symptoms were responding to a physicians' intervention. Indeed, patients sometimes preferred painful remedies "because they could *feel* them working"—a fact that makes it a little easier to understand why so many submitted to treatments, such as blistering or the use of powerful emetics, that must have been agonizing.[11]

At the same time, physicians assumed that various social groups experienced pain in different ways. Few thought of individuals as utterly unique in this era. Most took it for granted that human variations, where they existed, were capable of being classified, codified, and predicted—and doing so, of course, was a favorite Victorian pastime.[12] Imagining that certain kinds of people felt more pain than others (both physiologically and psychologically), privileged white spokespeople such as novelists, philosophers, and physicians classified sensitivity to pain in hierarchical terms. At the top were refined white women, their delicate nerve fibers so responsive to the slightest sensation that they were constantly overcome by headaches, flutterings of the heart, and fits of weeping.[13] This imagined chain of human sensitivity descended all the way down to those deemed "savage," whom many whites supposed to be practically immune from pain. Class, social condition, age, race, sex, nationality, and overall health were all crucial determinants in the arrangement of this hierarchy. In the minds of white commentators, black women were impervious to many of the sufferings that afflicted white ladies; above them on the chain were stoic white yeomen, supposedly less vulnerable to pain than educated and cultured white men, but more susceptible than either brutalized slaves or the toughened and debased Irish working class, paupers, criminals, and so on.[14] In line with this hierarchy of suffering, notes historian Martin Pernick, physicians dispensed anesthetics to some patients rather than others, based on beliefs about how much pain different individuals could or should bear.[15]

Popular Anglo-European travel writing helped to substantiate these views. For over a century, intrepid explorers had returned home bearing witness to the pain-free existence of primitive others. They described men who faced ritual mutilation with stolid indifference and women who gave birth effortlessly, briefly withdrawing for a quick, trouble-free labor before returning to work with an infant strapped to their backs.[16] These images of stoic savages seemed to confirm that social progress necessarily led to an increasing susceptibility to pain and suffering. Over time, suffering itself thus became a marker of whiteness, refinement, and class status, in turn signaling civilization and full humanity.

Whereas the experience of suffering offered a convenient yardstick for measuring superiority, a range of additional arguments, drawn from theology, medicine, and philosophy, lent added support to the idea that pain had a measure of value. Certain strands of Christianity emphasized pain as divine punishment for human sinfulness, a useful warning to mend one's ways. The diverse medical sects and theories that sprang up in the first half of the nineteenth century were similarly united in viewing pain as a helpful cautionary device. From hydropaths to homeopaths, all imagined that pain derived from and signaled a transgression in need of correction, despite their various assumptions about the source of transgression (with some pointing to the contravention of "natural laws" and others to failures in personal hygiene, intemperance, or faulty environments).[17]

Beyond these specific arguments lay an older and more amorphous valuation of pain, one that still exists today, although to a much more limited extent: that is that anything gained without suffering is worthless. Philosophers updated this timeless precept in the late eighteenth century by suggesting that pain and suffering were essential elements of human freedom. Scottish common-sense philosophers, in particular, argued that without consequences, freedom would be meaningless and autonomy correspondingly diminished. Freedom lay not in abolishing pain, in their view, but in the ability to make choices and to experience the costs or benefits of one's actions—a doctrine that was pervasive in nineteenth-century American religious and political thought.[18]

Yet while pain itself continued to hold an array of positive meanings in Victorian culture, the opposite held true for the purposeful infliction of suffering. By the early nineteenth century, the act of causing suffering or taking delight in another's pain had increasingly come to indicate primitiveness or perversity. Alongside their exotic tales of people living devoid of pain, travel writers had catalogued a litany of foreign practices—including cannibalism, head hunting, scalping, and human sacrifice—all seemingly designed to inflict maximum suffering on enemies. They used these ritualistic inflictions of pain as a sure indication that so-called primitive cultures were lacking in progress and enlightenment. Conversely, they assumed that advanced civilizations were fundamentally less aggressive and bloodthirsty, capable of dealing with transgressors or enemies through nonviolent statecraft or legal sanction.

A broad shift in modes of discipline, underway since the Enlightenment, helped to buttress these arguments. By the early nineteenth century, authorities no longer routinely demonstrated their power by publicly inflicting painful or deadly punishments. Whippings and executions in the town square— once relatively common spectacles in the Anglo-European world—had by this time given way to allegedly more humane prison sentences or other forms of private, legally sanctioned redress. A host of social movements had arisen simultaneously, aimed at curtailing the instrumental use of pain. Antiflogging societies had been formed to agitate against whipping sailors; pacifist societies were asserting the immorality of war; abolitionists had started speaking out against the cruelties of slaveholders; antidueling societies were critiquing the resort to pistols; childrearing experts had begun counseling parents to spare the rod; antivivisection societies had mobilized to limit the cruel treatment of animals; and reformers across the North were taking up the cause of all manner of powerless sufferers, from asylum inmates to schoolchildren.[19] Everywhere in the so-called civilized world, humanitarianism was on the rise.

This flourishing of sympathy generally relied on an extension of compassion to groups or individuals once considered unworthy of such regard. Yet at a time when many believed the disenfranchised felt no pain, how could someone judge whether another person was suffering in a fully sentient way that demanded sympathy and respect? Such judgments depended entirely on who was doing the judging. Martin Pernick identifies the way Victorians distinguished between "insensitivity" and "endurance." Whereas the "insensitive" supposedly lacked the human capacity to feel pain and were thus contemptible, those who "endured" did so in spite of their agony, nobly conquering their pain and thereby becoming worthy of respect and compassion.[20] Deciding between these alleged states ultimately came down to subjective moral judgments (is this person worthy? Is he or she behaving as I would under like circumstances?), although this was not generally recognized at the time. What many Victorians clearly *did* see is just how crucial such judgments were in determining who received social, legal, and political rights. It is no accident that abolitionists linked their appeals so closely to images of slave bodies in agony or supplication. In order to gain white support, abolitionists first had to subvert slaveholders' pronouncements that their human property was content, incapable of fully registering the pain of family separation, oppression, or physical punishment. They did this by trying to demonstrate that what slaveholders depicted as slaves' insensitivity was actually either heroic endurance or intense agony.[21] In other words, they worked to turn the hierarchy of feeling on its head, picturing anguished slaves tormented by callous and debased white slave-owners.

Abolitionists were hardly alone in using this particular strategy. Diverse groups of Northern reformers in the antebellum years called for better treatment of powerless groups by pointing to instances of genuine anguish among those once thought of as insensate or depraved. Reform literature of the period is filled with vivid descriptions of suffering: long passages portraying the mortification of fallen women; gruesome accounts of asylum inmates shackled to walls and screaming in pain; heartrending scenes of young sailors debased by cruel treatment, yet eager for a kind word. Even animals were dramatically reimagined around this time. No longer did they appear as they had for centuries, as "bundles of lust, greed, and ferocity." Increasingly, reformers portrayed beasts that exhibited a range of feelings once reserved for humankind, from pride and fear, to grief and parental regard. Drawing from the currents of Romanticism, sentimentalism, and Protestant evangelicalism, reformers set out to make the pain of others visible, to legitimate the suffering of slaves, paupers, prostitutes, wives, the insane, and the disabled, in an effort to better their treatment.[22]

It might now seem obvious that reformers would seek to demonstrate and portray suffering among the oppressed in order to bring about political change. In fact, there was nothing either inevitable or timeless about using suffering in this way. The scenes of suffering that so pervaded Victorian culture came to be meaningful in a whole range of ways only because of the relatively new importance that philosophers, theologians, novelists, and others had, from the mid-eighteenth century onward, begun granting to sympathy in particular and to the role of emotions in determining moral sense more generally.

Some of the first thinkers to direct their attention to this subject were philosophers, among them the third earl of Shaftesbury Anthony Ashley Cooper, Francis Hutcheson and his star pupil Adam Smith, along with lesser luminaries of the Scottish common-sense tradition. Writing during a period when Britain's commercial empire was expanding, touching off a scramble for wealth and status, they had started to wonder what "glue" would bind individuals together as fixed hierarchies began to erode. What would now provide the underpinnings of civil society, they questioned, and how could moral behavior be both understood and facilitated in this more fluid world of individual profit-seeking? In debating these problems, most Scottish moralists rejected two influential ways of thinking about human nature then current: the first articulated by Thomas Hobbes, who pictured a perpetually warring humanity coming together only out of self-interest; the second represented by John Locke's image of unformed individuals as *tabula rasa*. Human nature for both Hobbes and Locke was amoral at best. To this rather discouraging vision, Shaftesbury and his followers responded by suggesting that every individual was endowed with an innate moral sense. To know right from wrong, they argued, people only had to examine their own subjective responses and then act according to the dictates of their emotions and intuitions—a more positive view of human nature that would come to be embraced by large numbers of Northerners.[23]

For these philosophers, dwelling on suffering was the best means of generating sympathy and thereby accessing and refining one's moral sense. Here they drew from the work of Adam Smith, whose enormously influential *Theory of Moral Sentiments* (1759) attributed a crucial role to sympathy in the creation of fellow feeling. Beginning with the premise that human beings exist within social worlds, Smith argued that morality developed as individuals sought to harmonize their feelings and passions in response to their fellows. This was a delicate process that involved precisely calibrating sentiments, expressions, manners, and emotions so that they aligned as closely as possible to one's interpretation of the feelings of others.[24] In other words, Smith recommended the cultivation of a refined sensibility. "Cultivation" is the appropriate metaphor to use here, for Scottish moralists believed that although God had planted the seeds of moral sense, an ethical community only developed where individuals nurtured their innate capacities. For Smith, the process of cultivating sensibility would necessarily be incomplete, given the impossibility of ever fully entering into another's feelings. Nevertheless, he memorably argued, when "our brother is upon the rack," it is still possible to form some "conception of what are his sensations." "By the imagination we place ourselves in his situation," he wrote, "we enter as it were into his body, and become in some measure the same person with him."[25] Such sympathetic connections, forged by willed acts of imagination and self-examination, were for Smith the basis of benevolent action and sociability.

These ideas might have been confined to the dusty bookshelves of gentlemen's libraries or to discussions among an educated elite if not for the fact that a similar interest in the place of sympathy and suffering in social life had simultaneously begun to pervade religion and culture. The emphasis that Scottish common-sense philosophers placed on an innate moral sense, accessed through emotion and intuition, dovetailed with the broad transformation in religious sensibilities that took place across the entire range of Protestant denominations in post-Revolutionary America, one that both helped to propel and received enormous impetus from the Second Great Awakening of the early nineteenth century. As many scholars have noted, most Protestant ministers and their congregants by this time had come to reject orthodox Calvinism's insistence on original sin and predestination, as well as the Calvinists' vengeful God who sanctified pain and eternal damnation as just desserts for the wicked. Nineteenth-century churchgoers instead embraced a much more optimistic creed, one that provided a space for free will in enabling salvation, held out hope of human perfection, and pictured a benevolent God working toward this end.[26]

This broad liberalization of Protestantism transformed the way many of the faithful conceived of suffering. Thinking about or experiencing suffering has always held an important role in Christian theology. The vision of Christ, beaten and bleeding on the cross, is supposed to engender humility and gratitude in Christians, inspiring them with the knowledge that by virtue of Christ's sufferings their sins had been redeemed. Both the Old and New Testaments depict suffering as the most direct path to salvation, sometimes also as proof of God's love (as in Hebrews 12:6: "whom the Lord loveth, he chasteneth"). As churchgoers began to imagine God more as a merciful, compassionate parent than a stern and vengeful patriarch, however, they ceased to dwell so often on his purposeful infliction of pain, or on the extravagant agonies of the Passion.[27]

Yet if they no longer concentrated on the pain that God meted out or suffered on their behalf, ordinary Protestants increasingly focused on everyday instances of suffering for two significant reasons. First, in generating religious knowledge and conversion, ministers had started to stress the importance of feeling and emotion rather than doctrinal study or rational reflection—a shift brought about in large part by the more positive image of individuals as repositories of an inborn moral sense. Whereas God had formed humankind with a moral core, most ministers, much like Scottish moralists, did not believe that accessing one's moral recesses was automatic or involuntary. Granting a significant role to free will in bringing about the conditions necessary for conversion, they advised the faithful that dwelling on instances of suffering helped to create sympathetic feelings, allowing the activation and development of moral sense. Ultimately, the goal they aimed for was the creation of hearts vulnerable to emotional appeal and thus prepared to accept God's grace. For the majority of nineteenth-century Northerners, who believed in the possibility of salvation, there was simply no greater imperative than such a preparation, particularly during wartime when death was so ever-present.

A second and related shift also helps to account for why Protestants increasingly turned their minds to routine instances of suffering. As historian Elizabeth Clark and others have noted, the nineteenth century witnessed an "innovation in pulpit storytelling." Ministers increasingly abandoned lengthy biblical exegesis and began looking beyond the Bible for their cautionary tales and moral precepts. Drawing strength from the broad democratization of American society, preaching now became far more anecdotal, relying on stories drawn from everyday life—especially those representing ordinary sufferers whose religious convictions allowed them to triumph over adversity. Telling their flocks to look to their own emotions as the ultimate source of moral guidance, preachers worked to generate powerful emotion by dwelling on the pitiful, poignant, and tragic.[28]

It would be difficult to overemphasize the strength and intensity of religious belief in antebellum America. Fueled by a series of massive revivals, various forms of evangelical Protestantism quickly gained mass converts in the first half of the century. Although it is notoriously difficult to put a precise figure on the number of active churchgoers in this period, it is certain that they constituted a sizable majority of the population. By 1860 approximately 4 million of the nation's 27 million free citizens were formal members of Protestant churches. Adding this figure to the majority who attended religious services before, or without, becoming members, and taking into account the number of Protestant churches, one historian notes that "had all the Protestant church buildings in America been filled on any given Sunday morning in 1860 more than two-thirds of the nation's population would have been in attendance."[29]

Still, these statistics only hint at the pervasive reach of evangelicalism by mid-century. This was a time when Christian beliefs permeated all aspects of American culture, forming a crucial frame of reference through which the majority understood their world. Religious observance suffused the rhythms of most people's social lives, which took place in and around Sunday sermons, weekend Bible classes, and daily readings of scripture at kitchen tables or before fireplaces. Ordinary people took religious instruction seriously, with even the most humble writers commonly discussing the texts of sermons in their private writings.[30] Those who avoided church likewise found it impossible to escape the teachings of what historian Sydney Ahlstrom terms the "quasi establishment" of American Protestantism. With substantial social prestige, religious leaders presided over virtually all important events and institutions in the antebellum North. Their "moral attitudes and basic teachings were honored by lawmakers, and dominated newspapers and text books," writes Ahlstrom. "The faculties and curriculum of the public schools and even state universities were molded according to [their] specifications." Until the post–Civil War era, religious spokesmen continued to pronounce on every issue or event with undeniable authority, despite—or partly because of—a widely feared rise of profanity and a growing influx of Catholic immigrants that followed in the wake of industrialization and urbanization.[31] When it came to understanding suffering, therefore, it was their voices and beliefs—not those of physicians, scientists, or agnostic intellectuals—that held the greatest weight.

An acceptance of divine providence lay at the core of evangelical belief, shaping the way the mass of ordinary people confronted affliction. According to providential thinking, God actively directed the course of daily events according to his own mysterious design. No suffering took place beyond his knowledge or outside his divine plan. Abraham Lincoln reflected this perspective in his second inaugural address when he told citizens that God had willed the previous four years of bloodshed. For Lincoln, God's plan to remove the sin of slavery would purify national politics.[32] Others expressed a closely related conviction that God had delivered suffering to chasten his people, to counteract their selfishness and materialism and create emotions that might bind society together through powerful feelings. The majority of Northerners held fast to their providential understandings of suffering throughout the war, believing that the nation was headed in a progressive direction despite the madness of the battlefields.[33]

Accepting that God did all things well, even if they could never hope to penetrate divine reasoning, true believers exhibited pious submission in the face of suffering, actively resigning themselves to God's will. Doing so enabled them to become inspirational figures, capable of mobilizing others with the strength of their beliefs. Historian Heather Curtis describes the way female invalids used pious suffering as a path to religious influence and prestige, relying on gendered notions of female submission and piety.[34] But in a period of widespread evangelical adherence, the same beliefs could easily be applied to pious male sufferers as well, drawing from a Christian tradition of male martyrdom of which Jesus was the ultimate exemplar.

As anyone familiar with Victorian literature will readily attest, readers at this time did not have to go far to find stories of admirable sufferers, nor did they have to attend church. They only had to pick up practically any book or magazine published from the early nineteenth century onward to read tales in which commendable victims demanded their sympathies. According to the extensive scholarship on Victorian sentimentalism, almost all of the most popular novels published in the first half of the century made it a great virtue and badge of class status for readers to shed tears over the less fortunate.[35] Sentimental novels offered readers something else as well: a world in which humble, patient victims regularly affected extraordinary transformations in their onlookers. Little Eva, the central character in Harriet Beecher Stowe's *Uncle Tom's Cabin*, is the best-known fictional sufferer who worked such a change. It was her angelic death that finally taught the young slave, Topsy, the virtues of goodness and religion—a transformation that both the violence of the slaveholder and the rationality of an educated New England matron had been powerless to achieve.[36] In the bestselling temperance tales of the era, drunkards likewise came to see the error of their ways after witnessing the damage they did to long-suffering wives and families. And in countless domestic novels, women educated husbands and children by exhibiting patience and selflessness in the face of wayward behavior. The act of suffering was consistently held up in Victorian fiction as the most powerful means to influence witnesses positively and effect their spiritual transformation. Just as regularly, Victorian writers depicted the contemplation of suffering as a way of inculcating and expressing refined sympathies and uplifting the soul.

The continual appeal of suffering in antebellum literature and religion points to one of the central paradoxes of Victorian culture: at the same time that many Northerners were seeking to eradicate the willful infliction of pain, they nonetheless continued to hold up certain kinds of suffering as inspirational to experience or to behold. If feeling pain in full measure reflected one's humanity, then witnessing pain likewise allowed for the cultivation and exhibition of the "right" kinds of sympathetic response, and being an ideal sufferer granted an ability to propagate religious faith. Causing intentional pain had come to be seen by the majority as debasing, but contemplating or embodying ideal suffering might still be ennobling, even sublime.

Large numbers of people in the first half of the nineteenth century, then, valued suffering—either as experience or spectacle—in ways that most people in the Anglo-European world no longer do. Doctors and their patients viewed pain as an integral aspect of medical treatment. Influential Scottish common-sense philosophers highlighted the value of suffering to freedom and pointed to an innate moral sense that could orient human beings toward compassion and benevolence if only they practiced sympathizing with those in distress. Privileged whites identified their vulnerability to pain and their response to suffering as a measure of superior humanity. Protestant ministers and their congregants dwelt on scenes of suffering as a way to access moral sense and heighten receptiveness to God's grace. And sentimental novelists aestheticized and idealized victimhood, often depicting exemplary suffering as a form of social power. All of these interpretations of the meaning and value of suffering, and others besides, help to account for why Northerners throughout the war so often represented or sought to embody idealized suffering. Despite the fact that we still hold certain kinds of suffering as worthy of contemplation or imitation, contemporary commentators no longer value suffering in the range of ways or with the intensity that many of our mid-nineteenth-century forebears did.

Yet this is not to say that every American in the past valued suffering in the same way. In the period before the Civil War, it was respectable Northern whites who most often contemplated, represented, and responded to scenes of suffering rather than those living in slaveholding regions of the country, for it was among the former group that the relatively new meanings placed on sympathy and sentiment were most important in constituting class and gender. While the social order and economy of the South continued to be based around slavery, the early nineteenth-century North witnessed the emergence of industrial capitalism and wage labor. New domestic ideals and arrangements provided the crucial ideological and material underpinning for this changing economic order.[37]

The transformation of domestic life among middle-class Northerners encompassed both a reordering of the ideal relations between family members and a new set of ideas relating to privacy and the importance of emotional bonds. Forsaking an earlier model of patriarchal authority, Northern commentators had come to depict marriage as a contract underpinned by love and mutual respect by the early nineteenth century. Childrearing experts had likewise started urging parents to treat children with utmost kindness. Instead of meting out physical punishment, they were now supposed to gain control over their offspring by giving or withholding intense affection and by inculcating guilt and shame, the idea being to instill an internal conscience in children that would exist even in parents' absence—a more suitable model for the increasingly anonymous, mobile, and heterogeneous society that middling Northerners now encountered.[38] With the rise of industrialism creating new distance between home and work for growing numbers of middle-class people, the task of rearing children and supervising home life increasingly fell to women. The ideal home—reconceived as a tranquil space, the antithesis of the marketplace—became the repository for all those qualities now supposedly lacking in public life, from altruism and morality to gentleness and nurture. Ostensibly governed by virtuous mothers, home was widely depicted in the North as the crucial site in which people learned the value of sympathetic connections.

Below the Mason-Dixon line, by contrast, white men continued to rule over farms and plantations, with work and home life remaining as closely linked as they had ever been. Slave-owners were hardly eager to give up the use of corporal punishment, so necessary in controlling their slave-labor force, just as they were less likely to idealize motherhood in light of their frequent need to destroy slave families on the auction block.[39] The antebellum South did not witness anything like the flourishing of reform activity that took place in the North aimed at alleviating various kinds of suffering. Nor did elite Southern men celebrate the private home as a tranquil space headed by virtuous mothers. Although there was a growing urban bourgeoisie in certain parts of the South, this group had neither the political clout nor cultural capital of their Northern counterparts.[40]

Of course, neither section of the country was homogenous. Given that large numbers of Northerners continued to work the land, and a sizable working-class population either performed paid work within their homes or lived in domestic situations far removed from genteel standards of privacy or propriety, it would be inappropriate to draw too sharp a distinction between North and South.[41] There were plenty of Northerners who took their pleasure in the rowdy street life and bawdy entertainments that might be found in any urban center, just as there were respectable Southerners who schooled their sons in self-control and looked askance at dueling, honor-bound planters.[42] Nevertheless, it would be just as reductive to believe that home and domesticity (and the sympathetic connections supposedly forged there) did not come to mean something very different for large numbers of people in those places where slavery—a system that organized human relationships and family life as much as labor—had been eradicated.[43]

The Civil War was a struggle not simply between two divergent economic systems. At issue were also the domestic relationships and sentiments that many Northerners believed these different economies produced.[44] When free-labor enthusiasts like Frederick Law Olmsted traveled to the antebellum South and returned home to vent their opposition to slavery in print, they were clear on what they saw as the debasement of family life, white morality, and Southern culture more broadly, which went along with an economy dependent upon slave labor. The picture that Olmsted painted of the South was one in which poor whites lived in single-room shacks with dirt floors and untended gardens; where blacks and whites mingled promiscuously; where roads were bad, schools and community life nonexistent, and whites, in general, lazy, immoral, and immune to violence.[45] The North's sense of moral superiority over the South, in other words, derived in large part from what free-labor defenders viewed as the more virtuous domestic arrangements that their society depended upon and produced. For Olmsted, Northern domesticity and free labor nurtured men of self-restraint and moral fiber, whereas the Southern slave system bred white men of abnormal self-indulgence and immorality—men who failed to respect the value of a hard day's work and gave free rein to the kind of violent passions that would incite the war.

These stereotypes of white Southern culture added another important layer of meaning to white Northern idealizations of wartime suffering and the responses it supposedly produced. For most pro-Union commentators, the way their soldiers suffered, and the manner in which white civilians responded, was precisely what distinguished their war effort from that of the Confederacy. If most Northern whites readily conceded that Southern soldiers were equally brave on the battlefield, it was because the moral superiority they sought to claim rested on character traits better exemplified by sufferers and their sympathizers than by combat participation: traits generated within decent Northern homes, such as self-control, piety, domestic sentiment, selflessness, or patriotic conviction. Holding up white Union soldiers as exemplary sufferers, and pointing to white Northern volunteers' more extensive and automatic response to men in pain, in other words, were some of the major ways that Northern whites constituted national identity during the war.

This book deals with idealistic stories revolving around Northerners' response to suffering, all of which were told by patriotic writers, thus mostly supporters of the Republican Party. The most vocal of these writers were middle-class whites. They wrote stories that were didactic, designed not only to exemplify but also to evoke particular kinds of behavior and emotions. In identifying only some types of suffering as meaningful, and in suggesting appropriate responses, they expressed a class-based and racialized interpretation of the war. In this limited sense, their writing was propagandistic: it was based on a set of convictions concerning the correct mode of suffering and sacrifice, and it was purposefully directed at persuading readers of the moral superiority of white Union soldiers, their supporters, and their cause.

Yet to read these stories as akin to modern propaganda is to miss the crucial historical context that gave Civil War tales of suffering their persuasive power. Put simply, people could more readily believe in didactic stories of suffering in the mid-nineteenth century because they thought of emotional persuasion largely in positive ways. This is no longer the case. To talk of propaganda today is to instantly conjure up powerful forces and technologies capable of infiltrating susceptible minds: purposeful campaigns sponsored by oppressive regimes, for instance, or a mature advertising industry employing what have become standard tools of mass persuasion and manipulation—insights drawn from modern disciplines like psychology, techniques designed to sell us things or promote certain identities, and modern devices like television and radio. We can no more escape the idea of insidious outside forces swaying entire populations than we can forget fascism, anti-communist hysteria, or consumer capitalism.

People living in the mid-nineteenth century, however, were largely unfamiliar with this connection between propaganda and the successful manipulation of emotions. They were no strangers to the fear of being influenced by powerful demagogues or designing conmen.[46] But they still believed that genuine emotions welled up spontaneously, reflecting an unmediated truth. They also took it for granted that both the health and bodies of debased individuals would eventually register their wickedness for all to see. Just as good emotions (those that were understood as appropriately controlled and earnestly expressed) were said to be reflected in one's physiognomy and health, so too did insincerity or lack of emotional restraint supposedly reveal themselves in the bumps on people's heads, the state of their internal organs, or the expressions on their faces. Little wonder that Northerners failed to see emotions as susceptible to government manipulation or persuasive marketing. For the most sophisticated visual technique employed by mid-nineteenth-century advertisers was the use of different typefaces or fonts. And the federal state was a weak force in most people's daily lives, at least until the beginning of the war.[47] If mobilization dramatically extended the government's reach and power, such changes did not automatically cause people to see themselves as victims of sinister campaigns of emotional suasion.[48] Until the post-bellum era, writing or speeches infused with intense sentiments were far more likely to evoke tears and applause than skepticism or ridicule, and rarely anxiety or unease.

Unlike later wars, there was no government agency in the mid-nineteenth century to direct the writing of emotional appeals in support of the Union cause. That task was eagerly undertaken by a wide range of civilian publicists, and by soldiers of all classes.[49] Civil War troops were also remarkably overt in their idealism and patriotism compared to their twentieth-century counterparts. For nineteenth-century soldiers, civic participation was a crucial element of their identities—something that defined them as men in an era before female suffrage. They went to war not as individuals, but as representatives of their families and communities. They marched off in locally raised regiments often filled with friends and family members and commanded by prominent local citizens. Just as important, within these regiments they imagined themselves to be self-governing individuals who had a crucial part to play in shaping the war's outcome. Universally referring to themselves as "the boys," the majority of Union soldiers conceived of a communal army, ideally led by commanders who respected their troops as thinking citizens, treating them with a firm but considerate hand and thus according them the respect and affection of a father toward his sons.[50]

By the twentieth century, American soldiers necessarily held quite different understandings of their wartime roles. Over the intervening years, the growth of technical expertise and scientific management, coupled with the massive expansion of government bureaucracy and business organization, had created a new sense of distance between average citizens and the centers of decision making. Soldiers now enlisted in a fully professionalized army, organized on a national level. Receiving a great deal more training than their forebears, most saw it as their job to perform their assigned task well, "not to stick their neck out." No longer imagining themselves as autonomous individuals whose singular actions could affect the war's outcome, soldiers increasingly became minor cogs in a gigantic wheel, a shift that is perfectly captured by their new self-identification as "GI Joes" (short for "government-issue Joe"), the implication being that each soldier was akin to a "standardized product fashioned on an assembly line," someone lacking in agency who was "passively managed from above." To express an effusive patriotism in such a context— to talk about suffering and dying for one's country—was to open oneself to potential ridicule. Fighting for unit cohesion or expressing avid commitment to one's comrades was standard in the writings of World War II enlistees, but their letters, diaries, and memoirs contain far less of the political idealism and overt patriotism that typified the writings of Union soldiers.[51]

The nineteenth-century faith in the power of the individual to effect social change also hinged on a belief that idealized characteristics could be embodied—that is, that one could adopt or become a certain kind of "character." Just as mid-nineteenth-century Americans viewed emotions as individually generated, they also believed that people were mostly in charge of shaping their own destinies. For respectable Northern men, willpower, self-control, and reason were critical tools necessary for forging a strong character.[52] A number of complicated developments over the past century, however, have altered the way identity is both shaped and understood, bringing into question this earlier faith in the possibility of creating an autonomous and stable character. As historians of consumer culture have shown, the late nineteenth-century advertising industry invented a raft of new techniques to manipulate and stimulate desires, linking those desires ever more closely to personal identity.[53] Related changes taking place around the same time—ranging from the spread of a more interdependent market economy to the rise of new disciplines like psychiatry—have likewise directed attention to the mutability and complexity of identity.[54] Few people now think of character as a state to be achieved once and for all as mid-nineteenth-century Northerners did; nor do most assume that their identity is entirely subject to willpower. Selfhood now tends to be understood in terms of a process that takes place over an entire lifetime, one that is open to constant revision, expressed differently in various social settings, and influenced by unconscious forces or genetic factors beyond one's control. This modern fascination with the complexities of identity has made any explanation in the past that fails to take such complexity into account seem simple-minded, just as it has increased our skepticism toward any narrative that appears overly didactic or conventional.

In order to think about why white Northerners so often told conventional stories about wartime suffering, we need to suspend this skepticism, but not for the purpose of looking back nostalgically on a romantic past populated by naive people who still had faith in values like patriotism and self-sacrifice and were thus implicitly superior to cynical moderns.[55] Instead, this is necessary in order to analyze the historical context that made idealized suffering so compelling to certain groups of people. This context includes both the meanings attributed to suffering and the politics of such attributions. Not every sufferer, or every mode of suffering, held equal weight during the war. When Northern commentators held up certain kinds of suffering as laudable, they invariably downgraded other, less visible forms of wartime distress. While extolling the agonies that white men suffered in the Union cause, for instance, the press tended to portray those of displaced black refugees or poverty-stricken Northern families as merely unfortunate. Likewise, Unionists could not help but define exemplary sufferers in opposition to those who registered their pain in less than ideal ways. In fact, a large part of the appeal in embodying or celebrating ideal suffering lay in the fact that such suffering allowed people to demonstrate superiority over others, to receive public accolades, or to demand consideration.

There is always a politics to sympathy. These politics are explored most fully in the literature on Victorian sentimentalism. As this literature points out, sentimentalism is often politically problematic, for it tends to ignore difference in order to lay the grounds for sympathetic identification. The sentimentalist is supposed to approach sufferers convinced in the belief that "this person could be me, therefore I should feel for him or her in the same way that I would feel for myself in like circumstances." Using sympathy as a basis for moral and ethical judgments, sentimentalists ignore what is outside their realm of experience. Historian Christine Stansell is one of many scholars who have highlighted the problem with this equation. After painting a vivid picture of the boisterous, sociable world inhabited by working-class women in early nineteenth-century New York, she notes that the objects of middle-class concern depicted in novels and charity reports were always pitiful, lonely seamstresses or widows fallen on hard times wasting away in isolated garrets. To become an object of genteel concern, it was necessary for the working class to be entirely detached from their social milieu. "By the very unsolitariness of their lives, most of the female laboring poor excluded themselves" from such middle-class consideration, she concludes. In a similar vein, Karen Sanchez Eppler points to the way white abolitionists routinely featured in their writings black characters shorn of all physical signs of race, depicting them instead with a range of stereotypically "white" features. Only to the extent that white readers could imagine a literal kinship with black sufferers, it seems, could they extend the bonds of sympathy.[56] In thinking about the implications of sentimental accounts of wounded soldiers published during the Civil War, the same criticism could easily be applied. These almost always pictured ideal sufferers as white and respectable, capable of drawing out tender feelings in others only in so far as they exhibited the appropriate manly self-control, piety, or effusions of domestic or patriotic sentiment.

Critics also point out that sentimental sympathy tends to be a one-way street, with relatively powerful sympathizers offering compassion to helpless victims, in the process registering their superior virtue.[57] Depicting sympathy as a spontaneous outpouring of worthy emotions, sentimentalism cloaks the material conditions that went into enabling a middle-class person to claim the role of sympathizer. Attention shifts away from class relations or the benefits accruing to sympathizers within unequal relationships and is instead focused on a celebration of their praiseworthy response to suffering. Again, a similar argument can be made regarding Civil War stories of white sufferers and their sympathizers, given the extent to which these tales so insistently praised patriotism and benevolence while deflecting attention from the conflict's unevenly spread burdens. These narratives of suffering were inseparable from larger discussions of wartime nationalism. To be an ideal Northern patriot during this war was to sacrifice self-interest in order to uphold the democratic republican system, either by suffering on behalf of the nation or by tending to those who suffered. According to Republican spokespeople, patriotism was virtuous and justifiable because a democratic republic based on free labor principles would eventually benefit everyone, offering all workers an equal chance in life. As Philip Shaw Paludan points out, Lincoln depicted the war as a "people's contest" that would advantage working-class men, in particular. Yet in linking the nation's cause so strongly to the cause of labor, he writes, wartime patriotism denied the specific needs of the poor and working class, undercutting labor unity, and making any attempt to specify the war's unequal costs seem like unnatural selfishness or disloyalty.[58] The stories examined in this book undoubtedly had a similar impact in allowing middle-class people to congratulate themselves on their benevolence while simultaneously turning away from the disproportionate suffering of the oppressed.

All of these criticisms and others can be made of Unionists' attempts to redeem suffering. It can even be rightly claimed that *any* idealization of wartime pain ultimately works to justify future conflicts.[59] Yet such blanket criticisms cannot say much about how, why, and to what effect Unionists gave meaning to suffering during this war in particular. On a grand scale, the idealization of suffering might have been profoundly conservative. But for those forced to live with war's realities, the effects of redeeming suffering were much more ambiguous—oppressive for some, yet, for others, providing a source of profound solace, identity, and inspiration.[60] The chapters that follow go to demonstrate this point, each focusing around a different story of idealized suffering, seeking to identify the range of different meanings and effects that such stories produced.

2

Heroic Martyrs

I see him charging in advance of all, fearless and true[,] his look fixed with high resolve—his face illuminated . . . with the light of coming sacrifice.
Joseph H. Clark to Olivia Bowditch, March 27, 1863

NATHANIEL BOWDITCH was an unlikely hero. In the war's first year, he enlisted in the First Massachusetts Cavalry Regiment as a second lieutenant. Two years later he was dead, killed in his first major encounter with the enemy. As soon as the funeral was over, Nathaniel's father, Henry, set to work on the first of eight elaborate memorials dedicated to his son's memory. Painstakingly, he hand-stitched and pasted original letters and documents onto thousands of separate folio pages, many of which were decorated with intricate borders or colorful initial letters. In separate volumes he placed the correspondence that Nathaniel sent to his family before and during his military service, along with the replies to these letters. Additional volumes contained leaves from his own wartime journals, hundreds of condolence letters, stories and images of fellow Massachusetts officers martyred in the conflict, and an extensive collection of patriotic song lyrics and poems. The time and energy that he expended for more than a decade on this memorial project is evident on every page.[1] It was all part of his plan to instruct present and future generations on the fitting response to his son's death. Imagining his descendants pouring over these materials, Bowditch addressed them by writing: "May I not hope" that "in this way the dear memory of the sweet, brave youth . . . may be forever fresh. . . . That it may serve . . . to stimulate all of them to efforts in behalf of all that is noble and good and brave in human action . . . to make them truly gentlemen & gentlewomen."[2]

Bowditch thus transformed his son into a heroic martyr whose behavior galvanized comrades and whose story inspired listeners by evoking their better natures. The tale he told was not unique. Officers' deaths were generally depicted during the Civil War in ways that were interchangeable, and his memorials were no exception. In myriad eulogies and newspaper accounts of battle, or in the sketches of military leaders that regularly rolled off the Northern presses, hundreds of Union officers were transformed into heroic martyrs over the course of the war, using narrative conventions that drew upon a narrow range of stock figures, repetitive adjectives, and standard phrasings. Ideal officers were always resolute, earnest, and indefatigable in the performance of their duties, their eyes sometimes flashing with enthusiasm, yet always cool and courageous under fire, leading their men into battle at the head of their columns.[3] Whereas military commanders in later wars controlled troop movements from afar, officers in this conflict were expected to direct their men on the field, and those who did so courageously and with utmost self-control represented the heights of wartime heroism.[4] If they died in the attempt, reports generally pictured them lingering only long enough to cheer their men on to victory, or to express their love of family and trust in God.[5] All could expect to receive the kind of commendation that greeted Nathaniel Bowditch's death. At his memorial service, the Reverend James Freeman Clark declared, "this family has in its midst a hero & saint—a martyr who shall be precious in all time—whose name shall stand prominent on this splendid page of American glory as long as the history of America shall be read."[6] The relatives of the Union dead were guaranteed similarly effusive praise, drawn from an equally pervasive idealization of homefront heroism and self-sacrifice.

The scholarship on Civil War soldiers and civilians typically aims to break down these conventions, providing more matter-of-fact accounts of the war, in which soldiers were not all brave, deaths were often inglorious, and homefront divisions were readily apparent. The material that Henry Bowditch collected offers much evidence to support a modern understanding of the Civil War as a conflict that exacerbated social divisions and exposed individual weaknesses. Nathaniel's correspondence makes it clear that war was not the glorious business he had imagined. He was unsure from the outset if he could exercise authority over his subordinates and continually fearful that he would let his family down. Sometimes his letters told of the pleasures and freedoms offered by army life, but just as often he wrote in boredom or despair. When his life finally ended, it was in a cavalry skirmish too insignificant to rate a mention in most general histories of the war. Such were the details that Henry Bowditch had to work with. They could easily have undermined his narrative. He might have concluded, as many did in later wars, that his son was a victim rather than a hero, his life sacrificed to military ineptitude, pointless carnage, or unrealistic, outmoded ideals. But neither he nor any of Nathaniel's other family members, friends, or comrades supposed that his sacrifice had been in vain.

Why did Bowditch's tale become one of heroic martyrdom? And why did so many Northerners who lost relatives in this war choose to repeat similar tales? The simplest answer is that they called upon a deep reservoir of myths and stories in which heroic warriors inspired others with their fearlessness and ardor. Expressing time-honored ideals of manhood—from bravery and daring to fortitude and tenacity—such stories can be found in every war fought from antiquity to our own time. Yet the Bowditchs and their kind did more than simply draw on the material their culture offered in order to make sense of their loss. They did not just tell their idealized story; they *lived* it, investing tremendous emotional energy in creating a tale of heroic martyrdom anew, making it speak to their own situations and embody their particular desires and beliefs. Understanding why so many Northern families repeated tales of heroic martyrdom thus requires going beyond the outlines of the stories themselves to look at how they were incorporated and used in individual lives. Demonstrating this fact, this chapter follows a single family as they pieced together and lived through the tale of a martyred son.

Their story remains a recognizable product of its time and place, even though it resembles those told about other men in other wars. Reflecting their particular circumstances, the Bowditchs created the tale of a son who held attributes central to middle-class Victorian respectability. Placing him within an illustrious lineage, and memorializing his wartime actions alongside their own, they revealed their assumption that men went to war not as individuals but as representatives of their family and class. They spent no time reflecting on Nathaniel's particular foibles, his likes or dislikes, or his unique disposition. Nor did they set out to create an original tale. The single, exceptional life held little meaning for this family. The point of their story lay in its conventionality, not its uniqueness. Believing in the power of suffering to unite listeners and arouse their worthiest impulses, they focused on the way their son struggled to maintain a certain character in the midst of war—equal parts moral rectitude, diligent effort, and abiding patriotism—all instilled and supported by, and thus representative of, his family as a whole. In their story, this was an achievement shared by every other martyred Union officer—a fact they made clear by placing Nathaniel's story alongside those of hundreds of equally brave Massachusetts officers who exhibited precisely the same characteristics and met similar fates. They offered motivation and encouragement to others in the form of a thoroughly bourgeois Victorian tale of ideals upheld even in the midst of doubts and discouragements, of willpower overcoming obstacles, and, most important, of a character only fully realized at the point of suffering and death—that supreme moment of truth for most nineteenth-century Protestants, when the soul confronted its maker and grieving relatives chose whether to bend to or rebel against God's will. This was a story that could be, indeed was designed to be, endlessly replicated by others as they sought to make themselves "truly gentlemen and gentlewomen."

It was the work of a lifetime for Nathaniel Bowditch to become a heroic martyr. Long before his memorial service declared him an outstanding family representative, he had already done his best to ensure that he would be remembered in this way. The stakes were high, for like many elite men, he was well used to carrying the weight of family expectations. He was the son of Henry Ingersoll and Olivia Yardley Bowditch, named in honor of his renowned grandfather, a self-taught mathematician whose *Practical Navigator* had become an instant classic, relied on by ships' captains the world over. Henry Bowditch had "grave doubts" about saddling Nathaniel with so unassailable an example, but he held high hopes for his first-born. "I looked forward with delight to the future, when he was to become my aid and comrade in professional life. My life had been moulded to that idea," he later remarked.[7] Expected to walk a path traced out for him from the beginning, Nathaniel had to contend not only with his grandfather's formidable reputation but also with his father's equally daunting career. Even before his son was born in December 1839, Henry Bowditch was one of the best-educated and most widely known physicians in the country, well on his way to becoming the nation's leading specialist in pulmonary diseases.[8]

Professional success did not bring vast wealth to this family, although it did come with prestige. Henry Bowditch was not rich, but he was among the nation's intellectual and cultural elite. His family was unusual in other ways as well. They were staunchly abolitionist long before most white Bostonians came around to their way of thinking. They were also religious freethinkers in a culture where most elites purchased their pews at a single church. The Bowditch parents took pride in their outsider status, moving as they did in circles deeply influenced by transcendentalism, in a city that formed the epicenter of American Romanticism. They were more traditional in their political beliefs. Patriotism was a birthright for this family, just as it was for many others. As Nathaniel had often been reminded in his youth, his forebears were nationalists during the Revolution and his grandfather had succeeded in representing the republic they helped to create on the world stage, demonstrating that a democracy was capable of producing self-made men who could compete with the greatest minds in Europe. Nathaniel was still finishing his education when the war began, but he had taken these lessons to heart, making his enlistment a foregone conclusion.

Before this day arrived, he had received the kind of intense nurturing that many middling and elite parents invested in their offspring in the economically volatile and increasingly mobile prewar decades. Ambitious for Nathaniel's future, his family avidly tracked his educational achievements, seeking constant updates on his scholarly progress. Unfortunately, it never seemed quick or sure enough to meet their expectations. When Henry Bowditch looked back over his son's life, he remembered Nathaniel as a boy with an "almost morbid disposition to self-depreciation, which has been a prominent feature in his character." Feeling that a practical, rather than a purely academic, course of instruction would better fit his fretful child for the career mapped out for him, Henry chose the Lawrence Scientific School over Harvard College, which would have been the more usual choice for a child of the Bostonian elite.[9] "Never let pleasure come in contact with duty," he warned Nathaniel as he took up his studies. "Let me hear ... that you are perfectly reliable—and that whatever either [of your professors] asks you to do, both will feel certain of your doing well." A stream of further advice, sent by his father, mother, and sister, followed him over the next few months: to make himself invaluable, to live up to the example set by his "excellent grandsire," to fit himself for the career his father had "foreshadowed," and (particularly from his mother and sister) to be ever thoughtful, moral, and religious. "No one ever made himself eminent in our profession without deep intense regular work," his father constantly admonished.[10]

Believing that his son required a good deal of help, Henry Bowditch wrote in October 1859 to Charles W. Eliot, then a little-known professor of physics and chemistry at Lawrence, asking him to take a "kindly interest" in Nathaniel's education. "I believe his moral tendencies are not evil but you will find him youthful in many respects.... I confess to you I would like to see a more lively zeal in the pursuits of learning than he now seems to have," he explained, adding, "he has not awakened to the pure delight of scientific study." He was in touch with Eliot again the following August, noting that his son was still a "mere boy" and pleading, "I wish your influence to hover around him during his next year."[11]

Figure 1. Nathaniel Bowditch in his cavalry uniform, appearing on the front page of his father's *Memorial Book.* (Courtesy of the Massachusetts Historical Society, Boston.)

A little over a year later, this "mere boy" would leave for war. Judging from his prewar letters, Nathaniel was sensitive and affectionate, but not especially gifted academically. His wartime correspondence confirms his father's belief that he was self-deprecating and immature, always trying his best but constantly worried that his best was insufficient. Despite an extensive education, his writing seems careless, with words and characters often transposed or missed entirely and spelling errors throughout (mistakes his mother pointed out to him, and which his father corrected in pencil before stitching Nathaniel's letters into his memorials).

Bowditch looks even less impressive when compared to Charles Francis Adams Jr., who shared a similar educational background, traveled in comparable Boston circles, and entered the same regiment. Historians tend to gravitate to soldiers like Adams, and it is not difficult to understand why. Unerringly forthright, Adams's writing style is witty, singular, and self-consciously literary, whereas Bowditch's letters are filled with recurring phrasings and bland description. Yet there is also another reason why historians so frequently cite Adams: he is a quintessential realist, entirely unsentimental.[12] Unlike Bowditch, he rarely mentions God, and his letters contain none of the stock phrases about duty and bravery so popular in this era. For Adams, accounts of heroic battlefield action were often absurd, produced by reporters writing for what he termed the "lying prints." When discussing suffering, either his own or that of others, he was just as dismissive of convention, usually relying on gallows humor or stiff-upper-lip bravado.[13] He almost never voiced a fervent patriotism, perhaps because his father, Charles Francis Adams Sr., then U.S. Minister to England, and his brother Henry both initially disapproved of his enlistment. Tough and irreverent, distrustful of the social pieties of his age, Adams seems entirely familiar to modern readers, not too different from the disillusioned doughboy or cynical GI of later wars.

Adams was not unique among Union officers in his irreverence and cynicism, but he was certainly far from ordinary. Secular-minded soldiers like him were a decided minority in the Union ranks. Most respectable Northern men explained their motivations for enlistment in terms of patriotic ideology and relied on a conventional language of duty, honor, courage, and sacrifice to describe their service.[14] As was the case with the majority of Northern men, Nathaniel Bowditch came from a deeply religious, close-knit family whose members enthusiastically followed politics and readily sanctioned his enlistment as their wartime representative. As such, they expected him to uphold the values he had been taught at home. These values included not only religious and patriotic convictions, but a whole series of attributes useful for respectable men in the mid-century economy—attributes that characterized the "cautious, prudent small-businessman" who might expect to build his success on how others assessed his temperament and disposition, such as reliability, a steady work ethic, upright morality, and self-control.[15] For the Bowditch parents, who had long counseled their son on his obligation to develop a strong character and make his family proud, heroism did not require extraordinary feats of daring, only the diligent and creditable performance of duty.

Families with less wealth and social prestige than the Bowditchs had their own ways of defining abstract concepts like duty and bravery. Northern companies were generally mustered in with great fanfare, treated to long speeches delivered by local dignitaries before being presented with a regimental flag, hand-stitched by a local women's group. Reminded that they represented their states, localities, and families, all were told to act courageously in battle and to live up to the heroic precedents set by the Revolutionary generation.[16] Such were the universal expectations. Yet if men of different classes heard the same words, they would have registered them differently. Union officers knew that they would be performing under great scrutiny, in service of widely renowned names. Their grandiose rhetoric of honor and self-sacrifice witnessed not only elite educations and cultural backgrounds but also an awareness of being lead actors in an impending drama. The form and content of working men's patriotic language was less self-important, although no less enthusiastic in its support for war. Male wage laborers who had lost out in the new industrial economy, in particular, were known to scoff at the idealistic pretensions of the elite, which clashed so decidedly with their personal knowledge of oppressive working conditions and harsh realities. Their notions of bravery were framed less in terms of lofty ideals and *noblesse oblige* than in cutting pretenders down to size, demonstrating toughness and prowess, and sometimes violently defending local honor or ethnic pride.[17]

When Henry Bowditch advised his son on the necessity of bravery in war, he emphasized instead the respectable values of the Northern bourgeoisie. The term he used was "fortitude," an expression encompassing not only a lack of fear, but also humble self-sacrifice in a virtuous cause, personal independence, assiduous and patient effort, reliability, and upright morality. "It is the part of fortitude (true manliness) to be unshaken by the fear of death to be constant and firm in adversity, intrepid amid dangers, to prefer to die honestly than to be preserved basely and love the noble cause rather than victory," he advised Nathaniel upon his enlistment. "Moreover, it is the part of true fortitude (manliness) to be willing to labor and to suffer," and "self reliance added to industry and patience add greatly to true manliness." Extending oft-repeated prewar advice, he once more reminded his son, "The great point in life ... is to make yourself a *reliable* man and officer," remaining "pure, good & manly, brave[,] religious ... submissive to all superiors."[18]

This eight-page letter was only one of several wordy missives that followed Nathaniel to the front. A month earlier, his father had written a twenty-four-page letter of advice, much of which told his son how to remain healthy and morally sound by exercising self-control and regularity in food and alcohol intake, cleanliness, bodily discharges, religious adherence, and the like. A fortnight previous, he forwarded another letter of instruction. Representing the minutely detailed nature of his advice as well as his deep interest in his son's military bearing, he counseled: "You look well on horseback, in every respect, but one. *Your stirrups are too short.* They lift your toes above your heels. Hence the latter seem thrown downwards & your knees seem pushed higher than elegant riding allows. You see, I want you *perfect* in all things."[19] It is unlikely that many working-class families would have issued such exhaustive guidance to departing relatives, and not simply because being in the ranks made a man less visible. Rather, elite parents like the Bowditchs were well aware that their comparatively sheltered sons were about to come into contact with diverse strangers, under new circumstances that would severely test the self-control they had worked so hard to instill. The reams of advice that Henry Bowditch sent to his son were a measure of this anxiety, not to mention an indication of how much an officer's behavior and bearing was seen to reflect upon his family.

Most middling and elite families did their utmost to remind male relatives that army life did not guarantee their anonymity—that they would be watching and monitoring still. Warned by one family friend that a third of the young men entering the army would no doubt "come home drunkards," Henry Bowditch wrote immediately to his son explaining that multiple friends had begun to inquire after him. "Thus, you perceive darling, that already the eyes of many whom perhaps you know not, are upon you. They will rate your honorable, faithful career. Be assured that whatever you do even in the darkest of night will be known," he cautioned. A month later, his mother sent a similar warning, noting that both an aunt and one of their poorer neighbors had made inquiries after him. "[T]hus you see dear the eyes of poor & rich, high & low are watching for you."[20]

Nathaniel probably did not need to be reminded that he was on constant display. If the Civil War had been fought a century or even half a century before, there would have been no telegraph or photography, no war reporters at the front instantly transmitting the latest battlefield news, no mass-circulation newspapers carrying their stories, and no mass of readers both literate and politically educated enough to understand them. All of these changes—the growth of democracy, the expansion of literacy and print culture, the increased availability and circulation of information—ensured that events on the battlefield and in camp quickly became news and rumor back home.[21] The fact that most Civil War regiments were raised locally and composed of numerous relatives and friends also meant that families could glean news and testimony from soldiers' letters and from men sent home to recruit or to recover from wounds—information undoubtedly far more detailed and constant than would have been available to those with relatives fighting either in earlier or later wars. From the moment Nathaniel left for the field, his family followed his every move, as he knew they would.

A dense web of kinship and personal relationships connected the Bowditchs to many of the men who served with their son. Those in the

ranks shared similar kinds of connections, but relatively influential families had additional resources for keeping in touch with absent army friends.
When Nathaniel became ill, for instance, his father traveled to his regiment,
meeting his officers and forming first-hand impressions. Genteel women like
Nathaniel's mother and fiancée also joined voluntary organizations like the
Sanitary Commission, sharing their letters and circulating news from camp
as they sat and sewed alongside other soldiers' relatives. Rumors about the
behavior of officers from the First Massachusetts Cavalry Regiment swirled
about these circles, discussed regularly and reported back to Nathaniel by
various family members. When his mother wrote to say, "any scrap of news
about you, will be devoured by your voracious family," she spoke an unqualified truth.[22]

Soldiers from such close-knit communities understood that they were being constantly monitored but they also knew that onlookers watched with a
purpose, often waiting for some indication of how a man would bear himself
in battle. This was no abstract concept. As Nathaniel's mother had informed
him, he had become a model for his younger brother, who dressed in one of
his old uniforms as he marched around the house pretending to be a soldier.
More pointedly, he had received word from his Uncle Vin "not [to] come
back without honor," and, from his Aunt Sarah, to bear his trials with "a
brave heart." He knew that even women entirely unknown to him were following his progress. Annie Houghton, a "school girl," apparently advised by
his fiancée that he would welcome a letter, sent a note two days before his
death which read: "I saw quite a complimentary little notice of Lieut. Clark,
in the paper a few weeks ago, but nothing as yet concerning you."[23] The den-
sity of these connections between soldiers and their communities, and the
daily pressures that such constant homefront monitoring brought to bear on
men at war, suggests just how crucial intimate relationships were in enforcing
wartime heroism.

From friends and relations, to elderly neighbors and well-meaning school-
girls, all were watching for some demonstration of bravery. Yet Nathaniel had
little opportunity to gratify his onlookers in the period before his death. Many
Civil War regiments in the first few years of the war spent the vast majority of
their time in drilling, marching, and camping. But those who joined cavalry
regiments particularly lacked avenues for heroic display.[24] While Confederate
cavalrymen accumulated glory by launching audacious and widely publicized
raids that literally ran circles around Union forces, Northern cavalry regiments languished. Until their reorganization in 1863, most were attached to
specific army corps and sent to perform mundane tasks such as scouting,
picket duty, guarding supply lines, and acting as orderlies for senior officers.

These were the thankless responsibilities that occupied the First Massachusetts Cavalry in its initial year of service.[25]

Given this situation, it was difficult for Nathaniel to live up to the many exhortations to demonstrate bravery and selflessness. But as soon as he thought his chance had come, he seized it. Incorrectly believing that he was about to be sent to the field, he wrote home in mid-1862 using words and sentiments typifying those of thousands of Union soldiers about to go into battle. Emphasizing his steadfast commitment to the cause and his trust in providence, he told his sister: "This is my first and it may be my last battle but I never entered into anything with a clearer conscience and a happier feeling than I do this. I have my trust in my Almighty Father and know that whatever happens to me is for the best." Letters like this one obviously reflect the gravity that writers felt, poised as they were on what might be their last moments on earth. But the men who wrote them were also attempting to shape the way distant observers and future generations perceived their actions. Bowditch knew that he could die without performing a single brave deed significant enough to warrant mention in a newspaper or official report. His letter could stand in for that deed, evidence of potential heroism. Aware that it would be read aloud by family and friends, his writing style was formal and grandiloquent, self-consciously shifting into third person as he envisaged his actions on the battlefield. "You may rest assured that your brother will not flinch from duty and if he is shot I trust that it will be with his face to the enemy," he told his sister. "I feel that a man who falls in this cause falls in a glorious one and one which he may be proud of. I am now truly thankful that I came to serve my country in this her hour of need." As he penned these lines he no doubt "meant what [he] said," to use James McPherson's phrase.[26] Yet letters like this one are not simply passive reflections of a writer's beliefs. Bowditch sought to constitute himself as a hero through his words—words that he knew might have to substitute for action, and which would surely outlive him should he die.

If there was one feature that defined Unionists' war writing it was an acute self-consciousness, shared by authors convinced they were in the midst of events that would reshape world history. Often enough President Lincoln had reminded Union troops that the global fate of democratic republicanism hinged on their success.[27] Both soldiers and civilians believed that their writing would be cherished by posterity, just as they had revered the words of the founding generation, whose deeds many believed they had finally surpassed. The conflict's "result, will overshadow this republic while it continues to live, and it will affect the future destiny of man . . . the world over," Henry Bowditch declared near war's end, "its influence on the future of man will be far greater than the Revolution of 1776."[28] Throughout the war, thousands of Northerners would voice the same conviction. Setting his thoughts down right before he went into battle, Nathaniel Bowditch's writing was suffused by the belief that he was living in an unprecedentedly heroic time, and that his final words were all that might distinguish him as a hero.

Being so often reminded that he stood for his entire family, he would have had their response in mind as much as his own place in history. Matching her son's steadfast patriotism, Olivia Bowditch replied to his letter with unconcealed approval, describing how she wept for joy to "hear you say you do not regret but rejoice at having gone to serve your country," and adding that tears were shed by other family members as they read his words. "Our hopes are bright for you darling that you will return to us safe and crowned with the laurels of the Christian Warrior but should God see fit to take you to his bosom before we see you again your words of truest courage & faith will be cherished as priceless amulets of comfort by us all."[29] Having proclaimed his status as a potential hero and received the accolades of his family for his words, there were really only two options open to this soldier: to return home "crowned with laurels," or to die trying.

Yet to declare an aspiration to become heroic and to live up to such assertions in light of daily realities like boredom, disease, and bad officers were two different things. Like most soldiers, Bowditch had periodic bouts of "the blues" that were serious enough for him to consider resigning his commission several times. His options narrowed to heroism or death not because of an abstract ideological commitment to the war effort, but because his family relationships made such commitments obligatory. Behind Bowditch's assertions of potential heroism lay a lifetime of family injunctions—to perform dutifully and creditably, to uphold the good name of his ancestors, to make his family proud—now reasserted by both parents all the more urgently in the context of war. As soon as he donned his uniform and right up until his death, Bowditch was plagued by doubts and anxieties, silenced only by his parents' unyielding commitment to keep him at his post.[30]

In fact, it seems highly doubtful that he would have ever made it into battle without this homefront encouragement. After enthusiastically heading off to take up his commission, he returned to Boston the next day "thoroughly depressed," having witnessed one of his new officers harshly discipline a subordinate. Thinking that he should immediately resign, he confessed to his father, "I am totally unfit for this work; I can never govern men." Describing this scene several years later, Henry Bowditch recalled his reply: "it is not the custom for any of us to give up an important object, until we have . . . gained it. . . . [Y]ou cannot, at present, resign with honor." Instead, he recommended that Nathaniel study his new duties avidly, trust in God and "all things will be well."[31] This was not the last time that Nathaniel needed to be reminded that giving up was beyond the pale. By March he had fallen ill. "I someti[m]es get discouraged for it seems to me as if I did not seem to get any better," he told his sister, after more than a week prostrated in his tent.[32]

Further gloomy letters sent to various family members followed this one, prompting Henry Bowditch to set off for Hilton Head to assess the situation first-hand. As soon as he arrived, father and son sat down to discuss the possibility of requesting a furlough or an honorable discharge on medical grounds. In his journal, Henry Bowditch recorded his strong desire for Nathaniel to "stay his appointed time" in the army. "I tried to describe what a rousing reception we would give the Regiment on its return; of the flowers which the girls would shower upon it—and the bright smiles & pleasant words that would everywhere greet it," he noted.[33] Unambiguously, he laid out the implications of an early discharge: no triumphant welcome, female adoration, or public appreciation.

Evidently Nathaniel agreed to remain, but at an emotional cost that comes through unmistakably in the description of their parting that Bowditch recorded for his wife. With "eager & repeated kisses," his son clung to his neck. "[G]iving him my blessing ... and often telling him how much we should feel pride in him & rejoice to think of his having gained a rigorous manhood by trial—I gave him my final kiss," he explained, describing how Nathaniel returned his embrace, kissing him repeatedly in a way that "seemed to me he could hardly bear to cease from ... doing."[34] The desperation of his son, alone among comparative strangers and weak from illness, was not lost on the Bowditch family. But trials such as these were to be borne with resignation, used as an opportunity to fortify oneself against future ordeals. This was the only path to "rigorous manhood," he implied, and the best way for his son to ensure that the family felt "pride" in his actions.[35]

The ennobling power of suffering, gaining a rigorous manhood through trial—expressions like these have struck some historians as evidence that elites came to embrace a new tough-minded approach to pain during the war.[36] Henry Bowditch's attitude toward his son, however, can hardly be characterized as callous indifference; his own emotions were much too conflicted and painful for that. In his journal he described standing on the wharf at Port Royal ready to leave for home as "thoughts of Nat of his illness—of the possibility of his being worse—and the total ignorance in which we all are as to the final termination of this war, swept instantly over me [and] my eyes instantly filled with tears."[37] His faith in the virtue of suffering reflected not hard-heartedness but a deeply held conviction widely shared by virtually all

Protestants in this period. In a letter that Olivia Bowditch wrote to her son some days later, she also told him: "Trust in your Heavenly Father my boy and ... depend upon it that trial is good for us, it elevates & ennobles our character if only taken as a direct lesson from God." "I know you feel this," she added, "but it is pleasant sometimes to have a load of encouragement & sympathy from those we love." Both parents believed that confronting and overcoming painful ordeals molded "character," just as they were convinced that God had delivered such trials for precisely this purpose and that their son would naturally read their words as a form of "encouragement and sympathy." So, too, did Katherine Putnam, Nathaniel's wartime fiancée, who sent him off to war with a pamphlet that read, "Let your motto this year be *Forward!* Patient in endurance, submissive in suffering; content with God's allotment."[38]

That many civilians endorsed suffering as a chance to enhance manly willpower does not mean that they were blind to war's realities. The Bowditch parents were quite ready to condemn any war-induced distress that seemed to them gratuitous or avoidable. In the first two years of the conflict, in fact, their positions on government policies and military leadership changed just as much as their son's did. Nathaniel had begun the war trying to follow every instruction diligently, but he had soon learned that his officers could be unreasonable. By mid-1862, he was writing home declaring his lieutenant colonel "a donkey" and his colonel a "drunkard" who cared so little for his men that he refused to order tents and forced them to live in "nasty straw pig-stys."[39] Initially, his parents were unwilling to credit these claims. Thinking that hard work and submission to authority would counter any obstacles, they censured his criticisms, warning him to "keep a bridle both on tongue & pen" and give due deference to his superiors.[40] Their perspective quickly changed in light of heated reports and gossip on the home front condemning inadequate provisions for the wounded, incompetence among senior officers, and a growing toll in human life.[41] By late 1862 Olivia Bowditch had begun to respond sympathetically instead of critically to her son's grievances about his regiment's leadership. "The facts you mention seem to be known everywhere," she explained, telling him that a petition signed by hundreds of mothers requesting the president remove incompetent officers had been making the rounds.[42]

Henry Bowditch had also concluded by early 1863 that inept elites were bungling certain aspects of the war. He drew his knowledge not only from letters and homefront gossip but also from first-hand experience. Answering a call from the Massachusetts governor for physicians to travel to the front and assess the care of the wounded, he headed to Centreville in 1862. Like thousands of other voluntary workers, he returned from the front outraged by what he had seen and eager to better conditions for suffering soldiers by publicizing their fate. Adding his voice to an already animated public campaign for the formation of a trained ambulance corps, he attacked the subject with missionary zeal. In articles written for medical journals, letters sent to government officials, a widely distributed pamphlet, and a visit to the president, he portrayed his experiences in impassioned language, describing how appalled he was to discover wounded men without food or water, attended by untrained, coarse, and drunken ambulance drivers who did not seem to care a whit for their charges.[43] Like his wife, he suspected that cruelty and mismanagement were rife. Yet neither of them became disillusioned with the war itself, even when the consequences affected them directly.

In the middle of his campaign to improve the care of wounded Union soldiers, Henry Bowditch learned that his own son was among their number. He would go on to use Nathaniel's experience of writhing in pain for hours on the battlefield before help arrived as an example of needless suffering that might be relieved by trained ambulance personnel. The wound his son received in battle, however, was a different matter. This kind of suffering was not cause for censure or complaint. It was a chance to reaffirm and deepen his religious faith and patriotic commitment. Bowditch made this clear only moments after learning of his son's death. He was in Washington at the time, on his way to visit Nathaniel's regiment, when a telegraph arrived bearing the news. He sat down immediately to write to his wife. "I thank God ... that if he was to die so soon that he died in behalf of our dear country—a sweet sacrifice to Liberty!" he told her. "I thank Heaven also for my own increased devotion to the cause of the country. If by any power I could restore Nat to life to be a poltroon or a vile copperhead—I would not accept the offer." When loyal Northerners wrote about grieving families, it was exactly this kind of religious affirmation and steadfast patriotism in the face of death that they attributed to the most worthy citizens. Henry Bowditch was determined to embody this ideal. Emphasizing his resolve to confront death without protest, he declared that he would "go tomorrow to camp and after as short delay as possible shall return to life & (made—oh! how blank) to my accustomed work."[44]

He covered four additional sheets, with dozens more sentences punctuated by dashes and brackets, as if to corral the grief that kept intruding on his resolution. It was an impossible task, but essential for a man who had so often lectured his son on the virtues of suffering. A further letter written that evening reflected the same struggle for control, the same wayward despair unsettling efforts to bow down before political necessity and divine will. "Oh darling how bounteous God has been to have given us such a son," he wrote, before his determination to hold back distress crumbled, only to be reasserted over and again. "—Oh alas I shall never kiss the dear child more. My heart seems almost breaking—Yet I could not ask a more noble life or a more noble death—Why do I complain? And yet my whole nature yearns to see & hear him once again.... [M]ay his example cheer us all onward in the paths of duty to which we respectively belong Oh alas! alas! my tears have been my constant companion." Remarkably, Bowditch saw this fluctuation between resignation and despair as a great failing, even on the first day of his bereavement. Two days later, he apologized to his wife for what he deemed a display of "inconstancy," reassuring her, "Now I feel better, calmer."[45]

Behind these efforts to hold grief at bay there was a clear and uncompromising logic. Giving vent to unrestrained sorrow was not only to revolt against God's will, but also to deny death meaning, or at least the kind of meaning that made sense to Henry Bowditch. Repeatedly in these letters he sought to remind himself and his wife that God had given them a son who lived and died in an inspirational way. To fail to *be* inspired, to succumb instead to sadness and grief, was for him an admission that death was futile. In order to demonstrate that there was some reason for this calamity, some significance or plan behind it, he had to model death's inspirational potential, even to himself. And the way to do this was to demonstrate calm acceptance of loss and through that to confirm the sincerity and worthiness, the unshakable truth, of his political and religious convictions.

Such acts of self-abnegation and self-control were for many Northerners both a duty and a form of heroism, akin to the sacrifices made by men on the field. As historians have suggested, the war expanded avenues for women's civic participation and understandings of their civic duties.[46] Yet the idea that one of the highest forms of female patriotism lay in sacrificing male relatives in war remained strong throughout this conflict, particularly among elites. As one wealthy Bostonian woman wrote in her diary in late 1862, "I am convinced that the duty of women is as definite as well as arduous in this struggle for liberty, as the duty of men. Their patriotism must enable them to give all they hold in the cause of freedom," she argued, and to "keep up the courage of the nation by their cheerfulness and firmness." Olivia Bowditch had often personified this standard, telling her son at one point that "Mothers of Heroes must learn to be brave," and, like her husband, urging him to remain in the army and bear his sufferings gladly.[47] After his death she continued to believe that a "worthy" woman should celebrate rather than mourn the passing of a heroic son, writing to a friend in May of that year "if his comrades saw my silent tears they would not think me a worthy mother of such a hero, but I do not repine or murmur. I only feel an aching void, more sometimes than others."[48]

Among the almost 200 friends and acquaintances who sent condolence letters after hearing of the Bowditchs' loss, most reflected the same belief that celebrating death's inspirational potential required the suppression of grief. "[B]ear it properly and say 'thy will be done,'" counseled one of Livy's friends, urging her to rejoice in "such a life as his—and the noble heroic brothers who have fallen in the fight for right and liberty." Another female friend wrote to her mother, "what a privilege is yours to have offered up your son to your country's good, and to have had the sacrifice accepted." Yet another, Feraline Fox, talked of the "feeling of exultation" that her friend should experience "over the glorious death of a soldier fighting for his native land." These may have been platitudes, but they were not hollow ones. Fox's own brother had been severely wounded the previous year and would shortly die. "I can scarcely feel more perfect sympathy with you than I do now," she told her friend, "for death is very near us all at this time."[49] What stands out most strikingly in these condolence letters is the conviction that the most comforting and appropriate form of sympathy to offer at such a delicate moment was an affirmation of the writer's patriotism, a demonstration that death had, in fact, proved inspirational and useful.

The grief of friends was insufficient for the Bowditch family. Like many afflicted relatives, they immediately went in search of information to prove that their son really had died in an inspirational way. Henry Bowditch began by interviewing dozens of Nathaniel's comrades, filling page after page of hastily scribbled notes that detailed his efforts for his wife and three younger children who waited at home. One after another, these officers described how Nathaniel had rode far ahead of his column into battle, his saber aloft, unseating more than one Confederate cavalryman before suddenly finding himself outflanked and wounded on the ground. They described how he faced down his enemies, declaring that he would "never surrender," even as they stripped him of weapons and left him for dead. And they reported that he accepted his injuries in an equally heroic fashion, cheerfully and uncomplainingly. Several told how, when given a cup of water, he passed it on to "a more suffering but unknown comrade who lay by his side." Others confirmed that on his deathbed he expressed contentment at having been wounded "in the discharge of duty."[50] Bowditch and his wife sought further details to flesh out these stories. What were his feelings and how did he look on his way to Kelly's Ford? What were his precise movements during the battle? Who had seen their son give water to a wounded comrade and what words were exchanged? They wrote to anyone involved, begging for information. And they searched for any mention of Kelly's Ford in the press, carefully preserving articles from eleven different newspapers, published in five different states.[51]

Nathaniel almost certainly acted on his deathbed in the way his comrades described. Letter-writers tended to be scrupulously honest in specifying the last words and gestures of the dying, which were the most important details that families looked for in assessing the state of the soul at the point of death. One simply did not lie about matters as critical as these, even if to provide comfort to stricken relatives. This fact is attested to by the large number of soldiers' condolence letters that described wordless or painful deaths, which would have brought little solace to families who sought evidence that the dying were aware of and reconciled to their fate.[52]

This is not to claim that Nathaniel's comrades offered the whole truth. They told stories about him and, like all stories, the ones they told involved a "complex process of selection, ordering and highlighting" that gave prominence to some aspects of reality over others. Their stories not only aimed to make sense of Bowditch's sacrifice, but also reflected a perspective the teller could live with, one that offered a "subjective orientation of the self within the social relations of its world, enabling it to be imaginatively entered-into and inhabited."[53] Such perspectives were inevitably shaped by pre-existing repertoires of stories and cultural understandings of admirable battlefield behavior. Many who fought in the Civil War, particularly men of the officer class, had grown to manhood delighting in Sir Walter Scott's romantic tales of chivalry, or thrilling to Lord Tennyson's idealistic recounting of doomed British courage on the Crimean battlefields, as well as reading and hearing constantly of the self-sacrificing virtues of the Revolutionary generation.[54] When Nathaniel's comrades narrated his story, they emphasized not the unpleasant details—the gore, pain, or misery that was likely right before their eyes—nor did they focus on anything that was unique or exceptional about him. Instead, they told his tale in a way that indicated their own investment in conventional Victorian stories of battlefield martyrdom where the dying were animated by religious convictions and noble ideals. Joseph Clark, a lieutenant only briefly acquainted with Nathaniel, offered just such a story when he wrote to Olivia Bowditch of his own accord shortly after hearing of her son's death. "The whole scene rises before me," he began:

I see him charging in advance of all, fearless and true his look fixed with high resolve—his face illuminated, perhaps, with the light of coming sacrifice—I seem to hear his sabre ring, as steel meets steel in the thick [of the] fight: he is surrounded but does not yield: truth and honor and justice fight with him and he who fights with such allies conquers though he falls. Again his sword sweeps flashing down striking for the right— and then he dies—dies in the fulfillment of his fair promise. . . . [H]e has not lived in vain—for every such effort brings Heaven nearer earth.[55]

Such romanticized accounts of battlefield heroism were written and read not only by patriotic civilians, who churned them out by the tens of thousands, but also by officers themselves, often, and without any need of civilian prompting.[56]

Heroic war narratives like the one Clark imagined took shape in the first half of the nineteenth century, as writers began to transform popular perceptions of military life. Updating a late eighteenth-century image of warriors as brutal and licentious, widely read British authors in the early Victorian era had increasingly come to focus on the lives of idealistic Christian soldiers, drawing heavily from the then–immensely fashionable revival of chivalry.[57] For middle-class and elite British writers and their audiences, tales of military figures who were gentlemanly and virtuous helped to justify imperial ventures and uphold the moral superiority of elites, responding to critics of colonialism and class conflict by depicting worthy leaders who could simultaneously blend "Anglo-Saxon authority, superiority and martial prowess, with Protestant religious zeal and moral righteousness."[58]

Well-heeled Northerners like Henry Bowditch were no less concerned with upholding class-inflected versions of wartime heroism. In telling his son's story, Bowditch portrayed him as a representative of his "race," referring to a lineage of elite Bostonians and Bowditch gentlemen. It was therefore crucial for him to place Nathaniel's story in a wider context, which he did by creating an additional volume commemorating hundreds of other Massachusetts officers who died alongside his son. To accompany this volume, Bowditch hunted up as many images of these men as he could find. In line with the phrenological and craniological studies of the day, which held that character, temperament, race, and class background could be read through skull size and shape, facial features and expression, he suggested that such an array of faces revealed "fine specimens of the sons of our state . . . indicative of high-toned character." Imagining future generations of elites receiving the benefit of such models, he wrote in the preface to this volume: "May the young men of my race emulate the examples of these dead in a most noble cause."[59]

Bowditch and others like him had become interested in urging their fellow elites to replicate worthy figures like these because, much like their counterparts in Britain, they had become deeply concerned with the rising tide of self-interest and class conflict. In the prewar decades, they had watched as the social influence and moral leadership of Northeastern elites was challenged by a dramatic expansion of the white male franchise, rising levels of immigration and economic competition, and a mobile population that had taken many citizens far away from the oversight of established authorities.[60]

Historian George Fredrickson once suggested that wartime philanthropy provided a golden opportunity for "those patrician elements which had been vainly seeking a function in American society" to demonstrate their social relevance.[61]

A similar case could be made for idealized war narratives like the one created by Henry Bowditch, which celebrated the idealism and self-sacrifice of middle-class and elite Unionists. Bowditch framed his son's memorial with a quote from Sir Phillip Sydney ("Joyful is Woe for a noble cause, and welcome all its miseries"), the Elizabethan hero wounded at the battle of Zetphen in 1586 who had been immortalized not only for his glorious death but also for offering water to a wounded commoner who lay dying beside him.[62] For Bowditch, such acts of bravery and selflessness demonstrated the intrinsic leadership capacity and moral virtue of well-bred men. Emphasizing the way his son embodied the conventions of heroic martyrdom, he pictured him holding out his canteen to a wounded private, declaring his patriotic convictions, and stifling any signs of distress.

The Bowditch family found some consolation in these methodically collected details of heroism, but it never seemed to be enough. As Henry Bowditch told one of his friends, fellow physician J. N. Borland, the vision of his son's worthy behavior helped lessen his sorrow, yet only to the extent that it could be imagined as the source of instruction and stimulation: "[A]s I tremblingly hope, that his memory may tend to arouse in some slight degree, the dead, sleeping energies of the North," he told Borland, "I find a serene hope, glowing within me, that he has not gone in vain if, by his death, I can hope, that even one man can be made truly loyal, then his death has *not* been in vain."[63] Twice he raised the specter of a futile death, even as he denied the possibility with emphasis. Three times he referred to his "hope" that his son's death would inspire others, even as the modest nature of his expectations ("in some slight degree," "even a single man") pointed to a doubt about just how much inspiration one death could be expected to generate.

What he seemed to need was evidence that his son's death actually had inspired "even one man" to become a devoted Unionist. As if seeking this evidence, he sat down a few days after his son's funeral to write letters to two other local physicians, both outspoken supporters of the Peace Democrats. To each, he offered a detailed rendition of Nathaniel's story, interspersed with declarations of how proud and grateful he was to be "the father of the young martyr." Then he made clear what their response to his tale should be: "It will nerve many hearts to *undoubting unswerving loyalty* to think that the dear young blood was shed in defense of the only National Life worth having."[64] Equating his own sacrifice with that of his son, he sent an unequivocal message to these skeptics; any response from them other than unswerving loyalty was a betrayal equally of the Union dead and their grieving families. Yet the fact remained that he could never be sure if he actually had altered their minds. He was therefore exultant a few days later when a note of sympathy arrived from the famous statesman Edward Everett, with whom he had only a nodding acquaintance. Here, finally, seemed to be the proof he craved that his son's behavior had had an impact. Treating this note as a piece of evidence, he recorded his own interpretation of its significance for posterity, writing in the margins: "Nothing but Nat's public display of bravery and the wide feeling in the community in consequence thereof could have induced Mr. E to write." This was proof, he held, of the "great respect and honor" accorded not only to his son, but also to "his parents."[65] Apparently, just as he sought an acknowledgment that his son had not "died in vain," so he looked for some verification that the family's actions were appreciated and inspiring.

The barely suppressed anxiety driving this quest to demonstrate the inspirational nature of heroism suggests that Henry Bowditch was well aware that wartime deaths were open to much less flattering interpretations—his son's death perhaps even more than most.[66] After all, why had Nathaniel rushed straight into the midst of the enemy, so far in advance of his men (he was at least "8 to 10 rods" ahead of his column, according to eyewitnesses)? The most obvious explanation was that he lost control of his horse. Trying to head off this conclusion, his father emphasized the compliance of Nathaniel's mount, describing the horse to one correspondent as "perfectly docile and fearless," although "more rapid than that of any other man's on the field" that day. He had more trouble finessing another plausible interpretation of his son's swift ride straight into enemy ranks: that he had been goaded into this rash act by fear of being labeled a coward. This charge was not so easily dealt with, for many knew all about Nathaniel's concerns on that score. Just a few months after proclaiming his intent to die with his "face to the enemy," he had written home describing his first brush with danger, explaining that he had been forced to retreat in the face of a large enemy skirmishing party. On returning to camp, he had received a dressing down by a superior for not discharging his weapon as he retreated. This censure was still fresh in his mind weeks later when he next wrote to his parents: "It makes me feel badly at times when I think of it because I am afraid that the men will think me a coward." Assuring them that his fellow officers did not hold this opinion, he ended by noting, "I have made up my mind that they shall never have cause to say anything of the kind again for if it ever is my lot to be in the same place again I will fire all my carbines if I fall in the attempt."[67]

Rather than trying to expunge the details of their son's doubts and discouragements, or his run-ins with superiors—all details well known to his comrades and, no doubt, many of their families—the Bowditchs used them as the basis for their story of a son who overcame all difficulties in order to do his duty. Yet, ultimately, this family's intricate knowledge of wartime realities, and the many documents left behind to reflect them, made their attempts to memorialize their son's heroism a fragile enterprise, constantly in need of reassertion because alternative stories lay so close to the surface.

The memorials that they created reveal a lurking fear that battlefield deaths might come to be seen as meaningless slaughter, but they also show why such interpretations failed to gain currency at this time. In this war, heroism held meaning insofar as a soldier displayed an admirable character that reflected well on his family and community. To become a heroic martyr, officers had to perform conscientiously, suffer physical or emotional torments without undue complaint, exhibit moral conviction and self-control at the point of death, and embody all of those other character traits that represented the worthiness of their family and class backgrounds. Unionists like Henry Bowditch believed that there could never be too many of the same stories told, where men performed in exactly this way. How else, after all, than by telling a tale in which civilians and soldiers all embraced the same admirable behavior, could he hope to educate others to adopt the same standards? Such a mission made this family's actions in war just as noteworthy as their son's. Henry Bowditch purposefully included the family's letters to show just how much homefront support and prodding went in to creating a heroic martyr. He was proud of that fact. He wanted to show that they held Nathaniel to a high standard of uncomplaining selflessness while expecting nothing less of themselves. As the Bowditch parents worked so hard to prove at the moment of their greatest loss, it was both the burden and expression of a truly virtuous elite to model suffering's inspirational potential.

The process of creating and sustaining the story of heroic martyrdom was pressing, vital, and uplifting for this family. Henry Bowditch spent his spare moments for a decade after the war sitting in his study, carefully pasting the thousands of documents he had collected into scrapbooks. Occasionally, Katherine Day Putnam, Nathaniel's fiancée, might have sat beside him as she drew intricate borders of flowers and ivy around the pages he created. She, too, was powerfully invested in the narrative of Nathaniel's heroism, spending the rest of her life dedicated to his memory, "forever supported by her perfect confidence of a final re-union with her beloved one in death," according to Bowditch. Swapping emotional letters with him about their mutual loss, she becoming Henry's "second daughter," and he her "second father," bound together by a desire to ensure that this one death was remembered and mourned.[68] When Putnam died in 1876, a scrapbook dedicated to her memory formed the final volume in a story of wartime martyrdom that linked generations of elites together, creating a family lore that could be passed down to those yet unborn.

Ensuring the continuation of this tale, the Bowditchs housed their volumes in a custom-made memorial cabinet designed by Putnam's brother-in law, which took pride of place in the family parlor. Reflecting the quintessential Victorian passion for collecting, cataloguing, and displaying items of natural and historical interest, they placed Nathaniel's story alongside items that evoked his prewar and wartime career, including specimens collected during his school years; his pistol, field glasses, sash, and spurs; pieces of spent artillery; histories of the Civil War, and the biographies of wartime leaders. Next to these items were objects that linked Nathaniel's military service to that of his famous grandfather, including a flintlock rifle and other "relics" from the Revolutionary past.[69] Enshrining Nathaniel's rather-mundane war story behind glass and connecting it to a broader patriotic and military heritage, Henry Bowditch and his family spent a good deal of their lives investing meaning in their tale of heroic martyrdom and making sure it would not be forgotten.

It is certainly true that people in later wars continued to memorialize family members, keeping faded pictures of men in uniform on mantelpieces, or decorating walls with guns or armor to keep alive memories of military service. Yet subsequent generations no longer remembered their sons as heroic martyrs in the same way, or for the same reasons, that Henry Bowditch did. For a modern family, the aim of remembering a son alongside his comrades would be to recall his specific friendships, particularities, and uniqueness, not to reveal his representativeness as a member of a specific class and family lineage. Nor would most families nowadays recall their own struggles alongside their son's, comprehending their suffering as part of what gave meaning to his—a counterpart to his own in terms of its inspirational potential. Perhaps most important, a modern family might celebrate a son's patriotism, but their efforts would necessarily involve an overtly defensive element, since stories of heroism are now openly contested by a wide range of well-publicized alternative narratives that focus on wartime atrocities or chart war's myriad and debilitating psychological effects. Henry Bowditch might have had to labor to ensure that his son's death would be interpreted as inspiration, not tragedy. But in this task he had resources that were largely unavailable to later generations. Foremost among them were a steadfast providentialism and an abiding sense that suffering held the potential to motivate, edify, and uplift.

3

Exceptional Sufferers

A wounded man, with both legs nearly shot off, was found in the woods, singing the Star-spangled Banner; but for this circumstance the surgeons say they would not have discovered him.

"Incidents of the Battle of Belmont," in *Rebellion Record*, ed. Frank Moore (1862)

DURING A BATTLE at Roanoke Island in February 1862, a shell hit Private John Lorenze of the Ninth Regiment New Jersey Volunteers, tearing off both of his legs. According to the army chaplain who recounted his story in a New York newspaper, he lost neither "consciousness nor self-control." As he was borne away on a litter, he joked with everyone he met, inspiring them all with "his encouraging words and happy manner." Even as the fragments of his legs were removed, he "retained his spirits and cheered the surgeons by his pleasant frame of mind."[1] Similar tales broadcasting the exceptional fortitude, cheerfulness, or piety of ordinary Union sufferers circulated widely during the war. They were related by nurses and voluntary workers in their letters, diaries, and memoirs; described in newspaper articles and hospital publications; and recounted by soldiers to their families and friends. Sometimes, these stories presented men who were upbeat and jovial, like Lorenze. At other times, the afflicted were peacefully resigned, moving onlookers to tears with their trust in God, devotion to family, or commitment to the cause. But, invariably, when Unionists wrote about their sick and wounded, they described suffering white enlistees as a profound source of patriotic and religious inspiration—for comrades, civilians, and occasionally even the enemy.

Public interest in the suffering of ordinary soldiers was still fairly novel at this time in the Anglo-European world. Prior to the late eighteenth century, no scribe had recorded their experiences for posterity, and no monument had been erected to honor their sacrifices. This is hardly surprising given that premodern armies were typically understood as refuges for mercenaries, vagabonds, and conscripts, whose stake in war was limited to a hope of plundering the defeated. Regular soldiers were seen as a breed apart, mostly feared and reviled by the populace. In the aftermath of battles, a few officers might have had their names etched in stone or immortalized in chronicles and ballads, but the remainder of the dead were simply left on the field to rot, or buried in mass graves, their names lost to history.[2]

This situation only began changing with the advent of modern wars, fought not for personal or dynastic glory but for the nation. Newly urged by their leaders to identify with the causes for which they fought, regular troops were transformed into citizen-soldiers serving on behalf of "the people." In death, they were duly transfigured into national martyrs.[3] This elevation of common soldiers reflected the broader social and political transformations of the time. By the mid-eighteenth century, an Enlightenment-inspired discourse of natural rights had begun to erode fixed hierarchies and status relationships. No longer could coercion and compulsion be relied on to fill military ranks. Nor could leaders depend on the slow progress of information or widespread illiteracy to cloak public knowledge of war's impact. Instead, they had to encourage men to *want* to fight, just as they had to ensure that wartime suffering, newly exposed to the glare of public scrutiny, would not come to be seen as unnecessary or excessive.

Partisan writers and political and military leaders in the Civil War North well understood this imperative. They knew that mobilizing men for war necessitated extending the concept of heroic martyrdom from elites to ordinary soldiers. The Union armies, after all, were largely comprised of volunteers, drawn from a society that prided itself on leading the world in extending the blessings of democracy to all white men. In this period, therefore, much as in later conflicts, leaders were quick to identify battlefield injuries and deaths as the ultimate symbol of patriotic self-sacrifice. Middle-class Northern writers and voluntary workers likewise recognized the need to lionize ordinary volunteers in order to sustain popular support for the Union. Their focus on the plight of common soldiers, so emblematic of modern wars, anticipated celebratory depictions of the doughboy and GI. But in contrast to subsequent conflicts, when a soldier's bravery was largely defined by his actions on the battlefield, Civil War Northerners conceptualized wartime heroism just as often in relation to the way men suffered.

Historians have overlooked the pervasiveness of tales that focused on the nonmartial character of Union enlistees.[4] Stories of their suffering did not simply emphasize what would become a standard link between soldiers' death or injury, civic virtue, and national regeneration. Instead, they drew attention to the *way* that ordinary white soldiers suffered, dwelling for instance on how men like John Lorenze responded to their wounds, or how they behaved while hospitalized. Unlike modern accounts of war in which some men register their stoicism by ignoring or downplaying the pain of injury, these Civil War stories drew from the full range of Victorian ideas of suffering: from the belief that witnessing ideal suffering held inspirational potential, to the conviction that a positive acceptance of pain registered one's moral fiber, religious faith, and national character. Many of these mid-nineteenth-century tales had religious overtones, with men facing anguish as Christ had done: not to exhibit endurance, as a modern soldier might do, but to impress, encourage, and redeem.

Likewise, more secular Civil War stories focusing on Union sufferers' pluck and self-control did not simply concentrate on generic masculine attributes like courage and tenacity; they drew meaning from the specific set of political and cultural understandings that Northern writers invested in suffering and the responses it evoked. In describing exceptional sufferers, Unionists routinely critiqued their enemies, juxtaposing men like John Lorenze to Rebel soldiers who bemoaned their fate, gave way to despair in the face of illness, or willingly renounced the Confederacy. Attributing these differences to their superior social system and a sanctified cause, they defined admirable suffering as a sign of God's favor and an expression of white Union soldiers' civic and masculine identity. Men on both sides were equally fearless in battle, they argued, but only those who fought on the side of right—impelled by a deep sense of duty and sustained by the moral character nurtured within Northern homes—could maintain their integrity in the face of pain and affliction. For many Unionists, stories of well-borne suffering demonstrated the righteousness of their cause and the character of its white defenders, as no tale of battlefield heroics could.

And what of suffering men themselves? No doubt, many found it impossible to live up to an ideal of exemplary suffering. But it would be a mistake to assume that this ideal was solely propagated from above, or that it bore no relation to Union soldiers' experiences with wounds or injuries. The fact is that few sufferers spoke out against the equation that middle-class writers routinely made between their plight and national regeneration. Nor did they challenge the notion that Union hospitals were filled with cheerfulness, piety, and patience. On the contrary, the diaries and letters of sick and wounded soldiers make clear that large numbers expressed their suffering in terms popularized by dominant stories, representing themselves as undaunted patriots and trying to remain genial or uncomplaining no matter their misfortune. Unlike their counterparts in later wars, Union soldiers experienced their afflictions in a culture that valued ideal suffering as edifying, uplifting, and beneficial to both oneself and society. Exemplary sufferers became the Civil War's quintessential patriots—men who embodied the Union cause—not simply because they suffered for their nation, but because they suffered *well*. By commendably bearing their illnesses and injuries, they revealed the strength of their characters, the force of their religion, and the depths of their civic commitment. Such understandings made it possible for men to view suffering not as a personal ordeal, but as a continuing form of political participation. By imagining well-borne suffering as evidence of the justice of their cause, patriotic writers limited the disillusionment that might have resulted from rising death tolls, allowing ordinary white soldiers to embrace heroic status both as warriors and as worthy sufferers.

The Civil War was the first conflict in which masses of accounts specifying the names and heroic sufferings of private soldiers were published before hostilities ended; it was the first, too, in which writers tried to produce patriotism by telling inspirational stories focused on how common soldiers bore their wounds and illnesses. No one at the time remarked on this innovation. For though they had never before appeared in such numbers or for such a purpose, the stories themselves were not new. Tales of heroic suffering among regular forces first emerged in America in the early nineteenth century, as orators and revisionist historians began venerating the hardships faced by George Washington's Continental Army at Valley Forge.[5] These writers helped to create a new national mythology that located the nation's origins in the brave endurance of ordinary men. But until mid-century, theirs was still a fairly circumscribed story. A general suspicion of regular forces lingered until the Civil War, derived, in part, from an enduring Anglo-American distrust of standing armies.[6] Most Americans thus showed little concern for the plight of ordinary regulars, even those in active service.[7]

Elsewhere, the story was rapidly changing. As newspapers began reporting on the dreadful circumstances confronting soldiers in the Crimean conflict of 1854–56, the British public turned its full attention to martial suffering as never before. Not coincidentally, this was the first time that journalists and photographers had been on hand to document front-line conditions. From their new vantage point, they quickly let the public know the extent of mismanagement and scarce provisions, detailing the massive rate of fatal disease that followed.[8] The widespread public indignation led to Parliamentary inquiries and a voluntary movement aimed at improving sanitary conditions in the Crimea.[9] On the other side of the Atlantic, American leaders were receiving a valuable lesson on how quickly the newspaper-reading public became inflamed by stories of unassuaged distress. Those familiar with reportage on the Crimean conflict might also have learned something else: although the press in this war tended to picture British regulars as pitiful and unfortunate victims, there were just enough accounts of inspirational patience or piety in the British ranks to serve as models for the stories that Northern writers would later turn out in the thousands.[10]

The Crimean War powerfully demonstrated the ability of telegraph, photography, and war reportage to highlight the costs of war quickly and graphically. These innovations ensured that no government from this point on could afford to seem indifferent to soldiers' welfare, particularly not in America with its uncensored press, its extensive franchise, and its reliance on literate volunteers who wrote often to friends and families. Yet while avenues for inquiring into wartime suffering had rapidly expanded in the prewar years, the state's ability to care for sufferers had not. Like every other arm of the military, the Union Army's Medical Department was drastically ill-prepared to wage a large-scale war. In 1861 it had fewer than 100 medical staff, a few small post hospitals, no plans for the evacuation of battlefield casualties, and a negligible supply of such necessities as bandages, surgical instruments, and ambulances.[11]

Predictably, a chorus of outrage over medical conditions in the Union army soon swelled. Even before the first shots were fired, newspapers were reporting on disease epidemics sweeping through crowds of men assembled into makeshift training camps. As the battles began, correspondents catalogued a litany of distress: injured men left on the field for days before help arrived; crude field hospitals where the wounded lacked food and bedding; men dying unaided or buried in unmarked graves; callous surgeons manhandling and misdiagnosing their patients. By far the greatest share of the misery was borne by enlistees. Union officers not only received superior food and accommodation but also better medical attention, usually in separate facilities paid for out of their higher wages—facts that newspaper correspondents often noted with dismay. Detailing the aftermath of one battle, for instance, an outraged report in the *Cincinnati Daily Inquirer* described hundreds of sick men "packed like hogs in narrow pens, and left to die in filth, darkness and neglect," while officers occupied the fine homes nearby.[12]

Given its reliance on volunteer forces, the government could not let such complaints of suffering among the rank-and-file go unanswered. Although it took time and a good deal of pressure exerted by the press and public, the army was partially successful in improving its medical treatment. By 1863 it had significantly enhanced the transportation and treatment of the sick and wounded by adding a trained ambulance corps, streamlined methods of supply, new procedures for selecting and evaluating medical personnel, and a vastly expanded system of government hospitals.[13] The injured might still wait days to be removed from the field and then spend weeks in improvised hospitals close to the battlefield without adequate food or facilities. But at least some of the sick and wounded were now transported within days to one of the several hundred new general hospitals located in urban centers, where they might enjoy landscaped gardens, dramatically improved diets and medical attendance, and various recreational diversions—from well-stocked libraries, printing presses, and bowling alleys to debating societies and Bible-study groups. Faced with a vocal press, a demanding public, and a literate army, military and government leaders were constantly reminded of the link between mitigating suffering and keeping up morale among soldiers and their families.

The state went far in improving conditions for suffering enlistees. But the daunting logistics of caring for mass casualties led to a continual reliance on civilian volunteers to provide hospitals with bedding, clothing, amusements, and food. Much to the chagrin of some military and medical officers, these volunteers simply refused to recognize the army's right to oversee the sick and injured. Demanding the prerogative of supervising their contributions, volunteers inspected army hospitals and established special diet kitchens to provide patients with nutritious meals. They arrived in droves at general hospitals to visit friends, hand out homemade food, or play piano. Even after the government expanded its hospital system and provided a trained ambulance corps, voluntary agencies continued to run their own smaller medical facilities, and to help with the removal of battlefield wounded, sponsoring specially designed railway cars and outfitting steamers to transport the wounded via rail and water. Women made up a disproportionate number of these civilians. In addition to the 3,200 nurses officially appointed by Dorothea Dix in her role as superintendent of women nurses, thousands of women served as paid and unpaid volunteers in Union military hospitals.[14] Some traveled to the front under the auspices of state or national relief agencies; family members went on their own authority to tend sick and injured relatives; and a few mavericks, such as Clara Barton, solicited supplies from their friends in the North and made their way to hospitals and battlefields. Without a doubt, this was the largest number of volunteers ever before mobilized during wartime.[15]

And from their number came a constant stream of accounts of exceptional suffering.

Most voluntary workers were white and middle class, with time and money enough to invest in benevolent work. They went virtually everywhere. Following the armies, they were on hand to deal with the aftermath of most battles, documenting what they saw for civilian audiences through newspaper articles, books, pamphlets, and speeches. Unfailingly, they bore witness to the remarkable way that ordinary Union men confronted misfortune. Speaking on behalf of "the boys," Jane Hoge, a prominent member of the Northwestern Sanitary Commission, proposed to "tell the simple story of the soldiers . . . of their heroism, long-suffering and patience, even unto death" in her memoir published shortly after war's end, claiming, "they form the most striking human exemplification of divine patience the world has ever seen." She was only one of many to justify her writing as a means of publicizing common soldiers' inspirational suffering. "To the Privates of the Army" read the dedication page of another, similar reminiscence published in 1864, "whose daring in danger; patience in privation; self-sacrifice in suffering; and loyalty in love for their country, have given to the world a noble example, worthy of all imitation."[16]

In referring to soldiers' "heroism" and "daring in danger," these authors gestured toward men's battlefield participation. Like most voluntary workers, however, their narratives were centrally concerned with the aftermath of battles rather than with their progress. Through a series of vignettes, most recounted how the sick and wounded conducted themselves in hospital or on their deathbeds, often mentioning men by name, detailing their manner and expressions, and frequently adding a physical description or perhaps a brief family or work history. Some went so far as to organize their work around a succession of worthy sufferers, as did the anonymous nurse who offered chapters devoted to stories of particular patients, with titles such as "Darlington," "Gavin," "Little Corning," and "Poor Jose."[17]

Rather than trying to conceal the magnitude of distress—which could hardly be denied—these writers typically included graphic accounts of extensive injuries and horrendous pain. But instead of employing these details to discuss the nature of war, voluntary workers used them to illustrate the extent of soldiers' patriotism. Time and again, they portrayed white Union soldiers confirming that their wounds were inflicted in a good cause, relying on sentimental detail for added pathos. Offering one such vignette, Hoge told readers of a wounded soldier who had left his farm in Illinois soon after reaching the age of enlistment. Beginning with a physical description that emphasized his youthful countenance ("as fair, as though he had never heard the din of battle"), she went on to portray his tender memories of home, his "bright blue eyes" filling with tears at the mention of his mother. Woven into her scene was a description of how this patient had spent weeks in hospital bandaged from head to foot after lying for days on the battlefield in an ice storm, finally having to be "chopped out" as he was "frozen so fast in the mud." Asked if he thought "it monstrous to be left so long without help?" he replied, "Of course not . . . *how could they help it, they had to take the fort.*" Now "smiling, happy and grateful," he described the joy he and his fellow sufferers felt as they lay in the mud listening to cannons announcing a Union victory. "*I tell you*, not a man of us that could speak, but cheered, and even the men with only stumps tried to raise them and huzza," he exclaimed.[18] Using vivid examples of suffering to highlight Union troops' undaunted patriotism, voluntary workers justified the war's carnage by insisting that even the most youthful men clearly understood that suffering was necessary for victory.

There is no denying the publicity value of these stories of exemplary suffering. Voluntary workers were often intensely patriotic, convinced that their job was not just to document wartime conditions but also to strike an upbeat note that could raise lagging confidence on the home front. Emphasizing the good-humored way that soldiers coped with distress was one way to accomplish this end. "Give him anything to be cheerful about, and he will improve the opportunity," wrote one volunteer, describing hospitalized soldiers for readers of the *Atlantic Monthly*. Even those "who have lost an arm or a leg are as jolly as they can be," he claimed, "so it happens that a camp of six thousand sick and wounded, which seems at a distance a concentration of human misery . . . when near does not look half so lugubrious as you expected; and you are tempted to accuse the sick men of having entered into a conspiracy to look unnaturally happy."[19] Here was a bright picture that readers might dwell on without too much distress.

Every day, the newspapers printed new tolls of dead and wounded, but at least one might glance at these lists and imagine hospitals filled with smiling men. Painting an equally rosy image, the *Philadelphia Inquirer*'s special correspondent described a trip northward on a steamer filled "with a mass of suffering humanity," all "patient and enduring." He singled out "JAMES MCCLARY, of Company E, Second Michigan, who has three balls in each leg, both arms broken, and back badly bruised, notwithstanding which he is in good spirits, talks freely, jokes with his nurses, and bears himself with great heroism." Writers described privates who whistled and sang heedless of wounds, others barely pausing to seek treatment for serious ailments before returning to the field, even one who supposedly played the fiddle during a forty-minute operation "without missing a note or moving a muscle."[20] To all on the home front who felt discouraged, these stories plainly sought to inspire them with the knowledge that soldiers were dealing admirably with their wartime reversals.

If they kept one eye on civilian morale, volunteers usually had the other on potential donors who might contribute to their organizations. Presenting the wounded to civilian contributors as the epitome of Christian selflessness was one of their most popular strategies. "Say, mister, there's a fellow right acrost there, he ain't had nothing to eat since the day before yesterday. I guess he'd like some o' that 'ere stuff," one injured man reportedly told Alfred Bloor, an assistant secretary with the Sanitary Commission.[21] Frederick Law Olmsted, the commission's general secretary, reported the same generous spirit, quoting the letters of a male subordinate whom the injured addressed with statements such as: "I guess that next fellow wants it mor'n I do," or "Won't you jus' go to that man over there first. . . . I hearn him kind o' groan jus' now; must be pretty bad hurt, I guess: I had'n't got anythin' only a flesh-wound!"[22] The format that both men used to relate these tales of remarkable selflessness drew from two other approaches favored by civilian volunteers: first, they arranged their recollections in the form of personal letters, written in the present tense and addressed to a specific correspondent (usually an aid society), a strategy that lent their words immediacy and authenticity. Second, they used a vernacular that marked Union privates as rustics thankful for the slightest attention—men made of the honest, unassuming stuff that marked the citizen-soldier. Allowing their readers to bask in the knowledge of helping the less fortunate, they reassured all their constituents that the wounded were generous and humble, well worthy of their aid.

Northern voluntary workers, motivated by patriotism and a need to raise funds, obviously saw what they wanted to see: thousands upon thousands of exemplary Union sufferers. They saw soldiers who were intensely patriotic even in the depths of agony, men who were self-effacing and patient, sustained by love of family and faith to the end. Given the obvious lack of realism in their accounts—for surely *some* Union soldiers suffered in less than admirable ways—modern readers might be forgiven for dismissing their writing as mere propaganda. Yet it is worthwhile noting that disparate civilians, newspaper reporters, army doctors—in fact, practically every Northerner who worked among the wounded—told precisely the same stories, focusing their tales not tangentially but centrally on how the sick and injured bore their fate. Writers lavished attention on what men said and how they acted on their deathbeds or in hospitals, often devoting the bulk of their attention to this topic. They did so in published and unpublished sources, written both during and immediately after war's end.[23]

Clearly, tales of exemplary suffering appealed for a reason. We cannot write them off as mere apologies for the slaughter. For they often highlighted, rather than minimized, the pain of the sick and injured, as did the tale above in describing wounded youths who lay frozen on the field for days with agonizing wounds. Indeed, the more graphic the details of the torment, the better to emphasize the point of the story: the exceptional suffering of these men. Rather than simply denying the costs of war, stories of exemplary suffering expressed what most Unionists saw as the conflict's underlying truth: victory depended on the nature of the white Union soldiery and the society they came from. Ultimately, they located military success not on the battlefields, but in the character of white soldiers and the emotional connections forged between soldiers and civilians, which they believed had sustained this character throughout the war. This fact becomes clear in placing stories of exemplary sufferers alongside those told about the Confederate wounded and black soldiers, both of whom became foils against which the virtues of white Union enlistees stood out in stark relief.

Pro-Union writers tended to be scathing in their assessments of how Confederates and their supporters responded to affliction. When they described wounded Rebels, Northern volunteers invariably described churlish, selfish, embittered men, juxtaposing their inappropriate reactions to white Union soldiers' idealized behavior. "It is very rarely that our brave *Union* soldiers complain, or bear impatiently their wounds," wrote one female hospital worker after describing the grumbling of injured Confederates. Another noted in her diary that a Confederate soldier sent to her ward was "pleasantly disposed and reconciled to his fate, unlike the others I have seen."[24] More critical yet, Union nurse Emily Souder told a friend that wounded Rebels were "without fortitude or much else that makes a man what he should be," adding in a further letter, "they bear their suffering very differently from our men. . . . They whine, cry, and complain." Reaching a similar conclusion, a male volunteer who compared the behavior of the two sides reported that among Rebel prisoners, "There is not only more whimpering, but more fretfulness and bitterness of spirit, evinced chiefly in want of regard [of] one for another." Nor were volunteers the only ones to critique the behavior of Confederate sufferers. The Northern press was equally forthright in its condemnation, with one article published in the *New York Herald* in mid-1862 reporting that even "slightly disabled" Confederates moaned and protested, demanding immediate treatment, while dauntless Union soldiers lay on the ground "with horrid and gaping wounds without a complaining word or look."[25]

Pro-Union writers attributed this peevishness to a lack of self-control and an inadequate patriotism. To many Northern minds, Confederate soldiers simply lacked the fortitude necessary to bear up under stress. In her wartime diary, one voluntary worker noted, "The chance of a Southerner to live after going to a hospital is not over a fourth as good as for one of our Northern boys." Although admitting that Confederate soldiers could be daring in battle, where they could draw enthusiasm from their comrades and from the inherent drama of the moment, she suggested that coping with affliction was a different matter entirely, requiring a "moral" strength available only to those who knew deep down that their actions were just. Southerners could thus "do more fighting with less food while in the field," she held, "but when the excitement is over they lose heart and die."[26] This was the same argument used by a Northern journalist in mid-1862, who described Union soldiers buoyed by their "noble cause," bearing their pain "with silent manliness," in contrast to "wounded rebels [who] often groaned piteously, deploring their fate." All of the army surgeons he had consulted allegedly agreed: Confederate troops were more likely to die after operations due to their feeble wills, and to "bloat and decompose much sooner after death" as a result of immoderate habits, such as constant drinking. For many Northerners, exemplary suffering was proof that Union soldiers were more self-disciplined and patriotic than their Confederate counterparts, confirming common perceptions of white Northern men as rational, adult citizens fighting against an overly passionate, irrational, and effeminate South.[27]

Those of a more religious frame of mind believed not only that admirable suffering evidenced superior willpower and patriotism, but also that it testified to God's presence, particularly if death hovered over the sufferer. For Christians, the last few hours before death had long been of utmost significance, the moment when the sufferer confronted God's judgment and all pretense and falsehood were stripped away. There were only two ways to exit the world: either the dying revealed the presence of grace through their serenity, or they signaled its absence by bemoaning their fate. For believers, the descent of calm acceptance marked the instant the soul began its transition, a fleeting moment when a window between the two worlds stood ajar, providing onlookers with clear evidence of an afterlife as well as reassurance that the dying had achieved salvation. Northern writers often glimpsed the hand of God as they watched the faces of dying Union soldiers, as did the nurse who described a fading patient as suffused by a "radiance . . . streaming through the open portal of eternity [telling] of the glory upon which his soul is entering."[28]

Yet the comfort that came from watching a loved one's calm, clear-eyed departure was clearly beyond the reach of most who lost relatives at this time. Battlefield deaths generally occurred too suddenly to leave time for reflection, while thousands died anonymously, receiving a "lonely impersonal burial in southern soil," thereby making it hard for relatives to imagine a loved one's last moments.[29] If it was impossible for them to reconstruct the deathbed behavior of their own family members, however, they could take solace in an extensive literature written by female nurses and civilian volunteers which was filled with examples of Union soldiers dying good deaths—a literature suggesting that all who died or suffered for the Union had necessarily been saved. Illustrating her war narrative with abundant scenes of admirable sufferers expressing their love of God and country, Jane Hoge told her readers, "This spirit was born with the army, and remained with it from the beginning to the end, and has baffled our investigation to discover its cause." She could only conclude: "It was one manifestation of God's power in the work of our national redemption."[30]

Unsurprisingly, Hoge's assumption that God sided with the Union was a pervasive one among Northerners. Most believed their model republic to have been ordained by God, which meant that Southern intransigence was both wrong and profane.[31] Nothing seemed to confirm this perspective more than evidence of Confederates moaning on their deathbeds or wailing in the face of suffering. If God had been with them, so the thinking went, they would have had the peace of mind to tolerate their burdens without protest. This was the neat circular logic used by writers like Hoge. What could explain their soldiers' unique patriotism and fortitude in suffering? Since only the truly pious were calm and resigned under affliction, then the answer must lie in a godly cause. And where was the evidence that the cause was sanctified? One need look no further than the patriotism and fortitude of Union sufferers.

Condemning the conduct of all dying and injured Rebels was only one way of endorsing this logic. Occasionally, Northern writers excluded Confederate enlistees from this censure, drawing upon a belief, widespread at the beginning of the war among Unionists, that elite slaveholders were mainly responsible for inciting sectional violence.[32] Thus, enemy officers in their accounts were generally haughty and immune from sympathetic overtures, bitterly railing against their fate to the end. But an occasional Confederate private appeared eager to revert to Unionism at the first sign of fraternal sentiment.[33] Writing for a soldier-readership, for instance, one veteran recounted the aftermath of a battle in which his regiment had participated. Coming upon a group of wounded Confederates, he described "a youth, of fragile form and girlish look, lying a little to the left of the rest," his "chestnut curls ... thrown rudely back from a forehead of pearly whiteness." Raising "his large, lustrous eyes, and extended a tiny hand with a beseeching countenance," he told those around him: "I am not a rebel, but they made me fight." Amid this "scene of carnage and death," he explained, "grim heroes who had repulsed the shock of a hundred rebel charges . . . uncovered their heads to the dying boy, and big tears stood in their eyes, while their hearts heaved with emotions that evinced their love for the beautiful and pure."[34] Demonstrating that the Northern war effort was motivated by principle rather than vengeance, he implied that inherently tenderhearted Union soldiers, like himself, were eager to forgive their enemies—or at least those they could imagine as feminized victims of a ruthless Confederate leadership.

Affirming that they maintained an instinctive tenderness, Northern writers claimed a virtual monopoly on the compassionate treatment of the wounded and dead. Tales of Rebel surgeons abandoning or mistreating their patients were one popular means of juxtaposing the varying humanity of the two sides. Describing himself confronting a shed filled with hundreds of wounded Confederates, one Northern volunteer described a Rebel surgeon casually lazing about smoking his pipe and "never showing sympathy enough to dress a single wound," "while our own soldiers acted as their nurses, treating them as tenderly as they could." More common yet were accounts of Confederate soldiers' cruelty. Barely a week went by without a Northern headline announcing some new "Rebel barbarity"—from the murder of unarmed civilians to the mutilation of the dead.[35]

Yet nothing demonstrated Southern depravity more plainly than the allegations of heartlessness heaped on white Southern women during the war. According to outraged Northern commentators, they swanned about in jewelry made from Union soldiers' bones. They drank from their enemy's carved-out skulls and carried purses fashioned out of their skin. No Union soldier's grave was safe from their desecration.[36] Nor, according to Northern reports, did they show any sympathy when directly confronted with suffering, even when those afflicted were from the Confederacy. Telling of a white Southern woman and her daughters sitting in their yard as it filled up with wounded men from both sides, another Union volunteer depicted herself working furiously to assuage distress while these callous women looked on, smoking their pipes, using snuff, and showing not "the slightest possible concern or interest in the dreadful scenes around . . . them."[37] Given common perceptions of women as naturally more tenderhearted than men, there was no better evidence of Southern corruption than these stories of cruel and unsympathetic women.

In the minds of most Northern writers, the origins of this heartless response to suffering clearly lay in the Southern social order. Primed by decades of abolitionist writing, they pointed out that slavery violated the sanctity of family life, precluding the proper ties of affection that bound together family members and, by extension, citizens in general. Relationships in a slave society were based not on sentiment but on hierarchy and brutality, they believed, making cruelty and violence a part of everyday life.[38] Endless stories portraying the intrinsic sympathy of Northerners epitomized a belief in the moral virtues of a free-labor society, just as tales of cruel Southern women and inherently compassionate Unionists shifted attention away from Northerners' own culpability in causing suffering.

As they trumpeted their superior civilization, however, white Northern writers were careful to portray exemplary suffering as an attribute predominantly confined to the men of their race and culture. Just as Confederates were said to lack the willpower that enabled admirable suffering, so slavery had supposedly corrupted the self-control of black men. In evidence, writers could point to the fact that black soldiers succumbed to much higher rates of fatal disease than white troops, a difference that most put down to a want of the right attitude.[39] On a tour through the wards of a "colored" hospital, for example, one volunteer testified to the "beautiful" demeanor of the patients, "so gentle, so polite, so grateful for the least kindness." Championing their aspirations for freedom, he saw much evidence "of a desire for mental improvement and religious life," but he went on to note that "they die quicker and from less cause than the white" because "[t]hey have not the same stubborn hopefulness and hilarity."[40]

This writer noticed and commented on black suffering, as did large numbers of Northern voluntary workers. Many were abolitionists who felt compassion for the plight of slaves or destitute freedmen and -women. But they did not connect black suffering and selfless devotion to the commonweal in the insistent way that they did for white Union soldiers. Take, for example, William Howell Reed's account of his travels among the wounded. His narrative included dozens of reports of white sufferers expressing political convictions, alongside only two vignettes recounting black deaths. One described an "old negro" dictating a last message to his wife: "the tears dropped one by one down upon his coarse beard as he tried to express his gratitude. He told me to write to his wife that 'he was happy'. . . and he felt that the good Father was very near, [then] the old man sank back upon his pillow to die." In this portrayal, as in a later one dealing with the death of a "friendless colored boy," black sufferers are patient and pious, but the subjects are too young or too old to have participated in battle. Although Reed devoted an entire chapter to the establishment of a "Colored Hospital" at City Point, he chose to focus not on the behavior of its soldier-inmates, as he did in scenes dealing with white troops, but rather on the exceptional character of its white nurse, Helen Gilson. Not coincidentally, he had earlier pictured Gilson lecturing a group of freedmen and -women on their need to learn the civic virtue and independence necessary for full citizenship. Like Reed, many white writers drew sympathetic portraits of black suffering—as sad and unfortunate, but ultimately private. What made their depictions of white sufferers so different was the image of these men bearing up selflessly for an abstract political good.[41]

White Northern volunteers also frequently relied on African American characters for comic relief, helping to further distance black suffering from political commitment. Returning from a trip to distribute supplies to soldiers stationed at Fort Donelson, Sarah Henshaw, a member of the Northwestern Sanitary Commission, recounted two incidents, "amid the smiles and tears of eager listeners." The smiles were all for the frivolous antics of a "colored boy," the "servant" to a Southern officer, who told of his impressions during the siege as he tried to evade Union shells: "I run one way, den t'oder way, balls com everywhar. . . . I didn't mind 'em much; 'pears like I got used to de *strong* balls. But whenever de *rotten balls* come—Golly! how I was skeered!" This farcical exchange denied her audience the chance to empathize with a slave held captive and forced to undergo the terror of a Union bombardment. Just as noteworthy, it gave added distinction to the white sufferer in Henshaw's next vignette. While her audience chuckled over the image of a black boy dodging shells likened to rotten fruit, she shifted to a solemn tone, set in "one of the miserable rooms where amputations were going on." As the surgeons did their work, a "fine-looking young man" stood leaning against a window for support. Finally unable to contain himself, he began rifling through the pile of severed limbs lying at the surgeons' feet. Drawing forth his own "pale, refined hand" from the jumble, he raised it above his head, crying, "Hurrah! hurrah! for the Stars and Stripes!"[42] Presenting war as a game for the carefree "colored boy," it was that much easier for Henshaw to emphasize the point she wanted to make in her next anecdote: no matter what class white Union soldiers came from, they soberly grasped, indeed celebrated, the sacrifices required to maintain their political system.

Through stories like these, then, Northern civilians helped to cement a commonplace understanding about the meaning of white Union enlistees' suffering. Exceptional sufferers typified all that was decent about a free-labor society and contemptible about their enemies. Those who suffered well— who retained their political commitments, their love of family, and their faith in God no matter what—revealed the kind of moral fiber cultivated within a civilized community. They demonstrated a self-control that only white men could attain, and they evinced a depth of political loyalty only available to those living within a democratic republic. Most important, they proved the divine righteousness of their cause, since only those with a clear conscience and God on their side could possibly suffer so well. In short, exemplary sufferers personified the Union.

———◆◆◆———

It was no easy matter for Union enlistees to suffer in the prescribed way, given the medical realities they confronted. As anyone who has read their letters and diaries will attest, these men found plenty to complain about when it came to their medical treatment. A significant portion simply did not trust trained physicians. "Whenever a man gets in the hospital he is in the killing pen," one private informed his family; another wrote to his brother that he would gladly "see half of the surgeons shot" after learning "how they butcher the poor wounded boys up."[43] Lying in his cot suffering from dysentery, Henry Sentell voiced a similar skepticism toward the medical profession as a whole. In one letter he told his parents that army doctors "do not care whither they killed or cured the boys," the following week complaining to his brother, "they are a *Lazy worthless set throughout the army* (with a few exceptions)." In part, this skepticism arose from the fact that most soldiers had little prior experience with trained physicians. Female kin still treated most illnesses in the prewar era, using patent medicines or folk remedies. Hospitals tended to accommodate only those without relatives, too poor or desperate to find help elsewhere. Given the hurried, often brutal nature of army medicine (not to mention most physicians' dubious credentials), it is not surprising that many men remained unimpressed with their introduction to professionalized care. "If ever I longed for a mother's care and a father's presence, it is now," wrote one ailing private to his parents, after registering distrust for his doctor's remedies.[44]

Constant complaints among the rank-and-file over the state of wartime medicine continued throughout the Civil War. Men frequently gave vent to their disgust over the lack of personal attention to their own or their comrades' sufferings. They wrote home bitterly railing against the unfeeling response from officers toward their distress, or the meager government facilities for the wounded. Patients lying in hospital beds found multiple additional causes for protest, ranging from deplorable hospital food and sheer boredom to lack of consideration from doctors or tardy letter writers.[45] Yet despite all of their legitimate grievances, there is one thing that Union soldiers rarely protested in their letters and diaries: their own suffering. To quite a remarkable degree, men worked to smother any signs of anguish and to voice positive acceptance of wounds or illnesses.

Even if it was not always possible for the sick and wounded to be good-humored and content, lapses could easily be explained away. Everyone in this period accepted that even the most worthy sufferer might scream and groan when in extreme pain—at the moment of being wounded, say, or during or immediately after an operation. And soldiers and civilian writers also commonly distinguished between men's conscious and unconscious responses to pain. When white Union soldiers were vocal in their agony, most judged them to be unconscious, a state only worthy of note in passing. Instead, they granted meaning only to what these sufferers did when they seemed to be in control of their actions. Just as spectators gave or withheld sympathy depending on their subjective interpretation of suffering—condemning one sufferer for exhibiting brute-like insensitivity, while praising another behaving in the same way for noble endurance—this distinction allowed wide latitude to onlookers in classifying who was, or was not, worthy of respect. Describing a dying patient, for instance, one female nurse observed: "While consciousness lasted, he firmly retained his self-control; but at last reason gave way, and the groans and distressing cries which for a few days preceded his death told over what a depth of agony his soul triumphed before his brain lost power."[46] If a Confederate patient had conducted himself in the same way, this nurse might have concluded that he lacked willpower or gratitude. But for her Union patient, she took it for granted that groans and cries evidenced pain that was suppressed with heroic endurance whenever possible. Union soldiers similarly divided sufferers' behavior into meaningful actions performed in periods of seeming consciousness and incoherent, largely irrelevant ones taking place in moments of apparent oblivion, as did the private who told this family that his brother had been "out of his head most of the time," on his deathbed, but "when he was in his write [*sic*] mind he wanted me to read the Bible to him."[47] Anything he said while "out of his head" was immaterial; all that mattered was that when he had apparently regained self-control, piety was foremost in his thoughts.

Yet the most worthy sufferers worked on suppressing any sign of dejection right from the outset. This fact is borne out by the behavior of Jonathan Stowe, a thirty-year-old farmer from Grafton, Massachusetts, who was one of the many thousands mortally wounded at the Battle of Antietam in September 1862. Immobilized by a leg wound as the fighting went on around him, Stowe took out his diary and recorded his fear of being hit again: "Battle O horrid battle. . . . Am in severe pain how the shells fly." He lay on the field all through the following day and part of the next, listening to the injured screaming for water. Finally the Union army advanced, sending in ambulances to take the wounded to a nearby barn now serving as a field hospital. Those most desperately in need found themselves inside, near where the few available surgeons were bending over tables extracting lead from flesh, or cutting off damaged limbs. Stowe waited on some straw just beyond in the open air, surrounded by hundreds of other sufferers. "How cheerful the boys appear. Many must loose [*sic*] their legs or arms but they do not murmur," he wrote the next day, right before his own leg was amputated.[48]

Lying there on the hard ground, alongside distressed men in various states of mutilation, it now seems improbable that what Stowe would find most worthy of note was his comrades' cheerfulness. But so it was. After his operation there was almost nothing to eat and few medical attendants. "People come in from all parts of the country. Stare at us but do not find time to do anything," he wrote on September 21. It took another two days for voluntary workers to arrive with supplies, and several more before he received a bed sack and anything to eat besides bread and milk. In the meantime, he did his best to help a nearby friend, one of the several dozen amputees waiting until they gained strength enough to bear the long ambulance ride northward. Most had diarrhea, but there were no chamber pots and no one to help. "We are so helpless that can do nothing to relieve nature without *long pains*," he wrote on September 26, having earlier described this situation as "ludicrous." This was the closest he came to directly condemning his appalling surroundings. Two days earlier, he recorded in his diary: "One week today fought and wounded. *Such a week*. Suffering all around. I cannot complain for others are as bad some worse." Nights were the most dreadful. The days were mostly hot but the weather turned frigid in the evenings, when the few nurses on hand left for the day. The sickening "smell from mortifying limbs" and the "horrid dreams & screams" of Stowe's comrade kept him awake as much as the agony of his own wound. Few men became better acquainted with the full extent of every horror that war could inflict; none had more reason to complain. Yet Stowe still found time in the four days before he died to praise those who finally came around to help him: the "kind hearted" chaplain who telegrammed his parents; the "patient and kind" male nurse who dressed his limb; the "earnest" "good" surgeon who advised him to forsake his temperance pledge and take brandy to save his life; and the female volunteers who at last dispensed decent food, seeming to "employ their whole time for us." A biographical sketch, written by a friend shortly after his death, depicted his final weeks of inspirational suffering. To a visiting comrade he announced, "Yes I have lost one leg but we drove the Rebels." On making inquiries among his nurses, the writer "learned he was uncomplaining rarely asking for anything to be done for him but very greatful [*sic*] for volunteered kindnesses," and "though suffering extreme agony was cheerful himself and ever ready with words to cheer the desponding ones around him."[49] Nothing was more important to Stowe than suffering in the right way—staying optimistic and tolerant, giving thanks to anyone who sympathized.

Before his enlistment in the Union army, Stowe had been an admired figure in his hometown, well known as a man of self-disciplined habits who studied the latest in agricultural improvements, took an active part in community life, and regularly attended church. His final weeks were of a piece with the rest of a life spent in the pursuit of spiritual and physical improvement and a respectable character. Like other reform-minded Northerners in the prewar decades, he took particular pride in staying healthy by eating wholesome food and refusing stimulants. This disciplined regimen explains the curious telegraph that he sent to his family right before his limb was amputated: "I am wounded pretty badly. Have lain 48 hours without dressing. . . . I rejoice that my health is good." Having dedicated himself to achieving control over mind and body, Stowe believed that he would now bear the strain of injury better than most. He remained convinced that willpower would see him through, even as he was informed that he could not live, telling his brother, "Oh yes I shall," only minutes before he died.[50]

For nineteenth-century men like Stowe, there were decided medical advantages to bearing up under pain. Both physicians and laypeople thought of patients' attitudes as crucial to the healing process. They saw "mind and body, emotions and physiological dysfunction, internal and external environment" as inseparably connected, writes Charles Rosenberg, granting volition a central role in overcoming disease or recovering from wounds.[51] Cheerfulness was typically depicted as a triumph of willpower, a sure sign that a patient had the physical and emotional control that could assure recovery. Pessimism or gloominess, by contrast, showed a lack of resolve that would inevitably hamper recuperation. As one Civil War nurse put it, despondency was the sure mark of a "hopeless case." Patients "were very likely not to recover if they made up their minds that they must die." Union soldiers were no less convinced of the health benefits of a positive attitude, often claiming in their correspondence that sickness and death inevitably flowed from despair.[52]

Alongside these medical rationales, religious soldiers like Stowe had an equally important reason to model exemplary suffering, for it offered a potent way to propagate their beliefs. In becoming a sufferer, men faced a moment of truth. Just as it was impossible to simulate a calm death, so they could not feign admirable suffering: a patient either believed that God had delivered suffering for a purpose and was buoyed by this knowledge, or he gave in to despair. By suffering well, Stowe witnessed the sincerity of his beliefs, revealing their power to conquer even the greatest hardship. He became an inspirational figure, imparting a message akin to that of Christ on the cross: no amount of suffering could extinguish true faith. At a time when the majority shared Stowe's Christianity, such faith-based understandings of suffering had wide appeal. Writing to a female friend from his hospital bed, William Dulach explained: "I am pretty lonesome here amongst strangers still I can bear it with all patience for I am aware that it was the hand of God and he knows best how to treat us to make us fit for heaven."[53] Epitomizing serene acceptance of providence, he expressed sentiments that were repeated in the letters of countless enlisted men.

Religious and political beliefs merged seamlessly for most Union troops. They imagined God actively directing the course of daily events, viewing themselves struggling in a cause that formed an intricate part of his design. Faith in God and Unionism were inseparable; a man simultaneously demonstrated both in suffering well. Exemplary suffering was thus just as impressive as battlefield bravery—sometimes more so—according to some Union troops. Writing for a hospital newspaper in June 1864, one patient asked rhetorically: "The Brave Soldier—Who is He?" His answer was that the highest form of bravery could only be found in hospitals. Men in battle were sustained by each other and by the excitement of the moment, he explained, whereas a sick and wounded troops could "draw inspiration" only from "faith of the Gospel and from justice of the cause for which he suffers."[54] If "God is with him," he continued:

> Then shall his soul be truly strong. Then shall no complaint escape his lips. An inward fire will burn within his soul, which will quicken every secret, manly impulse. . . . Added to this, let there be just views of this great struggle for National life. . . . Let him consider how all liberty, justice and righteousness are imperilled in this war for the Union. . . . Let him thus think and feel, and he shall find an inspiration of true bravery in the hours of waiting, lingering agony.[55]

Well-borne suffering required and demonstrated one's religious and political convictions for this writer. It went without saying that it was impossible to suffer well without such combined faith. Clearly, he was not interested in demonstrating a stoic detachment from pain, as a soldier might do in a more secular context. Rather, he pointed to "the hours of waiting, lingering agony," stressing the depths of inspiration needed to triumph over anguish in much the same way as did civilian volunteers who described torments endured the better to accentuate extraordinary suffering.

Others similarly contrasted the bravery required of men in hospitals compared to those on the battlefield. Writing in a different hospital newspaper near the end of the war, another Union soldier explained that battlefield courage "courts observation." It was essentially amoral, he pointed out, just as likely to "give its strength to evil . . . nerv[ing] the arm of the thief or the manslayer." The impressive behavior of sick and wounded Unionists was of a different order. Taking place beyond the limelight, sustained by no ulterior motive, their admirable response to affliction necessarily sprang from deep conviction. "Patience dwells only in the bosom of piety, and always beholds the face of [the] father in heaven," he concluded. Making a similar point by emphasizing the fleeting nature of battlefield courage, another writer explained in his local newspaper: "Man's nerve can inspire him to do one grand, heroic deed, but it requires wonderful grace to enable him to go patiently and persistently. . . . Courage is far more easy than patience; thousands have courage to dare who have not patience to endure."[56]

As historian Earl J. Hess explains, it was common for Union troops to distinguish between moral and physical courage. Whereas moral courage was thought to depend on inner resources and deliberate exertion, physical courage was understood as a more impulsive and thus less resilient emotion. In battle, the man of moral courage supposedly recognized the danger but consciously strove to overcome fear in order to do his duty, whereas the physically courageous soldier simply got caught up in the moment, prompted to act only by "the nervous stimulus of combat."[57] Drawing on a similar contrast, sick and wounded soldiers highlighted the underlying beliefs that animated exemplary suffering. Any man might be capable of momentary bravery, but only one sustained by genuine conviction could suffer well. As one patient summed up the situation in his hospital newspaper in January 1864: "No army of ancient or modern times—no army which Caesar, Alexander, or Napoleon ever led, has excelled the army of the Union in personal sufferings, patience, endurance, heroism and glorious military exploits."[58] Whereas "glorious military exploits" were obviously part of what defined an unparalleled army for this man, the "personal sufferings, patience, endurance, [and] heroism" of the rank-and-file were equally crucial, bound together in such a way that "heroism" might be expressed just as easily through "personal sufferings" as by battlefield participation.

Pious soldiers might have remained solemnly devout and patriotic in their affliction, yet there were also other, less religious modes of admirable suffering available to men in this era. As in the wars that preceded and followed this one, men of the officer class widely admired the upbeat *sangfroid* supposedly displayed by European military leaders such as the Duke of Wellington in the face of suffering. At the conclusion of the Battle of Waterloo, his second-in-command is said to have remarked, "By God, sir, I've lost my leg!" while he, barely glancing up from a survey of the field, coolly replied, "By God, sir, so you have!"[59] For many elites, such nonchalance in the midst of a crisis reflected the composure of those born to lead, occasioning awed respect rather than mirth. British and European officers had developed *sangfroid* into something of a stylized art by mid-century, drawing attention rather flamboyantly to the sardonic one-liner in any situation that would seem to demand a more agitated response. Union officers were quick to take their lead, as when General Daniel Sickles, fresh from losing a limb at Gettysburg, began a speech to a cheering crowd by saying: "Although I am now suffering some little inconvenience, owing to a casualty that occurred in a recent battle ..."[60] With his studied casualness, Sickles no doubt aimed to deliver his speech with what Victorian writers called "aplomb," a mix of poise and droll wit that indicated self-assured ease among inferiors.

Enlisted soldiers regularly aimed for the same breezy unconcern in relation to their wounds, though they did so in a more egalitarian context and thus to different effect. When they happily bantered about their injuries, or laughed off their ailments, the rank-and-file registered self-control no less than Sickles did. But their joviality was of a more down-to-earth variety, indicating that they were good sports, convivial and accommodating, and not taking themselves too seriously. Adopting an unaffected simplicity, they marked themselves as ideal republican citizens—men who were too independent and vigorous to be crushed by misfortune, and too frank and forthright to care for others' opinions. In the parlance of the day, they had "pluck," a term commonly applied to ordinary soldiers capable of admirable control in dangerous or trying situations. "'Pluck' is another name for the heroic endurance of torturing wounds, and is so frequently seen in our Wards, as to occasion no remark," explained one writer for the *Armory Square Hospital Gazette*. "The want of it in any case is noticed and wondered at, so high is the tone and spirit of our wounded heroes. A leg off is nothing."[61]

It would be all too easy to read irony into such statements today, particularly in the wake of World War I—a conflict that popularized a very different style of phlegmatic humor, designed specifically to highlight the gap between idealistic accounts of battle and gruesome realities of injury. But Civil War Northerners intended no satire in conjuring up a wounded man who faced injury with such "heroic endurance" that he barely noticing an amputated limb. Civil War enlistees might have had a well-developed sense of irony when it came to parodying puffed-up superiors, cowardly comrades, or ined-

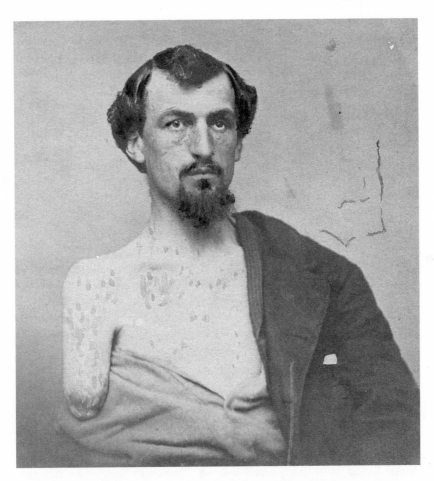

Figure 2. John F. Chase was one of many plucky Union enlistees. By his own account, he suffered forty-eight wounds during the Battle of Gettysburg (injuries he emphasized in this retouched photograph by drawing them in with pen). Having been given up for dead, he was thrown into a wagon filled with corpses on their way to burial trenches. But he regained consciousness, much to the wagon driver's astonishment, and immediately asked, "Did we win the battle?" Prioritizing the war effort instead of his own suffering, his response mirrored that of the countless exemplary sufferers who appeared in wartime poems, songs and stories. (Courtesy of William Oland Bourne Papers, Manuscript Division, Library of Congress, Washington, D.C.)

ible rations, but many unself-consciously suggested that "a leg off is nothing" in the expectation that readers would take their words seriously and simply be impressed by soldiers' characters.[62]

Whether the exemplary sufferer was an earnest believer, a plucky regular, or an imperturbable officer, self-control was key. Its importance for men at this time is just as evident in what they left unsaid as by what they wrote in diaries and letters. At best, hospitalized soldiers used a few words to describe how they felt about injuries or sickness.[63] It was obviously beside the point for them to chart their inner lives, either for themselves or for their families—to document, say, their changing mental or emotional responses to injury, or their distinctive experiences of suffering—in the way that soldiers injured in wartime routinely do today. In modern accounts of wartime suffering, the focus is invariably on men's psychological confrontation with injury or illness and with the idiosyncratic ways that traumatic experiences reshape self-perception.[64] Soldiers who refuse to discuss their sufferings are now understood as repressing their emotions, refusing to "come to terms" with experiences that will inevitably find release in subconscious, usually destructive ways.

For Union soldiers, detailing personal responses to illness was neither here nor there. No matter their class or context, they were remarkably taciturn when it came to describing the experience of being a sufferer. Even middle-class and elite soldiers—men who were generally more expansive on personal feelings than less-tutored peers, given their superior educations and literacy—rarely discussed the emotional impact of wounds or prolonged sickness.[65] Little wonder, since their culture placed small value on mining a deep interiority in ways that could highlight complex individuality. Exemplary sufferers were supposed to be instantly recognizable to others, exceptional not in their nature, temperament, or interior life but in their impressive ability to embody widely accepted standards. When their culture told tales of suffering, the aim was not to chart a sufferer's particular experience of pain and trauma. It was to explore what many saw as life's central conundrum: if God, in his inexplicable wisdom, chooses to bring down suffering down upon me, how will I respond? And how will my response affect those around me? Self-examination was simply immaterial to this understanding of suffering.

Union sufferers thus displayed their composure mainly through behavior rather than words, representing self-control only in silence. When they wrote to friends and family members, most were clear on the precise nature and location of wounds, usually noting the pain of being injured as well. Sending a fairly typical account to his mother soon after finding himself in hospital, Hiram Williams merely stated, "I expect you have heard of me being wounded. . . . I have lost my left foot and right toes. I suffered a great deal the first few days but this last week I have not had much pain. . . . I have not any more to say . . . this leaves me in good spirits." Several weeks later, he let her know: "I am in good health and nothing to complain of I [have] plenty to eat and good attendence. I dont know w[h]at more to tell you."[66] Factual and concise, he conveyed virtually nothing about his feelings, simply making the obvious point that he had suffered, but was now in good hands.

Undergoing an operation under nineteenth-century medical conditions would have left some without the strength to write much, but many of the injured had plenty to say on topics they deemed relevant. Telling his sister about a wound that would shortly prove fatal, George Rollins explained: "The ball entered just at the side of the Cap of the joint and is now in my arm—The sergeon cannot find it—I have been wounded one week and the wound is doing well—I have suffered considerable pain but 'tis not so bad now.'" This was all he revealed about his personal experiences of injury and suffering. But he did go on to pen a long and graphic account of the battle of Fredericksburg in which his wound was received.[67]

It is possible that Williams and Rollins wrote about their wounds only briefly because they chose not to worry their family members. Yet it is also the case that when injured men discussed their hospital treatment long after recovery was assured, they were just as likely to recount individual experiences of suffering in just a few words before moving on to discuss topics they considered more relevant. Many focused on praising those who had come to their aid, as had Jonathan Stowe, the soldier mentioned above who suffered a leg amputation during the Battle of Antietam. Elon Brown, for example, an enlistee wounded in the same fight, spent much of his time in hospital writing his memoirs. After taking note of his wound in passing, he recited the battles in which he participated and then went on to commend "the noble men and women (angels of mercy) who hastened to the field," stating, "I cannot express grattitude, in words sufficient, in the least, to indicate my feelings when I think of their good work. . . . I have witnessed their kindness in many other places and know from personal experience the emotions awakened by their deeds."[68] Concentrating his narrative of injury on the "emotions awakened" by a supportive public, rather than his own response to injury, he interpreted his wounds as an occasion to bear witness to, and perhaps promote, sympathetic bonds among citizens. So did many who described their injuries in public settings.

Another soldier who recounted his story in a pamphlet distributed among visitors to Philadelphia's Great Central Fair identified the numerous wounds inflicted on him during successive battles, including a cracked skull, extensive facial injuries, the amputation of a foot, partial blindness, and a severe injury to his right hand. Signing himself "Happy Jack," he ended his narrative by telling his audience, "I do not regret the sacrifice I have made for my God, my country and liberty," and he closed by thanking "the many friends who have shown me kindness."[69] Given the opportunity to tell his tale before a grateful audience, he opted for a spirited, lighthearted response to suffering, one that witnessed the selflessness of his military service by refusing pity and instead praising the behavior of others.

Exploring personal feelings or expressing regret of any kind in relation to their sufferings was simply a pointless exercise for most Union soldiers. Responding to a direct question about his recent amputation, the only facts William Newman thought worthy of note were those that concerned the physical nature of his injury. "[Y]ou wanted to Know all about my Leg," he replied to a female friend, "it is 6 month[s] to morrow Since my Leg was Amputated, it is taken of[f] below my Knee, and it is my right Leg." He did point to the severity of his wound, telling her, "I have got more pain now, then i had before it was healed. I have not left the Bed yet, nor have any hopes of leving it for the nex six month." But when his friend wrote back lamenting the war's devastation, Newman dismissed any such remorse. "I am sorry to hear that so many of our place got crippled since this War commenced but it cant be helpt," he replied, "if I was well to day, and had my Leg I should go back in to the Army & fight the rebs as long untill I got crippld again or the rebs came back in the Union."[70] In a similarly terse account of his injury, Benjamin Robb told his family that he had been "pretty severely wounded at the battle of chancelorville being struck in both legs." The "wound in the left thigh is not bad[,] the ball striking the bone and glancing off," he explained, "but the other one I think will lame me for life the bone being badly shatterd below the knee but I am satisfied for I was fighting for a just cause."[71] Such expressions of patriotic commitment let friends and family know that there was no point inquiring any further. A wound was "pretty severe" or "not so bad"; it was in the right limb or the left. Either way, it could not be helped now and was, in any case, all for the best.

All of these soldiers wrote about their injuries in a context that allowed little room for bitterness or regret, for they were constantly barraged by literature describing the exemplary behavior of other men.[72] Admitted to Armory Square Hospital in Washington, D.C., those who had been recently wounded could read about their fellow patients in the newspaper produced on the premises. "Franz Mitchel—Among the many severely wounded brought in yesterday . . . is pierced with twenty-three rebel bullets. He is cheerful and happy. May God preserve his life!" noted one such report.[73] No doubt, those with fewer wounds who may have been disposed to murmur were silently reproved by Franz Mitchel's cheerfulness.

Moreover, hospitalized soldiers were forced to contend not only with the onslaught of publicity given to admirable sufferers, but also with friends and communities who expected to see a dramatic improvement in their comportment as soon as the worst was over. This was made abundantly clear to James McWhinnie as he lay in Armory Square Hospital after having his leg amputated. The operation had left him dejected, lacking in appetite, and no doubt in extreme pain. Yet virtually every letter he received told him to cheer up. "Now Jim I know you are in a bad fix but you must keep up a good heart, don't let your spirits get down too far," counseled his uncle. A month later, a comrade from his regiment wrote to say, "Cheer up my boy. Look on the bright side of your prospective life & be not discouraged. . . . You have lost your limb but you have not lost your manhood . . . & no affliction of the body can rob you of the hope of a blissful immortality."[74]

This advice was apparently ineffective, for a female friend who visited McWhinnie in hospital informed his parents that he seemed "very blue," unleashing a further torrent of opinions from both parents on the appropriate mode of suffering. "I am sorry you do not look more on the bright side I am afraid you will get in the habit of it and it will be an ill companion through life," warned his mother. "I know sircumstances are disagreeable and wearisome and painful and we all feel deeply for you but pasiense and submison in afliction is a beautiful thing it recomends the sick person to [others] but when they see only a downcast countenance it acts on them and digusts them." Life, she reminded her son, was a constant "battle," and his current affliction was merely one of the many that he might have to confront in future. Like Nathaniel Bowditch's parents, this mother viewed suffering as a chance for her son to build a resolute character and to display an inspirational suffering that would attract others. And, much like Nathaniel Bowditch, this son quickly yielded to parental wishes, telling his brother the following week, "My spirits are good and I can talk considerable and laugh some. . . . Tell Mother I received her letter and a very good one it was too."[75]

As McWhinnie soon learned, there was always someone worse off. Nine months later, still in hospital, he told his family of one soldier who had lost both legs, another deprived of both arms, and yet another, wounded in multiple places, who now lacked sight, smell, and taste. "But he seems quite cheerful and makes no complaint. He says he even finds a cause of thankfulness for his loss in the inward change it has wrought in him," McWhinnie told his parents. "I declare I feel ashamed to think of the sympathy of my friends towards me when I saw them and talked with him."[76] Even if he studiously ignored those around him who did not live up to the ideal of exemplary suffering, McWhinnie's letters nonetheless demonstrate the weight that this ideal held for men in his situation. Not only did friends and relatives freely offer advice on how he should suffer, he was also confronted with numerous examples of men striving to embody this ideal, who provided the models against which he measured his own behavior.

There was virtually never a moment in this war when a man could be alone with his suffering. McWhinnie's friends and family received news about how he conducted himself in hospital. He took note of the way nearby patients dealt with their ailments. Suffering tended to be conspicuously public at this time, exposing the sick and injured to constant scrutiny. As soon as a battle had ended, civilians were generally waiting to remove the injured or to distribute provisions, ready to report what they had seen to civilians at home. Wounded men often found themselves suffering alongside others from their hometowns or local areas, who might similarly take note of their conduct. Once they had been removed from the battlefield, their exposure to the gaze of curious onlookers significantly increased. Whether soldiers were carried by train or boat, a profusion of spectators usually greeted the sick and wounded the moment they appeared in the North. In some major cities, local newspapers printed the arrival times of vehicles carrying patients. Voluntary workers traveling on hospital transports occasionally telegraphed ahead, preparing their organizations to be on hand at wharves or stations to pass out supplies. When their vehicles came into sight, bells rang out, alerting volunteer fire brigades and owners of carriages that they were needed to help ferry the sufferers to scattered hospitals.[77] Thousands lined the streets to watch the spectacle of soldiers being unloaded onto stretchers. One wounded man who disembarked from a hospital transport in Philadelphia amid this fray later recalled, "I saw the vast assemblage of men, women, children and vehicles. The people were all silent. The men, as the wounded were carried by, stood uncovered and many women were in tears."[78]

If there were no transports full of wounded men to meet, civilians could still get an indirect sense of how Union soldiers coped under distress, for many Northern communities deputized civilian representatives or local soldiers to report on wounded men from their vicinities. Residents of Tioga County, Pennsylvania, for example, were regularly updated on those from the vicinity who had been injured in recent battles. After detailing wounds, these reports invariably focused on the spirit prevailing among the soldier-patients. "Calvin Roosa, of Middlebury; shot through the right lung. Severe wound,

Figure 3. (opposite) Illustrators and printmakers did not seek to hide the enormous number of Union wounded. Instead, limbless soldiers featured prominently as patriotic icons on a wide range of Civil War material, such as this donation certificate for Philadelphia's Union Volunteer Refreshment Saloon. (Courtesy of the U.S. Sanitary Commission Papers, Manuscript Division, Library of Congress, Washington, D.C.)

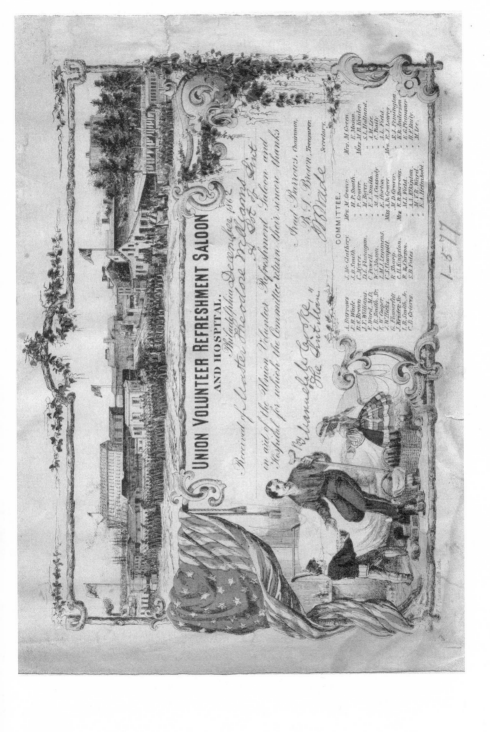

UNION VOLUNTEER REFRESHMENT SALOON
AND HOSPITAL.

Philadelphia December 1862

Received of Master Theodore W. Wyant First
of aid of the Union Volunteer Refreshment Saloon and
Hospital, for which the Committee return their sincere thanks

Anor. Barrows, Chairman.

R. S. Brown, Treasurer.

W. Wade, Secretary.

"By Annuals" for the
"The Institution"

COMMITTEE.

J. Barrows	J. McGuthery	Mrs. M. Green.
J. B. Wade	J. B. Smith.	H. P. Smith.
R. S. Brown	C. Ayres.	P. Green.
J. F. Williams	D. L. Flanigan.	Mrs. M. B. Steeler.
E. Beard	N. S. Moore.	M. Lee.
L. B. Smith, Jr.	L. H. J. Leatamens.	C. Bath.
S. W. Cooper.	C. S. Flampill.	J. L. Field.
S. W. Hicks.	R. Sharp.	Mrs. R. J. Lowry.
G. Vanorder.	C. Barrington.	Miss A. B. Green.
R. Barrows, Jr.	R. B. Drown.	M. D. Green.
L. B. Smith, Jr.	R. K. Drown.	Mrs. E. Anderson.
C. B. Grieves	S. B. Yates.	M. I. Field.
		M. L. Whinton.
		M. F. R. Ward.
		E. J. Helmbold.
		E. Moon.
		S. L. Holland.
		E. Horton.
		S. J. Penington.
		R. R. Penington.
		M. Lee.

but is doing well. . . . He is patient, and in pretty good spirits. . . . [P]rivate Riebsam, of Shippen, shot through both hips. He is severely hurt, but . . . is plucky too. . . . [S]ergeant Rogers, of Charleston; shot through the bowels . . . most severe on the list.—He is a strong man, and of great pluck, and may overcome the difficulty. . . . Josiah L. Butler, of Delmar . . . Wound very healthy . . . appetite good, spirits good, patience great, and full of hope. He is gaining fast."[79] Although military service had ended for many of these convalescents, they now had the opportunity to demonstrate to their civilian onlookers the spirit they took with them into battle.

This was an opportunity they could hardly avoid, given that they were on display no matter where they went. Assigned to a bed in an open ward, the average sick or injured enlistee could expect little privacy. During his stay at a hospital in York, Pennsylvania, William Rome noted in his diary, "the ladies are thicker than the soldiers here," adding several days later, "More than a Hundred here Every Day to bring provisions And Many other little Notions to the sick."[80] Women nurses described similarly frequent intrusions into their wards. In her diary in May 1864, Amanda Stearns explained, "the tide of visitors was tremendous; Dr. Bliss said there were fifteen hundred at supper-time; it seemed as if I were holding a reception." Even field hospitals were often crowded with visitors. When Mary Kelly went to nurse her husband—a wounded officer still too weak to be moved far from the battlefield—she was plagued by the raucous throng around her. "There are people here from every direction come to look after their friends," she wrote home. "This is the noisiest place ever any body was in."[81]

Oftentimes, the wounded were even more pointedly on display. Thousands of visitors to the Brooklyn and Long Island Sanitary Fair in early 1864 had an opportunity to examine wounded men close up, in an exhibition designed precisely for that purpose. Walking into the main fair building, they were confronted by a life-size painting of a camp scene depicting a U.S. Sanitary Commission (USSC) hospital tent with attendants ministering to their patients. To attest to the faithfulness of this representation, fair organizers set up an actual tent containing real sick and injured soldiers, shipped in from a nearby facility.[82] This was among the numerous opportunities available for those who wanted to mingle among the wounded. Walt Whitman, a frequent visitor to hospitals in and around the capital, described in his journal the sick and injured men packed into the Patent Office, one of the many buildings in Washington, D.C., temporarily transformed into hospital accommodations. The second floor was taken up with enormous glass cases, roughly eight feet apart, containing models of every kind of invention, proud monuments to human ingenuity. In between each case and in double rows running the length of the hall, there were beds filled with soldiers. Visitors might walk among these beds, or look down from the gallery above, which was also filled with patients. "It was a strange, solemn, and, with all its features of suffering and death, a sort of fascinating sight," Whitman remarked.[83]

He was not the only one enthralled by scenes of wartime distress. On a daily basis, most Northerners read or heard about the massive extent of the suffering and many wanted to observe this extraordinary spectacle close up. Thousands crowded into Matthew Brady's New York photography studio to study the first publicly displayed images of war casualties. Swarms of civilians headed off to battlegrounds to gain a firsthand view of war's aftermath. Wherever the sick and injured went, this fascination ensured that people would openly stare. Suffering from rheumatism of the legs, one private had to be transferred from one hospital to another, approximately a mile away. He made the journey on a stretcher, borne by hospital staff, who were hardly out of the gate before a crowd appeared pressing them with questions about the sufferer's ailment. In his correspondence, James McWhinnie related a similar experience. Heading off with two other one-legged comrades to their new hospital in New York City, they supposed that anonymity would be possible in the great metropolis, "but on the contrary," he told his family, "it seemed as if [we] had arrived in some one horse village where a lame soldier was a sight not to be lost."[84] People everywhere, it seems, felt compelled to gape in wonder at the unparalleled vision of suffering that the war had produced. Although there is no way to know precisely what they gleaned from these spectacles of suffering, one thing is clear: the Northern public felt that the war's suffering belonged to them. Writers continually bore witness to this suffering, the wounded were unself-consciously placed on display, and people stared frankly. No matter how dreadful the spectacle, suffering compelled awe and interest—scrutiny, not turning away.

———— ◆·••·◆ ————

In early 1867 a woman volunteer wrote a lengthy reminiscence about her wartime experiences. More than five years earlier, she had witnessed the aftermath of the battle of Belmont, Missouri, arriving in time to find the Union wounded still "scattered here and there," many having "lain twenty four hours" without food or water. Looking on these maimed forms, "lying prostate in their clothed gore," she could scarcely "realize that they were men." Similar horrors greeted her on other fields, she explained: from the "mangled multitudes" of Fort Donelson to the sixteen-year-old victim of a cannon explosion, reduced to "a charred mass of corrupted flesh," his scorched eye lids separated only with excruciating care; his burnt mouth finally teased open with drop after drop of beef tea. She did not spare her readers these gruesome realities. She laid them out, the better to emphasize the laudable suffering of Union troops and the merits of her own response. Drawing on all the conventional images of Union sufferers, she portrayed men "uncomplaining" in their pain, refusing her assistance "that it might be given another, more needy." She depicted one cheerful sufferer "gaily warbling 'Yankee Doodle'" as he hobbled along on his bullet-riddled legs, and another plucky amputee who insisted that he would sooner give up his remaining limb than set down his gun. Drawing in more a somber hue, she told of "poor Joe," the youth hideously wounded by cannon shot, who retained his pure, boyish spirit, becoming "an especial favorite" among the nurses. Alongside these ideal Union sufferers, she offered readers all of the equally conventional wartime depictions of the enemy: the cowardly Southern doctor who mistreated his Union patients; the haughty Confederate officer who shunned Northern volunteers' kind treatment and snubbed his nurses; and, finally, the young "rebel private" so overcome with her sympathetic overtures that he "wept bitter tears of repentance" at having joined an unjust cause. Demonstrating the purity of Northern compassion, she sent her heartfelt sympathy to the mothers of the Confederate wounded and pictured her fellow volunteers offering "words of Christian comfort" to men of both sides.[85] Suffering remained the central focus of her tale because it best expressed her truth about the war: that the Union victory was divinely ordained, upholding a superior culture that could be seen most clearly in the behavior of its white sufferers and their caregivers. That this story imagined the North's triumph as evidence of cultural superiority, not greater butchery, was, of course, part of its appeal.

White Union soldiers had their own incentives to uphold the ideals these stories expressed. In light of a pervasive emphasis on exemplary suffering, and the very public nature of their anguish, doing otherwise would have seemed anomalous. But if they suffered well, they became praiseworthy figures able to inspire others with the strength of their faith and the depths of their patriotism. They were held up as the embodiments of the Union war effort—whether as down-to-earth republican men or devout believers, ever ready to respond warmly to genuine sympathy, and ever loyal to their cause—the antithesis of the thoughtless Confederate privates whose principles could not sustain them, or the stuck-up Rebel officers, callous and obdurate, immune to fellow feeling. They helped to stave off death or deterioration as well, marking themselves off from the black troops who succumbed to despair, and demonstrating that their convictions shaped the core of who they were.

By the twentieth century, men lacked these same incentives, and they necessarily experienced suffering far differently than had nineteenth-century soldiers. In later conflicts, professional medical attendants would come to hold sole authority over the casualties of war. They now treat the sick and injured in sterile settings mostly closed to the public, perhaps with a room set aside specifically for visitors. They do not attribute lack of self-control or piety to men screaming in pain, nor urge patients to adopt a cheerful attitude or risk death.[86] And friends and family members no longer counsel soldiers in the days after their injuries to suffer in narrowly prescribed ways. How a man suffers—and how that suffering affects those around him—is no longer an intrinsic part of most war narratives. In a more secular modern context, the religious dimensions of soldiers' suffering lack the powerful resonance they once had. Suffering has gradually become a medicalized experience, divested of much of its political and cultural meaning. Social commentators still honor men who suffer uncomplainingly for their heroic fortitude. But they no longer dwell on exemplary suffering as a virtuous act or a public one that reflects the character of a soldier's race or nation. War wounds continue to be endowed with patriotic significance of a generic kind, but the experience of suffering—no longer a sign of political, religious, or moral virtue—has increasingly been transformed into one that men bear largely in private.

4

Labors of Love

*We will make them one great home to take the place of the many they have
left.... As they fight we will build this great house ... it shall be stocked with
everything that home can give and its love shall clothe and feed and tend them;
wherever they are ... in one form or other our love shall reach them.*

S. G. Cary, "Thirty Third Report of the New England Women's Auxiliary Association"
(1865)

Writing for the *Atlantic Monthly* in 1865, a Northern volunteer suggested
that the government could easily have provided the sick and wounded with
all of the services offered by volunteers throughout the war. What the government could *not* do, he argued, was to provide "so many bonds of love and
kindness to bind the soldier to his home, and to keep him always a loyal citizen." "If our army is ... more pure, more clement, more patriotic than other
armies,—if our soldier is everywhere and always a true-hearted citizen," he
proclaimed, "it is because the army and soldier have not been cast off from
public sympathy, but cherished and bound to every free institution and every
peaceful association by golden cords of love."[1] By sustaining men's attachments to the home front, women had saved the republic from militarism's
corrupting potential: despondency on one hand and brutality on the other.

When Unionists told stories about civilian efforts to alleviate wartime
suffering, they typically emphasized the personal, heartfelt nature of their
labors, telling tales in which soldiers' ability to suffer well inspired volunteers'
deepest love, and volunteers' love, in turn, aroused soldiers' noblest suffering. Whether they portrayed young soldiers turning from apathy or despair
after receiving homefront donations, or hardened troops morally transformed
through sympathetic nursing, stories about wartime voluntarism insisted that
women's most important war-work lay in extending "golden cords of love" to
the war zone.

Much like the stories examined in previous chapters, these ones drew from a wealth of enduring imagery. Emphasizing women's selfless devotion to soldiers, they shared themes in common with ancient and modern war narratives, from a stress on women's innate selflessness and compassion to a focus on their role in inspiring men's bravery, both as recipients of their protection and spectators for their deeds.[2] Yet as with stories of exemplary sufferers or heroic officers, these tales of civilian voluntarism also reverberated in ways specific to their time and place, lending a particular urgency to women's actions and a distinctive shape to their voluntarism. Unlike earlier and later conflicts, the Civil War took place at a time when many Unionists believed that women's moral influence over men was not just socially valuable but politically essential. Without such influence, America's republic would degenerate just as surely as its many failed antecedents. It was no trivial afterthought to extend "golden chords of love" to the war zone in such a context, for doing so complemented men's work on the battlefields in the most literal sense, with men fighting to protect republican democracy, and women working to preserve republican virtues. Moreover, home and family were the wellspring of patriotism according to most middle-class Unionists, such that the best soldiers were those who thought most often of home. Preserving men's domestic attachments thus had crucial military implications. Not only did women's love safeguard the character of the nation's citizenry, it also mobilized men for service and secured their lasting allegiance. Most important, the mass of Northern volunteers were true believers, convinced that this conflict had to be fought on two fronts at once: the first against the enemy, the second against the myriad temptations that drew soldiers away from God. Believing in the power of feminine influence to rouse men's better natures and transform their souls, most viewed women's efforts to keep home in men's thoughts as a sacred duty, at once serving political, military, and religious ends.

Northern voluntary efforts were fundamentally shaped by middle-class convictions about the significance of home and maternal influence. That is, volunteers did not just tell stories about the importance of preserving emotional connections with men, they formed efforts designed to do exactly that. Personalizing the goods they sent to the front, women broadcast the love they bore for Union soldiers. Working to domesticate the war zone, they adorned all the spaces that came under their control with homelike touches, from floral arrangements to well-laid tables. Indeed, practically every aspect of Northern voluntary work was directed at shoring up men's links to families and evoking memories of home, from women's manner of conducting battlefield relief and hospital work to their creation of soldiers' homes and lodges.[3]

The bulk of the historiography on Civil War voluntarism concentrates less on the voluntary movement as a whole than on the United States Sanitary Commission (USSC), the North's largest voluntary group. Historians diverge

in their understandings of this organization's purpose and long-term implications. In George Fredrickson's much-cited study, USSC leaders appear as
self-interested elites, concerned not so much with alleviating suffering as with
demonstrating the benefits of bureaucratic management. Their organization
marks the point at which amateur do-gooders, motivated by piety, paternalism, and zeal, began making way for experienced professionals who promoted
the standards of centralization, order, and efficiency.[4] In contrast, more recent
studies by historians Judith Giesberg and Jeanie Attie stress the divergent
agendas of male and female USSC workers. Refuting the idea that women
accepted male colleagues' methods, Giesberg depicts the war years as a time
when USSC women honed their organizational skills and built alliances that
would bear fruit in the post-bellum era, giving rise to a more militant, sex-
specific brand of benevolent activism.[5] Pointing to the gender conflicts that
plagued the USSC, Attie similarly notes that its female leaders resisted efforts
to undermine their authority, while women donors thwarted attempts to systematize and nationalize their voluntarism. By demonstrating the endurance
of traditional forms of female voluntarism, and exploring the gender conflicts
that shaped relationships among volunteers, this scholarship suggests that
the Civil War did not cause a thoroughgoing or uniform transformation in
civilian benevolence.

Nevertheless, this recent scholarship continues to treat tales depicting voluntarism as a labor of love as mere cant. As Giesberg points out, male volunteers used sentimental tales of voluntarism to deny the value of women's
labor. Bent on ignoring the fact that their female colleagues administered
large and complex organizations, she argues, USSC men instead portrayed
women as ministering angels, their work a product of their feminine natures
and thus not really work at all. Adopting a similar perspective, Attie argues
that these sentimental narratives helped men to depoliticize women's war-
work, thereby circumventing the challenge this work posed to the ideology
of separate spheres. Since USSC men were conservative elites interested in
expanding state power, she notes, tales of women's spontaneous benevolence
furthered nationalist aims as well, demonstrating that the Union had the support of women, supposedly "the least partisan and most virtuous members of
the community."[6]

It is indisputable that stories of women's devotion to the troops helped
to buttress an existing gender ideology and further nationalist ends. But it
should also be acknowledged that middle-class women themselves were
largely responsible for creating and broadcasting tales portraying their voluntarism as a labor of love. In light of their unprecedented mobilization and
the multifaceted nature of their war-work, it is worthwhile asking why these

particular stories maintained their appeal throughout this war. The answer lies not just in the obvious fact that women, like men, were deeply influenced by their culture's norms and values. This chapter suggests that sentimental stories about women's war-work resonated because they demonstrated the power of female influence and served as a vehicle for extending that influence. Long schooled in the transformative power of feminine emotion, many women sought to mobilize this power during the war, convinced that their efforts were vital in assisting the war effort and ensuring a stable polity. For large numbers of middle-class women, these sentimental stories did not mystify the "real" nature of their voluntarism. Rather, they helped to remind Americans just how crucial it was to extend women's moral authority into the public domain.

The Civil War North represents a high-water mark in wartime voluntarism. In no subsequent conflict were civilians so directly engaged in alleviating suffering. In later wars, the state would assume most of the auxiliary functions that volunteers took on at this time, narrowing the terrain on which civilians operated. In the Civil War, however, Unionists did not necessarily *want* the state to accept complete responsibility for soldiers. Imagining the war as a "people's contest," they chose to rely on a volunteer force rather than a professional army, just as they elected to depend on civilian volunteers to fill many support roles vital to the war effort. According to most benevolent women, the state simply could not provide the crucial emotional work their labor accomplished. No matter how efficient the Medical Department became, it could never remind soldiers of their homes and thereby save them from being transformed into mercenaries. Nor could it convince soldiers that the war was a mutual quest, engaged in by the entire community, thus countering daily reports of war profiteering, declining enlistments, or battlefield losses. Most crucially, nothing but personalized relief efforts could hope to counteract the increasingly inhumane, bureaucratic nature of the war itself. In the midst of what some scholars have dubbed the first "modern war," middle-class women determinedly sought to extend the felt connections between people on an intimate, local, and individual level.

Northern voluntarism initially grew out of dire necessity, springing from the chaos that existed in the early months of the war. Shortly after the fall of Fort Sumter in April 1861, troops had come flooding into the capital in response to a government appeal for 75,000 three-month militiamen. Several hundred thousand additional men were called service over the next few months, almost none arriving fully equipped with uniforms, weapons, and other necessities. Unable to deal with their requirements, the federal government looked to the states not just to raise but also to outfit regiments. State and local governments, in turn, called on civilians. In Pennsylvania, the Quartermaster General of Militia requested that women immediately "form associations in each county" to provide stockings and blankets for the troops.[7] Tens of thousands of women responded to similar requests sent out across the North, often by converting existing sewing clubs, church, and reform groups into soldiers' aid societies. In the war's first few weeks, according to one estimate, there were already 20,000 voluntary organizations catering to soldiers at work around the country.[8]

Scope for benevolent work remained even after the government increased its responsibility for provisioning the army. Privation in the ranks was widespread, despite the fact that Northern farms generated enough to feed the troops, and manufacturers were soon capable of equipping them without relying on foreign imports.[9] Insufficient or defective goods might still be caused by unscrupulous contractors, unforeseen disruptions to the supply lines, or officers' faulty paperwork. Whatever the cause, the results were the same: food arrived late or spoiled; shoes wore out on the march; uniforms made of "shoddy" disintegrated at the first sign of rain; and army rations remained woefully inadequate, especially for the sick and injured.[10]

Civilians worked to fill the many holes in the military's supply system and to furnish the needs of hospitalized men. Across the loyal states, voluntary organizations set up hundreds of soldiers' homes, private hospitals, and refreshment saloons. They created their own systems for supplying these institutions and ran their own hospital steamers and railroad carriages to help ferry injured men from the front.[11] They concocted dozens of fundraising ventures—ranging from the immense fortnight-long "sanitary fairs" held in Northern cities, to tens of thousands of smaller social events—the proceeds of which mostly funded hospital stores.[12] Volunteers tracked the fate of soldiers, following them into camp with Bibles, onto the battlefield with supplies, and into hospitals as nurses and visitors. They formed committees to lobby the government for an ambulance corps and to improve the army Medical Department, as well as raising money for soldiers' families, among a host of other activities.

Despite the claims of wartime propagandists, this flourishing of benevolence was neither unified nor harmonious. Volunteer groups mobilized simultaneously in thousands of different locations, drawing members from diverse backgrounds with varying, sometimes conflicting, aims and methods. They vied for official support, public largesse, and social prestige, such that the movement was riven by ideological conflicts and personal animosities. At the center of these conflicts was the USSC, a group whose male leaders had pretensions to unite all volunteers under a central hierarchy, national in scope and geared toward the efficient management of army health. Sanitary Commission leaders repeated the same mantra throughout the war: a centralized system for distributing voluntary supplies would aid military efficiency. Anything less would usurp official prerogatives, undermine discipline, and injure soldiers. If there was no check on women's benevolence, a few men would receive too much, burdening themselves with useless goods or eating themselves sick. Others would go without, and no stockpiles would exist for times of greatest need.[13] Failure to create a national organization of volunteers, moreover, would play straight into the enemy's hands, fostering "in contributor, agent and beneficiary alike, the very spirit of sectionalism and '*State-ish-ness*' to which we owe all our troubles."[14] Eager to centralize all voluntary efforts under their auspices, the USSC's male executive persistently underscored the connection between an orderly effort led by experienced men and triumphant nationalism, criticizing their competitors in the process.

Scholars have lavished considerable attention on the USSC's male leadership, using their perspective to discuss the nature of wartime voluntarism. In thinking about the shape of voluntarism overall, this emphasis is misplaced for three reasons. First, although the USSC's executive committee presented a relatively uniform outlook, the men and women active throughout this organization—whether as special relief agents, sanitary inspectors, associate secretaries, or nurses—held diverse viewpoints.[15] Some were "cosmopolitan rationalists," to use Jeanie Attie's phrase, that is, representatives of a New England, urban, mostly Unitarian social elite who supported scientific inquiry, elite-led institutions, and an expansion of state power. But many others spoke with noticeable religious and sentimental accents. Second, as recent scholarship points out, USSC men did not have a free hand to implement their agenda. They dealt with a largely female constituency, who had to be appeased lest they throw their support behind rival groups or stop donating entirely.[16] Finally, the USSC always competed with a host of other voluntary groups that, taken together, outnumbered and outspent this single organization. Examining the evolution of Northern voluntarism as a whole, it is possible to see that however much USSC men desired to create a fully professionalized, hierarchically ordered voluntary system, the mass of volunteers had their own ideas. Overwhelmingly, they supported forms of voluntarism that allowed them to reach soldiers directly, to display their affection, and to shore up the strength of men's relationships to the home front.

Much to the consternation of Sanitary Commission leaders, hundreds of organizations, both large and small, simply ignored their appeals, determined to conduct their own affairs on a local or state level. West of the Mississippi, a rival Western Sanitary Commission (WSC) supplied the majority of aid to soldiers and refugees in that area. Ignoring repeated entreaties from the USSC, this group refused to merge the two organizations. Instead, the prominent St. Louis business leaders and philanthropists in charge of the WSC established their own system of soldiers' homes and hospitals, employing a corps of around 300 female nurses to work in hospitals and on WSC hospital-steamers. With an extensive supply system roughly one-quarter the size of its larger rival, the WSC maintained its own agents for distributing goods at the front, in hospitals, and among Union refugees and former slaves.[17]

Elsewhere, sizable aid organizations also remained aloof from the USSC. The state of Indiana opted for an independent Sanitary Commission, created in March 1862 under the leadership of a local businessman. Iowa followed Indiana's lead, eventually adopting a compromise in response to lobbying from the rival associations: it established one depot at Chicago to funnel donations to the USSC and another at St. Louis, to supply the WSC. In Pennsylvania, the Philadelphia Ladies Aid Society and the Penn Relief Association retained their autonomy throughout the war, maintaining control over their supplies and frequently sending local women to assure their distribution at the front, as did the Union Relief Association of Baltimore and the New England Soldiers' Relief Association of New York.[18]

Countless civilians and smaller local groups likewise opted to direct their benevolence as they saw fit. It is impossible to know how many women's groups sent donations straight to local companies, for such ad hoc initiatives had no need for recordkeeping. But soldiers' letters make clear that the mails were filled with packages of homemade food and clothing making their way directly to friends and family at the front. It is just as difficult to determine the precise number of civilians who volunteered in the many initiatives that catered to soldiers passing through towns and urban centers. Judging by the scale of their work, their numbers were substantial. Almost all of the regiments making their way through Philadelphia stopped to partake of the free meals, bathing facilities, and reading rooms at the Cooper Shop Refreshment Saloon or the neighboring Union Volunteer Refreshment Saloon, privately funded ventures that were imitated in Baltimore, Pittsburgh, and elsewhere.[19] Local citizens also set up soldiers' rests or small hospitals throughout Union-held territory that were staffed by volunteers to care for furloughed or discharged soldiers too debilitated to make their way home.

One of the primary attractions of these autonomous ventures was that they enabled civilians to track the precise destination of their voluntary offerings, and often to receive direct thanks from the individual regiments, men, or hospitals that received them. In contrast, the USSC centralized and stockpiled donations, distributing them only after receiving an official request. Under the direction of a Department of General Relief, contributions of hospital supplies, clothing, medicines, and food were collected by twelve USSC branches that formed clearing depots for donations sent in by thousands of affiliated aid societies operating in villages and towns. At these branch depots, goods were unpacked, resorted, stamped with the USSC's seal, and then forwarded to central supply rooms in the West or East, where army medical officers or USSC representatives in the field could request them.[20]

This centralized system generated growing controversy by the war's second year, leading to increased competition among voluntary organizations. As the USSC expanded in size, charges of fraud and mismanagement plagued the organization. Soldiers returned from hospitals claiming to have purchased clothes donated to the Sanitary Commission or to have starved while hospital staff gorged on the food sent for their benefit. Critics began to denounce the salaries of USSC leaders and to decry its system of paid agents.[21] This anxiety coalesced midway through the war into support for the U.S. Christian Commission, a group formed in 1861 that drew together Protestant ministers and leaders of the YMCA, the American Tract Society, and a number of other evangelical religious groups. Having initially limited its work to the distribution of religious literature at the front, the Christian Commission began moving into the USSC's domain in late 1862, doling out hospital stores and supplies along with its Bibles and tracts.

Christian Commission publications touted their organization as a purely voluntary effort that reached out to soldiers directly. Contrasting their system with that of the Sanitary Commission, they initially eschewed paid employees, instead recruiting ministers to undertake short-term, unpaid tours at the front. Over a thousand Christian Commission ministers had been sent to the field by the end of 1862, a number that increased fivefold before fighting ceased. Busily campaigning for public support, Christian Commission publicists emphasized that goods donated to their organization went straight into soldiers' hands without mediation from officials, while the Sanitary Commission's system "destroyed the individuality of [women's] boxes by scattering their contents." Undertaking to make every local church organization a fee-paying auxiliary, the Christian Commission rapidly attracted the allegiance of several hundred women's groups.[22]

Because the USSC relied on public support, the organization had little choice but to personalize its mission in response to this challenge. While historians have noted this fact, few have appreciated just how extensive the changes were to the Sanitary Commission's initial program. Indeed, by the war's end, the USSC barely resembled the original plans of its male founders. These men had set out to demonstrate that individuals of the highest intelligence could assist the government in conducting the war on a firm "scientific basis." With this aim in mind they spent the war's first year focusing on preventative sanitary measures, such as monitoring hygienic conditions in camps and hospitals, conducting physical inspections to weed out unfit troops, and appraising army physicians of developments in medicine, surgery and disease prevention.[23] They certainly did not envision their organization serving mainly as a conduit between civilians and soldiers.[24] Women's collection of clothing, hospital stores, and food was to be merely a stopgap measure, a temporary expedient to mitigate soldiers' suffering while the government established its supply systems on a more stable basis. This is not what transpired. In order to appeal to the public and to respond to the needs of the moment, the USSC was compelled to shift its focus decisively over time, away from disease prevention and toward the personal ministry and monitoring of Union soldiers. By 1865 the Department of General Relief encompassed more than three-quarters of the USSC's workload, making the organization wholly dependent on women's efforts for their success. As this dependence increased, USSC activities grew ever more similar to the modes of benevolent activism they had initially belittled as overly sentimental and overtly pious.

Almost every aspect of the USSC's original design was modified in order to personalize relief efforts. Even before the Christian Commission began making serious inroads into their support, Sanitary Commission leaders set out to alter their system of battlefield relief to furnish the wounded with individual attention. Having first established a single depot near the headquarters of each army through which to dispense supplies, they altered this system in 1862 by introducing a Field Relief Corps. Under the direction of Lewis H. Steiner, each army corps was now provided with its own permanent field relief agent, supplied with government-owned horses and wagons stocked with the USSC's medical supplies, food, and stores.[25] Nevertheless, Steiner's men continued to act at a remove from the wounded, distributing supplies only after the request of army medical officers.[26] To close this remaining gap, a further innovation took place in mid-1864 with the formation of an Auxiliary Relief Corps led by Frank B. Fay, a Christian minister and former major of Chelsea, Massachusetts. Given charge of fifty men (mostly theological students), Fay organized his volunteers into small teams and placed them in direct relation to wounded soldiers. His men "understood that the corps was organized for personal ministry, and that this was to be provided with all the sympathy and devotion they would give a patient at home," Fay noted in his wartime diary.[27] Elaborating on the tasks undertaken by his men, one of their number explained that he would meet the wounded as they were carried from the field, providing them with food, bathing their wounds, and dispensing clean clothes. After conveying the wounded to hospitals or performing last rites for the dying, agents would then undertake nursing duties, such as cleaning the wards, writing letters, and reading to patients. The Sanitary Commission typically acclaimed this work as a way for families to establish a proxy on the battlefield, someone to provide "a sister's or a mother's care," as this agent expressed it.[28] Clearly, they worried about their image as a soulless bureaucracy more concerned with procedures than with individual soldiers, and they tailored their battlefield relief accordingly.

The USSC's message likewise took on increased sentimental and religious overtones as the war continued. Early in the conflict, commission publicists sometimes relied on rational appeals rather than emotion to make their case, as was evident in one plea they sent to insurance companies, which emphasized the monetary value of each soldier. Calculating the cost of his enlistment, outfit, training, bounty, pay, and rations, potential donors were advised that USSC efforts "saved the country ten times its cost by what it has done to economize the life, health, and efficiency of the army." Historians have used these pragmatic arguments to portray the USSC as a thoroughly bureaucratic venture that eschewed sentimentality.[29] But appeals to fiscal prudence mostly targeted the business community. When addressing women donors, USSC publications differed little from those of their rivals, typically offering lists of the number and type of goods distributed alongside heartrending tales of suffering men saved by well-timed supplies.

Much like other organizations, the USSC made heavy use of testimony from field agents bearing witness to the physical and emotional effects of women's goods on soldiers.[30] Quick to recognize the importance of first-hand evidence, branch society leaders solicited letters acknowledging the receipt of women's donations from surgeons and soldiers, which they published in city papers and reprinted in circulars mailed regularly to each of their auxiliaries.[31] Via such personal exhortations, the Sanitary Commission increasingly framed its message in terms popularized by evangelical revivals, such as when the Commission petitioned clergy throughout the Northwest "in Humanity's name and for the Redeemer's sake" to seek contributions and public support. Terming the results of these efforts a "great awakening," one USSC publicist noted that during the first months of 1863, the number of aid societies auxiliary to the Northwestern Branch increased from 250 to more than 2,000.[32] It did not take long for the Sanitary Commission leaders to comprehend that if they wanted their message to appeal, they had no choice but to frame their work as a religious mission directly affecting particular soldiers.

A host of additional initiatives catering to individual men reveal even more pointedly the USSC's growing concern with personalizing its services. In August 1861 the USSC established a Department of Special Relief in Washington, D.C., under the direction of Frederick Knapp, a Unitarian minister and cousin to USSC president Henry Bellows.[33] As Knapp explained in his first report, his mission was to supply food, shelter, and medical attention to soldiers arriving in the capital but too ill to continue to the front, as well as those waiting on army pay or discharges. He would go on to evolve a remarkably extensive system for monitoring these stray men. Some of Knapp's team of Special Relief Agents set themselves up at railway stations to keep a lookout for needy soldiers, whom they carried back to one of the numerous soldiers' homes that the USSC administered. Others concentrated on intercepting troops before they could fall in with bad company, visiting the paymaster's office twice daily to inquire after anyone submitting papers.[34] To deal with "sharpers," Knapp stationed detectives at railroad depots who handed out tens of thousands of small manuals (called "Soldier's Friends") filled with dire warnings about schemes for robbing the unwary, alongside information on USSC Homes and Lodges.[35] Next, he pioneered a system of "Sanitary Relief Couriers" to assist soldiers in reaching their homes. Any man showing up without means of leaving the city was given clean clothes, escorted to the nearest station, and provided with a ticket. For incapacitated men, Knapp offered personal escorts, responsible for obtaining their tickets, seeing to their needs on the train, and delivering them to their front doors. His agents were on hand at each railroad terminus to take soldiers to the next station or to transport the sick to nearby Commission Homes.[36] Here was voluntarism at its most intimate level, conveying Union soldiers directly from the war zone back to their waiting families.

As the conflict expanded in size, encompassing ever-larger numbers of men and ever-expanding death tolls, the USSC responded by creating an aid network that was ever more individualized. There were five Sanitary Commission Homes and Lodges in and around the capital by war's end, in addition to dozens of others established in Cleveland, Ohio, Memphis, Nashville, Louisville, Cairo (Ill.), Cincinnati, Alexandria (Va.), Boston, Chicago, and elsewhere, as well as a Home for Nurses and Soldiers' Wives and Mothers in Washington, D.C., and a Home for Nurses in Annapolis.[37] Claiming that military bureaucracy could only deal with armies in the aggregate, the organization worked to particularize each soldier so that family members could track his location and fate, setting up a special committee to ensure that reliable records would exist to document deaths in general hospitals; instituting a system for marking graves; and developing printed forms with space to list deceased soldiers' family members, place of burial, cause of death, and "dying requests"—a scheme clearly designed to minimize the anonymity of soldiers' deaths.[38] Constantly beset by worried family members searching for missing relatives, they also established a hospital directory in Washington, D.C., in late 1862, which recorded the names, locations, and medical conditions of soldiers in army hospitals. Branch offices were soon operating in Philadelphia, Louisville, and New York, tabulating daily reports from hundreds of army hospitals and responding to the flood of inquiries.[39] Concerning itself equally with the financial stability of Northern families, the USSC set up a Pension Bureau and War Claim Agency early the following year, which eventually encompassed a hundred subagencies dedicated to completing pension applications and providing free legal advice to invalid veterans or deceased soldiers' family members.[40] As these activities suggest, rather than moving away from modes of benevolence focused on mitigating suffering, USSC efforts evolved in the opposite direction—toward a personalized ministry that reached out to donors on an emotional level while offering individualized support for soldiers and their kin.

Voluntary organizations that operated outside of the USSC's purview provided a range of similar services that extended personalized care to those subsumed by a homogenizing army bureaucracy. Most major cities across the loyal states had soldiers' homes and lodges or sizable hospitals funded and managed by civilian donors. The Soldiers' Depot in New York, for instance, was originally designed to seek out and protect stray soldiers from that state. In April 1863 the newly appointed civilian managers rented several adjoining premises on the corner of Howard and Mercer streets, just off Broadway and not far from the docks and railroad depots that formed soldiers' entry point to the city. Fitting out these buildings with space for 650 men, they added a barbershop, dining and reception halls, a reading room, private apartments, and multiple dormitories and hospitals. Their operation had soon expanded across the country to encompass a system of "Military Couriers and Station Agents" who traveled on trains conveying soldiers between Washington and New York, performing a role similar to that of Knapp's couriers. Throughout Union-occupied territories, the Soldiers' Depot set up additional agencies, employing dozens of men to visit army hospitals and battlefields.[41] Likewise, the Citizens' Volunteer Hospital in Philadelphia began small and expanded quickly, accommodating approximately 200,000 soldiers during its three years of operation.[42] These substantial undertakings were designed not just to supplement government medical care but also to block the paths leading soldiers to vice or despair.

The managers and volunteers who staffed these ventures usually saw themselves as surrogate parents, dedicated to ensuring that troops returned to their families with their money and "self respect" intact, as Frederick Knapp put it. He described the USSC as akin to "the father of a home" seeking to ensure "the comfort and good of his children."[43] Like many wartime voluntary workers, he was an unswerving sentimentalist and a committed Christian, devoted to a belief that social unity and moral virtue could only come through emotional interactions between citizens (albeit paternalistic ones that supported his authority as a surrogate father). Evidence from Knapp's internal reports underscores this point, for they differed little from those he wrote for public consumption. Virtually every document he sent to the USSC's executive board stressed his heartfelt connections to the troops by highlighting his dealings with specific men. "He is a mere boy, of about eighteen, from a New Jersey regiment," he wrote of one soldier:

> He evidently struggles to be manly and brave, but his homesickness . . . masters him. We have thus frequent opportunity here in the Home to make note of what in the general excitement is almost unavoidably overlooked . . . namely, what a vast amount there is in the hearts of these soldiers of personal sacrifice, daily struggle to put down anxious feelings . . . tender thoughts of home checked in their utterance and hope silently waiting.[44]

Demonstrating his emotional connections to needy men, Knapp eagerly sought to plumb the depths of soldiers' "hearts." It may be true, as some scholars claim, that over time a number of male and female volunteers came to rely on a more detached, "masculine" language of scientific professionalism in describing their war-work.[45] But most continued to view benevolence as a Christian service, best administered by those who were earnestly committed to their charges.

Maintaining men's connections to home and emphasizing the sentiments animating benevolence was a central preoccupation of all voluntary groups, no matter how big or small. If some USSC leaders began the war with plans to institute a centralized, bureaucratic system that would demonstrate to the

Northern public the virtues of efficiency and order, their donors had other ideas. Forced to recognize that most voluntary workers desired intimate connections with soldiers and a system that allowed them to frame voluntarism as a personal exchange, the Sanitary Commission helped to facilitate the maintenance of emotional bonds between soldiers and the home front as much as did their competitors. Only by looking at the meanings that middle-class Northerners invested in domesticity is it possible to understand why so many sought to characterize their voluntarism as a labor of love.

⦿

While recovering in a Philadelphia army hospital in 1864 one Union soldier perfectly captured the significance of home for middling Northerners. Publishing "A Soldier's Thoughts of Home," in a newspaper produced on the premises, he enthused:

> Home! How the sound of that word flies through the portals of the soldier's ear, and finds a lodgement in the soldier's heart, illuminating its darkest recesses with the light [of] love and affection, inspiring him with nobler thoughts and better impulses, kindling anew the fires of patriotism and ambition, and animating him to deeds of bravery and daring.[46]

For this writer and countless others, home was the site of selfless emotions, and these emotions had clear civic and military effects. Merely to mention the word "home" produced a transformation, immediately bringing to mind an earlier schooling in "nobler thoughts and better impulses," as well as stimulating a desire to represent country and family on the battlefield.

This soldier's assumptions about the meaning of home were of recent origin, dating back only to the late eighteenth century. Assertions of patriarchal privilege had lost favor around this time, as revolutionary leaders embraced the principle of individual rights. Putting forth a new rationale for women's dependent status, Revolutionary-era thinkers revised negative judgments of feminine irrationality, carnality, and emotional excess, instead depicting women as the more morally virtuous sex, their tenderness and passivity unfitting them for political life. From their position in the private sphere, however, women were now granted new political responsibilities. Relying on a blend of liberalism, republicanism, and sensationalist psychology, social commentators invested novel importance in affection as "the glue of civil society," explains historian Jan Lewis. Through their natural affection, women would cultivate the ties that bound society together. And through their maternal roles, they would plant the seeds of civic virtue in their offspring.[47]

Concern over the republic's volatility made women's new roles especially crucial in the antebellum North. Until the end of the Civil War, people typically referred to the Union as an "experiment," pointing to an uncertain future in which the republic's survival was by no means assured. Widespread anxiety over the possibility of social disintegration had grown apace with increases in industrial production, social conflict, and political discord, forming a veritable cacophony by mid-century.[48] According to middle-class spokespeople, it was up to women to act as a vital counterbalance to an ever more amoral public sphere. While men engaged in the cutthroat pursuit of self-interest and the hurly-burly of politics, women were expected to safeguard cherished values, instilling self-control, moral purity, and civic mindedness in their children, and opening up a space for the expression of altruism, selflessness, and affection.

The links between motherhood and the survival of the republic elevated childrearing to a high-level concern. Self-proclaimed experts on the subject agreed by mid-century that children's characters were malleable. Drawing from sensationalist psychology and an evangelical concern with youthful conversion, they saw the first years of life as especially important in shaping future dispositions. Almost universally, they granted mothers the primary role in children's moral education. Women were expected to educate children through appeals to emotion rather than reason. And a vast body of child-rearing literature and sentimental writing told mothers how to acquire emotional influence over their offspring. First, they had to recognize that children learned by their mother's example: they would imitate her affections, her qualities, and her actions. It was therefore up to mothers to watch carefully their own behavior, "not . . . to teach virtue but to inspire it," as one advisor put it. Second, mothers had to ensure that children grasped the depth of their feelings, such that they appeared utterly devoted and yet entirely self-effacing. Describing the way women were enjoined to display selfless emotion, Lewis points to the fictional mother who arose early each morning to deliver her prayers "almost—but not quite—eluding the watchful eye of her child." Leading by example rather than stern enforcement (which might be construed as willful), the mother was supposed to craft a self overflowing with a deep emotion that escaped only inadvertently, in spite of her "extraordinary efforts [at] self-suppression."[49]

Women were promised immense power in exchange for their maternal self-denial. In line with the evangelical belief that social change could only come from individual conversions, mothers were constantly told that their influence held limitless potential to transform society. As Reverend John Abbott put it: "Mothers have as powerful an influence over the welfare of future generations, as all other earthly causes combined." Moreover, they were offered a form of immortality, an assurance of living forever within their children. Ultimately, the message underlying all maternal advice literature was that "women, like Christ," could be "instruments of someone else's salvation."[50]

Psychological theories and scientific developments in the first half of the century seemed to confirm the power of early impressions and maternal influence to shape the social order. Nineteenth-century understandings of the mind held that imagination was "essentially passive and mechanistic." Thoughts traveled along channels carved out by earlier memories, such that new viewpoints were formed via older associations, with the mind linking particular thoughts not just to an original association but also to the emotions attached to that association.[51] It was thus believed that the mere mention of particular words—especially emotionally charged ones like "mother" or "home"—could immediately conjure up the powerful feelings with which they were connected. The soldier quoted earlier waxing lyrical about home vividly expressed these beliefs. Picturing a mind comprised of distinct passageways, he described the term "home" speeding "through the portals" of his ear and finding "lodgement" in his heart, automatically unleashing a flood of associations strong enough to transform his behavior.

Whereas particular words held almost magical power to recreate emotional and moral states, powerful feelings were also thought capable of influencing from afar. Victorian commentators often described emotions as unbounded, seamlessly moving from one person to another via a mysterious process more often assumed than explained. It seemed to many by mid-century that there was an invisible connective force enigmatically at work in the world. Mesmerists by the 1840s were positing the existence of a "universal fluid" or electrical current that connected all matter, seen and unseen. Allegedly able to tap into this force, they staged spectacular displays that healed at a distance simply by moving their hands over patients' bodies. In equally impressive fashion, spirit mediums began accessing the supernatural realm around the same time. Claiming an ability to bring back messages from beyond the grave, they gained mass adherents by mid-century.[52]

Not coincidentally, widespread interest in invisible forms of communication arose just as a range of new scientific inventions began connecting people across space and time in novel ways: from the camera's ability to capture the past to the telegraph's capacity for relaying messages across vast distances.[53]

Doubtless, for many nineteenth-century people, the idea that one's emotional or moral state could jump across space, involuntarily communicating itself to others, seemed just as plausible as the act of sending a telegraph or taking a photograph. Thus did one wartime volunteer identify women's moral influence as "electric currents [running] along the invisible wires of sympathy," while another described voluntarism as "an irresistible moral contagion from heart to heart" that had "taught the value of liberty" and wove "a strong network of alliance between civil and military life."[54]

Of course, at the beginning of the war there was no guarantee that women's influence would extend to the army. Concerns were voiced as soon as the conflict began over how military life would affect the thousands of young soldiers streaming into army camps. What would happen to these men, many for the first time separated from parental oversight, compelled to associate with the wicked or corrupt, and obliged to adjust to military discipline and the infliction of violence? Would they return home brutalized by their experiences? Would they come back inured to vice or habituated to the subservience required of them as soldiers? From the perspective of middle-class civilians, war threatened not just the dissolution of the Union but also the moral corruption of its defenders.

Civilian volunteers immediately acknowledged that retaining men's family connections had critical military and social implications. Visiting Union soldiers' encampments in Washington, D.C., a few days after their disastrous rout at the first battle of Bull Run, one USSC official attributed the dejection of a New York regiment to the fact that nearby troops had been "feted and toasted" while they had been "neglected," indeed "positively maltreated," by the home front. "Let the New York women remember these boys," he told his brother. "If they continue to be badly used, they will discourage other of their fellows from adventuring in the cause of their country." In a similar vein, a volunteer working at the Volunteer Refreshment Saloon worried about a regiment of farmers' sons "who had had a considerable amount of moral training at home." Fearing these men would become "dispirited," if they believed "noone cared for them except as food for powder," he justified his own work as a means of demonstrating "that they were the cherished soldiers of the nation."[55] In a period when men represented their families in every sense—legally, socially, and politically—no one doubted that a lack of homefront support could have devastating implications for soldiers' morale.

The threat that divided families posed to the social order also greatly concerned middle-class volunteers. Never far from USSC leaders' minds was a lurking fear that alienated soldiers and their impoverished kin could become a rebellious mob. One of their first orders of business was thus to ensure that troops maintained financial links with the home front. For months they tossed around proposals to garnishee soldiers' wages on behalf of families, informing the secretary of war that they stood ready to act as a trustee to collect and allot men's pay (an offer ultimately declined as impractical).[56] Troops should be encouraged "in every possible way" to send home half to three-quarters of their army wages, they went on to warn the government, for ensuring a soldier's "continuing relation with his family" would preserve his "moral tone," keeping him from "the vices of camp, and from becoming a mere mercenary man-at-arms." Equally important, the government had to ensure timely payment of wages, lest soldiers' families become dependent on charity. "There is the danger of a great pauper class being thus created, especially in our large cities," cautioned one USSC report.[57] With an eye on the war's potential effects on social cohesion and class relations, voluntary organizations set out to strengthen Northern families and reinforce soldiers' domestic ties.

Middle-class women had their own stake in encouraging emotional links with the army. Most saw it as their responsibility to promote morality and work for men's salvation. Their claim to moral superiority rested on fulfilling this responsibility. The war offered an extended test of whether women's influence could reach beyond the confines of the home at a time of national crisis. Every story of a man saved from temptation by women's donations, and every tale of a cheerful sufferer whose moral fortitude triumphed over injury, demonstrated men's susceptibility to women's influence and affirmed the durability of domestic bonds. Encouraging soldiers to keep home at the forefront of their minds, women upheld their roles as moral guardians and confirmed the importance of the domestic sphere over which they presided.

Voluntary organizations quickly intuited that the best way to attract women's support was to emphasize their ability to nourish emotional attachments between soldiers and civilians. The Christian Commission was particularly masterful on this score. Its first public statement described the "gratuitous personal labor" of religious agents as a conduit through which "small packages of clothing, books, and medicines can be forwarded, and momentoes of social affection can be interchanged."[58] Identifying voluntary contributions as intimate gifts embodying home-front affection, it promised to act as a direct channel to soldiers, implicitly contrasting its small-scale, idiosyncratic distribution methods with the USSC's more remote and orderly system.[59]

Capitalizing on public anxiety with army life's corrupting influence, the Christian Commission also promoted itself as a way for civilians to exert moral guardianship over soldiers. To encourage religiosity in the ranks, the organization promised to circulate religious literature in camp; to create "religious associations" in each regiment; and to put "such associations in correspondence with the Christian public."True to its word, Christian Commission agents deluged troops with religious material and instruction. In 1864 alone, they distributed roughly one and a half million Bibles, almost the same number of hymn and psalm books, eight million "knapsack books" containing prayers and scripture, eighteen million religious newspapers, and over thirty-nine million pages of tracts. Fanning out across the war zone, agents conducted religious services and prayer meetings, many of which took place in the spacious Christian Commission chapels donated to many regiments by war's end.[60] The organization's publicity invariably imagined soldiers who were eager, even desperate, for such personal attention. Asserting the importance of individual ministry, they depicted young men surrounded by temptations, standing on the precipice of sin with nothing to stop them falling but the warm hand of the Christian Commission agent, extended in earnest sympathy.[61] To a home front keen to keep a watchful eye on the army, this message reassured that oversight was possible and that soldiers welcomed the effort.

Seeking to bolster this reassurance, voluntary organizations constantly reminding troops that they would one day return to civilian lives. "You are not regular soldiers; this is not your trade," reminded one tract addressed from "The Home to the Camp," by the American Unitarian Association. Assuring men that they were central to family life, this tract pictured time on the home front suspended as loving kin held their breath waiting for soldiers' return:

> We gather at our meals, or around the evening table, and your place is vacant. . . . There are great gaps in our hearts and our homes, which cannot be closed because of you. . . . The old places are kept open and warm for you. You are only absent, and we wait and watch; daily and nightly we pray for you.[62]

Working to strengthen men's emotional attachments to former lives at every turn, voluntary organizations rarely missed an opportunity to lend poignancy to their work, as did the Christian Commission when sending to the army tens of thousands of "comfort-bags" constructed by children's Sunday school classes and containing cheerful notes written in juvenile hands, along with articles for mending clothes and writing letters.[63]

Individual volunteers just as eagerly framed their message in ways designed to recall soldiers' memories of home and prepare them for a return to domestic life. Notes attached to women's offerings underscored the emotions behind their gifts, appealing for reciprocity. In a note pinned to her contribution, one volunteer wrote: "My son is in the army. Whoever is made warm by this quilt . . . let him remember his own mother's love." Another popular message slipped into hand-made socks evoked an image of domesticity restored:

> Brave sentry, on your lonely beat,
> May these blue stockings warm your feet,
> And when from wars and camps you part,
> May some fair knitter warm your heart.[64]

Just as often women drew attention to their own losses in their notes, merging soldiers and civilians together in sympathetic communion. Troops received articles with labels such as: "A pillow and sheet on which my wounded son was brought home from Cross Lanes," or "Three pairs of socks, sent home in the knapsack of a dear brother who fell at Antietam." Others reminded men of women's exertions on their behalf: "This blanket was carried by Milly Aldrich, who is ninety-three years old, down hill and up hill, one and a half miles, to be given to some soldier," explained one message.[65]

Alternatively, there were more insistent urgings for soldiers to recall former lives, as was the case with the volunteer who stitched a poem into the front of a hospital shirt, headed "To the Boy Who Don't Drink, Lie, or Steal":

> Soldier, brave, will it brighten the day,
> And shorten the march on the weary way,
> To know that at home the loving and true
> Are knitting and sewing and praying for you?
> Soft are the voices when speaking your name;
> Proud is their glory when hearing your fame;
> And the gladdest hours of their lives will be
> When they greet you after the victory.[66]

Emphasizing that the home front remained "loving and true," this woman offered domestic support as a reward for men of principled conduct. Like all the notes sent to soldiers, she designed hers to elicit their emotions. Using a sentimental image of women so devoted they thought only of men's return, so emotionally burdened they could only whisper loved ones' names; she personalized her offering in an effort to awaken soldiers' better natures.

To focus soldiers' attention on the affection embodied in their goods, volunteers used a range of additional methods. Some stitched their own names onto clothing or bedding. Others helped to construct "album quilts," consisting of patchwork squares made from the scraps of women's dresses, often adorned with the donor's name or "a patriotic sentiment or cheering couplet."

Recognizing civilians' desire to personalize their goods, one enterprising Vermont surgeon informed residents of that state that anyone fitting out a hospital bed could have his or her name inscribed on the bedstead, while hospital wards would be renamed after towns or counties that donated at least three dozen beds.[67] It was not enough for many volunteers simply to donate goods; they wanted to mark those goods as the product of a particular individual or township's care and affection to symbolize the emotion behind efforts to minister to the troops.[68]

Voluntary organizations were well aware that donors wanted evidence of their goods affecting soldiers. Their promotional literature tapped into this desire by repeating stories of men powerfully reminded of families on receiving even the smallest token from home. One voluntary worker appealed for donations by describing troops' reactions to the handmade gingerbread she was distributing, which "always brought the gushing tears and was, without fail, just like wife or mother's."[69] Equally common were tales of men astonished to discover that seemingly anonymous goods had, in fact, come straight from their families. Sanitary Commission official Alfred Bloor related one such incident in which a soldier uttered "quite a shriek of delight" upon being given a new handkerchief, exclaiming that it had been embroidered by the ladies' aid society in his hometown and was almost certainly the work of his sister.[70] Imagining a nation that retained its intimate connections despite the great distances separating men from their families, tales like these allowed the Sanitary Commission to downplay their anonymous methods, while offering donors a chance to imagine their goods going straight to friends in the army.

Occasional stories about miraculous coincidences only went so far in convincing donors that their goods had affected men. Seeking more concrete evidence of soldiers' appreciation, women often slipped notes into the goods they sent to the army in hopes of making a personal connection with recipients. After writing such a note, one woman was overjoyed at receiving a response from the soldier who now wore her hand-knitted socks. "It will be one of the oasis of my life, that letter of yours," she confided, "for it will remind me that I am doing a little."[71] Obviously this woman had an interest in seeing that her donation reached a worthy beneficiary in light of the many allegations of goods being misused. Yet, her fervid language—which not only depicted a thank you note as "the oasis of my life," but went on to discuss her devotion to soldiers and her longing to help them—implies that something more was at stake than a simple assurance that a package had reached its goal. The soldier who answered her letter not only confirmed the receipt of goods, he testified that an emotional exchange had taken place, one that he cared enough about to write to a stranger. For countless volunteers, imagined or actual emotional exchanges like this one were the currency that rewarded them for their efforts.

Given that hospital work was one of the most visible ways that women demonstrated devotion to the troops, nursing offered critical evidence of their ability to influence men emotionally. Most middle-class nurses structured hospital relationships along domestic lines, imagining themselves as maternal surrogates caring for affectionate boys. This allowed them to verify the importance of domesticity, while also presenting their relationship with male patients as familial, and thus asexual. At the same time, middle-class nurses could disassociate their work from wage labor by linking it to the domestic sphere, supposedly a realm of pure emotion, free from the taint of commerce. Just as important, in depicting their hospital work as a labor of love nurses gave their work meaning and value.[72]

Most women working in Civil War hospitals relied on patients for affirmation and support. Lacking professional training, they labored alongside sizable numbers of male officers who viewed them as intrusive or ineffectual. The only way they had to confirm their usefulness was through patients' responses. Nurses often said as much in their diaries and letters, as did one who told her sister: "I feel all the time of failure, of not coming up to the mark," later adding, "I think my poor men care for me."[73] For such women, the justification for their presence in hospitals lay in its emotional impact. Pointing to the healing power of feminine sympathy, they contrasted women's intuitive compassion and gentleness with the insensitivity bred by professionalism.[74] "Apothecary and medicine chest might be dispensed with," confidently asserted one nurse, "if an equal amount of genuine sympathy could be brought home to our stricken men."[75] Only men's acknowledgment of their abilities could support these claims about the healing power of women's ministrations.

The majority of enlisted men accepted nurses' attempts to create familial relationships and responded accordingly. In more than a hundred letters sent to nurse Sarah Ogden, her patients fondly reminisced about the care they received at her hospital on Broad and Cherry streets, Philadelphia. "I feel that I never can repay you for the kindness you showed towards me when I was suffering from my wounds down thare in my old Broad & Cherry home," wrote one soldier. Another noted, "often Due I think of the times that I had when I was in the city of Philadelphia it was just like a home to me."[76] These men both acknowledged and endorsed Ogden's attempts to create "a home." She loaned patients money, helped them obtain furloughs, and exchanged correspondence that, in a few instances, lasted through the war. Men responded by writing to Ogden, imploring her to visit their families, or making plans to call on her in the future.[77] "Home" for these soldiers and their nurses was not so much a physical space as a set of relationships based on emotional reciprocity.

There were a number of practical incentives for the sick and wounded to accept women nurses as maternal surrogates. Most men understood that gaining nurses' regard earned them added attention and sometimes extra food. "Visited my pet patients in the evening," wrote one nurse in her diary, adding later: "Played dominoes with two of my pet boys, after giving a number of them a nice relish at supper of dried beef and a can of . . . cherries."[78] Such attentions were no small matter for men languishing in hospital for months on end with few distractions and a bland diet. Just as important, patients sought emotional relationships with nurses because they recognized that these women were some of their most ardent supporters. Whereas army physicians tended to treat patients as "medical specimens," explains scholar Jane Schultz, nurses worked to "individualise suffering," remembering men's names, noting their personal details, and recording their dietary preferences. Sometimes they circumvented hospital rules in order to ally themselves with enlistees, such as by sneaking food to men against doctors' orders, or lavishing affection on those surgeons had given up for dead. Given that soldiers often felt themselves to be victims of insensitive doctors or bureaucratic red tape, Shultz argues, women nurses and their patients possessed "a solidarity born of a shared sense of oppression."[79] Picturing their modesty as opposed to physicians' conceit, their disinterestedness contrasting with men's selfish political and professional ambitions, nurses figured their presence as a vital corrective to a sometimes corrupt and arbitrary medical system.

Reinforcing their efforts at creating emotional relationships with their patients, women worked to make hospitals as homelike as possible. In virtually every general hospital, volunteer nurses decorated their wards and provided a range of diversions for their patients. Describing a visit to one field hospital close to the front, a male aid worker noted that the nurses had cut pictures from magazines and pasted them to the walls. Using colored cloth, they also decorated all of the tent poles, as well as pinning sprigs of evergreen over each bed in order, he wrote, to add a "home-like feeling to the wards."[80] Similar scenes greeted the wounded in most of the hundreds of wards in which women labored. Some planted gardens and flowerbeds outside their windows, soliciting "delicacies" for their patients and organizing festivals or other activities for their amusement. In Rebecca Pomroy's ward at Columbian College Hospital in Washington, D.C., the bay windows were filled with plants, the walls were adorned with pictures and moral mottoes spelled out in foliage, and Pomroy's workbox lay in the center of the room, prominently displayed on a large table. Nurses at Hammond Hospital at Point Lookout,

Maryland, similarly vied with each other in beautifying their work spaces: festooning them with cedar and holly wreathes; decorating furniture and walls; and creating artful arrangements of seaweed, pebbles, and shells collected from the nearby beach.[81]

Outside and around hospital wards, civilian volunteers also worked to erase the signs of war and remind men of home. Women planted gardens near the front lines to provide soldiers with fresh produce and to beautify the landscape. They sent canvassing committees into towns and villages, exhorting local farmers and gardeners to lay a "soldier's acre." Always, they described these efforts as a powerful reminder of civilians' emotional attachments to their soldiers. Putting his finger on the purpose behind these decorative touches, one volunteer noted the way homelike images quickly reached the "tender spot" in soldiers, instantly driving away the influences of camp.[82]

Nurses were not the only ones working to domesticate the war zone. Civilian donors did what they could to mitigate the anonymity of Civil War medicine. Tens of thousands of sick and wounded soldiers spent long periods recuperating in general hospitals—typically large complexes of buildings that resembled small towns rather than private spaces. While nurses personalized their wards, volunteers furnished equipment and funds to recall patients to civilian lives and past times. At the Armory Square Hospital in Washington, D.C., they appointed and staffed a library, a reading room, and a business college that trained soldiers for clerical work. Next, they raised money for a new hospital chapel where patients gathered for religious services, temperance meetings, and social events, or listened to local women serenade them.[83] Most general hospitals were equally well appointed, few going without lecture halls, libraries, reading rooms, night schools, bowling alleys, landscaped gardens, or other improvements, paid for by volunteers determined in their quest to remind soldiers of homefront solicitude.

From the perspective of hospitalized men, one of the most important reminders of home lay in the food that civilians provided. Swapping bland hospital diets for "home-cooked" meals, volunteers set up "specialized diet kitchens" to prepare a range of menus for men suffering particular ailments. This initiative eventually received endorsement from the War Department, with Christian Commission agent Annie Wittenmyer directing its implementation.[84] By 1864 she had appointed 157 "lady managers" who consulted with surgeons to determine the dietary preferences of men in approximately sixty of the military's general hospitals. Evidencing the way women aimed to individualize patient care and imbue spartan hospital surrounds with a measure of domestic comfort, one Christian Commission agent described the work as a way of bringing "to the bedside of every patient, in home-like preparation, such delicate food as might be prescribed." Activities like these demonstrated women's indisputable right "to the sphere which includes housekeeping, cooking and nursing," argued fellow aid worker Jane Hoge. Even in hospitals well managed by men there was "the same lack of home-like air, and indefinable tone of domestic comfort, that is seen in bachelors' mansions, no matter how lordly," she argued, going on to note: "A comfort-able, home-like meal, after thorough ablution, had a magical effect," which "in many instances . . . effected a cure."[85] Such comments suggest women's stake in domesticating military life. Men might be able to build the hospitals and shoulder the guns, but only women could create a home with its "magical" ability to comfort and cure. As volunteers like Hoge repeated throughout the war, the only way to limit militarism's corrupting potential was by extending women's domestic influence throughout the army.

Middle-class voluntary workers were not only interested in using femi-nine influence as a counterbalance to the roughness of army life, they also sought to model a properly ordered domesticity for the mass of ordinary enlistees. As soon as a man entered the Soldiers' Depot in New York, for instance, he was required to take a bath, have his head cleansed, and change into a clean set of clothes. This was not an unreasonable demand given that body lice infected most soldiers. But the intent went beyond sanitary con-siderations. "The strict attention to cleanliness, combined with the neat-ness, order and discipline of the building," wrote the Depot superintendent, will awaken "a feeling of self-respect in the men." He clearly felt that many enlisted men could do with such a lesson. Sarah Woodbridge, one of the managers of the USSC's Hartford Soldiers' Rest in Connecticut, shared his belief. She hoped that her neat and tidy institution—with its warm fire-place and tables covered in fresh white linen—would have a salutary "moral influence" over all who entered.[86] Neither writer singled out working-class soldiers as the specific group they were trying to reach, but the tone of their reports—which emphasized teaching men the need for discipline, cleanli-ness, and order—suggests that they imagined their lessons benefiting those who presumably had no prior knowledge of a well-managed home life. Their writings leave a distinct impression that middle-class volunteers saw the war as an opportunity to reach out to masses of working-class men—to instruct them in the intrinsic worth of bourgeois domesticity and build emotional connections that could demonstrate their worthy intent and fitness to act as men's moral guardians.

Casting themselves as parental substitutes, middle-class volunteers viewed it as their right to exert dominance over soldiers imagined as innocent chil-dren. When troops refused to exhibit the decorum these home-like spaces required, their managers' paternalism could easily shade into coercion. James Grimbs, a fourteen-year-old bugler, discovered this fact when he arrived at the Soldiers' Depot in New York in mid-1863 after receiving a discharge from the army. During a meeting with the superintendent, he mentioned that he had no friends in America and was thinking of using his remaining money to pay the fare back to his native Ireland. He then left for the evening in the company of an older male friend, entrusting his bags and most of this money to the Depot's staff. But when he returned the following day with his breath smelling strongly of alcohol, the superintendent refused to hand over his possessions. After Grimbs absconded again, the superintendent dispatched a police officer who tracked him to a "disreputable house," brought him back to the Depot, and forced him into bed. He was escorted straight to the harbor the next morning where the *Albert Gallatin* lay docked. Depot staff paid his fare home, changed the remainder of his money into British currency, and handed it over to the captain for safekeeping. The fact that Grimbs was underage probably added to this superintendent's heavy-handed paternalism. But it was also common for voluntary workers to pass judgments on soldiers' moral behavior or characters whatever their age, and to deny them assistance if they failed to measure up to invisible standards of respectability.[87]

Middle-class volunteers hoped their paternalism would result in a nation of morally virtuous men. Given their widespread belief in mother-love as the strongest and purest of feelings, capable of tapping into the goodness at the core of even the most depraved individual, it seemed obvious to them that reintroducing soldiers to homely environments held transformative power. At war's end they congratulated themselves on the success of their efforts. Union soldiers had not been corrupted, they proclaimed. Instead, they had emerged victorious and melted seamlessly back into civilian life. And the thanks for this outcome rested squarely with the emotional bonds that volunteers had established with soldiers throughout the war. As Thomas Gifford, secretary of the Citizens' Volunteer Hospital Association of Philadelphia, put it, his members had been motivated by pure love for their soldier-patients: "*Love* was the beacon light that guided us," he explained in his final report. And in future years, young soldiers would remember a time when they had been saved "from death's yawning abyss through *Love's* instrumentality."[88] Applauding its membership in similar terms, the final report of the USSC's New England Women's Auxiliary Association asked rhetorically what women had done to aid the war effort. They had built a "great house, spreading far and wide, sheltering all . . . stocked with everything that home can give," they answered. And wherever soldiers went, "in one form or other our love . . . reach[ed] them."[89] Like most Northern voluntary workers, they emphasized not the efficiency of their work but its emotional impact on men and its unparalleled ability to extend domestic influence even in the midst of war.

———◦·••◦———

In September 1862, having just crossed into Ohio after fighting in the South, Union enlistee William Garrett described the impact of female benevolence in a letter to his sister. Portraying himself as a man made callous by his time among a hostile population, he told of entering the Union "dirty ragged without shoes and broke down for want of sleep," wandering about town "not caring for any body," and expecting no one to care for him in return. "[W]hat do you think was the first remark I heard made," he asked. "[I]t was from a lady," exclaiming, "look at that poor soldier with no shoes I expect he was in the fight in Charlston." Further down the road, a "young lady" pressed him to accept a meal: "she invited me in and set me the best in town." Recounting the transformative effects of this sympathy, and identifying himself as a man susceptible to transformation and thus worthy of women's regard, he exclaimed: "I had to eat three times before I could get back on the boat. I felt ashamed of myself to think what I was started out for and then was treated by the ladies the way I was."[90] This was the impact women volunteers aimed for with their voluntarism: not simply to provide for men, but to convince them of an abiding attachment that would guarantee their moral transformation and eventual return to family life.

By gearing their voluntarism toward achieving such transformations, the mass of Northern volunteers believed they were performing vital political work. Only too well aware of the Union's fragility, they feared the war's potential to destabilize the social order, weaken soldiers' independence, and spread immorality. They imagined that by extending home care to the war zone, they had displayed the virtues of middle-class domesticity, helping to limit social conflict and offset the war's brutalizing impact on men. Convinced of the moral benefits of domesticity and mother love, they viewed even the simplest traces of home—a hand-sewn shirt, a piece of gingerbread, a comforting word—as a force that could immediately recall a man to an earlier state, no matter how dreadful his surroundings. Their emotions had acted as a "moral contagion" that spread throughout the Union armies, they believed, providing a bulwark against a fragmented and immoral society and guaranteeing a unity that was necessary both for victory and for a stable peace. Paying more than lip service to this belief, the majority of women volunteers structured their work around facilitating emotional exchanges with soldiers and reminding them that they would soon return to civilian life.

Arguably, the most important consequence of Civil War voluntarism on women's social activism lay in the conviction that women had, in fact, helped to save the nation by expanding their influence at a time of crisis. This belief led not in the direction of women's rights, but toward more militant efforts at moral suasion.

The Civil War produced no significant upsurge in support for female suffrage. Nor did it fundamentally alter beliefs about women's moral superiority.[91] In the immediate postwar era, the majority of socially active women remained committed to religious-based volunteer work that emphasized the importance of their influence and example.[92] They joined voluntary groups like the Woman's Christian Temperance Union, an organization that differed from its antecedents in admitting only women members. Participating in militant crusades against the purveyors of alcohol, such women smashed open barrels of liquor and directly challenged publicans and their customers.[93] Taking seriously the belief that women could remake the social order, they set out on a new mission to transform men's behavior.

The Civil War would not be the last conflict in which women were honored in sentimental terms. But the tides had shifted by the twentieth century, significantly altering the way people conceived of home and female influence.[94] Consider, for instance, one of the most popular tunes of World War I, "Keep the Home Fires Burning," which urged women:

Keep the Home Fires burning,
While your hearts are yearning.
Though your lads are far away
They dream of home.
There's a silver lining
Through the dark clouds shining,
Turn the dark cloud inside out
'Til the boys come home.[95]

This sentimental refrain appealed to women to act as soldiers' mainstay—to embody a home front that men were fighting to protect. But home by this time was no longer conceived as holding supreme power to influence men and ward off their corruption. A wide range of experts and specialized professions by the twentieth century now competed with women as guardians of social order and morality. And women themselves were no longer isolated from the formal political realm, given mass movements in favor of women's rights. Most important, no matter how much conservative commentators implored women to set society's moral tone, the stakes were necessarily lower. For it was clear to all after the Union's victory that the republic was in no danger of collapse. This success ensured not just national unity, but a stronger, more organic nationalism that made the dissolution of the United States virtually inconceivable. In keeping the home fires burning, twentieth-century women sustained homefront morale. But their Civil War predecessors imagined themselves doing much more: saving men from becoming mercenaries, upholding social order, preserving the republic from disintegration, and extending their domestic influence far and wide.

5

Noble Monuments

The American army has been watched over with a loving care which no army ever knew before . . . the exhibition of which must open a new era in the history of armies. No Government did this; no Government could do it. Only a people could do it profoundly in earnest to secure the triumph of a great national cause.

Robert MacKenzie, *America and Her Army* (1865)

BY THE TIME the Civil War came to a close, pro-Union commentators were united in viewing the North's success as the triumph of the more morally virtuous and civic-minded people. Newspaper articles, pamphlets, speeches, and histories all repeated the same story: typically, they began with a peace-loving society, untutored in the ways of war, blessed by a political system that fostered education, moral development, equal opportunity, and civic pride. When this system was threatened, Northerners spontaneously arose en masse, volunteering either to fight for the Union or minister to its defenders. At first naive, filled with bluster and self-confidence, their war fervor was soon chastened by suffering and stalemate. But as they settled in for a long struggle, they came to discover the depths of their patriotism, learning to renounce individualism for cooperative effort, materialism for national service. In the end, they demonstrated a steadfast patriotism unequaled in world history. Waging "a people's war"—fighting not for territory or glory but for a selfless political goal—their struggle was uniquely civilized, confirming for a global audience the moral decency of a Christian republic. The eventual passage of the Emancipation Act added credence to this tale of Northern transformation and moral superiority. For religious writers, providential design was clearly evident in the Union's triumph, but commentators often told the same tale with a more secular inflection.

In staking out the moral high ground, this understanding of the war had obvious attractions. Yet it was not preordained. Commentators might just as easily have touted the benefits of capitalist development by emphasizing their advanced industrial capacity. They might have made claims about the peerless bravery of their soldiers, the importance of centralized government, the timely injection of black soldiers into the military, or any of the other factors that could plausibly have been said to have contributed to their success. Instead, they chose to underscore their military naiveté, their moral decency, and their deepening civic-mindedness. They did this in the face of clear contradictions. Obviously, America was no novice at war-making, having recently acquired a sizable chunk of Mexico by force. Just as evidently, not all Northerners supported the Union: many were ambivalent or hostile to the war's continuance; soldiers had to be mobilized by bounties and the threat or reality of conscription; and support for voluntary organizations waxed and waned, drummed up by relentless publicity drives. Above all, the Union could be extolled as uniquely compassionate only by denying the massive slaughter it had inflicted.

Stories of Northern innocence suppressed these unpleasant realities, holding up a mirror that reflected a flattering image of the Union, and elite Unionists in particular. This was obviously part of their attraction, but their appeal also went much deeper. Middle-class commentators developed these stories in response to what they perceived to be widespread foreign hostility toward their cause. They believed, with Lincoln, that the global fate of democratic republicanism hung in the balance. And they wrote convinced that foreign audiences and legions of future generations would assess their efforts. Imagining that their words held monumental weight and historical import, most were more interested in distinguishing the spirit that propelled victory than in exploring complex social realities.

Modern scholars have done much to deconstruct these depictions of the Union war effort. There is a sizable literature detailing the strength of antiwar sentiment, charting the many factors that motivated enlistment, mapping out divisions on the home front, and exploring the complexities of foreign responses to American events.[1] But less work has gone into explaining why middle-class Northerner commentators continued to repeat stories that now seem so implausible. Yet even the soberest intellectuals at war's end celebrated the Union not so much for its skills on the battlefield as for its capacity to mobilize a virtuous citizenry and mitigate suffering. "The horrors and sufferings of war were inexpressibly grievous and repugnant to a nation that was daily growing more kind and tender-hearted," editorialized Charles Eliot Norton in the highbrow literary journal *North American Review* in 1866. The Union, he wrote, "longed to carry on war without misery; it hated to hurt even its enemies; . . . it strove with all its novel tenderness, not only to succor its own soldiers, but to treat even its enemies with a humanity which found little response in their natures." For Norton and many others, the most salient feature of the war effort lay not in its success in killing, but in its beneficial effects on developing a "moral community" dedicated to the "general welfare" and "the progress of civilization."[2]

To understand how such interpretations of the war effort evolved, it is necessary to put commentators like Norton in a transnational context. Their views were developed and elaborated over the course of the conflict in response to perceived hostility from abroad. In reality, British and European attitudes on American events were complex and fluctuating, shaped by domestic concerns and agendas. But aggrieved Unionists did not pause to parse the nuances of foreign opinion. They viewed any negative criticism as cause for immediate and thorough refutation, for the war threatened the most cherished of all American stories: the myth of the nation's exceptional role in world history.[3] Having long proclaimed America as a beacon on the hill, divinely ordained to instruct the Old World on the virtues of democratic republicanism, middling Northerners were used to congratulating themselves on creating a political system that fostered egalitarianism and economic progress while avoiding the class conflict and murderous rivalries of established monarchies. The war years forced them to contend with claims that the vaunted benefits of their political system were a hollow boast. Distilling many of the Confederacy's critiques of the North, foreign critics charged that the conflict revealed flaws intrinsic to democracies. Swayed by the prejudices and passions of the mob, a despotic Lincoln administration had allegedly raised an ignorant and brutal soldiery that unleashed a war of unrivaled ferocity. It was impossible for Unionists to ignore this commentary. America's republic was simply too novel to allow for complacency on this score: if hostile critics wanted to claim that war had exposed their nation's weaknesses, then it was up to Unionists to prove otherwise.

Pointing to the nature and extent of the Northern voluntarism became the favored means of defending the Union war effort. Just as Northern commentators portrayed their soldiers' cheerful suffering as evidence of a just cause, so they countered their critics by depicting the Unionist response to suffering as uniquely compassionate and resourceful. Inverting their opponents' arguments, they insisted that, instead of exposing an ill-bred and unprincipled citizenry, the conflict had in fact given rise to unprecedented levels of benevolence, such as *only* a democracy could produce. Nothing could be "better fitted to confirm the verdict of posterity as to the spirit and purpose with which the North waged and won this war for the Union," declared a

New York Times editorial in 1866, "than the grand social and national crusade against the horrors of war." Northern benevolence had firmly demonstrated "a popular heart incapable of a war for any but justice, freedom and national integrity."[4] Voluntary organizations thus came to be widely touted as "noble monuments," a uniquely republican phenomena capable of demonstrating before a global audience the moral virtues of the Union and its supporters.

Stories of Unionists' selfless patriotism and unstinting benevolence offered a powerful rebuttal to charges of inhumanity. But they had additional consequences, particularly in helping to shape the lessons that middle-class Northerners drew from the war. By interpreting victory as an endorsement of white unity and morality, they could overlook the fissures opened up by the conflict, such as mounting class conflict or the unequal distribution of suffering and distress. Having emphasized the centrality of voluntarism to national character, these commentators were also quick to urge self-help as a solution to the massive hardships faced by ex-slaves. Turning away from such troubling issues, they instead set their sights on restoring America's battered image in a global context.

When the official history of the U.S. Sanitary Commission was published in 1866, a *New York Times* columnist advertised the work as "a splendid vindication of Republican institutions" and "an unanswerable reply to the mean and mendacious attacks of the European Press on the motives and meaning of the war."[5] Several other reviewers suggested that the tired old story of military campaigns ("so many men, so many guns . . . an enemy in such and such a force") conveyed nothing of value about the conflict, while testimonials to Northern benevolence "really showed of what democracy was capable" and should thus be required reading at home *and* abroad.[6] Following up his published suggestion that the work be widely disseminated in Europe, yet another commentator sent a note to USSC president Henry Bellows, exhorting him to "send copies abroad. There are some people in Germany & England whom I would like to have see it."[7] As it happens, this prompting was unnecessary, since the USSC had already drawn up a list for the dissemination of their history that included prominent philanthropists, military leaders, aristocrats, and newspaper and journal editors throughout Europe.[8] A desire to counter hostile views of the Northern war effort, aired particularly in the British and French press, helps to explain why these reviewers were so eager for a foreign audience. Launching a bitter diatribe against the Union, foreign critics had assailed the basis of American identity, suggesting that the nation was heading down a path strewn with the ruins of failed republics. If some foreign commentators changed their tune over the course of the war, it was their "mean and mendacious attacks" that stuck in these writers' minds.

Even before Union and Confederate forces met on the battlefield, a number of British commentators were gleefully predicting the collapse of America's political system. In May 1861 Sir John Ramsden proclaimed to the British House of Commons that they "were now witnessing the bursting of the great republican bubble which had been so often held up to us as the model on which to recast our own English Constitution."[9] Only slightly less hostile to the Union war effort, the London *Times* declared the destruction of "the American colossus" a good "riddance [to] a nightmare. Excepting a few gentlemen of republican tendencies, we all expect, we nearly all wish, success to the Confederate cause."[10]

In the North, a widespread belief that the majority of the British elites were hostile to their cause provoked a level of Anglophobia unrivaled since the War of 1812. Every mean-spirited characterization of America and its political system was widely exposed in the Northern press and indignantly debated and refuted. Swapping insult for insult, the generally moderate *Harper's Weekly* was moved to assert that "the uniform, consistent policy of the British nation has been ever based on hostility to every other nation in the world.... At home and abroad, they hate every body, and are hated in return."[11] Hardly a week went by without a similar statement in the Northern press, while British and French papers obliged by providing a stream of discussion on the American conflict, attesting to European interests in the Americas and to the magnitude of the war.[12] Scouring this coverage, some Northern editors never seemed to tire of reporting on the most scathing of foreign claims.[13]

Unionists had good reason, of course, to keep a close eye on European sentiments. Preventing the British and French governments from granting diplomatic recognition to the Confederacy was the Lincoln administration's main foreign policy goal, since such a move would have been disastrous for the Union. It would not only have strengthened Southern morale and granted moral legitimacy to secession, but it might also have embroiled European nations in the war, as neutrals seeking to trade with the Confederacy inevitably challenged the Union blockade of Southern ports. Given that Britain and France depended heavily on Southern cotton in the antebellum years, Unionists feared that one or both nations might intervene in order to protect their trade with the South.[14] The British declaration of neutrality in May

1861, followed shortly by a similar French declaration, only fueled Northern apprehensions since many viewed these actions as a prelude to diplomatic recognition.[15]

Anxiety over diplomatic issues, however, cannot fully explain why Unionists were so eager to counter every foreign insult, nor does it justify the stridency of their retorts. Long after the question of intervention was settled, journalists continued to report at length on hostile or flattering foreign commentary relating to Northerners and their political system. The tenor of the journalistic coverage makes it clear that Unionists wanted to imagine British opinion as neatly divided between an oppressed working class that anxiously supported them, and a hostile aristocracy that actively promoted secession, for such an understanding perfectly complemented their interpretation of the war as a fight between democracy and tyranny.[16] Throughout the war, President Lincoln voiced the widely shared conviction that the fate of popular government rested on the Union's success. "The central idea pervading this struggle is the necessity that is upon us, of proving that popular government is not an absurdity," Lincoln famously announced in 1861. "We must settle this question now, whether in a free government the minority have the right to break up the government whenever they choose. If we fail it will go far to prove the incapability of the people to govern themselves."[17] One of the most popular tunes of the war, "When This Cruel War is Over," expressed similar sentiments, at the same time reminding Union soldiers that the eyes of the world were upon them:

> Let all nations see
> How we love the starry banner,
> Emblem of the free![18]

Concerns over European hostility replayed grievances long in the making. Ever since Alexis de Tocqueville penned his famous portrait of American democracy's leveling tendency and crass materialism in the early 1830s, British and European travel writers had been pronouncing harshly on differences between Old World and New. Analyzing this foreign commentary in a work published in 1864, the well-known Boston travel writer Henry Tuckerman complained that British authors invariably asserted a "depreciation of mind, manners, and enjoyment under the influence of democratic institutions." It was now an ideal time to set the record straight, he believed, to exonerate "the claims and character of our outraged nationality." His reviewers agreed. Not a single British author had adequately comprehended the situation in America, huffed one: "Hence the base jubilee at our recent internal dissentions, whose root—slavery—was planted by the English themselves. Hence their constant assertion that 'the republic is a failure.'" Writing only weeks before war's end, it might be supposed that there was no longer any need to defend the republic against claims of its inevitable demise. But such was not the case. Resentment against foreign criticism that predated the war only grew as it continued.[19]

Northern commentators were particularly keen to refute the suggestion that America's conflict was uniquely brutal. Having often stressed the peaceable nature of democracies in contrast to the ruthless power politics of monarchies, they were extremely touchy on this issue—all the more so because the war was undeniably one of the most extensive bloodbaths the world had ever seen. Was America setting a "mischievous example" to other nations with its gigantic war effort, asked the *New York Times* in late 1862? "The government of the United States is certainly the worst behaved in the world," it began in tones dripping with sarcasm, far worse than England, "with her feet upon Ireland, and her bayonets pressing against the breast of India," or the French emperor, filling his military camps while casting a covetous eye on Italy, Mexico, and China. Other European states were no better, "all paragons of peace-makers" who urged the North to abstain from bloodshed while crushing the poor under their own "colossal military systems." Ending on a self-pitying note, the author depicted an innocent North, "assailed and torn," while every European nation looked on, cheering its enemy in their "heartless work of revolution and ruin."[20]

In explaining why America's war had become so immense, numerous foreign critics pointed to democracy as the cause. With no restraining hand to stop them, federal soldiers had become a bloodthirsty mob leading the country into disaster. The London *Times*, voice of the British establishment, said as much on numerous occasions, noting in 1862: "The American Government is not able to rule of itself, but must seek its direction, not from the wise and prudent, but from the ignorant and violent."[21] John Roebuck, one of several outspoken pro-Confederate members of the British parliament, similarly praised Southerners as akin to English gentlemen in parliamentary debates while denouncing Northerners as "the scum and refuse of Europe."[22] Foreign editors prophesied doom, suggesting that the North's huge and unruly army could lead only in the direction of military despotism—a point on which they were seconded by Northern Democrats, who loudly protested the curtailment of civil liberties, hated draft laws, and expansion of government power. Having "constituted itself according to the flaming theories of democracy," the American republic was set to "die in a flood of blood and mire," wrote the editor of the Spanish newspaper *Pensamiento Español* in 1862, as was only to be expected from a nation corrupted by greed, and populated by the "dregs of all nations."[23]

Confederate propagandists did their best to foster these negative opinions of their enemies. The Union and Confederate governments had both sent envoys to Britain and France in 1861 to put forward their arguments for war. Henry Hotze, a paid Confederate agent, began his own journal, *The Index*, which fed pro-Confederate stories to the British press, as well as occasionally authoring pieces directly for the *Times* and other British publications. His counterpart, Edwin de Leon, was responsible for churning out a stream of similar material in France. Downplaying slavery's role in provoking the movement for Southern independence, both men focused on the more abstract issues of self-determination, free trade, and Southern military heroism, as did other Confederate propagandists. Directing their writing to audiences who typically knew little about Southern life, they conjured up an army of civilized Christian men schooled in traditional military virtues, assailed by a force of lowbred hirelings. The majority of Union soldiers were "foreign mercenaries," mostly "German and Irish emigrants," de Leon confidently asserted in one of his pseudonymously authored pamphlets, published in Paris in 1862. Reprinting their charges throughout the war, numerous British and French editors depicted the Union army as a motley crew motivated by bounties, engaged in a senseless struggle against the patrician leaders of the South. [24]

In reality, not all foreign spokespeople—or even all aristocrats—accepted the claim that Union soldiers were unprincipled hirelings. Some praised the federal war effort; others waited, unsure which side to support, and many more were likely disinterested or uninformed on the course of such distant events.[25] Nevertheless, Confederate propaganda had a good deal of influence overseas. As historian Hugh Dubrulle argues, the "semiofficial interpretation" of the Northern war effort among British "statesmen, journalists, foreign service personnel and soldiers" was that Union volunteers lacked discipline and leadership experience and were thus incapable of fighting a "limited war of skill." Consequently, they were forced to inaugurate a ruthless new mode of war-making that beat its enemy into submission by depending on superior numbers and material and attacking civilian populations. When these commentators looked back on the Civil War from the perspective of hindsight, Dubrulle writes, many spoke out against this "new style of warfare . . . and the democracy that served as its foundation," presenting "Confederate forces as a model for emulation," and "highlighting the social inequality that had produced traditional military virtues in the South." If a number of reform-minded journals and British radicals spoke favorably on behalf of federal troops, he writes, they were "outnumbered and out circulated by a press diverse in political outlook, yet united by an increasing distaste" for the kind of war the Union was fighting.[26]

These perspectives were particularly galling because they mirrored domestic concerns over the nation's direction. Northern writers had been expressing uneasiness for decades over the spread of the market economy and the attendant rise of social disorder, selfishness, and sin. At the same time, they had to contend with Southern caricatures of their society as unrefined and materialistic—"a conglomeration of greasy mechanics, filthy operatives, small-fisted farmers, and moon-struck theorists," as one Georgia newspaper put it in an 1856 article. At the beginning of the war, many questioned whether Northerners would be willing to sacrifice as much for the Union as Confederates did for their cause. And as the fighting persisted, middle-class Unionists continued wringing their hands over evidence of selfishness, profiteering, and disloyalty.[27] They were thus more than a little defensive when it came to charges that the Union had raised an army of unprincipled mercenaries fighting solely for profit.

To make matters worse, these criticisms struck a raw nerve by reviving a lingering fear of soldiers as agents of tyranny. Dating back to the Revolution, Americans had measured their distance from Europe by pointing to their miniscule army. Instead of raising a large force of professional soldiers, they had favored civilian militias, honoring an idealized George Washington who reluctantly exchanged plow for sword and then resigned his commission, in contrast to the hired mercenaries and career generals sent by the British to subvert American liberties. Yet during the course of the Civil War, more American men had taken up arms than in almost any previous conflict in world history. It was impossible to predict the results of this unprecedented development. As James McPherson points out, the generation engaged in this struggle had lived to see numerous governments like their own descend into chaos or despotism. Two French republics had collapsed in their lifetimes. Popular revolutions throughout Europe in 1848 had been crushed by conservative reactions, and republican governments had risen and fallen across Latin America. In "a world surrounded by kings, emperors, czars, dictators, theories of aristocracy and inequality," no one could be sure that America's republic would survive. When onlookers foresaw dangerous consequences from the wide scale militarization of the North, their views served only to reinforce pre-existing qualms over the republic's fragility.[28]

Pro-Union commentators defended their troops from such charges during the war by creating a sentimental and decidedly unmartial image of the Union army. In newspaper and magazine articles, readers could learn of men's daring in battle. But the predominant representation of "the boys" in popular wartime literature, music, and poetry was not of warriors but of young, white Christian men, beloved by family members. Usually pictured with blue eyes, golden hair, and pale brows, they were all the sons of mothers waiting anxiously for their return, or the fathers and husbands of respectable families. Examining the preponderance of sentimental war writing—from the masses of poems imagining dying soldiers' last thoughts, to the countless stories of bereft wives and mothers—scholar Alice Fahs points to the way this material demanded acknowledgment of the "lived, personal experience of war," particularly for women.[29] Yet, in a broader sense, it could not help but contribute to debates over soldiers' characters as well—debates shaped in the North by foreign and domestic critiques of Union troops. Imagining innocent boys thinking of home, God, and country as they marched into battle or waited for death, and families closely allied to the troops, Northern writers shaped a vision of their army as the antithesis of the hard-bitten conscripts and cynical mercenaries their critics thought them to be.

Passionate defenses of the Union army were also repeated endlessly in rejoinders aimed at foreign detractors, suggesting the extent to which middle-class writers felt it necessary to counter their critics directly. Robert Mackenzie, an expatriate American living in Glasgow, was one of numerous commentators who responded to what he described as "the wild caricatures" in the British press that pictured Union men "fighting in a frenzy of rage and hate," motivated only by "wicked lust for empire and thirst for blood." In a sixty-three-page pamphlet addressed to his adopted countrymen in early 1865, he offered a glowing tribute to federal troops. Drawing his material from the many laudatory accounts of Union soldiers published throughout the war, he described them as mostly educated, patriotic, Christian men who seldom drank or engaged in "gross sin," and who had seen the errors of their ways on the subject of racial equality (no trace of "the old and lamentable repugnance to the negro race" now being present in their ranks). For Mackenzie, the fact of the North's impending victory was not a strong enough response to the Union's critics. As he put it: "republican institutions [were] upon their trial." Loyal editors across the North had obviously reached the same conclusion, for as the war drew to a close few missed an opportunity to note that Northern men had not simply beaten their enemies, but demonstrated their exemplary characters, absolving democracy in the process.[30]

This is not to say that defenses of the Union army were solely addressed to foreigners. Insults could also be turned to advantage during the war, used to goad Northerners to prove their critics wrong. Charles Janeway Stillé, a U.S. Sanitary Commission publicist, employed this strategy in writing "How a Free People Conduct a Long War" in late 1862, one of the lowest points in the Union war effort. With a print run of 500,000 copies, his pamphlet became one of the most widely circulated of the Civil War, a prominence cemented by its reproduction in a March 1863 edition of *Harper's Weekly*.[31] Stillé's purpose was to bolster morale by reminding Northern readers of another series of bitterly fought campaigns—the Napoleonic wars—in which British forces gained victory only after numerous setbacks. At first, he seemed to court British approval, depicting the North's struggle as akin to their gallant stand against Napoleon. But then—after rehearsing foreign charges against Union forces—he went on to mount an irate defense on their behalf by damning English troops. "The British army is composed, as we all know, of the refuse of the population," Stillé began, their numbers swelled by masses of convicted prisoners, "taken from the hulks" despite their infamous crimes. What could be expected from such men? Nothing but "drunkenness, theft, marauding, a mutinous spirit under privations, and a fierce thirst for license." British forces were a "vile herd," the very antithesis of the "civilized, sober, well-educated American citizen."

Depicting the "American volunteer" as uniquely educated, intelligent and patriotic, "a figure hitherto wholly unknown in military history," Stillé's argument was hardly likely to appeal outside the Union. But war-weary Northern soldiers and civilians, not foreign readers, were his main audience. Recounting and then taking issue with foreign criticism was an ideal way for Stillé to counsel readers not just to stay the course, but also to prove themselves worthy in the face of their skeptics. The same could be said for the myriad tributes to Union soldiers written during the war: cloaking their prescriptions in a language of outraged victimhood, the Union's defenders let readers know exactly how they should behave in order to avoid national censure and disgrace.[32]

It would have been a great deal easier for Northerners to defend their soldiers as principled men fighting in a righteous cause, particularly in Britain, if emancipation had been a war aim from the beginning. Most Britons by this time were used to thinking of themselves as moral opponents of slavery. British ships had policed bans against the slave trade in the decades before the war; British audiences had cheered black American orators and the British crown had ensured that Canada remained a sanctuary for America's fugitive slaves. Having restyled their empire as a benevolent one, British citizens were loud in their denunciation of countries that profited from human bondage.[33] Yet ending slavery clearly formed no part of Lincoln's initial design. He made his views on the subject plain in the war's first year: the preservation of the Union—with or without slavery—was his sole objective. Demonstrating this commitment, he initially ordered military commanders to return fugitive slaves owned by loyal masters and disclaimed any intention of interfering with slavery in states that remained within the Union.

Some of those watching from afar took Lincoln at his word. Reporting his speeches alongside evidence of racial violence and discrimination in the North, they concluded that all talk about the Union standing up for liberty was absurd; the North was simply pursuing a vindictive war to subjugate the South. In the absence of emancipation as a war goal, foreign onlookers were free to ignore slavery as a factor in the conflict. They could instead view Confederates through a haze of romantic nationalism that rendered them not too different from Greek nationalists in the 1820s, or Italian revolutionaries under Garibaldi—both groups widely supported in Europe as beleaguered victims struggling to free themselves from oppressive regimes.

Yet when the Union finally did embrace emancipation, Unionists who supported the move were incensed to find that not all foreign critics rallied behind them. Harriet Beecher Stowe—one of many Northern abolitionists who supported the Union from the beginning in anticipation this shift—made her annoyance plain. She had become a widely celebrated figure in Britain after publishing *Uncle Tom's Cabin* in 1852, selling approximately a million and a half copies of her book and generating huge audiences on her publicity tours. On one of these trips in 1853, a number of women admirers had delivered a petition, initiated by the duchess of Sutherland and signed by more than half a million British women, which called on their American counterparts to renounce slavery as immoral and un-Christian. A decade later, smarting over anti-Union commentary in the British press, Stowe penned a pamphlet in reply that was reprinted in newspapers across Britain. Her point was simple and direct: now that the North had followed Britain's lead and declared their intent to liberate slaves, was it not time for British women to cheer the Union to victory? Picturing the North in a war against a "slaveholding conspiracy," giving "their blood in expiation of this great sin, begun by you in England, perpetuated by us in America," Stowe challenged: "Sisters, what have you done, and what do you mean to do?"[34]

Her reply met with a mixed response, according to historian Wendy Hamand. A number of British editors were sympathetic, applauding Stowe's message and urging support for the Union. But others voiced contempt for her position and cynicism regarding Lincoln's motives. They hypothesized that the Emancipation Proclamation was merely a clever ploy designed to incite a race war or pointed to its inadequacy in freeing only those slaves in areas not under Union control. "Where he has no power MR. LINCOLN will set the Negroes free; where he retains power he will consider them as slaves," concluded the *Times*. Setting himself up as "a sort of moral American Pope,"

Lincoln's real agenda was simply to encourage slaves to "murder the families of their masters while they were away at war."[35]

It is hard to know what, if any, effect Stowe's "Reply" had on British opinion. Scholars similarly continue to debate whether the Emancipation Proclamation fundamentally altered foreign attitudes. Most agree that it eventually did, especially after dire predictions of a racial armageddon proved mistaken. But, regardless of the realities of British and European sentiment, there remained a strong belief in the North that foreign elites stood firmly against the Union, eager for America's republic to fail. "There is certainly not one government in Europe but is now watching the war in this country, with the ardent prayer that the United States may be effectually split, crippled, and dismember'd by it," wrote Walt Whitman in his journal in 1864.[36]

If hostile foreigners could not be convinced of the purity of Northern motives, even after the Emancipation Proclamation, then new arguments were called for. And these were found by laying before the Union's critics the enormity of the North's wartime benevolence. In general, scholars have failed to appreciate the extent to which Northern writers relied on evidence of their voluntarism in an effort to vindicate their cause. Most have read the reams of publicity released by voluntary organizations and drawn on by Union publicists simply as domestic propaganda, written to mobilize support for the war or defend elite male leadership of voluntary efforts. As valid as these claims are, they miss middle-class writers' preoccupation with positioning their efforts in light of a transatlantic debate over the motives and meaning of the war—a debate that held considerable weight at a time before the spread of democracy was guaranteed, and one that helped substantially to shape interpretations of the Union's victory.

Voluntary organizations themselves provided the initial impetus to document the nature and extent of Northern benevolence. They had competed for support throughout the war by describing their activities in newspaper articles, public meetings, annual reports, and letters from the field. As the conflict reached its end, dozens of groups set about collecting and expanding on this material in an effort to memorialize their work. Lengthy tribute albums appeared, narrating the accomplishments of sanitary fairs, soldiers' aid societies, and local relief efforts.[37] Several oversized, lavishly bound volumes dealt specifically with women's benevolent activities, while a number of others sought to comprehend the entire range of wartime voluntarism. The Sanitary Commission, the Christian Commission, and the Western Sanitary Commission likewise all produced huge illustrated histories of their labors.[38]

The authors of these accounts all told the same basic story. Usually they began by describing the prewar era as a time when rampant materialism, political partisanship, and a host of other social ills threatened to rend the social fabric.[39] The attack on Fort Sumter then appears as a pivotal moment that awakened "an instant response in the nation's heart."[40] In Frank Goodrich's huge illustrated survey of wartime voluntarism, social disorder rapidly gave way to unity as a thousand villages simultaneously received telegraphed reports of the Confederate assault. Picturing a common scenario, Goodrich described the nation now "literally, acting as one man . . . incarnated in one thought, before itself and in the gaze of all mankind."[41] Driven by an instinctive aversion to suffering and innate patriotism, Northerners were said to have found a thousand novel ways to support of their troops. In James Moore's recounting of the Cooper Shop, the mere sight of hungry soldiers was enough to send local men and women rushing into the streets, armed with food from their own pantries, leading to innovative efforts to create Refreshment Saloons. Authors widely depicted this civilian movement as the flip side to an unprecedented enlistment of volunteer soldiers—the rebirth of a more cooperative public spirit that lay dormant in the antebellum years. Finally, no history of voluntarism was complete without an analysis of the size, scale and diversity of civilian activities, which were always affirmed as unmatched in world history.[42]

These stories were written by middle-class authors who had strongly backed the war effort and played an active role in the organizations they extolled. Prescriptive and self-congratulatory, they suppressed evidence of draft riots, declining enlistments, war profiteering, and other less-positive responses to the conflict, furthering the idea that support for the Union was natural and unanimous.[43] Sentimental anecdotes of meagerly clad wives spending their last few dollars on gloves for the troops, or grieving mothers transforming their only good curtains into hospital sheets, helped to drive this point home. The clear implication was that if even the poorest citizens recognized the need for sacrifice, then surely no one else had cause for complaint. Insisting that benevolence was universal, they rendered every sacrifice identical. In Frank Goodrich's *Tribute Book*, for instance, everyone gives his or her mite to the cause: poverty-stricken widows hand over their last scraps of food to the local aid society; children offer up their toys for the wounded; and a millionaire fits out his personal ship and bestows it on the government. "All were alike drawn to make some sacrifices, one of his person, perhaps his life, another of his

Figure 4. (opposite) Frontispiece to Frank B. Goodrich's *The Tribute Book*, depicting Unionists of all classes lining up to add their donations to the pile. The two panels on the lower part of the image connect Union benevolence to the biblical parables of the widow's mite and the good Samaritan.

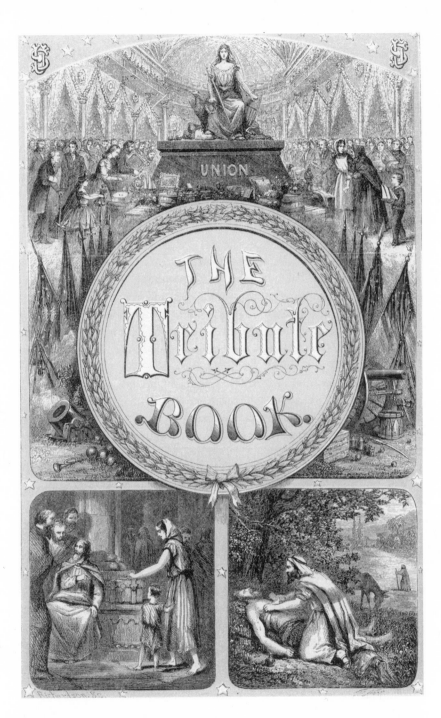

UNION

THE Tribute BOOK.

goods," Goodrich concludes.[44] In his reckoning, it made little difference that a penniless family faced starvation and a soldier death, while the millionaire could presumably afford a new ship. Holding up wartime sacrifices as equally worthy and all embracing, his tale of universal benevolence made any claim to unequal suffering seem aberrant and selfish.

Those who might have complained about this equation could ill afford a book like Goodrich's, with its extensive illustrations and leather binding. His work was addressed to a mostly privileged readership. While celebrating and promoting these readers' civic-mindedness, patriotism, and morality, Goodrich's work had the equally important function of reassuring them that foreign critics would now have to eat their words about Northern decadence. Estimating total wartime contributions at around $70 million, Goodrich proclaimed: "Let the world know the story of these millions, how they were gotten, how spent," and they would be forced to acknowledge: "there is a new thing under the sun."[45] Such frank boasts about the North's vast generosity were sounded practically every time an author addressed the subject of voluntarism, often appearing alongside detailed appendices that recorded the names of the mostly middle-class contributors and managers of aid organizations, listed donations received and estimated their value. Given that Goodrich's privileged audience had just lived through a period of mounting anger over conscription, inflation, and mass casualties, it must have been heartening for them to see their benevolence publicized in such a way. If they had suffered less than many at home, then they could at least be sure that depictions of Northern materialism were false, since they had given more to their troops in wartime than any of their foreign counterparts.

Pro-Union writers did not leave it up to chance for their story to find its way into foreign hands. A number addressed outside audiences directly with detailed recitations of everything the North was doing to aid its troops. Linus Brockett, a Connecticut-born publisher and committed Republican (he would later go on to author campaign biographies for Ulysses S. Grant and his running mate, Schuyler Colfax), produced one of these accounts in 1863 "for gratuitous circulation abroad." Detailing the wide variety of aid societies, religious organizations, and local relief efforts, he portrayed them as the spontaneous product of (often working-class) citizens who immediately banded together at the first sign of suffering. Taking aim at those who prophesied that war would bankrupt the nation or generate social discord, he held that Northern unity had only grown stronger after three years of war. Calls for funds "are met with so much promptness," he announced, "that the greatest difficult has been to direct the full flowing streams of charity." In place of the image of amoral, money-grubbing Yankees, so popular among Confederates and their European allies, he pictured instead a selflessness so wholehearted and instinctual that its supply was virtually boundless.[46]

A number of scholars have pointed to the many similar portrayals of spontaneous and unreserved benevolence in USSC publications, which routinely depicted women as the driving force behind the group's establishment. While this writing celebrated women's natural urge to limit suffering, it typically went on to lament the vast amount of misspent or misdirected energy taking place before the USSC was formed, picturing their organization stepping forward "ready to utilize all this passionate ardor, and to systematize all this promiscuous beneficence." As has rightly been noted, this story served to justify the bureaucratization of voluntarism and to celebrate the leadership of elite men who valiantly intervened to regulate women's chaotic efforts.[47]

Yet the commission's emphasis on an instinctive, popular benevolence was not aimed solely at promoting bureaucratic order and elite management. It was also directed at publicizing the fundamental decency of Northern democracy. In fact, among all the voluntary organizations operating during the war, the USSC was the most self-consciously interested in addressing the North's foreign critics. Its male leadership of scientists, physicians, sanitarians, and clergymen all participated in overlapping transatlantic networks that brought educated elites together to debate the latest developments in fields such as science, medicine, and philanthropy. They intended the scientific and medical treatises they wrote during the war to contribute to these debates. They also set up branches in Britain and France to publicize their work, as noted below, in addition to sending members abroad to report on scientific studies that purported to disprove negative assessments of Union forces. Keeping well abreast of foreign opinion, Sanitary Commission men rarely wrote with only a domestic audience in mind.

Scholars miss this context in assuming that the USSC was dedicated only to social control. According to historian George Fredrickson, the commission's leaders were fundamentally antidemocratic, viewing civilian benevolence "not as something embodied and expressed in their work, but as a great danger to the discipline of the army."[48] To support this point, he quotes a work published anonymously in 1863 by USSC worker Katherine Prescott Wormeley, who described the Commission as a "great teacher . . . guiding the national instincts; showing the value of order, and the dignity of work." But he neglects to cite the other half of Wormeley's statement, which goes on to claim that the organization "sprang from the nation, and that it becomes a teacher because the instincts of the nation have risen up and demanded to be taught." For Wormeley, the real lesson of organized benevolence lay not in the order and discipline it created, but in the way it harnessed and revealed what was already latent in the American political system. "An institution asking of the Government only permission to live," she writes, "planting itself firmly ... on the generosity of the people ... is a noble monument of the intelligence, the munificence, and the efficiency of a free people, and of the alacrity with which it responds when the right chord is rightly touched."[49] While USSC leaders believed that proper leadership was necessary to touch the "right chord," they also assumed that only a "free people" could respond appropriately, and only a voluntary organization basing itself on democratic principles could elicit this response. Emphasizing the way democratic citizens had instinctively mobilized to support their organization, the USSC set out to shape an image of the North as a civilized community in which morally virtuous citizens had come together on behalf of a shared goal.

Virtually every writer who addressed the topic of voluntarism shared this view. Interpreting the significance of their organizations in light of charges that democracies were ruled by ignoble passions, they emphasized an instinctive fellow feeling that overrode every base design. Northern benevolence was imagined in naturalistic terms, as a "great river," or a thousand "bubbling fountains," flowing from the wellspring of an innately decent society.[50] It was often held to be quite different from the philanthropy practiced elsewhere, where a privileged few gave alms in hopes of securing their good names. Britain might have brought forth one Florence Nightingale, crowed many Northern writers, but their society had produced a vast number of anonymous altruists, all motivated solely by their own consciences.[51] "No cold, colossal contribution here/Rears the tall shaft to stamp some brazen name;/The nameless millions pile their gifts sincere,/Nor ask nor wish to call the action fame," ran the stanza to one poem written to commemorate the work of the Union Volunteer Refreshment Saloon.[52]

For those interested in publicizing Northern voluntarism, nothing better confirmed their society's innate decency than the actions of middle-class white women. Patriotic men could easily be interpreted as politically partisan, given that the war's most vocal male supporters were allied with the Republican Party. But women were excluded from formal politics and thus untainted by selfish party considerations. Their moral and religious sense was held to be more acute than men's as well, having been nurtured in a domestic sphere removed from the marketplace. Comparing their actions to those of Confederate women thus became an ideal way for Northern authors to emphasize the virtues of democracy. In addition to the numerous depictions of Northern women's voluntarism in newspaper and journal articles, several volumes were given over to flattering portraits of their war work. In both Frank Moore's *Women of the War* and Linus Brockett and Mary Vaughan's *Woman's Work in the Civil War,* the entire female population of the North rose in a unified mass as soon as the fighting began. Interested only in tempering war's harshness, they did not stop to question men's political loyalties; their benevolence was impartial, seeking out friend and foe alike. Their counterparts in the South, by contrast, supposedly created no mass voluntary movement. With stunted compassion and unnatural partisanship, they instead became the Confederacy's fiercest supporters, dedicated only to urging their menfolk to greater violence.[53]

Sharply distinguishing the behavior of Northern women, middle-class writers applauded the culture that nurtured their innate morality and disinterestedness. As Charles Norton put it, hierarchical societies like the South were incapable of producing widespread benevolence because they lacked moral sense and communal feeling. "Freedom and equality on the one side, slavery on the other," he argued, "had wrought their effects on the souls of men." According to these memorialists, outside critics of Northern culture would simply have to yield in the face of women's example. A knowledge of their war work would secure a "proper understanding of our social life," and defend "the honour of our country," promised Brockett and Vaughan, or, as Moore put it, "there is no feature of the war more creditable to us as a nation."[54]

In explaining the extent of Northern benevolence, writers not only praised democracy for producing right-minded women, they also drew heavily on free-labor ideology, which held that the North guaranteed men an equal opportunity to engage in politics and the marketplace. According to one writer in the *North American Review,* his society could therefore boast a "higher moral standard" and greater social cohesion than anywhere else. Widespread material prosperity guaranteed that citizens cared for one another, he asserted, for only where individuals were free "from purely selfish wants" could they "appreciate the wants of others." Moreover, the North's system of popular education fostered an "intellectual cultivation" that allowed moral sentiments to flourish. Most crucially, democratic institutions lessened "factitious class divisions" by ensuring that each man had a stake in the country's future, sharing "in the direction of affairs according to his will and ability."[55] Using free-labor arguments to explain why the North had done more than any other society to alleviate suffering, this writer inverted foreign criticisms of democracy. Far from producing materialism and depravity, he argued, the North had given rise to an altruistic society precisely because it distributed wealth and power. Reiterating his conclusions, a *New York Times* editorial hoped that wartime voluntarism would prove "to the whole world, that . . . the Christian education of a self-governed people is adequate, not only to restrain their wild passions," but to "inspire them with ... self-sacrificing, generous devotion" toward the nation and its defenders.[56]

These were arguments that the men of the USSC had been trying to broadcast overseas ever since the beginning of the war. At first they did so by sending their publicity material to foreign editors. But by late 1863 it was clear that their message had failed to resonate, even among those who were directly interested in wartime philanthropy. In October of that year, Gustave Moynier and Henry Dunant organized the first International Geneva Congress, bringing together a group of European diplomats, army physicians, and philanthropists to formulate plans for the assistance of those wounded in war.[57] This was the most important humanitarian conference that had yet taken place in Europe, and Sanitary Commission leaders believed their example should have guided discussions. But American precedents received short shrift in the discussions that followed. "Difficulties that the Geneva Conference regarded as very serious and almost impassable, we have met and readily surmounted," opined the USSC's monthly bulletin in January 1864. A few months later, the same publication noted the extent to which the organization hankered after foreign acknowledgment. "We Americans are not yet quite rid of the habit of looking anxiously across the Atlantic for a word of approval ... as a child watches the eye of its mother," it explained, before gratefully quoting a British report on the commission's work.[58]

In an effort to spread details of this work abroad more effectively, the Sanitary Commission established a European Branch in Paris in November 1863, headed by Charles S. Bowles.[59] A few months later, a group of American expatriates living in London gathered to form the English Branch of the Sanitary Commission.[60] Under the chairmanship of American-born lawyer William M. Evarts, the English Branch rented accommodation in Trafalgar Square, opposite the headquarters of a pro-Confederate association, establishing a reading room stocked with USSC publications and American and English newspapers. Both branches would work closely for the rest of the war to publicize the extent of Northern voluntarism and distribute USSC literature widely.

The few historians who have noted these efforts have focused on their limited success in mobilizing foreign support for the Union.[61] Yet it is significant that they were attempted at all. In the midst of a war demanding every resource volunteers could muster, USSC leaders devoted substantial funds and energy to promoting the details of Northern voluntarism abroad. They were not chiefly interested in fundraising; nor were they primarily concerned with keeping Britain or France out of the war (the issue of formal intervention having been more-or-less settled long before they opened their foreign branches).[62]And if USSC leaders hoped to secure their historical legacy—an issue of obvious concern, given how much was spent on memorializing their activities at war's end—this was also not their sole objective, since the publicity they distributed overseas often stressed the broad sweep of voluntarism or more general arguments about Northern morality, rather than simply the commission's own successes. Instead, the USSC joined with other middle-class Unionists in a concerted effort to use Northern benevolence to assert the merits of their society and their cause. Whatever else they hoped to achieve, vindicating democracy was their chief aim.

Indeed, it is often hard to distinguish this objective from some of the work the USSC engaged in domestically. Along with its many other functions, for instance, the commission collected a massive array of statistics relating to various aspects of soldiers' health. From the war's earliest months, they began tabulating data on sickness and mortality among Union troops, comparing these figures to the rates of death and disease suffered by European armies in past conflicts. Using the differences between these figures to calculate the number of lives saved by their interventions, USSC leaders justified the organization's role in increasing military efficiency. However, cementing their credentials was only one part of their design. They also aimed to rebut hostile foreign opinion on the Union war effort, both by demonstrating the effectiveness and extent of Northern voluntarism, and by characterizing Union soldiers in positive ways.[63]

This intent is clearly evident in the USSC's remarkably extensive efforts to measure and describe the nation's military population. From early 1863 onwards, their Bureau of Vital Statistics—headed by Boston actuary Ezekiel B. Elliott until 1864, and then by Benjamin Gould—began investigating the "physical and social conditions" of Union troops. Their work extended well beyond the topic of army health, addressing issues such as soldiers' nativity, age, racial backgrounds, physical characteristics, and education levels. The bureau compiled its findings from the USSC's own inspections of Union recruits, and from millions of regimental returns that were stored in Washington and in state archives. They wrote to commanding officers to fill any gaps existing in these documents, such as the failure to report a soldier's place of birth. And they sent agents across the country armed with specially designed measuring implements, which were used to conduct thousands of studies charting the physical characteristics of different male cohorts, ranging from black soldiers to captured Confederate prisoners. Evaluating these measurements in light of similar data available on foreign populations, the USSC sought to identify those features unique to white Northern men, producing anthropological studies that would form the basis for new racialist theories in the postwar years.[64]

During the war, however, this work was used to rebut foreign criticisms of Union soldiers. Characterizing the Union army as overwhelmingly white, respectable, and native-born, Elliott produced a study of the age of Union volunteers. Countering the idea that these men were mostly hardened foreigners and city-born ruffians, he demonstrated that enlistees were predominantly young men drawn uniformly from across the North—not simply from urban areas where immigrants were known to predominate.[65] Taking over this work in 1864, Gould likewise tried to correct false allegations that appeared in "unfriendly foreign publications and addresses." Addressing himself to the perception of Union soldiers as an ignorant and brutish rabble, he also tabulated volunteers' education levels, highlighting the "unsurpassed zeal with which the most educated classes of the community bore their part in defense of their native land." Keen to promote these studies abroad, the USSC sent Elliott to present his findings at the International Statistical Congress in Berlin in 1863 and at the Society for the Promotion of Social Science in England thereafter. For good measure, they published his work in pamphlet form, sending copies to foreign dignitaries, libraries, scientific academies, and a host of others individuals and institutions, in locations ranging from London to St. Petersburg.[66]

The English Branch helped to circulate Elliott's work and organize his speaking engagements. As was the case domestically, USSC representatives finessed their arguments about the merits of voluntarism according to the specific audiences they addressed. Lecturing to elite male scientists, Elliott portrayed the USSC as an organization dedicated to promoting military efficiency and increasing medical and scientific knowledge. Following his lead, representatives of the English Branch did the same whenever the context demanded. Branch secretary Edmund Crisp Fisher delivered a paper several times on "Military Discipline and Volunteer Philanthropy" in late 1864 and early 1865, first at the Social Science Congress at York, then at London's Royal United Service Institute. In front of select groups of scientists and military officers, he rehearsed the standard claims about Northern voluntarism, pointing to its spontaneous organization and immense size to prove that the war was "not carried on, as many in Europe suppose, by the government of a minority." But he also drew attention to the USSC's role in increasing army discipline and supervising civilian benevolence, ensuring that sympathetic do-gooders were not allowed to weaken military authority. This was an argument calculated to appeal to British military and medical men who might find their own power challenged in like circumstances. Sending copies of his paper to British universities, statistical societies, hospital administrators, military officials, and "leading Englishmen," Fisher ensured that this viewpoint received a good airing among educated elites.[67]

When branch leaders addressed a broader public, however, they tended to portray their organization and the movement it spearheaded in quite a different light. Fisher's first order of business was to gain support among the expatriate American community across the United Kingdom. Sending out a circular to "leading Americans," he depicted the Sanitary Commission as a "purely benevolent" and entirely nonpartisan organization, wholly engaged in the "Christian work of humanity." Whatever political beliefs his readers held, he implied, they all could get behind a disinterested effort to minimize suffering. Using the same arguments in the articles he helped to insert into British newspapers, Fisher played up the idea that the USSC was simply doing God's work of finding and assuaging distress wherever it appeared. Given that the USSC was a wholly Northern agency that only assisted the stray enemy soldier who found himself behind Union lines, Fisher's espousal of impartiality was disingenuous at best. He hammered away at this point regardless, proudly pasting newspaper clippings into his diary that described the Commission extending its "humane assistance" just as "freely" to Confederate sufferers as to Northern soldiers.[68]

When Fisher addressed Americans living overseas, he tried to reel them in by boasting that the USSC was a "colossal volunteer association" which the "nations of Europe are seeking to emulate."[69] But he was more circumspect in appeals to the British public. Trying to win their favorable opinion, the branch commissioned Frederick Milne Edge, an English journalist and correspondent for the *London Daily News*, to write a work charting the USSC's successes. In a naked appeal to British patriotism, Edge's *A Woman's Example and a Nation's Work* portrayed the USSC arising directly from the famous work of English nurse Florence Nightingale in the Crimean War—a point somewhat undercut in the text itself, which spent only a few of its ninety pages on Nightingale's example, and the rest describing the work of the USSC.[70] Nevertheless, Edge did his best to evoke British sympathies, explaining, "As Englishmen, we must take pride in their success, for are not these Americans our own flesh and blood; and have they not profited in their labours by the example [we] set before them?" There were still plenty of statements about America's unprecedented benevolence in his book, but British readers were assured that its origins could be found in their own humanity. Patriotic Unionists back in America apparently felt that these arguments might have some traction abroad, for the Loyal Leagues (a group of organizations in Northern cities closely allied to the USSC and dedicated to funding pro-Republican literature) helped to send Edge on a book tour across Britain.[71]

The English Branch also went to some lengths to broadcast arguments about the admirable character of the Union army. When Robert McKenzie released his aforementioned *America and Her Armies* in 1865, warmly praising Union soldiers as educated, Christian men who were earnestly committed to their cause, Fisher obtained hundreds of copies, forwarding them to British editors, London bankers, members of the British cabinet and Privy Council, and bishops across the United Kingdom.[72] Neither Edge or McKenzie forefronted an image of the USSC as a top-down organization, dedicated to upholding military discipline. To a broader British public, the USSC was far more interested in emphasizing the moral virtues of the North and its defenders.

In fact, the English Branch scored its biggest publicity coup overseas not by publicizing details of the USSC's successes, but by condemning the Confederacy in relation to its treatment of prisoners of war. Nothing was more effective abroad in comparing Northern humanity and Southern barbarism than this explosive issue, which came complete with sensational reporting and graphic images. Effectively linking Northern voluntarism to the POW issue, the USSC portrayed the organization as an impartial judge dedicated to weighing the condition of prisoners on both sides. Unsurprisingly, they concluded that compassion was confined to the North; the Confederacy had not only failed to create organizations to alleviate suffering, but had sacrificed even a modicum of humanity with its fiendish cruelty toward powerless captives.

The POW controversy broke out in the North in 1864, roughly a year after both sides had ceased to exchange captured soldiers.[73] Prisons in the North and South by this time were typically filled well beyond capacity, their inmates forced to endure reeking, overcrowded buildings, epidemic disease, and constant hunger. The situation was made worse in the South by war-induced shortages of every basic necessity. Hardly capable of feeding their own population, Confederate authorities had little to spare for tens of thousands of Union POWs. This fact was brought home to Northerners after a small-scale prisoner exchange took place that year. Most of the returned men were hideously emaciated, some on the verge of death. Sending a committee to investigate their condition, Secretary of War Edwin Stanton immediately recognized the publicity value of their stories, having already made up his mind that the "civilized world" needed to see "the enormity of the crimes committed by the rebels toward our prisoners." His committee produced a lengthy report—complete with prisoners' testimony and eight photographs—which charged that the South had intentionally starved its prisoners, in "a predetermined plan, originating somewhere in the rebel counsels."[74]

The USSC confirmed these conclusions, having sent out its own committee to study the respective conditions of prisoners held in Northern and Southern jails. Its *Narrative of Privations and Sufferings of United States Officers and Soldiers while Prisoners of War in the Hands of Rebel Authorities* read like a legal brief, complete with eyewitness testimony from Sanitary Commission inspectors and physicians who had conducted physical examinations and recorded prisoners' testimony. Having traveled to Northern prisons, they asserted that Confederate captives had little to complain of, being provided with sufficient food, warmth, and medical care. Carrying out similar assessments of returned Union prisoners, they confidently declared that these men were not suffering from disease or the effects of war, but from deliberately inflicted starvation and ill treatment—claims buttressed with the inclusion of prisoners' photographs and medical reports.[75] With the authority of science and graphic imagery to support its claims, and funding from the Loyal League to defray the costs of publication and distribution, the USSC's report received extensive coverage in the Northern press. Images of the returned prisoners—their skeletal bodies covered only by loincloths and shown in full frontal poses—were soon turned into woodcuts and circulated widely by Northern editors, accompanying headlines, like the one appearing in a June 1864 edition of *Harper's Weekly*, that screamed: "further proofs of rebel inhumanity."[76]

Confederate propagandists in Europe knew full well that this issue had all the makings of a publicity nightmare for their cause. Trying to turn the controversy to their advantage, they went on the attack with a series of counterclaims, charging that Confederate prisoners were the real victims of brutality. It was the Union that bore responsibility for halting prisoner exchanges, they argued. And despite the North's abundant resources, Confederate men were starving by the hundreds in Northern jail cells. James Spence, a pro-Confederate lobbyist operating out of Liverpool (the center for Confederate shipbuilding and blockade running), was particularly active in making these claims. He had been working from early 1862 onwards to set up Southern Independence Associations in the United Kingdom—typically small-scale clubs comprising a handful of aristocrats, conservative parliamentarians, wealthy merchants, ship builders, and textile workers thrown out of a job by the North's blockade of Southern cotton. By 1865 thirty-one of these clubs had been established across England and Scotland, mostly in manufacturing districts.[77]

In October 1864 Spence helped to organize pro-Southern residents of Liverpool to stage a week long "Southern Bazaar" to raise money for soldiers held in Northern jails. He also set up a "Relief Fund for Local Southern Prisoners," seeking help for Confederates who had gained temporary asylum in Britain after escaping federal custody. Having raising approximately 25,000 pounds as a result of their efforts, according to Liverpool's *Daily Post*, the group wrote to the U.S. minister to Britain, Charles Francis Adams, demanding permission to examine Northern prisons and distribute funds to inmates. When Adams rebuffed their request, the group was confirmed in its belief that the North had something to hide. Lord Wharncliffe, one of the bazaar's aristocratic sponsors, joined with Spence in informing various British editors that the North's intransigence on the issue could only signal a desperate bid to conceal the systematic abuse of Southern captives.[78]

What Confederate propagandists lacked was hard evidence to support their declarations—the kind of evidence that the USSC had collected in abundance. A month after Spence held his Southern Bazaar, the English Branch wrote to the USSC leadership, noting that its report on the treatment of Union POWs needed wide circulation abroad. Meeting with Thomas Dudley, the U.S. consul at Liverpool, Branch secretary Edmund Fisher agreed to help him distribute 10,000 copies of the report to neutralize Spencer's activism. "You can't reach the English mind with argument," Dudley wrote to Fisher; "they can only be moved by acts like these of cruelty, surpassing anything that has been practiced in this age and only finding counterparts in the dark ages of the world."[79]

Fisher readily agreed, spending a good part of the remainder of the war engaged in distributing the USSC's *Narrative of Privations and Sufferings* and promoting its charges in the press. Tens of thousands of copies made their way across Britain and Europe under his direction. In December 1864 the U.S. consul at Bristol, Zebina Eastman, wrote to Fisher requesting additional copies to satisfy the "great demand" in his area, explaining, "Nothing that has been published, has produced such an effect on the sentiment of this community, and its free circulation, must be of great benefit to the Union Cause." Making the same point a month later, George Fogg, the U.S. legation in Berne, Switzerland, requested that Fisher arrange to have the report translated into French and German, for "no other arguments can ever so powerfully tell against the cause which commits & permits such atrocities."[80] Some foreign critics might have remained skeptical about the Union's moral purpose, despite evidence of its extensive voluntarism. But when coupled to sensational claims of Confederate cruelty—backed up by medical reports, photographs, and eyewitness testimony—such arguments became a great deal more convincing.

The USSC had done its best to advance claims about Northern morality and Southern barbarism overseas. Picking up the same arguments at war's end, middle-class Unionists repeated the mantra that their society's compassionate response to suffering was only possible in a democracy. Revealing their ongoing preoccupation with foreign condemnations of their war effort, they did not just celebrate Northern voluntarism per se; they extolled it as the symbol of a distinct culture far different from the one their critics imagined. Historian George Bancroft, for instance, wrote to the author of a weighty tome honoring the Christian Commission's work, declaring that such an organization was a "eulogy of free institutions," which "*could* not grow up, *would not be allowed* to grow up in any nation in Europe."[81] Chief Justice Salmon P. Chase was of the same opinion. Speaking before the House of Representatives in a ceremony held to mark the end of the Christian Commission's work, he maintained that "no such humane ministration of beneficence and loving-kindness was ever witnessed before in any age or country" or would it be possible "in any Christian land except our own," a viewpoint seconded by every other orator who spoke at the event.[82] Northern voluntarism was not just good in itself—it was a monument to "free institutions," the sign of a humane, Christian community.

These opinions formed part of a widespread faith that the Civil War had swept away all the problems and divisions of the past, knitting citizens more closely together through bonds of shared empathy and goodwill. Declaring that the North had shown the world how to wage a more "civilized" kind of warfare, Christian Commission memorialist Lemuel Moss was convinced that America had entered "a new era in the history of benevolence," with "millions of hearts, young and old" having learned "the blessedness of giving."[83] Sanitary Commission publicity was equally hopeful, picturing the urge to help "suffering fellow beings" as "more universally and more deeply felt among us than when the war began." Others provided a range of evidence to support their claims that selfishness was largely a thing of the past. Goodrich pointed out that Northerners' altruism had not been confined to the army but had instead begun to spread more widely, with vast sums given during the war to help educational institutions and churches. The impressive religious revivals that had taken within Union ranks offered another powerful sign that morality was ascendant, with millions of reformed men now set to return home "clothed with new power for good." Calculating the huge sums of money expended in the nation's support, and detailing the effects of this benevolence on both givers and receivers, middle-class authors justified their belief that society had permanently turned away from materialism and self-interest.[84]

These ideas fed into larger claims about the war's regenerative potential, sounded loudly as the armies began to disband. Less-religious commentators drew from the currents of romanticism, seeing in the intense emotions of the past few years a sign that people, once numbed by their workaday concerns, could now appreciate the importance of the nation and the worth of values like courage and patriotism. Everywhere people proclaimed that America's young republic had come into its own, emerging victorious from historic battles worthy of comparison to any campaigns of ancient or modern times. Its struggle "unparalleled in the history of warfare," according to one Union soldier, America had proven itself a power to be reckoned with before a global audience.[85] The nation's newly discovered might and unmatched sacrifices heralded for many a more cohesive society that would march into the future united in its quest to preserve the wartime values of self-sacrifice, patriotism, and social betterment.

Among religious commentators there was an even more pervasive faith that the conflict had produced lasting change. With slavery abolished and the people chastened by suffering, the nation had evidently been absolved of its sins, clearing the path for the second coming of Christ. "By bringing the nation to the consciousness of God's supremacy, and to the conviction of his truth and justice," wrote Reverend J. P. Thompson in the *New Englander*, the war had established his "kingdom in the souls of multitudes." Listening to the "voices of wailing," he heard "the prophecy of redemption." It was a prophesy with deep roots in American theology. For religious thinkers had long held that salvation could only come about through suffering, and that the nation was destined to play a major role in the re-establishment of God's earthly kingdom. Yet there was something new here as well. Antebellum Protestants had overwhelmingly interpreted the nation's mission as one of "moral persuasion, with evangelical piety and democratic institutions offering a contagious example to others," in the words of religious historian James Moorhead. Now they aligned religious fulfillment with the nation's secular military and political struggles. There was an intense and virtually unanimous conviction that the Union war effort was "hastening the day of the Lord," writes Moorhead, "that the war was not merely one sacred battle among many but was a climactic test of the redeemer nation and its millennial role." Exhilarated by their victory, the majority of believers foresaw that God would recompense their sufferings by restoring America as a chosen people and leading them to a new dawn. [86]

Given that the war ushered in the Gilded Age rather than the millennium, scholars have tended to discount these optimistic pronouncements, instead focusing on the war as a transitional moment that led to national consolidation, realized through increasingly centralized political power, a burgeoning bureaucracy, and an activist state. The fact that Unionists tended to embrace national consolidation as a corrective to state sovereignty has led many scholars to posit a more generalized wartime valorization of efficiency, organization, and order.[87] According to Wilfred McClay, for instance, the Grand Review where Union soldiers marched in lockstep past cheering onlookers is a perfect symbol for the nationalized, bureaucratized, and efficient modern nation-state that Americans supposedly championed as a result of the war.[88]

Yet, if one reads contemporary accounts of demobilization, a very different story emerges. What most Northerners celebrated, above all, was the moral rather than the military discipline of their armies. They placed the Grand Review in the context of critical foreign debates about the nature of their soldiers and the potential ramifications of their war, and they loudly proclaimed that peaceful and speedy demobilization witnessed the vast difference separating Americans from Europeans. At a Thanksgiving celebration held in Paris in December 1865, attended by President Andrew Johnson and assorted Union generals and expatriate Americans, every orator echoed the same theme. In the words of General Schofield, the "most important lessons taught by the late American war" were that

> people who have always enjoyed so great a degree of personal liberty as to be almost unconscious of even the existence of a Government over them in time of peace, have found this mild Government to be in time of civil war the strongest in the world (loud cheers). . . . But what is grandest of all . . . these vast armies, when their work was done, quietly disbanded, and . . . returned to the avocations of peace as quietly as the Christian returns from the sanctuary to his home on a Sabbath morning; and in all respects a better *citizen* than he was before.[89]

Rather than viewing efficiency and order as the major consequences of the war, most Northerners maintained an optimistic faith that the conflict had produced a more united, virtuous, and religious citizenry.[90]

This confidence raised expectations that were bound to end in disillusionment. It also left the nation drastically ill prepared to deal with the problems of Reconstruction.[91] Hopeful pronouncements about a more selfless and united society aside, very few middle-class Northerners emerged from war questioning the government's laissez-faire policies or critiquing their society's massive disparities in wealth and power. Their flattering self-conception had little to offer the mass of poverty-stricken African Americans who had recently emerged from a lifetime of servitude with nothing but the clothes on their backs. For the past four years, middle-class commentators had championed the resourcefulness and drive of ordinary democratic citizens. Their idealization of voluntarism acted as an anti-statist ideology, ensuring that, even as state power expanded, most Northerners remained reluctant to commit resources to help former slaves. Believing that social change would follow from individual conversions, most privileged Unionists saw reconstruction as a spiritual rather than a political problem—and one that the war had helped to resolve. As one orator promised returning soldiers, the nation had experienced "its second birth." "A future is given unto us, for re-construction, for beneficent action, for joy to suffering humanity, and for a world's redemption, such as our fathers knew not, and such as has been vouchsafed to no other people, since time began."[92] Providence had helped to secure a Union victory, and wartime benevolence had proved Northerners worthy. Reconstruction, according to this orator, was simply a matter of sustaining the "beneficent action" that Northerners had exhibited over the previous four years. How this was to be accomplished, he left to their individual consciences.

The plight of newly freed slaves was not high on the U.S. Sanitary Commission's list of priorities as they wound down their operations. They spared a few thousand dollars for one freedmen's aid association, but far more lavish sums went to publicizing the organization's work domestically and abroad. In mid-1866, the organization's president, Henry Bellows, received word that Paris intended to host a Grand Exposition to rival the one held in London fifteen years before. He wrote excitedly to colleagues, setting forth detailed plans to highlight America's gigantic voluntary movement, envisaging rooms filled with miniature models of hospital transports, sanitary wagons, and lodges; life-size replicas of feeding stations and aid rooms staffed by female attendants; shelves stocked with every item donated during the war; and maps, photographs, drawings and broadsides depicting sanitary fairs, volunteer hospitals, and a range of other topics. Money "could not be more humanely & wisely expended than in making our experience *tell* on the world," he wrote, "It would be for the honour & glory of our country," as much as for that of "our constituent."[93]

Bellows' grand plans came to fruition over the following year. While the American government, still reeling from the shock of war, made a poor showing at the Paris Expo, its few exhibitions largely confined to an out-of-the-way annex, the USSC emerged triumphant.[94] Occupying an entire building to itself—usefully situated across from the Comite Internationale's much less inspiring display of sanitary initiatives collected from across Europe—the

USSC put on an impressive show, complete with all of the exhibitions that Bellows had imagined, and many more besides.[95] It was awarded a Grand Prix for its efforts, one of only a few dozen given out that year. Bellows was ecstatic. The USSC had finally secured an appropriately grand stage to broadcast to the world the extent and nature of American voluntarism. Tens of thousands had come to see this benevolence close up, and hundreds had been handed copies of many of the volumes cited in this chapter—from Frank Moore's *Women's Work* to Goodrich's *Tribute Book*. Writing to John Blatchford, Bellows hoped that the exhibitions, "so instructive as an illustration of the democratic method of free Institutions," would "act as one of the chief stimulants to the study & admiration of political liberty & Social Equality."[96]

Bellows—and many of his fellow Northern elites—eagerly sought international recognition of Union voluntarism because foreign critiques of the war effort struck so close to the bone. In arguing that the conflict exposed weaknesses inherent in America's republic, foreign criticism echoed the concerns of many in the North who feared the war's potential to incite popular unrest, produce further social inequalities, create a dictatorial government, or brutalize the populace. These were not unreasonable fears. The government had dramatically expanded its reach during the war, draft riots had occurred in numerous towns and cities, and the struggle had become savage beyond all expectation. The story of the North's war effort as benevolent and unified—a magnanimous and civilized response to wartime suffering unprecedented in world history—helped to drown out voices of dissent. And this was a mission the Republican administration could get behind. When the USSC's exhibition returned from Paris, it was proudly displayed in the capital's Rotunda, allowing visitors to gaze on their achievements and congratulate themselves on winning the respect of a once-doubting Europe.[97]

6

Honorable Scars

Were such a thing possible, as the restoration of my arm, I would not have it restored. I consider it an honor and am proud of it.
Henry C. Allen

TWO YEARS BEFORE the USSC staged its exhibition of Northern voluntarism in the capital's Rotunda, a very different set of wartime memories were on display in Washington, D.C. At Seaton Hall in May 1866, William Bourne, a former minister and hospital visitor turned newspaper editor, was showcasing hundreds of manuscripts produced by Union veterans who had lost their right arms in the war. They were the product of two penmanship competitions he had established in the war's immediate aftermath, aimed at helping maimed veterans find work. Proudly displaying his entrants' achievements, Bourne placed their manuscripts on long tables spanning the length of the hall, each accompanied by the author's photograph. Most of the images pictured coat sleeves taken up to reveal a missing limb, although a few displayed shirtless torsos with gaping wounds. Wandering up and down the hall, enthusiastically inspecting this unique display, renowned author Fanny Fern was overcome with intense feelings, not of despondency but of national pride. Proclaiming the exhibition a "purely *American* idea," she applauded its demonstration of ordinary men's self-sufficiency and optimism in the face of suffering, declaring in a *New York Tribune* article: "As a moral lesson I would have had every boy and girl in the land taken there to see the power of the mind over the body."[1]

This was exactly the response Bourne had hoped to produce. He saw his competitions as a way of lauding inspirational suffering and promoting self-sufficiency—demonstrating that America's wounded men had not succumbed to despair. His competitions echoed the dominant spirit of the age in their inventive can-do approach to problem solving and their emphasis on literacy and education, both widely heralded in the North as characteristic of American democracy. They also epitomized central tenets of the Northern bourgeoisie with their faith in individual willpower and their assumption that wartime problems were best addressed by benevolent individuals and voluntary action, not recourse to political, legal or social change. Most of all, by seeking out and publishing ordinary men's stories of suffering, Bourne's efforts reflected a characteristic Victorian enthusiasm for tales about characters who triumphed in the face of adversity, remaining true to their religious, moral, and political principles and bearing witness of the results.

There were both similarities and differences between the story that Bourne aimed to tell and the ones his contestants set down in their manuscripts. Bourne's immediate goal was to help amputees find white-collar jobs—a task he thought best accomplished by awarding left-handed penmen with the tidiest "business hand."[2] While his preferred story encompassed efforts at self-improvement and social elevation, many of those who entered his competition did not share his enthusiasm for such themes. The majority were farmers or laborers who had little or no interest in bettering their writing. Some probably hoped to garner a prize regardless, yet many explained that they entered the competition not to win, but in order to tell their stories. It was "the duty of *every* member of the left arm'd corps ... to add something to the collection," wrote one entrant.[3] For amputees were the bearers of the war's physical memory and thus its most obvious patriots and spokesmen, he believed. Taking this role to heart, large numbers of entrants boldly put forward their opinions on political issues or lectured comrades on the need for diligence and determination in confronting setbacks. If Bourne aimed to promote the value of a middling vocation, many of his entrants instead embraced the only chance they might ever have to explain the nature of their service and the meaning of their injuries in a public setting.

The unique set of almost 400 manuscripts produced by these men offers a rare opportunity to examine the way maimed veterans interpreted and expressed their understandings of suffering in the immediate postwar era. Writing for public consumption, usually in hopes of impressing the judges (most of whom were Union generals), the writers sought to put their best foot forward, trying to fashion themselves as exemplary sufferers. Their narratives thus provide access to the dominant mores surrounding injury and sacrifice, revealing how masses of ordinary veterans believed ideal sufferers should behave, even if such ideals proved hard to live up to in practice.

Most writers discussed their sacrifices in positive terms, drawing on three dominant narratives of redemptive suffering. They explored their wounding as an event that instructed onlookers in the true meaning of civic commitment, allowed them to achieve religious insight, or strengthened their character. Those focusing on civic commitment emphasized their willing participation in war, stressing that a democratic republic needed virtuous men prepared to surrender comforts for the common good. They expressed pride in sacrificing (or "giving") a limb for the cause they championed, marking themselves as ideal citizen-soldiers who stood in contrast to hired mercenaries or conscripted troops. Others depicted suffering in religious terms. Explaining that their blood had been shed to save a political system ordained by God, they resigned themselves to his will, offering an inspirational example of martyrdom through their Christ-like patience and unyielding faith. Finally, numerous men portrayed the ability to endure suffering as the ultimate test of self-governing manhood. Arguing that willpower had enabled them to survive amputation, they now exhibited the same willful effort in disciplining their maimed bodies and learning how to write. Identifying the value of suffering in a political, religious or personal sense—and sometimes all three at once—these amputees incorporated bodily loss into a sense of civic and masculine identity.

The Civil War produced a wide range of devastating injuries, most of which went unheralded in the postwar years. Those who could transform physical loss into expressions of patriotic commitment, Christian fortitude, or self-discipline were the lucky ones. Others needed daily assistance, failed to find work, or found it impossible to triumph over extreme pain. Surrounded by the stories of mutilated veterans who had mustered the resolve to thrive in the face of injury, an inability to cope could only be interpreted as a character flaw. Inevitably, the value that the culture placed on willpower in overcoming adversity made failures out of some men, directing attention to a powerful ideal of self-help and away from wounded veterans' specific financial, social, or physical situations. But complaints from those who fared poorly went largely unheard in the post-bellum years, as Northerners celebrated their victory and heaped praise on veterans who got on with their lives.

In comparison to later American conflicts, the Civil War produced an enormous number of amputees.[4] According to official statistics, almost 22,000 Union soldiers survived an amputation, although in all likelihood the number of such men was much larger.[5] Most were compelled to seek paid work. Although the government provided pensions to amputees, one-armed men received a mere $15 a month in 1866—barely enough to keep body and soul together, let alone support a family.[6] It was obvious that something further had to be done to aid maimed patriots. But middle-class Northerners worried over the form and extent of additional public assistance. Their responses were colored by prewar attitudes toward the needy, which tended to blame those in poverty for their own plight, as well as by newer concerns about the debilitating effects of army life on manly independence. Afraid of augmenting the growing numbers of dependent poor, Northern politicians and public commentators generally agreed that the best course was to help injured veterans help themselves.[7]

A number of voluntary initiatives aimed at employing disabled soldiers sprang up in Northern cities at war's end. In several large cities, wounded veterans could register at employment agencies operated by the Sanitary Commission.[8] Messenger services staffed entirely by amputees also provided work for a small number of those living in New York, Boston, and Philadelphia.[9] Others found jobs with the federal government, which gave preference in civil offices to appropriately trained and honorably discharged veterans. However, the state provided nothing comparable to the rehabilitation hospitals or training schemes that catered to veterans injured in subsequent wars.[10] And even the improvised, limited assistance provided to disabled Civil War veterans turned out to be short-lived. By mid-1866 the army had closed its remaining hospitals, and most of the employment bureaus had ceased operations, leaving disabled men largely to fend for themselves.

William Bourne had an intimate knowledge of the difficulties that injured men faced in adapting to civilian life. He was also an old hand at social activism. Born into a family of committed abolitionists, Bourne had thrown himself into educational and labor reform in the prewar decades. When the Central Park Hospital in New York opened its doors to sick and injured soldiers in the summer of 1862, he signed on as a volunteer. Bourne became a regular visitor around the wards over the next two years, befriending the men and conducting religious services. In his diary, he recorded the names and personal details of his patients, some of whom kept in touch after their discharge. He also began publishing a newspaper called *The Soldier's Friend* in December 1864, filling its pages with details of bounty and pension laws, reports on newly formed veterans' organizations, and a range of other useful information, alongside his own patriotic verse.[11]

Concerned primarily with finding work for disabled soldiers, Bourne led by example, hiring amputees to sell *The Soldier's Friend* in the railway cars and streets of New York. From the earliest editions he lectured those missing a limb on the benefits of self-help. "Make up in mind what you have lost in body," he advised, suggesting, "Your will can carry you farther on one leg than you can travel without it on two." If the will was more important to manhood than bodily integrity, Bourne implied that it could only be demonstrated by vaunting oneself into white-collar employment: "There are hundreds of good clerks who have lost a right hand, but who are to[o] inert to learn to write with the left," he declared.[12] To remedy this situation, he published details of a penmanship competition in June 1865, offering premiums of $1,000 to "the Left-Armed Soldiers of the Union," as "an inducement to that class of wounded . . . to fit themselves for lucrative and honorable positions." By the time judging began in February 1866, he had received some 270 manuscripts, a response so enthusiastic that he organized a further round of prizes, adding an additional 120 entries the following July.[13]

Interest in Bourne's competition was not spread uniformly among left-armed veterans. Only a few commissioned officers chose to write manuscripts, perhaps put off by the condescending tone of uplift that infused the entire enterprise.[14] Competing at penmanship was also out of the question for most black soldiers, since the vast majority had only recently escaped from slavery, under which an education was legally denied them. Even among literate African Americans, Bourne's competition was irrelevant. As Will Thomas, one of the two black soldiers who put pen to paper, noted, "I dont expect to secure a position as *clerk*, that being proscribed on account of my *color*."[15] Thomas knew only too well that black soldiers injured in the line of duty faced a unique set of difficulties in civilian life that a penmanship competition was ill-designed to address.

For his predominantly white entrants, Bourne provided instructions that were broad enough to provide plenty of scope for individual variations. Contestants were advised that manuscripts should include personal and military details, together with a "brief" literary specimen either "original or selected." Readers of *The Soldier's Friend* learned further that "essays on patriotic themes, and especially narratives of the writer's experience in the service . . . are preferred." From the outset, contestants also knew that they were writing for a public audience, since Bourne planned to exhibit the manuscripts and use the proceeds to publish a memorial volume that each entrant would receive.[16]

In the glare of a public spotlight, several entrants claimed center stage with manuscripts running to dozens of pages. Colonel W. Davis, the highest-ranking participant and one of the more prolific writers, for instance, submitted a third-person narrative detailing his impressive ancestry and various prewar accomplishments.[17] But most participants were more modest. A few provided one or two sparse sheets simply listing a name, rank, and list

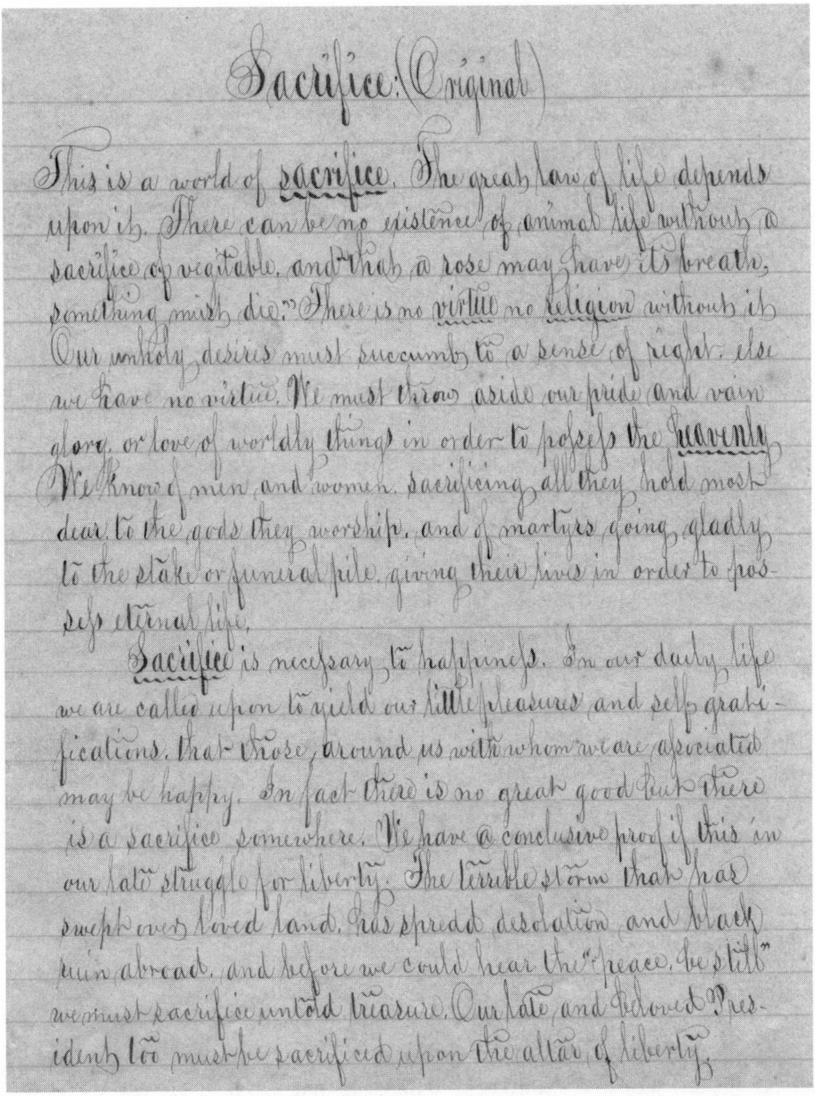

Sacrifice. (Original)

This is a world of sacrifice. The great law of life depends upon it. There can be no existence of animal life without a sacrifice of vegetable, and that a rose may have its breath, something must die? There is no virtue no religion without it. Our unholy desires must succumb to a sense of right. else we have no virtue. We must throw aside our pride and vain glory, or love of worldly things in order to possess the heavenly. We know of men and women sacrificing all they hold most dear to the gods they worship. and of martyrs going gladly to the stake or funeral pile. giving their lives in order to possess eternal life.

Sacrifice is necessary to happiness. In our daily life we are called upon to yield our little pleasures and self gratifications. that those around us with whom we are associated may be happy. In fact there is no great good but there is a sacrifice somewhere. We have a conclusive proof of this in our late struggle for liberty. The terrible storm that has swept over loved land. has spread desolation and black ruin abroad. and before we could hear the "peace. be still" we must sacrifice untold treasure. Our late, and beloved President too must be sacrificed upon the altar of liberty.

Figure 5. First page of Henry H. Chaffee's entry to Bourne's left-handed penmanship competition, endorsing the virtues of "Sacrifice." (Courtesy of William Oland Bourne Papers, Manuscript Division, Library of Congress, Washington, D.C.)

of battles. Roughly a dozen men copied lines of poetry or political speeches (Lincoln's being the favorite). Several opted out of the role of narrator entirely, instead allowing transcribed military reports or discharge papers to speak on their behalf. And the largest number followed the organizer's stated preference and recounted their military histories, usually beginning with enlistment and ending with discharge from the military, with only an occasional brief reference to prewar occupations or postwar lives.

These men created their narratives in view of an imagined audience and in light of pre-existing stories of amputees. All knew that there was generous prize money offered.[18] Although awards were made solely on the basis of penmanship quality, rather than on what participants actually wrote, competing for relatively large sums in a public forum—and a specifically patriotic one at that—would have influenced the way men told their stories.[19] Aware that their words would be read and displayed, participants framed their response to injury in light of how they interpreted public expectations, just as they would continue to do in their daily lives. Their narratives thus evidence their authors' understandings of and negotiations within a particular cultural milieu—one in which limbless soldiers were already well-represented figures, with images, poems, and stories featuring amputees circulating widely during the war.

Two main depictions of amputees predominated in wartime culture. First, mutilated soldiers often appeared in poems, songs, or stories as pitiful figures who had made disproportionate sacrifices only to be forgotten by an ungrateful public. *The Empty Sleeve*, a cheap pamphlet written in verse form to be sold by needy veterans, for instance, painted a grim picture of life as a one-armed man:

'Tis but a common story, I shall to you unfold,
Yet 'tis no less important because so often told.
'Tis of an humble soldier who bore throughout the wars,
The flag of freedom's conflict, and bears to-day the scars;
And of his wife and children, all famishing and poor,
Because the crippled parent can never labor more.

Poverty was the fate of most amputees, not just an unlucky few, this author insisted. And this fact stood as an indictment of privileged Northerners:

O men of wealth and station, O men of high degree!
Whose lot is power and plenty, this ought not so to be.

For you the soldier periled his life in manhood's pride;
It was for you he battled, and for you it was he died.[20]

Such portrayals of unfortunate amputees suffering from the indifference of the wealthy abounded in wartime culture.[21] Men with missing limbs had so obviously sacrificed for the Union that their shattered state was the perfect vehicle for writers seeking to show that the poor had been saddled with the long-term costs of war. Given the inadequacy of pensions or jobs for one-armed men who lacked powerful friends or families, this was a justifiable critique. But it only went so far. These complaints almost never extended to criticism of the war itself, rarely, if ever, picturing men who regretted going into battle. Nor did they offer specific remedies (save for an implied need for larger pensions). They simply insisted on recognition and sympathy for amputees as the conflict's most evident victims. Moreover, most of the sad wartime tales of amputees lacked even this modest social critique. Instead, they depicted amputation in bittersweet terms—as an occasion for sadness, but also one calling for profound gratitude that a limb rather than a life was taken.[22] In both cases, amputees represented a singular class of veterans— men whose wounds confirmed their service and demanded acknowledgment and grateful remembrance—yet not a class that formed a rallying point for antiwar sentiment or called for structural changes to address poverty or warfare more broadly.

Wartime representations of amputees as unfortunate men deserving appreciation and reward influenced how some of Bourne's entrants represented themselves. The link was often direct and obvious, with men narrating their histories using almost identical imagery or words to those produced by wartime poets and authors. Like published wartime narratives, which refrained from criticizing the Union war effort, amputees did not speak out against the war itself, despite their evident suffering. Condemnation of the state's manner of dealing with the war's victims was similarly restricted to a handful of personal appeals for employment or higher pensions. Even these few who voiced concerns about their personal plight were clearly constrained by a culture that valued self-help, willpower, and unflinching patriotism above all else. They knew that their tales would be put on show, and they led their readers only so far as they believed they would follow.

Indeed, it would have been unorthodox for Bourne's contestants to complain too loudly about their lot, for doing so would have undermined a second depiction of Union amputees—one far more pervasive than that of the sad and neglected victim. During the conflict, limbless soldiers had often been held up as the epitome of inner strength, patriotism, and self-control—men of action who needed no assistance since they barely noticed their missing limbs. In newspaper articles and military reports commenting on Union officers wounded in battle, the emphasis was generally on their steely resolve in confronting injury. This was the case in the reports written by a junior officer serving under Colonel William Bartlett, who lost a leg in the war's first year. Bartlett reportedly drilled his men for hours at a time as he stood on his remaining limb, refusing a more comfortable position on horseback. "There is a will about this," remarked his subordinate. "It is this quiet, intense determination, this fixedness of will, that makes us desire Colonel Bartlett, with but one leg, for our commander, over any other man with the full complement of limbs."[23] Accounts like this one were ubiquitous and impossible for fellow amputees to ignore.

The same strict self-control was just as evident in reports describing how Union officers initially responded to their wounds. They invariably maintained their composure, kept the cause foremost in their minds, and rallied their troops before taking care of themselves. Here is how the press portrayed General Oliver Otis Howard's conduct at Fair Oaks:

> Howard exposed himself like the commonest soldier, until at last he was struck by a ball, which shattered his arm. Instantly waving the mutilated member aloft as a pennon, he cheered on his men to the charge, and was then borne from the field.[24]

If contemporary accounts are to be believed, the sight of Union officers waving their bloody stumps in the air to inspire their men was a common one. And it was equally common for Union officers to signal an undaunted spirit by making light of their injuries at the first opportunity. On his way home to recover from his wounds, Howard reportedly met with General Philip Kearny, who had lost an arm during the Mexican-American War. Sharing a joke that was much repeated among fellow Union amputees, Howard suggested they "might buy their gloves together in future."[25] With officers so sanguine about their injuries, how could their men behave otherwise? Akin to the steady stream of exemplary sufferers in the wartime press (discussed in chapter 3), the portrayal of amputees as upbeat and impervious to regret predominated. The majority of Bourne's contestants drew on these wartime tales as they narrated their experiences, proudly recounting their own displays of patriotism, self-control, and optimism.

Amputation was not understood at this time as a disability so profound that it invalidated a man's capacity to act as a soldier. Colonel Bartlett and

General Howard remained in service despite their missing limbs. So did the majority of Union amputees. In future wars, losing a limb meant an automatic discharge for the vast majority of soldiers. But well over two-thirds of Union troops who survived an amputation remained on duty, usually as members of the Invalid Reserve Corps (later renamed the Veteran Reserve Corps), with only around 5,800 seeking an immediate discharge.[26] Specifically designed to reward only those who were "meritorious and deserving," the VRC was organized into two battalions. Amputees were assigned to the second battalion, authorized to carry swords and revolvers, and sent to perform hospital or clerical duties or to guard warehouses, offices, and supply depots.[27] Companies of soldiers in this battalion were also often put to work guarding prisoners, conscripts, stragglers, and deserters, underscoring their roles as trustworthy patriots.[28] *out of 22,000 known amputees.*

Humorous stories focused on amputees helped to further normalize their position in society. In 1869, shortly after Bourne's competitions, author A. F. Hill published the comical tale of a one-legged veteran's travels around the country, which drew upon his personal experiences (Hill suffered a leg amputation after the Battle of Antietam).[29] *John Smith's Funny Adventures on a Crutch* is written in the first-person by the pseudonymous Smith—the quintessential phlegmatic veteran, and a common man, as his name suggests. The narrative opens with a brief acknowledgment of amputation as "one of the most painful things in the world," before going on to spurn pity by depicting a character who had endured anguish but emerged with humor intact: "As I now look back on that dismal scene," Smith relates:

I cannot help smiling; —now, when I can skate as fast as any one, on my solitary foot, swim as well as I ever could, climb like a squirrel, jump on a saddled horse and ride at any pace I please, place a hand on a fence as high as my head and spring over in a quarter of a second, or walk twenty-five or thirty miles a day—all this with one good leg, a crutch and a cane!

These improbable scenarios were told for comical effect, but the author's overall point was clear: pity was inappropriate and unnecessary, since the loss of a limb had not destroyed Smith's spirit or limited his mobility. Hill emphasized this point throughout his novel, claiming his injury as a mark of frontline service and a chance for displaying a resilient character immune to setbacks.[30]

Focusing on manly willpower triumphing over adversity, veterans masked the complex emotions occasioned by amputation. Denying any association with victimhood, Hill went to the other extreme in creating a character who was, if anything, improved through the loss of a limb. Yet the multitude of complicated feelings he worked to erase can still be glimpsed beneath the surface of his text. At one point, Hill records a revealing dream sequence, where his central character imagines that he is in the company of "a very black African, armed with an axe." Alone in the wilderness, the two men are confronted by an enormous bear. Smith's black companion immediately drops the axe and makes for a nearby "tree stump," leaving him alone to cope with the marauding animal. Since there is no chance of a quick escape for the one-legged Smith, he throws down his crutch and snatches up the axe, cutting off both of the bear's paws in defending himself. As the incensed animal waves its bloody limbs and careens in his direction, Smith looks to find safety on the tree stump, but finds the "scared nigger" occupying all the space, "his thick lips mumbling unintelligible words of fright, and his white eyes starting out so that they could have been knocked off with a club, without touching his flat nose." The imagined scene, he writes, "was so unprecedentedly ludicrous, that terrified, as I fancied I was, I laughed outright . . . and so awoke."

It needs little analysis to conclude that this scene reveals greater ambivalence about the loss of a limb than Hill's text would otherwise suggest. In this dream, after all, Smith is inadvertently forced to shield a black companion from danger. Facing the prospect of being killed by the bear's bloody stumps—none-too-subtle symbols for his own wound—he is denied refuge on another "stump" by an unworthy black man, suggesting a good deal of animosity toward the Union struggle as an emancipationist war. His final recourse and, indeed, his salvation, lies in humor—but it is humor that is, not coincidentally, at the black character's expense. Only by demeaning his black companion as passive, absurd, and timorous can he maintain his identity as a heroic white man and thereby keep at bay his feelings of rage, fear, and helplessness.[31] Whether in this scene Hill simply imagined what his character might dream, or reported in a more autobiographical vein, he nonetheless evoked a range of emotions—terror, dread, fury, and racial animus—that had to be suppressed in order for his character's buoyant outlook to survive.

Bourne's entrants were no more willing than Hill to discuss the range of emotions caused by their injuries. Yet at least a dozen men complained of their unfortunate situations, with roughly half this number expressing resentment against more fortunate competitors or tacitly critiquing the competition itself. Pointing to the class bias inherent in a contest that effectively rewarded those with advanced schooling, Joseph Egolf plaintively remarked that many would be at a disadvantage, having had no "opportunities to acquire an education." More forthrightly, Charles Jackson told of working long hours seven days a week as a factory watchman, leaving little time to prepare his manuscript. "Perhaps the rest of the competitors have the advantage of me and do not have to sit up evenings with their eyes half closed, to do their writing," he noted. Others made similar points with greater poignancy. Opening with a self-effacingly apology for their awkward scrawl, they admitted they held out no hope of winning a prize and then proceeded to recount lives of great hardship. "My parents being poor I was compeled to labor when under other circumstances I should have attended School," wrote one, another commenting that from the time he lost his arm, he was "destined to struggle for an existence with my left arm alone, with no trade, no profession, no means and no wealthy friends."[32]

These writers drew on the wartime trope of the pitiable but worthy amputee in seeking to evoke readers' sympathies. A few spoke out for higher pensions or more government jobs for the wounded, but none called for broader changes (say, pensions tied to financial need rather than military rank, or state-based educational programs for amputees).[33] Instead, they presented themselves as humble and industrious men who were willing to labor if only given a chance. Aware that their left-handed manuscripts automatically defined them as hardworking and diligent, several went so far as to address potential employers directly. "I have no business," wrote John Koster. "Being by trade a Paper Maker, I would like a Position as foreman of a Mill." Likewise, William Kipling wrote at the end of his narrative: "If this should meet the eye of any kind person who can get me some permanent employment I shall feel thankful."[34] In this era of patronage politics, it was clear to these men that jobs flowed to men with personal contacts or established reputations.[35] So rather than making demands or claiming rights, they represented themselves as deserving of consideration by potential benefactors. It was a successful strategy in the context of this competition, for Bourne apparently hunted up employment for jobless entrants. And at least one impressed onlooker—the principal of the Northwestern Business College in Illinois—offered free scholarships to one-armed contestants living in the West (although Bourne wrote back explaining that all of his manuscript writers were now engaged in "some business pursuit" and suggesting that men be allowed to "name a disabled *substitute*").[36]

There were obviously some tangible reasons for ordinary men to enter these penmanship competitions, even aside from the possibility of prize money. They promised employment opportunities or the prospect of securing a wealthy patron. They also offered marginalized men a rare public stage from which to voice frustration with others' unfair advantages. As they did so, at least a few of Bourne's contestants rejected his implicit claim to be the champion of *all* wounded men. In pointing to the middle-class bias of his competition, or in rejecting penmanship as irrelevant to their working lives, a handful of left-handed writers launched justifiable, if tacit, critiques against what was essentially a paternalistic enterprise, run by a well-meaning but judgmental sponsor who minced no words in stressing the value of a middling vocation and the need for wounded veterans to pull themselves up by the bootstraps.

For greater numbers of entrants, however, the appeal of Bourne's competition lay in the fact that it enabled them to claim a particular form of identity—not as soldiers who happened to have been wounded, but as members of a unique group whose injuries witnessed their patriotism and demonstrated their inspirational suffering. Among the hundreds of manuscripts Bourne received, only a tiny handful of men wrote about their wounds in terms of the pain of injury, the tedium and misery of hospital life, or the devastating effects of bodily dismemberment. Most instead claimed a moral authority that came directly from their wounds. Telling positive stories of overcoming pain and misery, they described becoming better men in the process, with lessons to impart to their society. Emphasizing an unwavering religious faith, firm political commitments, or a resilient manhood, their stories vividly depict the way Victorian notions of redemptive suffering helped to shape the identities of men wounded during the Civil War.

The majority of these amputees interpreted their suffering in religious terms. Emphasizing their submission to God's will, they often drew on sentimental wartime tales that tugged at readers' heartstrings by picturing sufferers who were sorrowful but resigned. Evoking the two themes most popular in sentimental literature—domestic feeling and worthy victimhood—one amputee wrote:

> Home, double dear since so nearly lost, to thee I inscribe these few unlettered lines—so feebly written by a trembling left hand . . . may no murmuring breath escape the lips of him, who even with the fearful loss of his right arm, helped to achieve such glorious results.[37]

Stressing his pitiable condition alongside his manly achievements, this writer laid claim to the power of redemptive suffering. Many did the same, exemplifying serene acceptance or a humble piety, and sometimes endowing their wounds with the capacity to inspire spiritual awakening or self-sacrifice in others.[38] Their providential understandings of suffering left little room for resentment or irony. After serving throughout the entire war, Alfred Tuttle had his arm shot off outside Appomattox Court House, one day before Lee's surrender. If the injustice of this situation struck Tuttle, it did not find its way into his text. Instead, he merely noted: "I have great reason to be thankful that I did not meet the fate of thousands of my comrads, whose bones lay ble[a]ching on southern Battle Fields."[39] Perceiving their glass half full, men like Tuttle praised a merciful God, offering readers worthy examples of selflessness and piety.

Making the full extent of a spiritual triumph clear meant acknowledging the torments that had to be overcome in achieving resignation. Representing the depths of their despair enabled some of Bourne's entrants to emphasize the distance they traveled in reconciling themselves to God's will. Phineas Whitehouse was one of several men who described a journey from anguish to acceptance in an ode to his lost arm. He started by speaking of his misery as he looked down at the "piteous wreck" of what was "once an arm." But then he went on:

> What matters it, one arm its task has ended?
> 'Tis well, it may be, why should I repine?
> For Life's stern conflicts I am still defended,
> While, true and faithful, one stout arm is mine.

> With that, and Heaven to aid me, let me labor
> With cheerful heart, whate'er my lot may be;
> And though may rust the rifle and the sabre,
> May that lone arm a final 'victory' see! [40]

Beginning with desolation and focusing attention on the awful spectacle of his maimed stump, Whitehouse's final show of jaunty resilience and faith appeared all the more impressive.

Religious soldiers often expressed a sentimental attachment to their lost limbs, readily drawing on domestic imagery. Reaching for a metaphor to describe their grief, many pictured amputated limbs as lost family members or sadly mourned "best friends," suggesting the centrality of the family to Victorian men's lives. Whitehouse came close to representing his remaining arm as a person with a mind of its own ("true and faithful"). Similarly, Alfred Randolph pictured an arm that could feel. One stanza of his poem reads:

> Goodby, right arm! no more thou'lt start
> Eager to greet my friend,
> Yet this poor one that's near my heart
> No colder clasp will lend.

And should my country ever need
A guard so maimed as I
It would be just as proud to bleed
Goodby; right arm! goodby![41]

Others described missing arms that could speak, and a few charted fully conscious limbs endowed with will and memory. Ira Borshears began his manuscript by describing the "innocent childhood" of his right arm, his "companion and helper." As his limb "grew apace with the days and years," it became
an "apt scholar and learned the use of many things." Now, having "served
its owner and his country well," his limb "sleeps in death," its "virtues and
untimely loss" now "recorded, by the inheritor of its labors, the lone Left
Hand."[42] Similarly attributing full consciousness to his limbs, Henry Palmer
noted that upon being wounded, his right arm became "wayward and unman-
ageable," while his left "sought immediate promotion":

> My right arm, as if conscious of approaching dissolution, seemingly be-
> queathed unto the left arm, all the properties of which it died, seized and
> possessed. The seal of this last Will and Testament was the bloodseal of
> amputation—Patriotism, Love of Country, and Equal Rights were the
> subscribing witnesses to the instrument—The body from which the arm
> was severed, was the Executor—In Heaven's Court the Will was proved,
> allowed and recorded.[43]

These images of arms that could speak, think, or feel are more than a curious trope. In one sense, they register a conventional Victorian modesty: one
was not supposed to speak too readily about the self at this time for fear of
being seen as self-centered or egotistical.[44] Describing a lost limb as a friend
or family member allowed writers to express the pathos of losing an arm—to
remind readers of a limb's critical functions, its connections to scenes of family life—all the while seeming to keep the emphasis on another rather than
oneself. Just as important, by personifying an arm and rendering loss in terms
of a death scene, writers could grieve without relating grief to a permanent
state inherent to their injuries. For the period of mourning associated with
funerals inevitably came to an end. So, too, would their grief for their missing
limbs. In depicting themselves as bereft friends or relatives, amputees asked
readers to draw from their own experiences of bereavement, and to comprehend the loss of a limb in terms of empathy rather than condescension.

While a number of Bourne's 400 entrants lamented their tough circumstances, or represented themselves as sorrowful yet resigned, only a single

contestant openly complained that amputation had robbed him of sexual and racial power. Having joined the Union army as one of a small minority of draftees, Thomas Perrine perhaps had more reason than most to resent his injury. Clearly well educated, he submitted an original poem in ornate Spencerian script, which read in part:

Awful day! that took away
My arm and sweetheart too: —
An empty sleeve, an empty heart —
'Twould make a darkey blue.

These negroes all, Judge Taney said,
"A White man's rights do lack."
The rebels left no right to me —
I might as well be black.[45]

Here, Perrine implied that the loss of his arm had reduced him to the level of a slave, limiting his appeal to women and rendering his political rights as a white man mute by extending them to African Americans. Yet he made the point with droll wit, using what passed for humor at the time. It was no easier for Perrine than for A. F. Hill, it seems, to seriously dispute to the notion that limbless men faced their impediments with a light heart.

Perrine's depiction of amputation as a challenge to manhood would become standard in later wars. In the aftermath of World War I, scholars have shown, veterans and social commentators generally construed the loss of a limb as a mark of feminization or humiliation.[46] Several historians have drawn from this literature to reach similar conclusions about the Civil War. In her study of the medical discourse surrounding the phenomenon of phantom limbs, manifested in painful or twitching sensations in lost body parts, Erin O'Connor argues that the "fraudulent body language" of the amputee rendered him "effeminate," akin to the hysterical female. Likewise, although Lisa Herschbach begins her examination of the artificial limb industry in the post-bellum North by noting that amputation represented both "manly heroism and effeminate dependency," she emphasizes the latter.[47] Both authors claim that prosthesis resolved the threat to manhood caused by amputation, at the same time reconstructing maimed veterans as industrial laborers in a way that elided the distinction between man and machine.

If artificial-limb manufacturers made these arguments, however, they had minimal impact on the way most amputees understood their injuries. Despite the fact that the federal government provided artificial limbs to its soldiers free of charge, the majority of limbless men never even attempted to have a prosthetic device fitted.[48] Among those who did take up the government's offer, large numbers later reported to pension officials that they soon abandoned their mechanical limbs, because they were useless, painful, or both.[49] Of course, some amputees may have remained unaware of the state's largesse. In other cases, amputation had been performed so close to the shoulder or hip joint that fitting a prosthetic device was impossible. But that still leaves the majority, who apparently had no wish to hide their injuries or to use a mechanical device to compensate for their physical loss. As one study examining hundreds of postwar photographs of Civil War amputees points out, almost all of the men pictured effectively drew attention to missing arms or legs by taking up empty sleeves and trouser legs and attaching them to other parts of their clothing.[50]

A large number of those who entered Bourne's competition plainly asserted that their wounds engendered feelings of self-respect rather than embarrassment, suggesting that a missing limb was not necessarily cause for shame at this time. Whereas four writers expressed unqualified regret over losing an arm, dozens insisted that they had sacrificed their limbs willingly for the national cause. "If i had a dozen arms like it was i would [have] given them all soner than have the states torn from this glorious Union which our forefathers fought for," claimed one. With similar equanimity, Charles Coleman reasoned: "I cannot but feel happy to think that I lost my arm in so good a cause and for so just a government," a point seconded by Lewis Kline, who wrote, "I feel satisfied and contented with my lot, Knowing in what capacity, and for what I sacrificed my limb."[51]

These men could express pride in their mutilated bodies in large part because the dominant Victorian ideal of white manhood did not privilege a man's strength or size. As historians of manhood note, the extension of the capitalist marketplace in the antebellum North had drawn men into a new world of ceaseless striving. Those aspiring to respectability in this novel economy had increasingly begun directing their energies toward self-improvement and self-discipline, believing that hard work rather than talent was the key to social advancement. Definitions of improving and mastering the self required, above all, the control of bodily desires and passions through the development of a strong character and resolute will.[52] Ideal manhood was thus seen to hinge on self-discipline rather than physicality, with middling white men defining their identities in contrast to those who supposedly lacked self-control, namely women and men of "lesser" races and classes.

For amputees who accepted this dominant gender ideal, injury could constitute evidence of manhood rather than its negation, for it gave tangible proof of willpower in action. In fact, the commonest theme in the manuscripts sent to Bourne concerns the importance of confronting injury with determination and self-control. Some focused on how their time in the military had given them the strength of will they needed to cope as a one-armed man, as did Louis Boos, who pictured army life giving him "an experience of hardships, troubles and sufferings." Adopting the tone of a knowing elder with a message to impart, he declared: "Discipline will improve a young man," teaching him "not to be troubled about what were previously heavy grievances." Rufus Robinson similarly urged comrades to follow his lead by drawing on the self-discipline they learned in the army in order to educate themselves. "Our experience has taught us that we little knew what could be achieved by us physically, until we entered the field as soldiers, and the same rules apply to us mentally," he claimed. Instead of emphasizing how soldiering caused their injuries, they credited military life with their successful rehabilitation.[53]

Robinson and Boos saw no contradiction between physical disability and soldiering. In fact, they drew a direct parallel between the traits required of good soldiers and those that men needed to succeed in civilian life. In line with this perspective, J. Cavanaugh explained that writing was much like military service in its demand for long hours of bodily training, mental discipline, and perseverance. Having spent his every leisure moment trying to master left-handed writing, he dropped his pen "time and again in despair," finally offering his manuscript as proof that "Persevereance will accomplish wonders in writing, as well as in War":

[At] Cold Harbour (where I had the honour to loose an Arm) Grant tells us in his Report, that the results of those terable Battles, did not come up to his expectations fully, but he still persevered, and the result finally was the Bottling up, of Lee and his Army at Richmond.[54]

Comparing himself to the Union's most renowned general, Cavanaugh apparently saw victory less as a matter of military training or leadership ability than the outcome of character traits like determination and self-discipline that were shared by Union enlistees and commanders alike.

Others followed Cavanaugh's lead: they wrote of the long hours spent in practice; of wrestling with despondency as they worked to discipline awkward left hands; and, finally, of the rewards that flowed from their exertions. Their emphasis on writing as an act of self-mastery was particular to the Victorian era. Whereas students in the eighteenth century learned to write by transcribing model alphabets or phrases, writing masters in the nineteenth century, as historian Tamara Thornton has shown, increasingly focused on the importance of disciplining the body by regulating hand position, posture, and physical movement. Penmanship thus came to be widely seen as a "process of character formation," Thornton notes, "both in the literal sense of making letters and in the figurative sense of constructing a self."[55]

This belief in penmanship as a physical act signifying a strong character is reflected in G. H. Long's description of left-handed writing as the "most difficult job I ever attempted." Emphasizing his determination to succeed, and the bodily toll his efforts exacted, he described how he forced himself to pick up a pen just two weeks after his amputation, heedless of the fact that "every word I wrote made me sweat." By dint of constant practice, he managed to secure a position as a clerk, noting that despite a few difficulties with his writing, "I overcame it all, and can now get along very well." He closed by quoting an expression lifted straight from the popular self-help manuals of the day that counseled men on how to achieve success in life, noting: "patience and perseverance [will] accomplish all things." With a similar self-help motto to impart, Lewis Kline told others to "take heart and go to work body and soul," for "where there is a will, there is always a way!" Offering their manuscripts as evidence of strong characters, these writers measured their manhood using the most accepted yardstick of the day.[56]

Long and Kline probably came from fairly humble backgrounds (a point difficult to confirm since they offered few personal details). Nonetheless, they endorsed a bourgeois emphasis on self-cultivation, depicting themselves on the path toward personal and social improvement that Bourne aimed to promote.[57] The character traits they valued—diligence, patience, self-discipline, perseverance—were vital for men engaged in white-collar employment at mid-century, which generally required literacy skills, attention to detail, and long hours spent behind a desk. Respectable middling men like Long and Kline—eager for self-improvement and confident that their diligence would be recouped in a salaried position—readily adopted the era's language of uplift, convinced that others should follow their lead.[58]

In contrast, a number of letter-writers subscribed to a rough democratic manhood—widely embraced by wage laborers in the urban North—that valorized the qualities of tenacity, brute strength, and physical courage over self-discipline and patience. A few manuscripts center on dramatic examples of courage under fire or stoic endurance in the face of injury. Two or three soldiers described hopping straight off the operating table and returning to watch the progress of a battle. And one proudly reported that he lay unflinchingly as a Confederate surgeon sawed off his arm without the use of anesthetics. Relaying these scenes without lengthy commentary or description, the

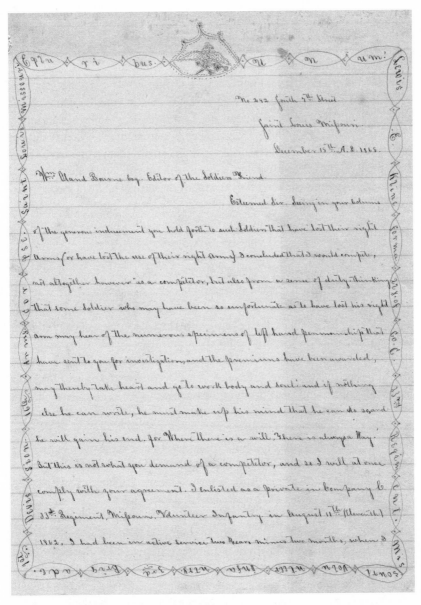

Figure 6. First page of Lewis E. Kline's sample of left-handed penmanship, using some of the popular self-help mottos of the day. (Courtesy of William Oland Bourne Papers, Manuscript Division, Library of Congress, Washington, D.C.)

writers left the impression of plucky men who had already proved their worth and no longer felt any need to brag.

One of these men was Henry Allen, who had been a mechanic before the war.[59] Using a blunt tone suggesting he was not given to contradiction, he baldly asserted: "the taking away of my right arm . . . was necessary, to constitute *me* a perfect man." Having vowed to "bring a mark home with me, to show that I had been [near] danger," he wrote, "I have that mark, and so conspicuous, that all can see it."[60] For Allen, a "perfect man" obviously did not need a perfect body; what he needed was a clear mark that testified to bravery. By the 1860s, the necessity of demonstrating manhood in physical terms had become increasingly pressing for manual workers: they had watched as their independence and autonomy were eroded over the previous decades by the emergence of industrialization and wage labor. Perhaps because he enjoyed little scope for shaping a proud identity in his working life, Allen instead emphasized his injury as a sign that he was brave enough to stare death in the eye or withstand the severest pain.

Yet even veterans like Allen shared one crucial belief with those who endorsed a more middle-class version of ideal manhood. Along with every other amputee who wrote about the meaning of his injuries, Allen yoked his definition of manhood firmly to his political commitments. Calling his wound an "honorable scar," he referred simultaneously to his daring under fire and to the cause in which he fought. Rhapsodizing over the war wound, Phil Faulk made this connection clear, deeming "veteran scars":

enduring, priceless momentoes of glory won in the deadly breach. . . . [They] speak of deeds of noble daring performed, where none but true and brave could venture. They proclaim your patriotism in language more eloquent than human tongue. They picture the price of liberty and union, and are richer ornaments than the purest gold.[61]

These "scars" were not precious or honorable because they demonstrated bravery, but because they symbolized bravery animated by a political commitment to protect "liberty and union."[62]

By the late nineteenth century, veterans on both sides of the conflict would come together to celebrate a manly courage detached from the political issues involved in the war.[63] But in the conflict's immediate aftermath, this was decidedly not the case. Much like the middle-class memorialists described in the previous chapter, volunteer soldiers of all classes typically believed that their political system was novel and volatile, arrayed against forces from within and without. They did not know that history would see democracy gain the moral ascendancy over other forms of political organization. They took seriously the idea that they had saved "the last best hope on earth" for republican democracy, to use Lincoln's memorable phrase.[64] When Faulk expressed pride in his wounded body, his pride came from a belief that injured veterans had stood up "nobly, voluntarily in defence of [our] country's free government." Continuing on in this vein for several pages, he expressed in the most florid prose what other amputees put more simply. "I went because I thought it my Duty to go and I served three years for my country," stated George Dale. "I stood up for my rites untill I lost my rite arm" and was "willing to sacrifise my life for such a great cause as we were engaged in."[65] It was this "great cause" that amputees pointed to as they validated their sufferings and demanded that civilians do likewise.

Arguing that the Union had been saved by their sacrifices, left-handed penman utilized the multiple meaning of arms: as individual limbs, weapons, or parts of the military attached to the body of the Union. John Bryson wrote:

Victory has crowned our arms at last! . . .
Those traitor hands were powerless to *destroy*
This glorious Union, which *our fathers* gave
. . . And though thou'st stabbed us to the very core, . . .
Our Union will arise, secure in every part.[66]

Alfred Whitehouse similarly reminded his audience:

The right arm's gone
the nation yet remains
Tho many perished,
yet we are saved,
The right, will triumph over wrong,
Tho it leave us but one left arm strong.[67]

Both by shouldering arms, and through the redemptive sacrifice of their right limbs, they claimed to have ensured the integrity of the Union. Only by doing so, they argued, could they preserve their rights as members of that union. "When we think of the rights and priviledges defended and forever preserved . . . we [cannot] for a moment regret even the loss of our strong right arm. . . . The strong right arm of the government is yet in its full vigor," noted Charles Horne. Or, as another put it, despite losing a right arm, he maintained his "right to cast a vote."[68]

The rights these veterans had saved were central components of all men's

Figure 7. Alfred D. Whitehouse won a premium of $20 in the first left-handed penmanship competition staged in 1866, making him ineligible for prizes in the second competition held the following year. He nonetheless displayed his improved mastery of writing by submitting this second entry—an impressive sample of ornamental penmanship that referred simultaneously to his missing arm and to the enduring "arms" of the nation. (William Oland Bourne Papers, Courtesy of Manuscript Division, Library of Congress, Washington, D.C.)

identities in the Civil War era. Political privileges had become an emblem of white manhood by mid-century, as masses of men began participating in the vibrant culture of electioneering and partisan politics that took shape after the 1830s as older restrictions on male voting rights were lifted across the country. This new political culture largely excluded African American men—many of the new states carved out of the northwestern territories having passed full suffrage for white men only, and race-based discrimination having increased across the North more broadly with the rise of biological theories of racial inferiority. Women, of course, were also universally barred from voting. Where there had once been multiple categories of nonvoters—servants, non-propertied men, most women, and other dependents groups—now formal political participation was open to all white men, sharply distinguishing them from the mass of disenfranchised women and excluded African Americans.[69] As Bourne's contestants acknowledged, this aspect of their manhood was assured regardless of their missing limbs.

Bourne took the lead from his entrants in suggesting that amputees had protected manhood rights. When visitors in New York and Washington came to view the work of the "Left Armed Corps," they entered a hall with banners on each side of the room. On one side, they declared: "The Army and Body you may Sever, But Our Glorious Union Never," and "We lost Our Right Hand for Our Rights." On the other side, they read: "Our Disabled Soldiers Have Kept the Union from Being Disabled," and "See the Conquering Heroes Come. The Left Hand. The Empty Sleeve. All Americans Together Not a Fetter in the Clime."[70] By accepting disability and ending slavery, Bourne made clear, amputees had ensured a powerful nation where men's political rights were secure. His banners went further, hinting at a new political climate in which "All Americans," both black and white, were now on an equal footing. If a few of his white contestants balked at this image, most had reconciled themselves over the previous few years to the necessity of emancipation. In the optimistic glow of victory, the white Northern majority joined with Bourne in looking forward to a new era in race relations.

A number of contestants also anticipated a less partisan, more unified nation. Drawing on the tales of benevolence laid out in the previous chapter, many praised the work of Northern civilians, depicting their injuries not as an individual event but as part of a larger story of sacrifice that had been crucial to the war's outcome. Some remembered the work of their nurses and volunteers who kept hospitals supplied and staffed.[71] A few men devoted their entire manuscripts to honoring "the Ladies." Others pointed out that "scarcely a family in the country" had escaped war's impact.[72] Rather than particularizing individual sacrifices, they offered tributes to patriotic Northerners, suggesting that the suffering accompanying mass death had linked soldiers and civilians together through bonds of mutual sympathy.

One notable aspect of this praise is that not a single writer pointed to the crucial support provided by a particular family member, directing their acclaim instead solely at an abstract benevolence. Yet many wives or female kin were surely forced to earn extra income to recoup amputees' lost earning potential or to help them with tasks like cutting up food, bathing, and dressing. In striking contrast to later wars, the Civil War produced little anxious commentary regarding injured veterans' difficulties in adjusting to postwar society, and virtually no discussion of the role of wives or sweethearts in rehabilitating men.[73] By the twentieth century, when female self-sacrifice and the availability of domestic labor could no longer be assumed, wives became the central focus in descriptions of amputees' treatment and rehabilitation, constantly reminded that it was their job to shore up amputees' self-esteem.[74] If the Civil War wounded were eager to extol women's sacrifices in a general sense, they ignored specific wifely labors, which might easily evoke a helpless dependency.

Relying on others was anathema to the Victorian ideal of self-help. Left-handed penmen went to great lengths in distancing themselves from any suggestion of dependency. Holding a hard line in favor of self-reliance, some expressed disgust with comrades who openly solicited sympathy or aid. Castigating unemployed veterans, Phineas Whitehouse lectured, "If there remains a spark of that patriotism that prompted you to seize the musket, or a semblance of that manhood you exhibited on the field of battle . . . You will rather seek at once for permanent, honorable employment." Henry Allen had equally harsh words to say about the one-legged soldier he saw begging in the street. "I made up my mind that he was an indolent fellow before he went to war. There is no man who has lost an arm or a leg . . . but can earn a good support with the limbs left him," he wrote. As the war's most obvious patriots, amputees were supposed to embody the self-reliance and determination that characterized their military experience. "We are the living monuments of the late cruel and bloody Rebellion," wrote Jonathan Allison, and now "prepare to act another part in the great drama of life," by deciding on a livelihood "as becomes soldiers or good citizens." For Allison, volunteering for war and fulfilling one's duty as a "good citizen" by seeking an independent living was one and the same thing.[75]

By demonstrating their independent spirit, Union amputees distinguished themselves as ideal citizen-soldiers. Everyone who attended the exhibition of left-handed manuscripts agreed on this point. Addressing a crowd gathered at the opening of the second exhibit—which included General Grant, Theodore Roosevelt Sr., and New York governor Reuben Fenton—House Speaker Schuyler Colfax echoed Fanny Fern when he emphasized the way the competition "proved how American energy could triumph over adverse circumstances." Following him to the podium was Major General Nathaniel Banks, who also highlighted the unique intelligence and self-reliance that Union amputees manifested in their one-armed manuscripts. Calling to mind the chaotic violence that had plagued many European states in the wake of war, he praised Union soldiers' readiness to go quietly back to their homes and eagerly devote themselves to "civil pursuits," no matter their situations. Believing that European audiences could benefit by witnessing this exceptional display of self-discipline and civic virtue, Bourne got together with several veterans groups to confer with the secretary of state over the possibility of sending the exhibition to Paris. Unlike the Sanitary Commission, however, he was apparently unable to raise the money to realize his plan.[76]

What happened to the men who entered Bourne's competition after the cheering died down? In most cases, it is impossible to know, just as it is difficult to judge the extent to which amputees, in general, succeeded in embodying the spirit of self-help that so many championed at this time. Reading amputees' manuscripts alongside pension records, however, helps to reveal the massive toll that injury exacted in a culture that revered self-reliance and cheerful endurance. "I suppose there is no language fully adequate to describe the extent of inconvenience," wrote John Thompson. "To be compelled just in the prime of life (when teaming with anticipations of future prosperity and pleasure) to consent to be a permanent cripple for life . . . is a matter of no small moment." Considering Thompson's condition, this was a dramatic understatement. According to his pension application, he lived for the next eleven months with multiple pieces of shrapnel lodged near his hip joint, experiencing the "severest pain conceivable" as they worked their way to the surface of his skin. He died in 1874, apparently of blood poisoning from his wounds, one of the many uncounted casualties of the Civil War.[77]

Others eventually succumbed to the emotional toll that their injuries exacted. In his manuscript, Dorus Bates advised fellow left-armed soldiers to "never get the blues," telling them, "you will have to go but a short distance to find some poor fellow that is more unfortunate than yourself." But Bates was unable to take his own advice. A boyhood friend later described him as "full of life hope and ambition . . . up to the time he lost his arm." After this "his constant theme was regret at the necessity of being placed on the retired list of the army as it must necessitate his being thrown out of the line of promotion." He was married in 1877, and the following year saw the birth of his first child, but Bates remained unemployed throughout, finally committing suicide two years after his daughter was born.[78]

Equally sad circumstances surrounded the competition's top prizewinner, Franklin Durrah. He would never go on to take up a clerical job, as Bourne

anticipated. Not long after Durrah finished his manuscript, a physician declared him "deranged" and had him sent to an insane asylum. For most of the
next forty years, he lived with his mother Eliza in Centre Street, Philadelphia,
periodically spending time in different mental institutions. He wandered the
streets muttering to himself, cursing and behaving violently toward his neighbors; his mother was forced to become his constant attendant, able to leave
him alone for only short periods for fear of what he might do. "No one can say
how far his wound was instrumental in causing loss of his mind," one doctor
told pension officials in the late 1870s, yet he added, "the arm was all that he
appeared crazy upon."[79]

Pension files are replete with distressing stories of men who suffered griev-
ously for decades after the war, and of family members who underwent their
own trials as a result. But they also reveal a curious anomaly in relation to
Civil War amputees. By 1893 the federal government was spending a gigantic
41.5 percent of its annual income on roughly a million Civil War pension-
ers. Yet only 9,000 amputees ever applied for the pensions to which they
were automatically entitled.[80] From the late 1870s onward, pension legislation
specified that successful applicants were eligible to receive retrospective payments in a lump sum, dating back to discharge from the service, in addition
to ongoing payments.[81] Given the pervasive discussions of pension legislation in the press and within veterans' groups, it seems unlikely that anyone
would have remained unaware about such entitlements. Yet large numbers of
limbless men were apparently willing to forego thousands of dollars, despite
a climate of broad acceptance for pensions, at least among fellow veterans.

Perhaps this is because Civil War amputees continued to be held up well
into the late nineteenth century as embodiments of patriotic virtue, stalwart
independence, or enduring faith. Numerous Union officers who lost an arm in
service went on to prominent careers, garnering praise for their extraordinary
ability to triumph over adversity. Oliver Otis Howard, for instance, headed the
Freedman's Bureau before leading U.S. troops in military encounters against
the Nez Perce Indians of the Northwest in the mid-1870s. A deeply religious
man, he continued to maintain that his lost limb taught him patience and
increased his devotion to God, amply compensating for his suffering.[82]

Those more impressed by displays of physical bravery could point to John
Wesley Powell, who lost an arm at Shiloh while commanding his regiment.
The ultimate one-armed man of action, Powell led widely publicized expeditions into Colorado in the late 1860s and 1870s as director of the U.S.
Geographical Survey. Hailed as one of the most important scientific ventures
of the era, Powell's expeditions involved him in navigating rapids, narrowly
escaping death at the hands of hostile Indians, and scrambling up mountains;
at one point forced to use his remaining arm to hang from a rock ledge, 400

feet above the Colorado River. In newspaper and magazine articles, the loss of an arm appeared but a minor inconvenience for the intrepid Powell.[83]

Possessing a visible war wound could also be politically effective in the decades after the war, when Civil War veterans constituted a large percentage of the voting population. Four years after suffering an arm amputation at Gettysburg, Lucius Fairchild was elected Wisconsin's governor. He would go on to become the leading spokesman for Union veterans as a whole, not only as "commander-in chief" of the Grand Army of the Republic, the largest veterans' organization in the North, but also as head of the Military Order of the Loyal Legion, a more exclusive group originally composed of Union officers. Often at the forefront of movements to build monuments honoring the war dead, he was a tireless speaker at veterans' events, usually discoursing on his favorite themes of patriotism and loyalty. Always, according to his biographer, he drew on "the symbolic power of 'the Empty Sleeve,'" gaining political clout from his unassailable war wound.[84]

Of course, these famous amputees were far outnumbered by those who spent their lives in relative obscurity. They, too, were often admired figures. The popular Civil War historian Bruce Catton offered a glimpse into the life of one humble amputee in a memoir written in the early 1960s. As a young boy growing up in rural Michigan in the early twentieth century, Catton was intrigued by the elderly Civil War veterans in his midst, who seemed to him "grave and dignified, pillars of the community." He was particularly respectful of one veteran, an amputee who arrived in town each summer to peddle berries. "It never once entered my childish head to feel sorry for him," Catton explains, "On the contrary, I thought he was rather lucky. He carried with him forever the visible sign that he had fought for his country and been wounded in its service." By the twentieth century, it was no longer fitting to think of a war wound in such romantic terms. Catton went on to renounce his childish enthusiasm for combat in his memoir, explaining that he had spent his career trying to demystify experiences like those of the one-armed berry peddler by revealing the horrors that they suffered.[85] Yet in thinking back to an earlier time, he inadvertently captured a moment when, no doubt picking up on the reaction of those around him, he had looked at a maimed veteran and felt only awed respect.

Around the turn of the century, author Mark Twain paid a visit to Daniel Sickles, perhaps the most famous of all Union amputees.[86] He described

Sickles—a controversial figure and a proud ladies' man—surrounded by manly trappings: floors covered with weapons and the stuffed heads of wild game; drawers overflowing with women's stockings and gloves, left behind by his many lovers. Sickles was proudest, though, of his missing leg. "I am perfectly sure that if he had to part with either of them," Twain wrote in reference to the general's limbs, "he would part with the one that he has got."[87] Twain understood the immense political mileage Sickles gained from his lost limb: he was renowned, in part, for being a Union amputee. Those with less fame got their share of attention, too. Boys like Bruce Catton gathered around them, eager to hear their stories. They were invited to head veterans' parades and to speak to children's classes, revered as the Union's greatest patriots. In a culture that defined self-control, religious faith, and civic virtue as central to manhood, and in which soldiers and civilians defined their war as a historic moral victory, amputation did not necessarily induce feelings of effeminacy or shame. It could easily evoke the opposite.

Injured servicemen in many subsequent conflicts would be extolled as heroic figures—their wounds celebrated as badges of honor. But this status became far harder for wounded men to maintain at a later date and also much more open to contestation. Take the experiences of those who lost limbs during World War I.[88] As was the case in the Civil War, the maimed were initially viewed through a lens of sentimental patriotism that figured them as the nation's greatest defenders. But public sympathy dissipated not long after demobilization in most countries, and the limbless soon came to view their state as one of dependence, emasculation, even freakishness. Images of the war-wounded in the aftermath of this conflict were shaped by what historian Robert Whalen has identified as a bifurcated memory of war. On the one hand, heroic war narratives retained some of their luster—reflected in works like Ernst Junger's *Storm of Steel*, in which the nightmare of battle forged a more virulent German manhood. On the other hand, melancholy, fury, disillusionment, and disgust existed in abundance, too, often symbolized by limbless men whose shattered state became an apt symbol for war's devastating effects. In the drawings and paintings of Otto Dix and his fellow Berliner George Grosz, or in the work of playwright Ernst Toller, injured veterans were tragic or frightening figures—angry, potentially violent, and often grotesque.[89] They became a fit subject not for jocular tales like *John Smith's Funny Adventures on a Crutch*, but for black comedy that tacitly juxtaposed their maimed bodies against the romantic illusions of prewar battlefield ideals.

Heroic war narratives were openly contested in most countries after World War I. And economic depression from the mid-1920s onward soon lessened public sympathy for the war-wounded. In Britain, Germany, Australia, and elsewhere, veterans groups openly fought among themselves and against the state for the right to claim a share of shrinking public funds and civilian consideration.[90] In many countries the war-wounded came to be widely feared as a disruptive force—which, indeed, they sometimes turned out to be. Disabled ex-servicemen in Germany marched in the streets, highlighting what they saw as the nation's betrayal by staging grisly public spectacles of massed war wounds. Signs of anger and antisocial violence among returned Australian servicemen likewise alarmed public officials, who fretted over the possibility that such men might turn toward Bolshevism.[91] As the public grappled with the onset of the Great Depression, there were still some who viewed wounded veterans as heroes, but many also feared them as a dangerous group of embittered, damaged men.

After America's Civil War there were no corresponding images of amputees as frightening or grotesque figures. Northerners did not fear the wounded as a threat to public order or state authority, despite their worries that such men might sink into a helpless dependency. Their lack of concern proved to be justified. Having fought to protect national integrity and the authority of the government, the majority of Union veterans remained firmly on the side of law and order in the postwar years. Amputees created no political movement to lobby the government, nor did they clash with other groups of veterans. They had no need to do so, for their fellow soldiers continued to uphold their claim that a missing limb symbolized frontline service and exemplary patriotism.

In the aftermath of later wars, altered understandings of what it meant to be a man also made it more difficult for the limbless to regard their condition in positive ways. By the twentieth century, brawn and strength topped the list of manly attributes.[92] And the limbless could no longer find comfortable refuge in political participation as something that differentiated them from women. Discussions of amputees after both world wars acknowledged this new context, focusing on the feelings of effeminacy engendered by amputation and the crucial role of women in shoring up maimed men's self-esteem.[93] It would thus be hard to imagine a wounded veteran in the modern day remarking, as one Civil War writer did, that amputation "was necessary . . . to constitute *me* a perfect man." These words would simply have rung hollow at a later date.[94]

Staging a competition like Bourne's would be just as unlikely in the modern era. By the early twentieth century, disability was increasingly defined in terms of economic productivity, in light of a shift toward the rationalized, scientific management of production and new ideas about the importance of physical well-being on mental states.[95] There were optimistic spectacles of amputees after both world wars, but these now focused on the glories of modern science and engineering, picturing the limbless as fortunate recipients of prosthetic arms and legs, not men dedicated to controlling their remaining limbs. The prime object on display in Bourne's competition—the character of the wounded themselves—was now of secondary importance.

To a striking degree, Bourne's contestants imagined themselves in charge of their own destinies. The growing professionalization of science and medicine necessarily weakened wounded men's sense that they, rather than their doctors, controlled their recoveries. The rise of disciplines like psychology and psychiatry further transformed understandings of disability. Specialists from these disciplines produced masses of studies dealing with amputees' physical and psychological rehabilitation, addressed both to the medical community and to wounded men and their families. Their work echoed some of the themes that appealed to Bourne's entrants, such as the need for amputees to exert willpower or keep up a cheerful front. But now it was doctors and psychologists, not the wounded themselves, promoting this message. And a new emphasis on men's complex emotional and mental responses to injury had changed what it meant for the wounded to exercise self-control. For the psychological literature produced in the twentieth century reimagined amputees, in a sense, as incurable and unique—their ongoing feelings about their wounds inevitably shaping their identities in ways that set them apart from the able-bodied. They might exert willpower to stave off negative feelings, but the long-term psychological issues were presumed to be constant. The situation was different for Civil War soldiers. Some were obviously unable to overcome injuries, either emotionally or physically. But in operating outside a psycho-scientific framework, men could plausibly claim that their wounds were simply physical marks, not psychic injuries that shaped their entire being.

Civil War soldiers framed their injuries as an opportunity to demonstrate the control of mind or spirit over wayward bodies. They imagined their tales as inspiring examples of self-control, religious faith, and civic virtue. Their stories made sense in the immediate postwar context, when Northerners still celebrated their war effort as a historic victory that would benefit men like the ones these amputees held themselves up to be. In the coming decades, new war stories would take shape, reflecting a world that they could not have imagined.

Epilogue

The book for the army is a war-song, not a hospital sketch.
Oliver Wendell Holmes, "The Soldier's Faith" (1895)

SOMETIME IN THE early twentieth century, Edith Harwood, the grand-daughter of a Union veteran, fondly recalled attending the "Old Soldiers' Campfires" held annually in the small country town of Wapello, Iowa, as former comrades gathered from across the state to reminisce about their war experiences. They spent the day alone before being treated to a chicken pie dinner served by the Women's Relief Corps, an auxiliary to the Union veterans' group, the Grand Army of the Republic (GAR). Then they made their way to the GAR Hall above the post office, where local citizens had assembled. Flag bearers came in first, followed by men playing military airs on fife and drum. Finally the elderly veterans appeared, dressed in their best suits and keeping perfect step as they marched up to their seats of honor on the stage. "[A]ll history seemed to move down that center aisle . . . Shiloh, Vicksburg . . . the Emancipation Proclamation, George Washington, Paul Revere, the Spirit of Seventy-Six, and Glory Hallelujah rolled into one," Harwood enthused. She sat in her chair nervously watching her mother, the president of the Women's Relief Corp and the only woman on stage. After the welcome speeches, the crowd joined in singing Civil War tunes, including sentimental favorites like "Just Before the Battle, Mother" and "Tenting Tonight on the Old Camp Ground." Afterwards, the old soldiers took to the podium, where they spoke at length about current affairs (an aspect of the program that Harwood admittedly found more than a little dull). Capturing the tone of the men's speeches—which apparently dealt with the need for patriotic self-sacrifice—her grandfather called them "flag waving and eagle soaring." The evenings always ended with Harwood's mother reciting verses and stories popular from an earlier time. She knew the oft-repeated encores by heart: tales of lonely Union pickets pining for their families as they lay dying, or poems like "Driving Home the Cows," which told of a father who thought all three of his sons had died in the war, looking up from his work one day to see his youngest child walking toward him, his empty coat sleeve swaying in the breeze. By far the best-loved story was that of a one-legged veteran who had been arrested for vagrancy, only to find himself in a courtroom presided over by a Union officer he had saved in battle. Gravely pronouncing his ruling, the judge declared: "The sentence is that all your life—your bunk will be the best room in my humble home." There were few dry eyes in the hall once Harwood's mother was done.[1]

As rituals like the Old Soldiers' Campfires reveal, war stories filled with pathos and patriotism never entirely disappeared. They were still around in the early twentieth century, as, indeed, they are today, ready to be updated for every new conflict. But history had moved on by the time Harwood sat listening to what she called Civil War "tear jerkers." The turn-of-the-century context had sapped much of the meaning from the stories recounted in this book. Some were no longer told at all; others existed in anemic form, their persuasive power undermined by alternative war narratives and new ways of understanding suffering and sympathy, manhood and womanhood, civic participation and national identity. People continued to revel in periodic doses of wartime sentimentality, but they returned home to a society quite different from the one that Northerners had envisioned in 1865.

There was a fundamental optimism underlying popular Civil War tales that idealized Northerners' response to suffering. They imagined that exemplary sufferers could positively influence observers by modeling strong characters and religious convictions. They supposed that benevolence could erase social divisions and selfishness, confirming the value of America's democratic republic for a global audience. And they anticipated that a God-ordained victory would bring about a society in which honorable men would thrive and selfless women would continue to wield salutary moral influence. Northerners' optimism collapsed as none of these idealistic predictions came to pass. The war itself had unleashed forces that gathered strength in the postwar decades—including business consolidation, rapid industrialization, and class and racial conflict—bringing into question many of the assumptions that underpinned older tales of suffering and benevolence.

The Republicans' free-labor ideology had promised white Union soldiers that victory would be its own reward—that a union free of slavery would provide success for anyone of diligence and moral fiber. Instead, opportunities for ordinary men to earn an independent livelihood declined markedly in the postwar years, as the rewards of reunification disappeared into the pockets of Gilded Age elites. Stories that idealized Union soldiers' response to suffering lost much of their appeal in this more secular, cutthroat age. So did tales of women valiantly shoring up men's characters and saving the nation from impending collapse. By the century's end, as America's power came to span the globe, it became harder to recall that the nation's republican political system had once seemed truly imperiled; few felt any pressing need to defend the nation's political system from its critics. Women's place in this political order had shifted dramatically as well. Many remained content serving dinner to aging veterans or playing second fiddle to men, as did Harwood's mother. But vast numbers now demanded suffrage, convinced that men could only be influenced by legislative change. Looking out at a more heterogeneous, worldly, conflict-ridden society, many white Northerners relinquished the belief that their side had once been morally superior to its enemies, instead embracing their Confederate foes. Both men and women would update their war stories later in the century to take account of this altered landscape. Tales of exemplary Union sufferers, selfless volunteers, and unprecedented benevolence would be few and far between in their new memories of the war.

———◦•┼•◦———

Dramatically accelerating social, economic, and cultural change led to the declining appeal of Civil War narratives of suffering and sympathy. Scholars often cite war narratives created in the late nineteenth century as a straightforward reflection of how participants understood the war. Yet what such sources typically reveal is the extent to which Northerners had discarded older narratives in favor of new ones more relevant to their contemporary concerns and preoccupations. It becomes easier to see why the stories recounted in this book lost their appeal when one considers just how vast and rapid were the changes in postwar America.

Broad economic trends in this period fundamentally altered Northerners' understandings of themselves and their place in the society. Most of the men who fought in the Civil War came from small towns or rural villages and worked the land. Even those employed in manufacturing typically labored in factories or mills small enough for owners to keep a paternalistic eye on their employees.[2] The pace of industrialism and urbanization sped up markedly in the decades after the war. By the 1890s manufacturing output had outstripped agriculture productivity, transforming the United States from a second-rate industrial power into a world leader. Cities expanded just as rapidly, with more than one in five Americans living in areas with populations over 100,000 by the turn of the century. Equally seismic shifts accompanied these ones. Where economic independence had once been a realistic goal for a large portion of the white male population in the North—either in the form of owning a farm or mastering a trade—the vast majority by the 1880s and 1890s would spend their lives as wageworkers, salaried employees, or tenant farmers. Most would never meet their employers, for the tens of thousands of small-scale manufacturing establishments that existed before the war had increasingly been taken over by corporations that engaged armies of workers and maintained a stranglehold over entire industries.[3] The world that most Union soldiers believed they were fighting to protect—a world of boundless opportunities for ordinary men to earn an independent living—became largely illusory within three decades of victory.

The Gilded Age is well known for its ruthless economic rivalries, widespread corruption, and class conflict. These were years when robber barons made fortunes by crushing their rivals and passing underhand deals to secure monopolies or drive up stock prices, all the while flaunting their opulence. At the same time, masses of ordinary people were buffeted by economic woes. A financial panic in 1873 saw the closure of thousands of businesses and masses of layoffs, touching off a recurring cycle of depressions that lasted until the late 1890s. By the end of 1874, there were at least a million unemployed men, some of them waiting in the breadlines that had become a new feature of the urban landscape. Workers responded to this volatile economic climate by forming the first nationwide labor unions, expressing a growing militancy through strikes—thousands of which took place in 1870s and 1880s, mostly notably in 1877 as railroad workers across the country battled with state militia and federal troops, leaving hundreds dead. Meanwhile, the hopes that veterans had placed in the presidency of former Union general Ulysses S. Grant turned to outrage as his administration was plagued with one corruption scandal after another.[4]

In these conflict-ridden times, white Northerners increasingly turned a blind eye to the racial strife that was taking place in the former Confederate states. The situation had been different in the early years of Reconstruction, when support for black suffrage had been widespread. But within just a few years, as historian Nina Silber has shown, this hopefulness gave way to a tendency "to scapegoat the black politician and voter for all the problems of the South."[5] Supposing that political rights and market forces would be sufficient to reconstruct race relations in the former Confederacy, most white Northerners were unwilling to confront the deep structural inequalities and race hatred that black men and women faced. They would have heard reports about the numerous race riots (seventy-eight in all) that occurred in Southern towns and cities, mostly in election years, in the decade following war's end. They might have read about the reign of terror unleashed by the Ku Klux Klan, including the lynching of some 400 African Americans between 1868 and 1871.[6] But the signs of political corruption and impending bankruptcy of state governments across the South by the mid-1870s had convinced many Northerners that any further effort to alter the country's racial hierarchy was doomed to failure.

As their attitudes toward black Southerners hardened, privileged white Northerners displayed growing compassion for Southern elites. Looking out at the rampant materialism and shady dealings of the Gilded Age, the old South's planter class—impoverished and disenfranchised as a result of their struggle—seemed to be the one group that existed outside the corrupt sphere of politics and commerce. To many Northern whites, they had come to seem like the real victims of war, while former slaves were recast as profiting from their ruin. An updated vision of slavery underlay this new perspective, drawn from the Lost Cause myth widely propagated in the postwar South. According to this myth, the Old South was a land of idyllic plantations occupied by gracious men and elegant ladies, served by a force of loyal and contented "servants." Reimagining slavery as a benign institution, Northern elites who fretted about the mounting class tensions in their own backyards evinced a growing nostalgia for the leisurely, preindustrial lifestyle of the Old South's planter class, notes Silber, especially the "authoritative yet harmonious" relationship they supposedly had with their subordinates.[7]

A widespread acceptance of the Lost Cause myth in the North tended to render the Union's victory a hollow one, bringing into question key assumptions that had lent persuasive power to the stories dealt with in the preceding chapters. When Lost Cause proponents wrote about the Confederate cause in the postwar years, they claimed that any attempt to defend their slaveholding society was hopeless from the outset (a belief that no one, of course, held when the war commenced). The Confederacy was defeated, according to this myth, only because it was forced into an unequal fight against an enemy equipped with superior industrial capacity and greater population. As for slavery, they assumed that it was destined to wither away eventually, hardly requiring a cataclysmic war to bring freedom to slaves who were, in the meanwhile, quite satisfied with their lot.[8] The conviction that Unionists had won a critical struggle that preserved democratic republicanism, saved the country for free labor, and maintained America's exceptional role on the world stage hardly made sense in the light of a belief that slavery was destined to end of its own accord, and the North destined to triumph, not by virtue of moral superiority but by advanced size and strength.

Of course, not every Northerner accepted the myth of the Lost Cause. Frederick Douglass and other African American spokespeople joined with former abolitionists in remembering the war as an ideological struggle over the meaning of citizenship and democracy and a triumph for the more virtuous side.[9] A sizable number of Union veterans endorsed their perspective, as they would continue to do throughout their lives. They were particularly active in promoting ongoing loyalty to the Northern cause—defined in terms of ending slavery or preserving the Union. Broadcasting their message widely in the last decades of the century, they sent members to talk to schoolchildren and launched campaigns to ensure that history textbooks presented Unionist interpretations of the war. As Edith Harwood discovered while attending her grandfather's Old Soldiers' Campfire meetings in Iowa, it also remained commonplace for aging veterans to deliver "flag waving and eagle soaring" speeches within their local communities for half a century after the war.

Nevertheless, in Northern culture more broadly, there was a distinct retreat from partisan questions of causation and culpability and toward a focus on the war's military history in the final decades of the century. By the 1880s magazine and journal editors had discovered a burgeoning market for such material. Soliciting eyewitness accounts of major battles from Union and Confederate generals, *Century* magazine almost doubled its circulation, reaching 225,000 readers a month by the middle years of the decade.[10] Numerous publications tried to mirror this success by printing material on the war's battles and leaders. They found a group of loyal readers in former Union soldiers, who began joining veterans' organizations in large numbers in these decades, particularly the GAR.[11] Although some veterans continued defending older arguments about the virtues of the Northern cause, most focused on the conflict's military history within their GAR posts and at campfire meetings, recollecting the details of army life or discussing the merits of particular strategies or commanders, and only rarely touching on the larger causes and consequences of the war.[12]

This heightened interest in the war's military history muted an emphasis on the shared suffering and sympathy between soldiers and civilians that had been commonplace during the war. In popular literature by the 1880s, there was a striking turn away from tales that dealt with war-induced distress or life on the home front, as Alice Fahs has shown. Henceforth, the only Civil War stories published on such topics tended to be nostalgic yarns about the Old South or romances that pictured reconciliation through marriages between Northern men and Southern belles.[13] Within their organizations, veterans also found little time to discuss wartime relationships between war zone and home front. Their groups were specifically designed as exclusive worlds that marked their members off from the rest of society. It would not have done for them to focus on the families who sustained Union troops, the volunteers who supported them, or the civilians who endured wartime loss and privation as well. Only battlefield experience lent veterans their unique status, and this became the core of their postwar reminiscences. Occasionally, they spared a thought for the mass of bereaved civilians, listening, as Edith Harwood's fellow citizens did, to sentimental wartime poems about bereft families. But at the meetings that she attended, no one apparently recalled tales of selfless women, exemplary sufferers, or unstinting benevolence. Instead, their favorite story—that of the one-legged veteran taken in by his former officer—spoke of a very different kind of emotional connection that revolved around an undying brotherhood between Union veterans, no matter their class or situation.

The appeal of combat and military fellowship had advanced so far by the late nineteenth century that some Union veterans had begun to argue that battlefield experience was the *only* important outcome of the Civil War. In an address to a Harvard University graduating class in 1895, Oliver Wendell Holmes memorably articulated this new position. Expressing disgust at the "wallowing ease" of modern life, he celebrated participation in battle as the ultimate male experience—the only way a man could feel "the passion of life at its top." Those who fought beside him had not done so to support any particular principle or outcome, he argued. They had simply followed a "soldier's faith" that was entirely self-referential. "The faith is true and adorable which leads a soldier to throw away his life in obedience to a blindly accepted duty, in a cause which he little understands, in a plan of campaign of which he has no notion, under tactics of which he does not see the use," Holmes told his listeners. Real war might be "horrible and dull," he went on, but it carried a "divine" message, serving to remind men living in a "snug, over-safe corner of the world" that "struggle for life" was part of the natural order and they should thus be ready to confront danger whenever it appeared. Prioritizing the battlefield as a testing ground for masculinity, Holmes specifically repudiated wartime tales in which Union soldiers demonstrated their characters not just in battle, but also in suffering. "The book for the army is a war-song, not a hospital sketch," he concluded.[14] Undoubtedly he was referring to the reams of material produced in an earlier era that focused on the nonmartial aspects of the Civil War, recounting the heroic martyrdom of Union officers, the exceptional suffering of their troops, the impressive character of limbless veterans, or the self-sacrifice of their caregivers.

Holmes's "soldier's faith"—with its overt secularism, its stress on physicality, and its vision of life as an endless struggle—was a distinct product of the late nineteenth century. Such faith was little in evidence during the Civil War, when the majority of Union soldiers endorsed perspectives like those of Bourne's one-armed writers. They typically viewed their suffering as an opportunity to demonstrate religious convictions or manly character, justifying their service in light of a specific cause. They did not liken themselves to soldiers engaged in previous conflicts, much less to Confederate troops, for they imagined that the North's democratic culture had produced a uniquely educated and virtuous citizenry who fully understood the issues underlying the conflict. In fact, they saw their service as the very antithesis of Holmes's unreasoning obedience. It was only later in the century—long after the Union victory was secure, religious fervor had waned, and new ideals of admirable manhood were ascendant among Northern elites—that Holmes's outlook could gain credence.

Scholars have described the last quarter of the century as a time of "strange formlessness," or even "crisis" in Protestant religiosity. One explanation, according to Sydney Ahlstrom, is that "evangelicalism was no longer calling the tune—or more accurately, that fewer people were heeding the call."[15] Wartime experiences themselves did not cause this shift, however much they might have undermined the already shaky piety of a few elites like Holmes. Rather, postwar urban and industrial expansion dramatically undermined the old Protestant Establishment—an expansion driven in large part by new waves of immigration, which helped to double the nation's population in the thirty years after the war. Whereas roughly five million people had crossed the Atlantic between 1815 and 1860, twice this number of immigrants arrived in the United States in the years between 1860 and 1890, with millions more following them over the next few decades.[16] Most of these newcomers ended up in Northern cities. Although Protestant leaders tried to reach them by holding periodic revivals, as they had done in the Civil War era, their message held limited appeal to the mass of non-English-speaking migrants who arrived with their own beliefs systems and quickly established separate religious communities.

Older religious outlooks came under challenge from other directions as well, most notably from Charles Darwin's *The Origin of the Species*, a work that had negligible impact in America prior to the 1870s. Thereafter, Darwinism inevitably weakened confidence in a beneficent, orderly universe supervised down to the minutest level by a loving God. In place of providential design,

Darwin imagined a world following the amoral dictates of evolution; instead of moral freedom he emphasized biological determinism; and in lieu of a well-ordered nature he posited an endless war of weak against strong. His work would help to expand the prestige of scientific techniques over the ensuing decades, influencing a broad range of fields by promoting attention to "origins, histories [and] developments."[17] Within this new intellectual landscape, the authority of religious leaders was marginal at best.

The application of Darwin's theories to humankind undermined this authority still further, for Social Darwinists contended that moral stewardship and benevolent outreach—goals that underpinned evangelical activism—were not just unnecessary but positively harmful. Self-taught philosopher Herbert Spencer is best known for applying evolutionary arguments to humanity. Imagining the course of human history as a vast struggle between different social groups, he coined the term "survival of the fittest" to rationalize what he saw as inevitable hierarchies of power. If society's weakest members fell by the wayside, he argued, this was all for the best, for the culling of America's most fragile members would only leave the remaining population stronger in the long run. Attempts to mitigate this situation by benevolent do-gooders were unconscionable in his view. "To aid the bad in multiplying is, in effect, the same as maliciously providing for our descendants a multitude of enemies," he wrote.[18] Although not universally embraced, such arguments were profoundly influential in late nineteenth-century popular culture, offering an easy-to-grasp vision that seemed to encapsulate an age of ruthless acquisitiveness and open rivalry between social groups and imperial powers. This was a context ill-suited to boasting about the North's wartime voluntary efforts and unstinting generosity.

The views of Social Darwinists were particularly compelling for privileged and powerful men like Oliver Wendell Holmes. Having witnessed the rise of immigrant-led political machines, nationwide labor unions and farmers' cooperatives, and renewed imperial rivalries, they had begun to fret that "over civilization" was rendering elites unfit to compete with other races, classes, and nations in the global struggle for survival. They now urged their sons to prove their virility by taking up rugged sports like boxing and football—pastimes once reserved solely for working-class youths.[19] Rejecting sentimentalism and refinement as emasculating, elite whites increasingly renounced older ideals of manhood based on self-restraint, spirituality, and moral character in favor of new models that privileged physical size and strength, aggressive drives, and potent sexuality.[20] To their minds, the Civil War became a heroic time when men had been able to escape the confines of bourgeois domesticity and test their mettle in combat.[21]

End-of-the-century war stories celebrated the rugged soldier rather than the exemplary sufferer, often following Holmes in directly refuting earlier tales of war. Descriptions of the wounded now appeared, if at all, as brutal realities unredeemed by religious, patriotic, or familial sentiment. Publishing his version of the battle of Spotsylvania in 1887, for instance, Union veteran Frank Wilkeson described bodies blown apart, their organs "torn out and slung in ribbons and shreds on the ground," or men knocked down by shells, who "staggered aimlessly round and round . . . as sheep afflicted with grubs in the brain do." Continuing on in this vein for several pages, Wilkeson's detached tone signified his own ability to face death and pain with unflinching stoicism. The wounded Union soldiers in his tale were far different from inspirational wartime sufferers sustained by family, faith, and cause. In fact, Wilkeson made a point of contesting such war stories, noting that none of the men who died around him "cried aloud, none called on wife, or mother, or father." Instead, they lay "with set jaws, waiting for the end. They moaned and groaned as they suffered, but none of them flunked." Only a few "delirious" men "babbled of their homes," Wilkeson noted, whereas the rest "braced themselves and died in a manly manner."[22] Reversing wartime arguments, he measured a "manly" death solely by reference to physical endurance in the face of pain.

Stoic suffering was not confined to Union troops in Wilkeson's account. In fact, he specifically honored Confederate soldiers for dying in a "manly way." Having rejected an earlier emphasis on Union sufferers' superior self-control and moral virtue, the way was clear for veterans like him to embrace their former enemies. Large numbers did so in the last decade of the century, coming together to celebrate a military heroism that knew no sectional lines. Black Union soldiers were notably absent from the Blue and Grey Reunions held to commemorate Civil War anniversaries, nor did they participate in the cooperative fundraising drives in which some Union veterans helped erect monuments to the Confederate dead. Reconciliation was a whites-only affair, representing not just the weakening of sectional divisions, but a deepening racial divide as Jim Crow laws spread across the country.[23]

Just as white veterans updated their war stories to focus on battlefield heroism, a corresponding development took place in women's war memories. During the war itself, Northern women had been honored en masse: as family members who sustained men, as selfless nurses or grief-stricken wives and mothers, or as volunteers who propped up manly character and limited the conflict's brutalizing effects. By the 1880s and 1890s, however, the only women whose voices continued to be heard were those who had traveled to the war zone. Rather than exalting women's ability to influence men through emotion and piety, these updated war narratives tended to focus on the women themselves, highlighting their professionalism, competency, or extraordinary goodness. Making fewer claims about Northern womanhood's overall contributions to Union victory, their war stories now focused on the admirable character and capabilities of particular individuals.[24]

The altered focus of women's late nineteenth-century memoirs is evident without even opening their books. Those who wrote during the war titled their works to reflect contents that venerated Union soldiers' exemplary suffering. Jane Hoge, for instance, called her 1867 war memoir *The Boys in Blue: or Heroes of the Rank and File*, whereas her wartime coworker Mary Livermore clearly had other themes in mind two decades later, when she headed her reminiscences: *My Story of the War: A Woman's Narrative of Four Years Personal Experience*. Ostensibly, both women claimed to speak on behalf of soldiers, each dedicating their volumes to Union veterans and to the honored dead. But Hoge's work represented an earlier interest in tales of hospital life that focused squarely on Unionists' exemplary suffering and the ability of sympathetic women to evoke such responses. Livermore concentrated instead on her own and other women's wartime experiences. The same is true for Annie Wittenmyer's 1895 memoir, *Under the Guns*, a title that referred to moments when the author was imperiled by enemy fire. Even Adelaide Smith's *Reminiscences of an Army Nurse*, published in the early twentieth century, offered a narrative of hospital life almost completely devoid of patients. Most of the drama in Smith's story occurred outside the hospital, with only a few pages devoted to a description of "Some Patients."[25] Much as veterans' memoirs had come to emphasize battlefield daring and stoic endurance, late nineteenth-century female memorialists offered accounts of their intrepid adventures on the front lines, paying little attention to the larger causes or consequences of the struggle.[26]

This altered focus reflected a broader transition among socially active women in the last two decades of the century. Even fairly conservative groups by this time, such as the Woman's Christian Temperance Union and the Women's Relief Corp, had begun to support calls for female suffrage, overcoming their earlier concern that the women's rights movement threatened to corrupt the private realm.[27] Confronting the host of complex problems caused by industrialization, urbanization, and immigration, it had become abundantly clear that no amount of indirect moral suasion could adequately redress contemporary ills. Women's consciousness of their interests as a group had increased markedly, too, as the political realm increasingly came to be seen as an arena in which competing social groups fought for their own advantage.[28]

As women began demanding a direct voice in politics, women writers updated their war memoirs to celebrate their own or their coworkers' proficiency and skill, tacitly endorsing demands for gender equality. Men's exemplary suffering—once the main focus on women's war writings—was marginalized as a result. Ironically, this shift negated earlier arguments about women's crucial role in ensuring national integrity. Rather than picturing the idealized home front as a bulwark against the republic's disintegration, the central focus shifted to women's myriad abilities, with the Civil War simply as a backdrop for their heroic actions. Take, for instance, Mary Livermore's 1886 memoir—one of the few later accounts that focused not on a handful of remarkable women but on the mass of women war-workers. In this work, women's thoughts and actions have moved to center stage. A few stray statements about Union soldiers' exemplary spirit are scattered throughout, but the first story of a specific Union sufferer appears several hundred pages into her text.[29] It recounts the tale of men wounded at Fort Donelson, which Livermore and her coworker Jane Hoge had written and spoken about often during the war. When Hoge set this story down in her 1867 memoir she portrayed the appearance and personal backgrounds of her male characters, describing how they expressed an undaunted patriotism by raising their amputated limbs to cheer as the fort was taken. Even after spending days frozen on the battlefield, the soldiers in her tale remained cheerful and patient, communicating a deep love of home and cause by growing teary-eyed at the mention of their families and focusing their attention on the battle's outcome rather than their own suffering.[30]

None of these details made it into Livermore's story. Writing several decades later, she briefly described one "patient sufferer" who gave a "nonchalant answer" to her indignant query about his treatment, then she went on to concentrate on her own responses to the scene around her. Sickened by the stench of blood and the sight of grisly injuries, Livermore had to leave the room several times until she finally overpowered her "weakness," having determined to hold herself "in iron control, until I had become habituated to the manifold shocking sights that are the outcome of the wicked business men call war."[31] The details of soldiers' wounds no longer appear as a means of emphasizing the heroism of the wounded. Instead, they now highlight Livermore's resolve and provide a vehicle for condemning men's violent propensities. The battle in which these men were wounded, she writes, was

> but one of countless thousands which men had waged with one another, in which hundreds of millions had been slain—transfixed with lances, hewn in pieces with battle-axes, torn in fragments with plunging shot,

or deadly canister, or fiendish bombs, mowed down with raking fires of leaden sleet, engulfed in the explosion of subterranean mines, impaled on gleaming bayonets, dying on the field, of wounds, fever, neglect,—forgotten, uncared for, a prey to the vulture, and devoured by the jackal and wild beast. While the mothers who bore these men, and the wives who loved them, lived on, suffering a prolonged death, finding the sweetness of life changed to cruel bitterness because of their bereavement.[32]

This striking passage contrasts markedly with earlier writing that extolled women for motivating patriotism and sustaining the Union cause. In Livermore's updated reading, Union soldiers are not suffering in a virtuous struggle: the battle they are wounded in is merely one in a long, undifferentiated list of barbarous events. Women, likewise, have been transformed from men's most ardent supporters into the innocent victims of their violence.

By the 1890s the pacifism reflected in this passage had gained wide support among socially active women, forming one facet of a broader critique of immoral male behavior.[33] While most held on to their faith in women's moral superiority, they no longer believed in their ability to reform men by example. To many, men had instead come to seem incorrigible—unworthy of holding the reins of power. One only had to look about at the rampant political corruption or the millions of women and children living in squalor while factory owners thrived to find a searing indictment of the social world they had created. There are thus very few innocent, pious male sufferers in Livermore's account. Accepting newer definitions of manhood that recast displays of emotion in men in negative terms, the men who weep in her account do not reveal their love of family, cause, or country; they simply show their weakness as men. One older sufferer she describes as "a mere puling, weeping baby." Another who "almost shrieked in his mental distress," she commanded to "die like a man, and not like a coward."[34] Proceeding to tell this wounded soldier about "Christ's mission on earth," she concluded: "I made little impression on the dying man." Some historians have used such scenes as evidence of growing wartime insensitivity, or the renunciation of sentimentality among women war-workers in favor of detached professionalism.[35] They are more appropriately seen as a reflection of late nineteenth-century culture in which women were no longer content to support men or to rely on their ability to influence them indirectly. Having devoted decades to campaigning for temperance and women's suffrage, Livermore was far less interested in discussing the meaning of the war than in using her memoir to highlight women's capacities and endorse their role in public life.[36]

Just as veterans rewrote their war stories to emphasize a shared martial valor, so women writers produced updated accounts that stressed their wartime accomplishments. There seemed little now to recommend older tales that had once demonstrated the virtues of the Union and its defenders by focusing on exemplary sufferers and universal benevolence. As America's democratic republic grew in strength, perceived threats to national existence shifted accordingly. Where respectable Northern commentators had worried at one time that antidemocratic forces and excessive self-interest were imperiling the Union, the fears that arose over the next fifty years—from an alleged increase in degenerate stock, to competition among nations for imperial supremacy—seemed to demand strong leadership or progressive legislation more than a virtuous citizenry. Influenced by the rise of new ideals of manhood, ministers in the late nineteenth century were far more likely to stress the need for a militant, physically active brand of Christianity than to praise men who exhibited resignation and patience in the face of suffering.[37] And women were no longer satisfied in their supportive, subordinate roles. As science and medicine gained in prestige, the intricate connection that Victorian men had once drawn between mind and body—where recovery from injury was understood as wholly contingent on a strong character and a resolute will—lost out to an emphasis on surgical and medical skill. In this new age of brawny men and dedicated suffragists, flush industrialists and spreading urban slums, lynch mobs and Social Darwinists, scientific discoveries and corporate consolidation, older wartime tales seemed naive at best. Suffering soldiers and their selfless caregivers thus made way for a glorification of daring men and equally daring women.

Notes

PROLOGUE

1. "How a Soldier Died," *West Philadelphia Hospital Register* (U.S. Army Hospital, West Philadelphia, Pa.), December 16, 1864, 64.

2. John Peck, *War, the Army and Victorian Literature* (Houndsmills: Macmillan Press, 1998), 14.

3. George M. Fredrickson, *The Inner Civil War: Northern Intellectuals and the Crisis of the Union* (New York: Harper and Row, 1965), viii.

4. On antiwar sentiment in the North, see Jean H. Baker, *Affairs of Party: The Political Culture of Northern Democrats in the Mid-Nineteenth Century* (Ithaca, N.Y.: Cornell University Press, 1983), and Frank L. Klement, *The Limits of Dissent: Clement L. Vallandingham and the Civil War* (1970; New York: Fordham University Press, 1998).

5. Mark Grimsley, *The Hard Hand of War: Union Military Policy Toward Southern Civilians, 1861–1865* (Cambridge: Cambridge University Press, 1995), deals with the transformation of Union war goals. On the changing nature of warfare, see Brent Nosworthy, *Bloody Crucible of Courage: Fighting Methods and Combat Experience in the American Civil War* (New York: Carroll and Graf, 2003).

6. Heather Cox Richardson, *The Greatest Nation of the Earth: Republican Economic Policies During the Civil War* (Cambridge: Harvard University Press, 1997), Richard F. Bensel, *Yankee Leviathan: The Origins of Central State Authority in America, 1859–1877* (New York: Cambridge University Press, 1990), and Leonard P. Curry, *Blueprint for Modern America: Non-Military Legislation of the First Civil War Congress* (Nashville: Vanderbilt University Press, 1968), are among the many works that canvass the war's

economic and political impact. Likewise, there is a sizable literature examining the way the conflict reshaped the relationship between citizens and the state, including Drew Gilpin Faust, *This Republic of Suffering: Death and the American Civil War* (New York: Knopf, 2008), chaps. 3–4; and James McPherson, *Lincoln and the Second American Revolution* (New York: Oxford University Press, 1990).

7. Fredrickson, *Inner Civil War*; Gerald Linderman, *The Experience of Combat in the American Civil War* (New York: Free Press, 1987), 2. Faust, *This Republic of Suffering*, chap. 6, places the religious skepticism voiced by prominent intellectuals in a longer historical context, as does Anne C. Rose, *Victorian America and the Civil War* (New York: Cambridge University Press, 1992), 13 and passim. For Rose, the war was a "cornerstone in the Victorians' redefinition of sacred values in secular terms," although not in a straightforward sense. Rather than acting as the sole catalyst for change, the war reinforced pre-existing social and intellectual trends, she argues, namely the evolution of bureaucracy and individualism, religious disengagement, and the growing prestige of alternative frames of reference such as scientific rationalism or self-gratification attained through work, leisure, or romantic love. Faust's argument is similarly nuanced. She notes that for some, the war encouraged novel ways of thinking that had already begun taking shape in antebellum America, while others remained resolutely sentimental and wedded to their religious convictions. Nonetheless, the rhetorical weight of her argument privileges change over continuity. Wartime suffering "transformed the mid-nineteenth century's growing sense of religious doubt into a crisis of belief that propelled many Americans to redefine or even reject their faith in a benevolent and responsive deity," she concludes (210).

8. Two recent Pulitzer Prize–winning books on the Civil War, for example, tell a quintessentially modern tale of idealism betrayed by war's harsh realities: Geraldine Brooks, *March* (New York: Fourth Estate, 2005), and Louis Menand, *The Metaphysical Club: A Story of Ideas in America* (New York: Farrar, Straus, and Giroux, 2001). Menand is bluntest in his assessment, arguing that the war "swept away almost the whole intellectual culture of the North," a claim based solely on an analysis of Oliver Wendell Holmes and his cohort of fellow Harvard intellectuals (x).

9. One of the earliest critics of Civil War literature was Rebecca Washington Smith, who asserted that the conflict produced few works of "distinction" because the "majority of writers reflected the idealistic, patriotic tradition" of the time. "The Civil War and Its Aftermath in American Fiction, 1861–1899," Ph.D. diss., University of Chicago, 1932, 56. Later scholars who have echoed her critique of the era's artistic output include Steven Conn, "Narrative Trauma and Civil War History Painting, or Why Are These Pictures So Terrible?" *History and Theory* 41 (December 2002): 17–42; David Lundberg, "The American Literature of War: The Civil War, World War I, and World War II," *American Quarterly* 36, no. 3 (1984): 373–88; Thomas C. Leonard, *Above the Battle: War-Making in America from Appomattox to Versailles* (New York: Oxford University Press, 1978); Daniel Aaron, *The Unwritten War: American Writers and the Civil War* (New York: Knopf, 1973); Edmund Wilson, *Patriotic Gore: Studies in the Literature of the American Civil War* (London: Hogarth Press, 1987); and Richard Lively, *Fiction Fights the Civil*

War: An Unfinished Chapter in the Literary History of the American People (Chapel Hill: University of North Carolina Press, 1957). Alice Fahs's work has injected more subtlety into the assessment of Civil War writing. Treating sentimental war literature as more than a denial of reality, she notes that wartime writers did not simply shy away from the carnage. Instead, they dealt with it from an intimate perspective, especially by exploring the "tension between the needs of the nation and the needs of the individual." *The Imagined Civil War: Popular Literature of the North and South, 1861–1865* (Chapel Hill: University of North Carolina Press, 2001), 12.

10. In particular, see James McPherson, *For Cause and Comrades: Why Men Fought in the Civil War* (New York: Oxford University Press, 1997), and Earl J. Hess, *The Union Soldier in Battle: Enduring the Ordeal of Combat* (Lawrence: University Press of Kansas, 1997). On the shift to realistic war literature in the wake of World War I, see Paul Fussell, *The Great War and Modern Memory* (New York: Oxford University Press, 1975); Eric J. Leed, *No Man's Land: Combat and Identity in World War I* (New York: Cambridge University Press, 1979); and Modris Eksteins, *Rites of Spring: The Great War and the Birth of the Modern Age* (New York: Anchor Books, 1989).

11. World War I did not completely disrupt the idealistic war narratives of the past, as noted by J. M. Winter, *Sites of Memory, Sites of Mourning. The Place of the Great War in European Cultural History* (New York: Cambridge University Press, 1995), and Joanna Bourke, *Dismembering the Male: Men's Bodies, Britain and the Great War* (London: Reaktion Books 1996). Nevertheless, in comparison to the Civil War, twentieth-century authors and artists produced vastly more work that expressed disillusionment, disgust, ambivalence, or alienation toward war. Their updated war narratives reflected a shift toward literary realism across the English-speaking world in the late nineteenth century. It is commonplace for scholars to imply that the Civil War itself somehow contributed to this shift. Yet they rarely analyze the link directly by comparing writing published before, during, and after the war. Evidence is usually offered instead from sources published long after war's end, ignoring the impact of intervening decades or transnational literary trends in reshaping memory and literary styles. By contrast, J. Matthew Gallman, "'Touched with Fire?' Two Philadelphia Novelists Remember the Civil War," in *More than a Contest Between Armies: Essays on the Civil War Era*, ed. James Marten and A. Kristen Foster (Kent, Ohio: Kent State University Press, 2008), 250–71, points to the war's negligible impact on two Northern authors.

12. Steven E. Woodworth, *While God Is Marching On: The Religious World of Civil War Soldiers* (Lawrence: University Press of Kansas, 2001), chap. 12.

13. Mark S. Schantz, *Awaiting the Heavenly Country: The Civil War and America's Culture of Death* (Ithaca, N.Y.: Cornell University Press, 2008); Woodworth, *While God Is Marching On*, 292–93.

14. My goal of embedding particular stories in specific contexts led me to focus only on Unionists' narratives. Similar stories may well have appealed to Confederates. While it is outside the scope of this book, an interesting study remains to be written on such tales, which would need to be understood within very different systems—of class, economy, race, religion, and gender—than those considered here.

15. In particular, David W. Blight, *Race and Reunion: The Civil War in American Memory* (Cambridge: Belknap Press of Harvard University Press, 2001); and Kirk Savage, *Standing Soldiers, Kneeling Slaves: Race, War, and Monument in Nineteenth-Century America* (Princeton, N.J.: Princeton University Press, 1997).

CHAPTER ONE

1. David B. Morris, *The Culture of Pain* (Berkeley: University of California Press, 1998), 2–3.

2. Judith Walzer Leavitt, *Brought to Bed: Childbearing in America, 1750–1950* (New York: Oxford University Press, 1986), chap. 1.

3. Daniel E. Sutherland, *The Expansion of Everyday Life, 1860–1876* (New York: Harper and Row, 1990), 127; Gary Laderman, *Sacred Remains: American Attitudes toward Death, 1799–1883* (New Haven: Yale University Press, 1996), 24–25, also surveys literature on mortality rates in the antebellum North. For working-class men's concern with workplace injury and death, see Joshua R. Greenberg, *Advocating the Man: Masculinity, Organized Labor, and the Market Revolution in New York, 1800–1840* (New York: Columbia University Press/Gutenberg, 2007), chap. 1. On the fragility of working-class lives in the antebellum North see Edward Pessen, *Riches, Class, and Power Before the Civil War* (Lexington, Mass.: D. C. Heath, 1972), chap. 3.

4. Schantz, *Awaiting the Heavenly Country*, 4.

5. On mortality differentials in urban and rural areas, see Michael R. Haines, "The Population of the United States, 1790–1920," in *The Cambridge Economic History of the United States*, ed. Robert E. Gallman (Cambridge: Cambridge University Press, 2000), 180–87.

6. Elliott Gorn, *The Manly Art: Bare Knuckle Prize Fighting in America* (Ithaca, N.Y.: Cornell University Press, 1986), chap. 4, esp. 144–47, depicts working-class men's embrace of blood sports as a rejection of middle-class values. On the growing popularity of murder narratives, see Amy Gilman Srebnick, *The Mysterious Death of Mary Rogers: Sex and Culture in Nineteenth-Century New York* (New York: Oxford University Press, 1995), esp. chap. 4. Michael Denning, *Mechanic Accents: Dime Novels and Working-Class Culture in America* (repr., London: Verso, 1998), chap. 1, points to the rise of cheap, mass-produced dime novels and sensational fiction in the 1840s and 1850s.

7. Laderman, *Sacred Remains*, 36, 41–42, 78.

8. Charles E. Rosenberg, "Health in the Home: A Tradition of Print and Practice," in his edited collection, *Right Living: An Anglo-American Tradition of Self-Help Medicine and Hygiene* (Baltimore: Johns Hopkins University Press, 2003), 1–20. On homeopathy and the water-cure movement, see Martin Kaufman, *Homeopathy in America: The Rise and Fall of a Medical Heresy* (Baltimore: Johns Hopkins University Press, 1971), and Susan E. Cayleff, *Wash and Be Healed: The Water-Cure Movement and Women's Health* (Philadelphia: Temple University Press, 1987).

9. Charles E. Rosenberg, "The Therapeutic Revolution: Medicine, Meaning, and Social Change in Nineteenth-Century America," in *The Therapeutic Revolution: Essays in the Social History of Medicine*, ed. Morris J. Vogel and Charles E. Rosenberg (Philadelphia: University of Pennsylvania Press, 1979), 8.

10. Martin S. Pernick, *A Calculus of Suffering: Pain, Professionalism and Anesthesia in Nineteenth-Century America* (New York: Columbia University Press, 1985), chap. 3 and p. 43. A similar point is made by Alison Winter, *Mesmerized: Powers of Mind in Victorian Britain* (Chicago: University of Chicago Press, 1998), chap. 7, and Heather D. Curtis, *Faith in the Great Physician: Suffering and Divine Healing in American Culture, 1860–1900* (Baltimore: Johns Hopkins University Press, 2007), 27.

11. Pernick, *Calculus of Suffering*, 45 (emphasis in original). On this point, see also Curtis, *Faith in the Great Physician*, 29, and Rosenberg, "The Therapeutic Revolution," 14. As the latter notes, such therapies retained their popularity among both physicians and their patients until well after the Civil War.

12. Walter E. Houghton, *The Victorian Frame of Mind, 1830–1870* (New Haven: Yale University Press, 1957), 14.

13. G. J. Barker-Benfield. *The Culture of Sensibility: Sex and Society in Eighteenth-Century Britain* (Chicago: University of Chicago Press, 1992), 1–28, describes how eighteenth-century thinkers elaborated a gendered view of the body's nervous system.

14. Victorian writers disagreed on whether insensitivity to pain was rooted in biology or based on variable environmental factors, such as upbringing or social situation. Even those who accepted environmental arguments, however, generally assumed that insensitivity might take generations to overcome, believing, as most did in this period, in the heritability of acquired characteristics. It is difficult to assess whether working-class Northerners shared these beliefs about differential suffering. Yet it is clear that where privileged writers put a negative value on others' ability to bear pain, this valuation could easily be reversed. Many scholars, for instance, have discussed the way urban working-class men viewed the capacity to withstand pain in positive terms, defining themselves in opposition to what they saw as overly effete middle-class manhood.

15. Pernick, *Calculus of Suffering*, chap. 9, analyzes the selective use of anesthesia by American physicians before 1880, based on their perception of how much suffering was warranted in specific cases.

16. Jennifer L. Morgan, "'Some Could Suckle Over Their Shoulder': Male Travelers, Female Bodies, and the Gendering of Racial Ideology, 1500–1700," *William and Mary Quarterly* 54, no. 1 (1997): 171, 186–90. Travel writing was enormously popular in the first half of the century, with "only religious writings exceeded in quantity the number of travel books reviewed and the number of travel narratives published in American journals," according to Larzer Ziff, *Return Passages: Great American Travel Writing, 1780–1910* (New Haven: Yale University Press, 2000), 59.

17. On the rise of competing medical sects and theories in antebellum America, see James H. Cassedy, *Medicine and American Growth, 1800–1860* (Madison: University of Wisconsin Press, 1986), chap. 1; and John S. Haller, *American Medicine in Transition, 1840–1910* (Urbana: University of Illinois Press, 1981), chap. 4.

18. Henry F. May, *The Enlightenment in America* (New York: Oxford University Press, 1976), 348, notes that Scottish common-sense philosophy "reigned supreme in American colleges" until the Civil War. See also Pernick, *Calculus of Suffering*, 62.

19. There is a sizable literature on the evolution of humanitarianism, including James

Turner, *Reckoning with the Beast: Animals, Pain and Humanity in the Victorian Mind* (Baltimore: Johns Hopkins University Press, 1980), 1–14; and Karen Halttunen's *Murder Most Foul: The Killer and the American Gothic Imagination* (Cambridge: Harvard University Press, 1998), chap 3. Halttunen's work not only charts the rise of a humanitarian sensibility, but also examines its unintended flip-side: the new shock value and sexual allure that pain began to hold (represented by the rise of sensational fiction and sadomasochistic pornography), in a culture that had redefined suffering as forbidden and thus obscene. Authors interested in using scenes of suffering to generate humanitarianism were not unaware of the potential for their work to incite titillating voyeurism instead. Sentimental authors dealt with this issue by picturing characters who visibly manifested sympathy through strong emotion and bodily reaction (the quivering lip, flushed face, or quick tear being the most common), baldly seeking from readers a similarly physical response and thereby "educating" them in the appropriate attitudes toward others' distress. The "emotional vocabulary" of sentimental novels, as John Mullan, in *Sentiment and Sociability: The Language of Feeling in the Eighteenth Century* (Oxford: Clarendon Press, 2000), chap. 3, explains, was powerful precisely because physical signs, unlike words, were supposedly incapable of being misconstrued. As noted below, new understandings of emotional susceptibility increasingly made illegitimate all such attempts to manipulate sentiment.

20. Pernick, *Calculus of Suffering*, 161–62. David B. Morris, "About Suffering: Voice, Genre, and Moral Community," in *Social Suffering*, ed. Arthur Kleinman, Veena Das, and Margaret Lock (Berkeley: University of California Press, 1997), 40, makes a similar point, noting that suffering is "not a raw datum, a natural phenomenon we can identify and measure, but a social status that we extend or withhold. We extend or withhold it depending largely on whether the suffer falls within our moral community."

21. Elizabeth B. Clark, "'The Sacred Rights of the Weak': Pain, Sympathy, and the Culture of Individual Rights in Antebellum America," *Journal of American History* 82, no. 2 (1995): 463–93.

22. Ibid., 484; Myra C. Glenn, *Campaigns Against Corporal Punishment: Prisoners, Sailors, Women and Children in Antebellum America* (Albany: State University of New York Press, 1984), chaps. 2–3; David Perkins, *Romanticism and Animal Rights* (Cambridge: Cambridge University Press, 2003), 3, and passim; and Turner, *Reckoning with the Beast*.

23. John Dwyer, *Virtuous Discourse: Sensibility and Community in Late Eighteenth-Century Scotland* (Edinburgh: John Donald Publishers, 1987), chaps. 1–6, esp. 52–65; Mullan, *Sentiment and Sociability*, chap. 1. These ideas were broadly disseminated through literature, poetry, plays, and other art forms, as discussed in Julia A. Stern, *The Plight of Feeling: Sympathy and Dissent in the Early American Novel* (Chicago: University of Chicago Press, 1997); Elizabeth Barnes, *States of Sympathy: Seduction and Democracy in the American Novel* (New York: Columbia University Press, 1997); and Janet Todd, *Sensibility: An Introduction* (London: Methuen, 1986). See also Martha Tomhave Blauvelt, "The Work of the Heart: Emotion in the 1805–35 Diary of Sarah Connell Ayer," *Journal of Social History* 35, no. 3 (Spring 2002): 577–92, for a more intimate portrayal

at how the culture of sensibility shaped the private writings of one woman in the early Republic.

24. On Smith's later shift away from popular opinion as an appropriate basis for assessing moral sense, see Dwyer, *Virtuous Discourse*, chap. 7.

25. Adam Smith, *The Theory of Moral Sentiments*, ed. D. D. Raphael and A. L. Macfie (1759; Indianapolis: Liberty Fund, 1982), 9. Clark, "Sacred Rights of the Weak," 478 n. 40, notes that Smith's text was reprinted in Boston, New York, and Philadelphia in 1817, 1821, and 1822 respectively. On the influence of this work in the United States, see also May, *Enlightenment in America*, 346–48.

26. On the religious changes wrought by the Second Great Awakening, see Jon Butler, *Awash in a Sea of Faith: Christianizing the American People* (Cambridge: Harvard University Press, 1990); Nathan O. Hatch, *The Democratization of American Christianity* (New Haven: Yale University Press, 1989); and Timothy L. Smith, *Revivalism and Social Reform: American Protestantism on the Eve of the Civil War* (Baltimore: Johns Hopkins University Press, 1980).

27. Susan Curtis, "The Son of Man and God the Father: The Social Gospel and Victorian Masculinity," in *Meanings for Manhood: Constructions of Masculinity in Victorian America*, ed. Mark C. Carnes and Clyde Griffin (Chicago: University of Chicago Press, 1990), 73, details the softer image of God that prevailed among American Protestants by mid-century.

28. Clark, "Sacred Rights of the Weak," 480.

29. Woodworth, *While God Is Marching On*, 26. See also Gardiner H. Shattuck, *A Shield and Hiding Place: The Religious Life of the Civil War Armies* (Macon, Ga.: Mercer University Press, 1978). On the difficulty of counting believers, see Sydney E. Ahlstrom, *A Religious History of the American People*, 2nd ed. (New Haven: Yale University Press, 2004), 517. As he notes, Methodists attracted most adherents by mid-century (well over a million members by the 1840s and an "incalculable number of regular hearers"), closely followed by Baptists, then Presbyterians, Congregationalists, and a range of other Protestant denominations (437).

30. Lewis O. Saum, *The Popular Mood of Pre–Civil War America* (Westport, Conn.: Greenwood Press, 1980), 34.

31. Ahlstrom, *A Religious History*, 556 and chaps. 33–34.

32. Ronald C. White Jr., "Lincoln's Sermon on the Mount: The Second Inaugural," in *Religion and the American Civil War*, ed. Randall M. Miller, Harry S. Stout, and Charles Reagan Wilson (New York: Oxford University Press, 1998), 208–25, charts Lincoln's growing apocalypticism over the course of the war.

33. James H. Moorhead, *American Apocalypse: Yankee Protestants and the Civil War, 1860–1869* (New Haven: Yale University Press, 1978). Saum, *The Popular Mood*, 57.

34. Curtis, *Faith in the Great Physician*, 33.

35. See note 60 below for a discussion of scholarship on Victorian sentimentalism.

36. Richard H. Brodhead, *Cultures of Letters: Scenes of Reading and Writing in Nineteenth-Century America* (Chicago: University of Chicago Press, 1993), 38–42.

37. As Mary P. Ryan, *Cradle of the Middle Class: The Family in Oneida County, New*

York, 1790–1865 (New York: Cambridge University Press, 1981), 153, 184–85, argues the development of the privatized nuclear family did more than provide the unpaid labor that underpinned capitalist development. After mid-century, as the older route to middling success—the independent proprietorship of artisans, shopkeepers, and farmers—had given way to white-collar occupations, native-born middling Northern whites were far less capable of reinventing class status in children by bequeathing specific skills, property, or land. Within the newly privatized domestic sphere, however, parents were able to craft strategies and inculcate traits of character deemed essential to middle-class achievement and respectability, for instance by limiting family size, keeping children at home longer, extending their educations, and adopting child-rearing practices intended to ensure self-monitoring and self-control. Likewise, domestic ideals furnished the ideological justification for this new capitalist order. As scholars, such as Lori Merish, *Sentimental Materialism: Gender, Commodity Culture and Nineteenth-Century American Literature* (Durham, N.C.: Duke University Press, 2000), 4, point out, the domestic sphere came to be defined as the site of spontaneous emotions and moral values only by suppressing its "marketplace orientation." Identifying (or, rather, mystifying) the economic and sexual division of labor as natural and morally worthy, the middle class held up the sentimental home and the free labor system as libratory realms in comparison to the more obvious exploitation at the heart of slavery. On the political impact of sentimentalizing domesticity, see also the brilliant work of Jeanne Boydston, *Home and Work: Housework, Wages, and the Ideology of Labor in the Early Republic* (New York: Oxford University Press, 1990).

38. Jan Lewis, "Mother's Love: The Construction of an Emotion in Nineteenth-Century America," in *Social History and Issues in Human Consciousness: Some Interdisciplinary Connections*, ed., Andrew Barnes and Peter Stearns (New York: New York University Press, 1989), 209–29; and Ruth H. Bloch, "American Feminine Ideals in Transition: The Rise of Moral Motherhood, 1785–1815," *Feminist Studies* 4 (1978): 100–126.

39. On patriarchal rule in the antebellum South, see Drew Gilpin Faust, *Mothers of Invention: Women of the Slaveholding South in the Civil War* (Chapel Hill: University of North Carolina Press, 1996), 32; Stephanie McCurry, *Masters of Small Worlds: Yeoman Households, Gender Relations, and the Political Culture of the Antebellum South Carolina Low Country* (New York: Oxford University Press, 1995), 85–91; and LeeAnn Whites, *The Civil War as a Crisis in Gender: Augusta, Georgia, 1860–1890* (Athens: University of Georgia Press, 1995), chap. 1.

40. Jonathan Daniel Wells, *The Origins of the Southern Middle Class, 1800–1861* (Chapel Hill: University of North Carolina Press, 2004).

41. On a distinctive Southern honor culture, see Bertram Wyatt-Brown, *Honor and Violence in the Old South* (New York: Oxford University Press, 1986); and Kenneth S. Greenberg, *Honor and Slavery: Lies, Duels, Noses, Masks, Dressing as a Woman, Gifts, Strangers, Humanitarianism, Death, Slave Rebellions, the Proslavery Argument, Baseball, Hunting and Gambling in the Old South* (Princeton. N.J.: Princeton University Press, 1996); and Nicole Etcheson, "Manliness and the Political Culture of the Old Northwest, 1790–1860," *Journal of the Early Republic* 15, no. 1 (Spring 1995): 59–77.

42. Scholarship on nineteenth-century urban subcultures includes Shane White and Graham White, *Stylin': African American Expressive Culture from Its Beginnings to the Zoot Suit* (Ithaca, N.Y.: Cornell University Press, 1998); Srebnick, *The Mysterious Death of Mary Rogers*, chap. 3; and Christine Stansell, *City of Women: Sex and Class in New York, 1789–1860* (Urbana: University of Illinois Press, 1987).

43. Northern working-class men were just as likely as those in the middle class to sentimentalize home and family, notes Boydston, *Home and Work*, chap. 7.

44. It is unfeasible to reduce comparisons between North and South to a quantitative assessment of the number of slave-owners or the percentage of Northern whites who adhered to middle-class domestic standards (or were morally opposed to slavery for that matter)—a model that some historians rely on to dispute the idea that the North and South differed in reality. What such attempts at quantification ignore is the way people interpreted their reality. Free labor spokesmen like Olmsted argued that allowing any number of slave-owners and slaves into the free territories would inevitably debase free labor, just as he believed that slavery had debased the entirety of Southern culture, not just those who owned slaves. For Olmsted, as for many white Northern men who supported the Republicans, an opposition to slavery's expansion was fully compatible with an intense racism, notes Eric Foner, *Free Soil, Free Labor, Free Men: The Ideology of the Republican Party Before the Civil War* (London: Oxford University Press, 1970), chap. 2. It was commonplace for both antebellum Northerners and Southerners to assert that the two regions were culturally incompatible. On such perceptions and the realities that underlay them, see also James M. McPherson, "Antebellum Southern Exceptionalism: A New Look at An Old Question," *Civil War History* 29, no. 3 (2004): 230–44.

45. Frederick Law Olmsted, *The Cotton Kingdom; A Traveller's Observations on Cotton and Slavery in the American Slave States*, ed. Arthur M. Schlesinger (New York: Knopf, 1953), 17–19, 21–22, 160–63.

46. Karen Halttunen, *Confidence Men and Painted Women: A Study of Middle-Class Culture in America, 1830–1870* (New Haven: Yale University Press, 1982), chap. 1.

47. On the physical manifestations of emotion, see John F. Kasson, *Rudeness and Civility: Manners in Nineteenth-Century Urban America* (New York: Hill and Wang, 1990), 98, and John D. Davies, *Phrenology: Fad and Science; A Nineteenth-Century American Crusade* (1955; Hamden, Conn.: Archon Books, 1971). On political identities, see Phillip Shaw Paludan, *"A People's Contest": The Union and Civil War, 1861–1865* (New York: Harper and Row, 1988), 12–13, and Reid Mitchell, *The Vacant Chair: The Northern Soldier Leaves Home* (New York: Oxford University Press, 1993), chap. 2

48. This is not to argue that large numbers of Northerners did not view the Republican-controlled government as a newly intrusive and powerful agent that could directly affect their lives, as demonstrated by Iver Bernstein, *The New York City Draft Riots: Their Significance for American Society and Politics in the Age of the Civil War* (New York: Oxford University Press, 1990), merely that they did not view such changes as a result of emotional manipulation.

49. Melinda Lawson, *Patriot Fires: Forging a New American Nationalism in the Civil War North* (Lawrence: University Press of Kansas, 2002).

50. Thomas E. Rodgers, "Billy Yank and G.I. Joe: An Exploratory Essay on the Sociopolitical Dimensions of Soldier Motivation," *Journal of Military History* 69 (January 2005): 93–121; Mitchell, *The Vacant Chair*, 43–52.

51. Rodgers, "Billy Yank and G.I. Joe," 113, 114–19.

52. The free-labor ideology embraced by Northern Republicans reflected this belief. According to its spokesmen, a free-labor system provided all workers with the possibility of social advancement. Anyone who fell behind, as Lincoln often asserted, need look no further than his own weak will or faulty character. Foner, *Free Soil, Free Labor*, chap. 1. On Victorian conceptions of manly character, see also Anthony Rotundo, *American Manhood: Transformations of Masculinity from the Revolution to the Modern Era* (New York: Basic Books 1993), 10–30.

53. Peter N. Stearns, "Stages of Consumption: Recent Work on the Issues of Periodization," *Journal of Modern History* 69, no. 1 (March 1997): 102–17, surveys the extensive literature on the growth of consumer culture in Western societies, as well as mapping out differences between the early phases of consumer culture dating back to the seventeenth century, and the development of modern consumerism around the turn of the twentieth century. On the creation of new identities and desires facilitated by the rise of consumer capitalism, see Nan Enstad, *Ladies of Labor, Girls of Adventure: Working Women, Popular Culture, and Labor Politics at the Turn of the Twentieth Century* (New York: Columbia University Press, 1999); William Leach, *Land of Desire: Merchants, Power and the Rise of a New American Culture* (New York: Pantheon Books, 1993); and Kathy Peiss, *Cheap Amusements: Working Women and Leisure in Turn-of-the Century New York* (Philadelphia: Temple University Press, 1986). On the evolution of advertising, see Jackson Lears, *Fables of Abundance: A Cultural History of Advertising in America* (New York: Basic Books, 1994).

54. T. J. Jackson Lears, "From Salvation to Self-Realization: Advertising and the Therapeutic Roots of the Consumer Culture, 1880–1930," in *The Culture of Consumption: Critical Essays in American History, 1880–1980*, ed. Richard Wightman Fox and T.J. Jackson Lears (New York: Pantheon Books, 1983), 1–38.

55. Some of the recent literature on Civil War soldiers tends in this direction. After concluding that many "willingly made extraordinary sacrifices, even of life itself, for the principles they perceived to be at stake in the war," for instance, McPherson, *For Cause and Comrades*, 178, ends by asking whether "Americans today would be willing to make similar sacrifices."

56. Stansell, *City of Women*, 73; Karen Sanchez-Eppler, "Bodily Bonds: The Intersecting Rhetorics of Feminism and Abolition," *Representations* 24 (Fall 1988): 28–59. Likewise, Laura Wexler, "Tender Violence: Literary Eavesdropping, Domestic Fiction, and Educational Reform," in *The Culture of Sentiment: Race, Gender, and Sentimentality in Nineteenth-Century America*, ed. Shirley Samuels (New York: Oxford University Press, 1992), 9–38, focuses on the way sentimental sympathy facilitated cultural assimilationist practices directed at freed slaves and Indians, a point reinforced by Susan M. Ryan, *The Grammar of Good Intentions: Race and the Antebellum Culture of Benevolence* (Ithaca, N.Y.: Cornell University Press, 2003).

57. Merish, *Sentimental Materialism*, 4.

58. Paludan, *"A People's Contest,"* chap. 8. Wartime mobilization also necessitated a close partnership between the Republican administration and private enterprise in the construction of new railroads or the manufacture of supplies. Federal legislation benefiting private corporations rather than consumers, such as the provision of free land to railroad companies or a taxation system heavily weighted toward excise taxes on consumer goods, was likewise obscured by wartime patriotism. Given the way a shared patriotic agenda temporarily aligned the goals of government and private enterprise during the war, it was all too easy to avoid thinking about the "possibility that private gain was not necessarily public benefit," Paludan notes (137).

59. Fanny Nudelman, *John Brown's Body: Slavery, Violence, and the Culture of War* (Chapel Hill: University of North Carolina Press, 2004).

60. The politics of sentimentalism has been subject to extensive debate. Older works, such as Herbert Ross Brown, *The Sentimental Novel in America, 1789–1860* (Durham, N.C.: Duke University Press, 1940); or E. Douglas Branch, *The Sentimental Years, 1836–1860* (New York: D. Appleton-Century, 1934), were largely dismissive, treating sentimental sympathy as maudlin and politically ineffective. Challenges to this perspective, including Jane P. Tompkins, *Sensational Designs: The Cultural Work of American Fiction, 1790–1860* (New York: Oxford University Press, 1985), Cathy N. Davidson, *Revolution and the Word: The Rise of the Novel in America* (New York: Oxford University Press, 1986); and Nina Baym, *American Women Writers and the Work of History, 1790–1860* (New Brunswick, N.J.: Rutgers University Press, 1995), sought instead to take sentimentalism seriously as a affirmation of (usually white) female power and agency, and a subversion of the division between public and private life. Subsequent studies, such as those noted in note 56 above, have challenged this revisionist literature. My own perspective aligns with those who refuse to judge sentimentalism as wholly "good" or "bad," in either a literary or political sense—that is, as evidence of artistic failure or false-consciousness. This is not an evasion but an acknowledgment that any discourse is open to multiple interpretations and can generate a range of effects. The political impact of sentimental sympathy has, in fact, been demonstrably contradictory. As Clark, "Sacred Rights of the Weak," 492–93, notes, for example, the Constitution and Bill of Rights failed to offer protection from physical coercion to weak parties in status relationships. Arguments positing equality in suffering gradually, albeit imperfectly, inscribed into law the idea that freedom from physical pain was a fundamental human right. "The spare liberal notion of bodily autonomy made its way into the courts cloaked in sentimental garb," she argues. Yet this shift was double-edged. Proliferating images of slaves' suffering may have set African Americans apart as a group, constituting rather than erasing difference from white sympathizers. Moreover, an emphasis on freedom from pain, Clark notes, "provided a poor stand-in for a more comprehensive vision of social and economic justice: private wrongs beget private remedies." For further discussion of sentimentalism's multiple effects, see Lauren Berlant, "Poor Eliza," *American Literature* 70, no. 3 (Sept. 1998): 635–68; and Jeffrey Steele, "The Gender and Racial Politics of Mourning in Antebellum America," in *An Emotional History of*

the United States, ed. Peter N. Stearns and Jan Lewis (New York: New York University Press, 1998), 91–106.

CHAPTER TWO

1. Henry I. Bowditch Papers, Massachusetts Historical Society, Boston. The first of these memorials is an illuminated manuscript, approximately a thousand pages in length, containing material extracted from seven additional volumes that Bowditch and other family members worked on between 1863 and 1877. It is hereafter cited as "Memorial Book" to distinguish it from the manuscript volumes containing original material, henceforth referred to as MD (for "Manuscript Documents"), vols. 1–7. Of these volumes, the first holds original copies of correspondence sent by and to Nathaniel from the 1850s up until the time of his death. Material relating to the cavalry battle in which he died, along with testimonials from his officers, forms the second volume, while a third contains hundreds of condolence letters. The fourth consists of Henry Bowditch's wartime journals and material relating to his volunteer work. The fifth and sixth are filled, respectively, with wartime poems, song lyrics, and miscellaneous writings (titled "Waifs"), and with stories of several hundred Massachusetts soldiers, almost all of them officers, who died in the war (titled "Brief Memoranda of Our Martyr Soldiers"). This last-mentioned volume is accompanied by two further albums containing approximately 100 *carte de visites* of the men memorialized therein. Henry Bowditch completed the seventh memorial in 1876, upon the death of Katherine Day Putnam, Nathaniel's wartime fiancée, who is the subject of this volume. In addition, Bowditch extracted material for a short biography of his son, fifty copies of which he had privately printed for distribution among friends and relatives. *Memorial* [of Nathaniel Ingersoll Bowditch] (Boston: privately printed by John Wilson and Son, 1865). The Bowditchs housed these volumes in a custom-made memorial cabinet, described below. Adding to this private collection, family friends commissioned stained-glass memorial windows in Bowditch's memory in two separate Boston churches.

2. Bowditch used these words in a "Memorial Cabinet Catalogue," created to describe the contents of the memorial cabinet. See also a twenty-six-page "Dedicatory Epistle to the Descendants of Our Family in the Twentieth Century," in the preface to MD 1.

3. *Harper's Weekly*, the leading Northern magazine in this period, regularly published officers' biographies or accounts of battle, for instance, using the kind of standard depictions of heroism described here. Likewise, Northern newspapers on a daily basis offered stories of battles and sketches of heroic officers relying on the same conventions. Gerald F. Linderman, *Embattled Courage: The Experience of Combat in the American Civil War* (New York: Free Press, 1987), suggests that the idea of courage as heroic action undertaken without fear, particularly represented by officers riding ahead of their men into battle, markedly diminished by the last two years of war as men came to understand the follies of exposing themselves to danger. If he had surveyed newspapers, compilations of military biographies, or officers' commendations of their men published in *The War of the Rebellion, A Compilation of the Official Records of Union and Confederate Armies*, 128

vols. (Washington, D.C., 1880–1901) (hereafter *Official Records*), however, he would have found no such change. In reality, soldiers may have come to accept that adopting defensive cover was no cause for shame, but the officer who "coolly" exposed himself to enemy fire remained the beau ideal of heroism, as popular in the war's last year as in its first. To cite just two examples picked at random from the *Philadelphia Inquirer*, see the obituary of "General Alexander Hays at Gettysburg," May 19, 1864, killed while riding "at the head of his column, cheering and sustaining it against an overwhelming force of the enemy," or the report of "The First Battle Before Atlanta," July 28, 1864, depicting Hooker "in the hottest of the battle, always hailed by enthusiastic cheers, and by the very magnetism of his personal presence infusing such a spirit into his soldiers."

4. James M. McPherson, *Battle Cry of Freedom: The Civil War Era* (New York: Oxford University Press, 1988), 476, 330, notes the problems officers had in coordinating enormous armies in the preradio era—a feat accomplished with bugle calls, flags, and officers' personal leadership in the field. In sharp distinction to twentieth-century warfare, he notes: "In both armies the proportion of officers killed in action was about 15 percent higher than the proportion of enlisted men killed." Civil War generals suffered even higher combat casualties, having a 50 percent greater chance of being killed than a private.

5. Evidence of such conventions abound in MD 6, for instance.

6. Rev. James Freeman Clarke to Henry I. Bowditch, March 23, 1863, MD 2.

7. Mark Rothenberg, "Bowditch, Nathaniel (1773–1838)," in *American National Biography*, ed. John A. Garraty and Mark C. Carnes, 24 vols. (New York: Oxford University Press, 1999), 3:270–72; *Memorial*, 5. Bowditch discusses these doubts in a preface written on January 23, 1870, in Memorial Book.

8. Henry Ingersoll Bowditch (1808–92) attended Harvard Medical School, earning an M.D. in 1832 before traveling to Paris to continue his training. Warmly welcomed among scientific circles on the Continent as a result of his father's wide fame, he spent the majority of his time studying under leading French physician Pierre Charles Alexander Louis, who was then pioneering a new mode of clinical practice involving correlating the results of auscultation, bedside observation, and autopsy findings using his own statistical method. After his first year under Louis' mentorship, Bowditch was joined by another Bostonian, Oliver Wendell Holmes (1809–94). Both men returned to their native state to propagate Louis' ideas, leading the call for the adoption of empiricist methods. A prolific medical writer, Bowditch published numerous medical textbooks. By the time his son Nathaniel was entering his twenties, Henry had also helped to found the American Medical Association and taken up a post as a professor of clinical medicine at Harvard. John Harley Warner, "Bowditch, Henry Ingersoll," in *American National Biography*, ed. Garraty and Carnes, 3:269–70.

9. *Memorial*, 3. The Lawrence School was established in the mid-1840s and was closely allied to, and later merged with, Harvard University. Louis Menand's *The Metaphysical Club*, 102–12, details the school's teaching methods. A letter from Olivia Bowditch dated August 26, 1860 (MD 1), implies that the decision to send Nathaniel to Lawrence rested on a belief that he was not "fit" for a Harvard education.

10. Henry Bowditch, March 9 and April 11, 1859. Further injunctions along the same lines can be found in Henry Bowditch, February 27, 1860; Livy Bowditch, April 1, April 16, and May 20, 1859; and Olivia Bowditch, April 20 and August 26, 1860, MD 1. Nathaniel's sister, Olivia Yardley Bowditch, was named after their mother. I have used her nickname, Livy, to distinguish her letters.

11. Henry Bowditch to Charles W. Eliot, October 14, 1859, and August 22, 1860, MD 1.

12. Fredrickson (*Inner Civil War*, chap. 11) was one of the first scholars to rely on Adams as representative of a shift in soldiers' attitudes toward war. Soldiers like Adams, he argues, repudiated idealistic accounts of heroism, duty, and patriotism for a celebration of the "strenuous life" of soldiering, one revolving around values such as endurance, tenacity, and pragmatism.

13. Worthington Chauncey Ford, ed., *A Cycle of Adams Letters, 1861–1862*, 2 vols. (Boston: Houghton Mifflin, 1920). Quote from 1:157.

14. McPherson, *For Cause and Comrades*, 100 and passim. On the centrality of politics and religion to the lives of mid-nineteenth-century Northern men more broadly, see Woodworth, *While God Is Marching On*; Mitchell, *The Vacant Chair*, chap. 2; and Paludan, *"A People's Contest,"* 12–13.

15. Ryan, *Cradle of the Middle Class*, 161.

16. Stanton P. Allen, *Down in Dixie: Life in a Cavalry Regiment in the War Days* (Boston: D. Lothrop Company, 1893), 105, recalls one such sendoff given to his Massachusetts Cavalry Regiment.

17. On working-class urban men articulating a standard of bravery that sharply differed from that held by most in the Northern middle classes, see Gorn, *The Manly Art*, 107.

18. Henry Bowditch, January 24, 1862, MD 1 (emphasis in original).

19. Henry Bowditch, December 27, 1861, and January 14, 1862, MD 1 (emphasis in original).

20. Henry Bowditch, January 14, 1862, and Olivia Yardley Bowditch, February 18, 1862, MD 1.

21. This was the first major conflict in which the consequences of battles were almost immediately registered and experienced on the home front, drawing civilians into events as they occurred. To get a sense of just how novel this shift was, Peck, *War, the Army and Victorian Literature*, chap. 1, notes that in the previous decade when the British were fighting in the Crimea, it still took more than three weeks for the public to be made aware of the disastrous charge of the Light Brigade.

22. Olivia Yardley Bowditch, January 31, 1862, MD 1.

23. Ibid.; Lucy Bowditch, January 25, 1863, and Annie M. Haughton, March 15 [1863], MD 1.

24. According to historian Stephen Starr, in *The Union Cavalry in the Civil War*, 2 vols. (Baton Rouge: Louisiana University Press, 1979), 1:66, 109, 211, Union commanders initially gave little thought to the cavalry's role in the war. Busy organizing vast armies of infantry, most were unenthusiastic about the prospect of mounted regiments

because they were costly to equip, of untried strategic value in the field, and they raised the uncomfortable prospect of pitting Southerners renowned for their horsemanship against the North's decidedly less-experienced urbanites and farm boys. On the early organization and reorganization of cavalry regiments, see also 1:235–38.

25. Ibid., 1:247. After weeks of drilling in Maryland, Nathaniel's battalion was dispatched to join General Hunter's Expeditionary Corps, which had taken control of Beaufort, South Carolina, the sea islands off the coast, together with the forts at Hilton Head. Here they remained in camp until August 1862. That month, Nathaniel's battalion was ordered to Virginia and attached to the Army of the Potomac, where he came close enough to hear the Battle of Antietam in September, participating in his first skirmish at Aquia Creek the same month. But no orders came to engage the enemy. By year's end, the regiment was thoroughly demoralized. Men were writing dejected letters home complaining of boredom, squalor, and lack of supplies, and a near mutiny was set to break out among some of the regimental officers, according to Benjamin W. Crowninshield, *A History of the First Regiment of Massachusetts Cavalry Volunteers* (Boston: Houghton Mifflin, 1891), chaps. 3–4, and Bliss Perry, ed., *Life and Letters of Henry Lee Higginson* (Boston: Atlantic Monthly Press, 1921), 175. Nathaniel saw his enemies once in a brief encounter, but he was not ordered into battle until May 17 the following year.

26. Nathaniel Bowditch, May 28, 1862, MD 1; McPherson, *For Cause and Comrades*, 28, 100.

27. For example, "Speech to the One Hundred Sixty-Fourth Ohio Regiment," August 18, 1864, in *Collected Works of Abraham Lincoln*, ed. Roy P. Basler, 8 vols. (New Brunswick, N.J.: Rutgers University Press, 1953–55), 7:504–5.

28. George B. Forgie, *Patricide in the House Divided: A Psychological Interpretation of Lincoln and His Age* (New York: W. W. Norton, 1979), chap. 6; preface to MD 1.

29. Olivia Yardley Bowditch, June 16, 1862, MD 1.

30. In relation to other soldiers, Nathaniel probably lacked self-confidence and assertiveness and thus needed more homefront prodding than many. Certainly his family was more patriotic than some. To a greater or lesser degree, however, most men's political commitments in this period were not bloodless ideas but convictions emerging out of and shaped by the daily exchanges that went on not only between comrades but also among friends and families and those who represented them at war. On this point, see Judith Lee Hallock, "The Role of the Community in Civil War Desertion," *Civil War History* 29 (1983): 123–34, who suggests that desertion was far more likely among soldiers from "less cohesive communities," that is, those that had high rates of population turnover and provided low levels of support to soldiers and their families. See also Joan E. Cashin, "Deserters, Civilians, and Draft Resistance in the North," in *The War Was You and Me: Civilians in the American Civil War*, ed. Joan E. Cashin (Princeton, N.J.: Princeton University Press, 2002), 262–85.

31. Quoted in *Memorial*, 8. Bowditch relates this story in several places, including one letter written to an old classmate, George S. Hilliard, March 28, 1863, MD 3.

32. Nathaniel Bowditch, March 20, 1862, MD 2.

33. Henry Bowditch journals, [April 4 or 5, 1862], MD 4. It appears likely that a page between entries dated April 4 and April 6 has been torn out.

34. Henry Bowditch journals, undated entry [April 5, 1862], MD 4. During his stay at Hilton Head, Bowditch specifically addressed his journal entries to his wife and forwarded them back to her, as the entry for April 7, 1862, makes clear.

35. Bowditch also sent a follow-up note using the same words, dated April 5, 1862, MD 4. They had their desired effect. The following day, Nathaniel sent a note to his mother, apologizing for his previous letters written in a "blue mood." MD 2.

36. Fredrickson, *Inner Civil War*, chaps. 6–7.

37. Henry Bowditch journals, April 7, 1862, MD 4.

38. Noted in "Memorial Cabinet Catalogue."

39. Nathaniel Bowditch, June 1 and October 27, 1862. See also letters sent to various family members dated November 3, December 7, 14, and 19, 1862, and January 16 and 19, 1863, MD 2. His regiment was initially commanded by Colonel Robert Williams, a former instructor of cavalry at West Point. His next in command was Lieutenant-Colonel Horace Binney Sargent, a Harvard graduate. These were the two officers that Bowditch complained of in his letters. Sargent replaced Williams as colonel when the latter resigned near the end of 1862. Most of the officers who initially commanded the battalions comprising this regiment were fellow Harvard alumni, used to getting their own way. Before the regiment even left for the South, these men had already begun sending home complaints about the quality of their commanders. According to Crowninshield (*History of the First Regiment of Massachusetts Cavalry*, 42–46), when the governor appointed Williams and Sargent, his decision "astonished and dissatisfied" the company officers, who believed field commanders would be chosen from among their number. Discontent spread, and "a mutiny broke out, the effects of which were never wholly eradicated." Attempting to quell the unrest, Williams wounded one private and dismissed numerous officers, with Boston newspapers following the story at length. First Lieutenant Charles Francis Adams was one regimental officer who had little respect for either Williams or Sargent. See Ford, *A Cycle of Adams Letters*, 97, and Charles Francis Adams, *An Autobiography* (Boston: Houghton Mifflin, 1916), 138. On similar discontent among other officers in the regiment, see Perry, *Life and Letters of Henry Lee Higginson*, 158.

40. Olivia Bowditch, January 7 and February 18, 1862, MD 1. Initially, both parents were staunch supporters of the regiment's colonel, leading to debates and disputes with neighbors, as Olivia Bowditch described in letters dated April 9 and 16, 1862.

41. Robert W. Frost and Nancy D. Frost, eds., *Picket Pins and Sabers: The Civil War Letters of John Burden Weston* (Ashland, Ky.: Economy Printers, 1971), 36, provides one perspective from an enlisted man in the First Massachusetts Cavalry. Weston, a former carriage-maker, wrote home on March 11, 1863, complaining bitterly about his officers, believing them "the meanest" in any regiment and wishing to see half of them "tied up by the thumbs by a detail of niggers" and starved "untill every bone in their old carcusses are broken in inch pieces."

42. Olivia Bowditch, October 24, 1862, MD 1. Making it clear that the rumor mill

was churning away in Boston, she wrote again on January 18 to ask: "Is it true that such things occur around you as officers stabbing their men, and that for very trivial offences the men suffer most awful punishments such as hanging by their thumbs till nearly dead, having their heads shaved at this inclement season & [being] deprived of their *pay!!*" A week later, on January 25, she wrote expressing a wish to get "50 privates" to tell her what they really felt.

43. Henry I. Bowditch, "The Ambulance System," *Medical and Surgical Reporter*, October 11, 1862, 50, reprinted from *Boston Medical and Surgical Journal*, October 9, 1862. The Quartermaster's Department responded to Bowditch's assertions on October 30, 1862, *Official Records*, series 3, vol. 2, pt. 1, 697–703. Edward Bowditch to "Dear Mother and Livy," October 15, 1862, MD 5, described accompanying his father on trips to visit the president and General McClellan to discuss his proposals. After his son's death, Bowditch published *A Brief Plea for an Ambulance System for the Army of the United States, as Drawn from the Extra Sufferings of the Late Lieut. Bowditch and a Wounded Comrade* (Boston: Ticknor and Fields, 1863). Calls for the reform of the ambulance system were already widespread by this time, as noted in "The Ambulance System," *Medical and Surgical Reporter*, October 11, 1862.

44. Henry Bowditch, March 19, 1863, MD 2.

45. Ibid.; Henry Bowditch, March 21, 1863, MD 2.

46. On this point, see for example, Nina Silber, *Daughters of the Union: Northern Women Fight the Civil War* (Cambridge: Harvard University Press, 2005); Lynde Cullen Sizer, *The Political Work of Northern Women Writers and the Civil War, 1850–1872* (Chapel Hill: University of North Carolina Press, 2000); Judith Ann Giesberg, *Civil War Sisterhood: The U.S. Sanitary Commission and Women's Politics in Transition* (Boston: Northeastern University Press, 2000); Jeanie Attie, *Patriotic Toil: Northern Women and the American Civil War* (Ithaca, N.Y.: Cornell University Press, 1998); Elizabeth D. Leonard, *Yankee Women: Gender Battles in the Civil War* (New York: W. W. Norton, 1994); and Lori D. Ginzberg, *Women and the Work of Benevolence: Morality, Politics, and Class in the Nineteenth-Century United States* (New Haven: Yale University Press, 1990).

47. P.A.M. Taylor, ed., *More Than Common Powers of Perception: The Diary of Elizabeth Rogers Mason Cabot* (Boston: Beacon Press, 1991), entry dated October 4, 1862, p. 234; Olivia Bowditch, June 10, 1862, MD 1.

48. Olivia Yardley Bowditch to Mrs. William Henry Thayer, May 3, 1863, cited in Vincent Yardley Bowditch, *Life and Correspondence of Henry Ingersoll Bowditch*, 2 vols. (Boston: Houghton Mifflin, 1902), 2:20.

49. Mary R. Hudson to "Livy my dear child," March 10, 1863; Mrs. A. G. Walley to Olivia Bowditch, undated; Fairy F. Fox to Livy Bowditch, March 21, 1863: all in MD 3.

50. Henry Bowditch to "Darling," March 21, 1863, MD 2.

51. See, for example, Henry Pickering Bowditch to Henry Bowditch, April 12, 1863; George H. Wheeler to Henry Bowditch, May 4, 1863, MD 2.

52. Drew Gilpin Faust, "The Civil War Soldier and the Art of Dying," *Journal of Southern History* 67 (February 2001): 63–90.

53. Graham Dawson, *Soldier Heroes: British Adventure, Empire and the Imagining of Masculinities* (London: Routledge, 1994), 22–23.

54. Alfred Tennyson's "The Charge of the Light Brigade" was one of the most widely admired war poems of the 1850s, according to Peck, *War, the Army and Victorian Literature*, 19. Frank Luther Mott, in *Golden Multitudes: The Story of Best Sellers in the United States* (New York: Macmillan, 1947), 105–6, confirms Tennyson's enormous popularity among all classes of Americans in this period. As Mott also notes (65–70), Walter Scott claimed an equally diverse but far larger readership for his novels, with *Ivanhoe* (1819) being by far the best loved. It is likely that Scott's broad appeal rested on the diverse standards of heroism that his male characters allowed readers to embrace vicariously. In *Ivanhoe*, readers could identify with the high-minded chivalry and lofty standards of honor and gallantry represented by the novel's main character, or they might relate to the simpler virtues of untitled men such as Friar Tuck or Robin Hood, who were less splendidly arrayed, paternalistic, and full of lofty idealism, but equally brave and a good deal more democratic, freewheeling, and independent. Stories of Revolutionary heroes were just as compelling for antebellum readers, as noted by Forgie, *Patricide in the House Divided*, 33–57, and Mott, *Golden Multitudes*, 96.

55. Joseph H. Clark to Olivia Bowditch, March 27, 1863, MD 2.

56. Similar descriptions of idealized death scenes written by soldiers can be found in MD 3 and 6.

57. Dawson, *Soldier Heroes*, 61–64; Mark Girouard, *The Return to Camelot: Chivalry and the English Gentleman* (New Haven: Yale University Press, 1981), 35–36, 132–36, examines chivalry's appeal among middle-class Britons in the 1850s, suggesting that many embraced the idealism and deferential social relations of chivalric codes out of concern that their class had abandoned social stewardship for the self-interested pursuit of wealth, generating social unrest and class division.

58. Dawson, *Soldier Heroes*, 83.

59. MD 6.

60. On such prewar anxieties, see the prologue to Paludan, *"A People's Contest."*

61. Fredrickson, *Inner Civil War*, 100. Rose, *Victorian America and the Civil War*, 1–16, and chap. 1, offers a different interpretation. Unlike those who point to widespread religious fervor in the middle decades of the century, she notes that some middle-class Americans around this time experienced a "religious crisis." Religion, for such people, had lost much of the spontaneity and influence it had had in their youths, for it now competed with their many secular pursuits—particularly, satisfying careers, new forms of leisure, romantic attachments, and political allegiances. Drawing from a declension narrative, represented, for instance, in Ann Douglas's *The Feminization of American Culture* (New York: Knopf, 1977), Rose tends to interpret the increased emotionality and waning interest in doctrinal dispute or intellectual religious discussion among nineteenth-century Protestants as a loss rigor and faith—an argument now widely disputed. Yet her work is still useful for interpreting religiosity among middle-class Northerners during the Civil War. They clearly did not abandon their religious practices, yet in their romantic striving for personal fulfillment and material gain they "dimly sensed

the increasing marginality of religion in the modern world," she argues (38). The war temporarily resolved this religious crisis, offering the realization of personal glory, ambition, and intense experience within a framework of high-minded devotion to the commonweal. Her account thus acknowledges the sometimes inconsistent or ambivalent religiosity of middle-class civilians that is slighted in Fredrickson's account. As she suggests, many among the middle class wholeheartedly embraced religious interpretations of the war, yet the conflict simultaneously revealed the importance of secular political, military, or bureaucratic means of resolving social disputes.

62. *Memorial*, t.p., verso.

63. Henry Bowditch to Dr. J. N. Borland, March 23, 1863, MD 3.

64. Henry Bowditch to Dr. De Wolf, March 23 and 24, 1863, and George S. Hilliard, March 28, 1863 (emphasis in original). A note in Bowditch's hand, dated September 1864, states that both men were "copperheads" and he hoped "to do something towards their conversion" (MD 3).

65. Edward Everett to Henry Bowditch, March 27, 1863, MD 3.

66. Both in camp and back in Boston, it seems, there was much talk of lives needlessly sacrificed. One letter, written by an officer in the First Massachusetts, revealed his concern that Bowditch's death might be interpreted in such a light. He told his father: "The poor fellow has lost his life, it is true, but in the best cause . . . & in a War like this, not a single life is *fruitlessly thrown away* & it pains me heartily to hear such things said, or to see them written. Any life lost in a War waged for such magnificent results as this War aims at, is *well laid down*, not fruitlessly thrown away." H. Pelham Curtis to "Dear Father," March 18, 1863, attached in an undated note from Margaret S. Curtis to "My dear Mrs. Bowditch," MD 2.

67. Henry Bowditch to George S. Hillard, March 28, 1863, MD 3; Nathaniel Bowditch to Olivia Yardley Bowditch, September 7, 1863, MD 2; Nathaniel Bowditch, October 2, 1862, MD 2. Henry Bowditch made inquiries about this incident after his son's death, which came to the attention of the regiment's colonel. Shortly after he left for Boston, this officer wrote to explain: "I was much pained by being told that Nat was stimulated to meet his fate, by the sting of censure, which he received from *me*." Denying that he had delivered any rebuke six months earlier, he traced the report back "to an intriguing and turbulent spirit in the Regiment" which, he claimed, had exposed him to "gross and slanderous *falsehoods*." Horace B. Sargent to Henry Ingersoll Bowditch, March 22, 1863, MD 2.

68. MD 7.

69. "Memorial Cabinet Catalogue."

CHAPTER THREE

1. "John Lorenze," *The Independent* (New York), March 27, 1862, 6.

2. George Mosse, *Fallen Soldiers: Reshaping the Memory of the World Wars* (New York: Oxford University Press, 1990), 9–10. See also Yuval Noah Harari, *The Ultimate Experience: Battlefield Revelations and the Making of Modern War Culture, 1450–2000* (New York: Palgrave Macmillan, 2008).

3. Mosse, *Fallen Soldiers*, 16–18. See also David Bell, *The First Total War: Napoleon's Europe and the Birth of Warfare as We Know It* (Boston: Houghton Mifflin Harcourt, 2007); and Adam Zamoyski, *Holy Madness: Romantics, Patriots and Revolutionaries, 1776–1871* (London: Phoenix Press, 1999).

4. One recent exception is Fahs, *Imagined Civil War*.

5. John Resch, *Suffering Soldiers: Revolutionary War Veterans, Moral Sentiment, and Political Culture in the Early Republic* (Amherst: University of Massachusetts Press, 1999), 2–5, chap. 3, notes that Valley Forge did not become a byword for the heroic suffering of ordinary soldiers until after the turn of the nineteenth century, when revisionist historians (often Federalists engaged in partisan battles over the need for increased defense spending) began depicting Continental Army soldiers as the real heroes of the Revolution. Prior to that time, he argues, Washington's troops were more likely to be feared as a potentially dangerous rabble than admired for their heroic fortitude, with patriots celebrating their victory as the triumph of a hardy, self-sacrificing citizenry, not a force of regular soldiers. The lack of immediate interest in the sufferings of troops who enlisted during the Revolution is evidenced by the fact that of the roughly 3,000 men who died at Valley Forge, the grave of only one (an officer) was marked, according to Thomas W. Laqueur's "Memory and Naming in the Great War," in *Commemorations: The Politics of National Identity*, ed. John R. Gillis (Princeton, N.J.: Princeton University Press, 1994), 158. Until well into the nineteenth century, there was no move to erect memorials to regular soldiers who fought in the Revolution, or to preserve areas such as Valley Forge.

6. On antimilitarism in the post-Revolutionary era, see Marcus Cunliffe, *Soldiers and Civilians: The Martial Spirit in America, 1775–1865* (London: Eyre and Spottiswoode, 1968), chap. 4. The low public esteem for regulars prior to the Civil War also rested on the fact that most enlistees were poor or foreign-born. As Cunliffe notes, these sentiments did not translate into contempt for all things military, as evidenced by the election of numerous presidents with military backgrounds, or by the continued (if controversial) funding for military academies such as West Point. But until the Civil War, public praise and interest concentrated almost solely on military elites rather than their men.

7. During the Mexican-American War, stories identifying enlistees and volunteers by name and praising their admirable suffering did not regularly appear in American newspapers. Nor did the state show much interest in memorializing their suffering. According to John R. Neff, in *Honoring the Civil War Dead: Commemoration and the Problem of Reconciliation* (Lawrence: University Press of Kansas, 2005), 28, Congress established an American cemetery in Mexico City in 1850, but only slightly more than 5 percent of all casualties were named and re-interred in the new burial grounds. Yet I have come across one exception to this general disinterest in the suffering of ordinary servicemen. From the 1820s onward, a great deal of public attention concentrated on American sailors (not coincidentally, far more likely to be young and native-born). At this time, middle-class benevolent workers in port cities began organizing societies aimed at uplifting sailors' moral characters and ministering to their widows and orphans, imitating similar British efforts, as described by T. Phillips in "Bethel Flag," *The Religious Intelligencer*, June 2, 1821, 12, or "Anniversary of the American Seamen's Friend Society,"

National Era, May 19, 1853, 79. In the decades before the Civil War, a massive number of newspaper and magazine columns catalogued the unenviable lot of young seamen, generally picturing them as harshly treated, pitiable figures. Quite possibly, this coverage influenced later representations of soldiers and sailors, although more work in this area remains to be done.

8. Approximately four British regulars died from disease in the Crimean War for every one killed in battle. Compared to previous conflicts, this ratio of disease fatalities to battlefield deaths was not unusual (the comparable ratio for British forces fighting in the Napoleonic wars earlier in the century being twice as high). Public shock over disease rates in the Crimea resulted not only from newspaper reportage on the subject, but also from a new nineteenth-century interest in the collection of statistics and demographic data more generally. As one contemporary American observer noted, states had previously either failed to collect and record casualty figures, or declined to publicize their findings. Edward S. Dunster, "The Comparative Mortality in Armies from Wounds and Disease," in *Contributions Relating to the Causation and Prevention of Disease, and to Camp Diseases* (New York: Published for the U.S. Sanitary Commission by Hurd and Houghton, 1867), 170.

9. On the influence of war reporters and newspaper coverage in shaping public opinion in Britain, see Winfried Baumgart, *The Crimean War* (New York: Oxford, 2000), 15–16, 97, 141.

10. Ulrich Keller, *The Ultimate Spectacle: A Visual History of the Crimean War* (London: Gordon and Breach, 2001), chap. 5, describes stories in British press representing privates as ideal sufferers. Given the extent to which American editors filled their publications with material extracted from British sources, it seems likely that these tales made their way to the United States, although I have made no detailed examination the Northern press coverage of the Crimean war.

11. George Worthington Adams, *Doctors in Blue: The Medical History of the Union Army in the Civil War* (New York: Henry Schuman, 1952), 4–5.

12. "The Situation of the Wounded," *Cincinnati Daily Inquirer,* March 4, 1863, 1.

13. Adams, *Doctors in Blue,* 4–5. On wartime medical care, see also Jane E. Schultz, *Women at the Front: Hospital Workers in Civil War America* (Chapel Hill: University of North Carolina Press, 2004); Alfred J. Bollet, *Civil War Medicine: Challenges and Triumphs* (Tucson, Ariz.: Galen Press, 2002); Robert E. Denney, *Civil War Medicine: Care and Comfort of the Wounded* (New York: Sterling Publications, 1994); and Stuart Brooks, *Civil War Medicine* (Springfield, Ill.: Charles C. Thomas, 1966).

14. Schultz, *Women at the Front,* 21, 39–40, estimates that over 20,000 women worked in Union military hospitals as nurses, cooks, and laundresses.

15. Scholarship on Northern voluntarism includes Giesberg, *Civil War Sisterhood;* Attie, *Patriotic Toil;* Matthew Gallman, *Mastering Wartime: A Social History of Philadelphia During the Civil War* (New York: Cambridge University Press, 1990); Robert H. Bremner, *The Public Good: Philanthropy and Welfare in the Civil War Era* (New York: Knopf, 1980). As Barton C. Hacker, in "Women and Military Institutions in Early Modern Europe: A Reconnaissance," *Signs* 6, no. 4 (Summer 1981): 643–71, notes, it

was once commonplace for masses of women to accompany armies—in the capacity of prostitutes, sutlers, cooks, nurses, laundresses, and wives—often in numbers exceeding that of combatants. Only in the mid-nineteenth century, as armies began to assume control over nonmilitary support services, did army life become masculinized. In addition to this time-honored practice of civilians accompanying soldiers in auxiliary capacities, however, the Civil War also generated an unprecedented range of voluntary efforts directed at maintaining soldiers' health, well-being, and morale, examined in greater detail in the following chapter.

16. Mrs. A. H. [Jane Currie Blaikie] Hoge, *The Boys in Blue: or Heroes of the "Rank and File"* (New York: E. B. Treat and Co., 1867), 35–37; *Notes of Hospital Life from November, 1861, to August, 1863* (Philadelphia: J. B. Lippincott and Co., 1864), vi.

17. *Notes of Hospital Life.*

18. Hoge, *The Boys in Blue*, 40–41 (emphasis in original). Hoge broadcast this incident widely through her wartime lectures, for example, "Address Delivered by Mrs. Hoge of the North Western Sanitary Commission at a Meeting of Ladies, Held at Packer Institute, Brooklyn, L. I., March, 1865 in aid of the Great North Western Fair" (New York: Sanford, Harroun and Co., Steam Printing House, 1865); reprinted as no. 88 in *Documents of the U.S. Sanitary Commission* (hereafter *Documents*), 2 vols. (New York: n.p., 1866), 2:4–5.

19. G. Reynolds, "A Fortnight with the Sanitary," *Atlantic Monthly* 15 (1865): 243.

20. "Arrival of Wounded Soldiers on the 'State of Maine,'" *Philadelphia Inquirer,* June 5, 1862, 1; "Incidents of the Fort Donelson Fight," and "A Man of Nerve," in *Anecdotes, Poetry, and Incidents of the War: North and South, 1861–1865*, ed. Frank Moore (New York: Printed for the Subscribers, 1866), 82, 56. Newspapers also frequently published tales in which Union soldiers happily bantered about their wounds. See, for instance, "After the Battle," *Chicago Tribune*, May 25, 1864, 3; J.C.R., "The Dying Sergeant," *The Independent* (New York), May 19, 1864, 1; "Miscellaneous Incidents," *New York Herald*, June 20, 1864, 1; "Hooker's Army," *New York Herald*, June 9, 1863,1; and "Why the Soldier Was Happy," *Saturday Evening Post*, November 15, 1862, 2.

21. This extract was taken from letters originally sent to a women's aid society in Pennsylvania, which were later serialized in the *Saturday Evening Post,* June 4, 11, and 18, 1864, and then reprinted in Alfred J. Bloor, *Letters from the Army of the Potomac, Written During the Month of May, 1864 to Several of the Supply Correspondents of the U.S. Sanitary Commission* (Washington, D.C.: McGill and Witherow, 1864), 7.

22. Quoted in Frederick Law Olmsted, *Hospital Transports: A Memoir of the Embarkation of the Sick and Wounded from the Peninsula of Virginia in the Summer of 1862* (Boston: Ticknor and Fields, 1863), 115. The same letter appears in an *Atlantic Monthly* article, and is reprinted as "Scenes in Hospitals," *Sanitary Reporter* (Louisville, Ky.), March 15, 1864, 161–62.

23. All of the examples cited above come from published sources. But volunteers were just as likely to describe exemplary suffering in their private writings. To give just an instance, John Hancock Douglas (an associate secretary with the USSC) wrote to his brother about his visits to dozens of hospitals, describing a universal "cheerfulness"

among the inmates. Indicating that he did depict misery when he saw it, Douglas had earlier told his brother about the "sad & demoralized condition" of Union troops after the first battle of Bull Run. Douglas to his brother, October 25, 1861, John Hancock Douglas Collection, Library of Congress, Manuscript Division, Washington, D.C.

24. Quotes from Mrs. H. [Anna Morris Holstein], *Three Years in Field Hospitals of the Army of the Potomac* (Philadelphia: J. B. Lippincott and Co., 1867), 47; and Amanda A. Stearns, *The Lady Nurse of Ward E* (New York: Baker and Taylor Co., 1909), 249 (emphasis in original). The latter work consists of letters written during the war.

25. Mrs. Edmund A. Souder [nee Emily Bliss (Thatcher)], *Leaves from the Battle-field of Gettysburg* (Philadelphia: C. Sherman, Son and Co., 1864), 33–34, 48; Olmsted, *Hospital Transports*, 120; "Want of Patience of Wounded Rebels," *New York Herald*, June 6, 1862, 1.

26. Quoted in Elvira J. Powers, *Hospital Pencillings; Being a Diary While in Jefferson General Hospital, Jeffersonville, Ind., and Others at Nashville, Tennessee as Matron and Visitor* (Boston: Edward L. Mitchell, 1866), 18.

27. "Terrible Suffering of Wounded Volunteers Before Richmond," *Philadelphia Inquirer*, June 6, 1862, 8. On Northern images of Southern effeminacy, see Nina Silber, "Intemperate Men, Spiteful Women, and Jefferson Davis," in *Divided Houses: Gender and the Civil War*, eds. Catherine Clinton and Nina Silber (New York: Oxford University Press, 1992), 285.

28. Faust, "The Civil War Soldier and the Art of Dying," 63–90; and Lewis O. Saum, "Death in the Popular Mind of Pre-Civil War America," *American Quarterly* 26 (1974): 488; "Hospital Memories I," *Atlantic Monthly* 20 (August 1867): 155.

29. Laderman, *Sacred Remains*, 124.

30. Hoge, *Boys in Blue*, 53.

31. Woodworth, *While God Is Marching On*, chap. 6.

32. Grimsley, *The Hard Hand of War*, 9.

33. For example, William Howell Reed, *Hospital Life in the Army of the Potomac* (Boston: William V. Spencer, 1866), 191–92; or "Conversations with the Rebel Wounded," *Philadelphia Inquirer*, May 14, 1862, p. 4.

34. "The Dying Rebel," *United States Service Magazine* 4 (1865): 464.

35. Reed, *Hospital Life*, 170. To cite just a few examples from the *Philadelphia Inquirer*, "Rebel Barbarities in East Tennessee—Innocent Men Hanged—Children Shot and Women Tortured to Death," July 25, 1863, 2; and "A Repulsive Scene," February 8, 1864, 2, on Confederate soldiers mutilating the bodies of the Union dead.

36. Samuel B. Shepard to "Friend Thomas," July 20, 1862, quoted in *Yankee Correspondence: Civil War Letters Between New England Soldiers and the Home Front*, ed. Nina Silber and Mary Beth Sievens (Charlottesville: University Press of Virginia, 1996), 66, for instance, claimed to have entered a Southern home with "footstools made of the skulls, & pipes of the thigh bones, & purses made of the skins of Northern mechanics and farmers." "The Graves of Union Soldiers Desecrated," *Philadelphia Inquirer*, July 5, 1862, 1, told of Confederate women "playing merrily" on top of Union soldiers' remains. Such stories gained traction in light of investigations made by the Committee on the

Conduct of the War, which publicized allegations of Confederate atrocities, as noted by Bruce Tap in *Over Lincoln's Shoulder: The Committee on the Conduct of the War* (Lawrence: University Press of Kansas, 1998), chap. 2.

37. Quoted in Lemuel Moss, *Annals of the United States Christian Commission* (Philadelphia: J. B. Lippincott and Co., 1868), 474.

38. LeeAnne Whites, "The Civil War as a Crisis in Gender," in *Divided Houses*, ed. Clinton and Silber, 3–21;

39. Ira Berlin, ed., *Freedom: A Documentary History of Emancipation* (Cambridge: Cambridge University Press, 1982), 633, explores some of the reasons for the higher disease fatalities among black soldiers as compared to white ones.

40. Reynolds, "A Fortnight with the Sanitary," 243. General Fry shared this opinion, concluding, "the greater susceptibility of the colored man to disease arose from lack of heart, hope, and mental activity," and noting that this belief was "supported by the opinions of surgeons of boards of enrollment on the abstract question of the physical fitness of the colored men examined by them." Provost-Marshall-General's Bureau Report, March 17, 1866, to E. M. Stanton, Secretary of War, *Official Records*, ser. 3, vol. 5, pt. 1, p. 669.

41. Reed, *Hospital Life*, 121, 138–39, 51–53. I have only turned up one story depicting black sufferers as both cheerful and selflessly patriotic in the mainstream Northern press: "The Colored Troops in Charleston Harbor," *Philadelphia Inquirer*, July 29, 1863, 2. On the other hand, as Schultz (*Women at the Front*, 98) notes, it was not unheard of for white women working in Union hospitals to offer portraits of black soldiers' inspirational suffering. Esther Hill Hawks, a white female physician who ministered to black soldiers on the Sea Islands, for instance, described the heroism of wounded black soldiers from the 54th Massachusetts Infantry Regiment, noting, "The only thing that sustained us was the patient endurance of those stricken heroes . . . with their ghastly wounds [so] cheerful & courageous." At the same time, however, Hawks emphasized the way black soldiers fought for racial equality and uplift, quoting one patient, Charley Reason, who explained that he suffered "*not* for my country, I never had any, but to gain one," and another who emphasized that he was ready "to give my other arm, or my life if necessary, for my race!" Quoted in Gerald Schwartz, *A Woman Doctor's Civil War: Esther Hill Hawks' Diary* (Columbia, S.C.: University of South Carolina Press, 1984), 51, 54.

42. Sarah Edwards Henshaw, *Our Branch and Its Tributaries: Being a History of the Work of the Northern Sanitary Commission and Its Auxiliaries During the War of the Rebellion* (Chicago: Alfred L. Sewell, 1868), 55–56.

43. Clement Potts to his mother and grandmother, February 8, 1862, Clement D. Potts Papers, *Harrisburg Civil War Round Table Collection*, ser. 2 (hereafter HCWRC), and Newton Adams to his brother, July 11, 1864, Newton Adams Papers, *Civil War Times Illustrated Collection*, Military History Institute, Carlisle, Pa. (hereafter CWTIC). Similarly, see Watson Goodrich to "My Dear friend Alvin," October 13, 1861, Watson Goodrich Letters, Filson Historical Society, Louisville, Ky.; and William Eastman to "Dear Father, Mother, Sisters & Brother," October 1861, William Eastman Correspon-

dence, Massachusetts Historical Society, Boston, both of whom accused their physicians of causing comrades' deaths.

44. Henry Sentell to "Dear Parents," May 18, 1862, and "My Dear Brother," May 24, 1862, Sentell Family Papers, New York Historical Society, New York (emphasis in original); Rosenberg, "Health in the Home," chap. 1; Henry H. Robbins to "Dear Father," July 11, 1862, Henry H. Robbins Papers, Massachusetts Historical Society, Boston.

45. Charles Perkins to his brother, July 17, 1862, Charles E. Perkins Papers, CWTIC.

46. Anon., "Hospital Memories II," *Atlantic Monthly* 20 (September 1867): 330

47. Charles Laforest Dunham to his family, January 10, 1863, quoted in *Through the South with a Union Soldier*, ed. Arthur H. DeRosier Jr. (Johnson City, Tenn.: Publications of the East Tennessee State University Research Advisory Council, 1969), 51. He did note the following month that his brother talked about home in his sleep, and that he "went off [died] very easy."

48. Jonathan P. Stowe Diary, Jonathan P. Stowe Papers (hereafter Stowe Papers), CWTIC.

49. Ibid.; undated "Biographical Sketch" in Stowe Papers. This sketch is attached to a partly completed eulogy delivered at Stowe's funeral, which contains identical sentences, indicating that both documents were produced shortly after his death. They are typed copies of the original (probably prepared by Stowe's descendants), thus spelling may have been altered over time.

50. "Biographical Sketch," and note dated September 19, 1862, Jonathan P. Stowe Diary, Stowe Papers.

51. Charles Rosenberg, "Body and Mind in Nineteenth-Century Medicine: Some Clinical Origins of the Neurosis Construct," *Bulletin of the History of Medicine* 63 (1989): 185–97.

52. Sarah E. Edmonds, *Nurse and Spy in the Union Army: Comprising the Adventures and Experience of a Woman in Hospitals, Camps, and Battle-Fields* (Hartford, Conn.: W. S. Williams and Co., 1865), 60; Frances M. Clarke, "So Lonesome I Could Die: Nostalgia and Debates Over Emotional Control in the Civil War North," *Journal of Social History* 41, no. 2 (Winter 2007): 253–82.

53. William Dulach to "My Respected Friend Elizabeth," November 19, 1862, William Dulach Letters, Filson Historical Society.

54. J.H.K., "The Brave Soldier—Who Is He?" *Armory Square Hospital Gazette* (Washington, D.C.), June 4, 1864, 2.

55. Ibid.

56. Anon., "Patience," *The Haversack* (St. John's College Hospital, Annapolis, MD) October 12, 1864, 3; *Lebanon Courier* (Lebanon County, Pa.), April 25, 1861, 1.

57. Hess, *Union Soldier in Battle*, 79.

58. Anon. "The Private Soldier," *Armory Square Hospital Gazette*, January 27, 1864, 3.

59. Quoted in Peck, *War, the Army and Victorian Literature*, 51.

60. Daniel Sickles, quoted in W. A. Swanberg, *Sickles the Incredible* (New York: Scribner's, 1956), 231.

61. Alfred H. Holt, *Phrase and Word Origins: A Study of Familiar Expressions* (1936;

New York: Dover Publications, 1961), 200. "Pluck," *Armory Square Hospital Gazette*, August 13, 1864, 2. In all likelihood, this article was written by one of the women nurses who worked at the hospital, their unsigned pieces sometimes appearing alongside those of patients.

62. Stephen Garton, *The Cost of War: Australians Return* (Melbourne: Oxford University Press Australia, 1996), 31–32, discusses how Australian veterans of both world wars developed a language rich in ironic humor in order to express and simultaneously deflect war's horrors. Their humor was "of a debunking kind," he writes, "mocking, sending up, and sharpening the divide between home and front." I elaborate further on the distinction being drawn here in my final chapter.

63. This claim is based on my analysis of the personal papers of several hundred sick and wounded soldiers, only a fraction of which is cited in this chapter.

64. Take, for example, a story of wartime injury recently narrated by magazine correspondent Michael Weisskopf, who lost a hand while reporting on the war in Iraq, "My Right Hand," *Time*, October 2, 2006. It is not simply that Weisskopf is more forthcoming than a mid-nineteenth-century soldier would be about what it was like to be injured in wartime; rather, that his changing self-image as he struggles to come to terms with his wound *is* the story.

65. On differences in the language used by working-class and middle-class letter writers, see Marilyn Motz, *True Sisterhood: Michigan Women and Their Kin, 1820–1920* (Albany: State University of New York, 1983), 76–81.

66. Hiram Williams to "Dear Mother," April 22 and May 7, 1865, Hiram Williams Papers, HCWRC.

67. George Rollins to his sister, December 20, 1862, George Rollins Papers, CWTIC.

68. Elon Brown Memoir, CWTIC.

69. "Soldier Life of John W. Whaples," *The Haversack* (Philadelphia: Published by the Committee on Hospitals for the [Philadelphia] Great Central Fair for the U.S. Sanitary Commission, Henry B. Ashmead, 1864), 15–16.

70. William Newman to "Dear Friend," November 20, 1864, and to "My Dear Friend Almira," December 13, 1864, Almira Winchell Papers, GLC4706, Gilder Lehrman Institute, Pierpont Morgan Library, New York.

71. Benjamin Robb to "Dear Sir," June 1, 1863, Benjamin F. Robb Papers, CWTIC.

72. Hospitalized patients were often urged to conform to an ideal cheerful suffering. Addressing himself "to the Sick and Wounded," for instance, John F. W. Ware, in "The Home to the Hospital: Addressed to the Sick and Wounded of the Army of the Union," Army Series no. 6, *Tracts of the American Unitarian Association* (Boston: American Unitarian Association, 1862), 15–16, informed readers that that "mere dogged patience, the bracing of the will or the nerves to bear quietly" was not enough: "The hospital needs *cheerfulness*." "That is only half courage which bears up under dangers and hardships," he insisted. "The highest courage lies in cheerful bearing." Expressing the same conviction, another praised the cheerful sufferer as one whose superior courage evidenced "a resolute and constant habit, a firm virtue founded in principle and character." Charles

Eliot Norton, "The Soldier of the Good Cause," Army Series no. 2, *Tracts of the American Unitarian Association*, 11.

73. *Armory Square Hospital Gazette*, May 8, 1864, 3.

74. Uncle Hugh to "Dear Nephew," May 23, 1863, and P. P. [Farnham] to "Dear Friend & Bro," June 27, 1863, James McWhinnie Papers (hereafter McWhinnie Papers), Massachusetts Historical Society.

75. Letter to "Dear James," from his mother, July 9, 1863, and James McWhinnie to "Dear Brother David," July 16, 1863, McWhinnie Papers. Three days later his mother apologized for her letter, stating she should "have remember[e]d that you were in a great deal of suf[f]ering and weakness and that it was not perhaps the proper time to say so much."

76. James McWhinnie to "Dear Father, Brothers & Sisters," April 19, 1864, McWhinnie Papers.

77. The *Philadelphia Inquirer*, for example, regularly announced the arrival of steamers carrying the wounded, sometimes listing patients by name and detailing the hospitals to which they had been sent, as well as describing the immense crowds that gathered. See, for instance, "Arrival of the Sick and Wounded," April 25, 1862, 1; "Wounded Soldiers," May 2, 1862, 8; "Arrival of Wounded Volunteers," June 9, 1862; "Ambulances and the Soldiers," June 15, 1864, 3; "Arrival of Sick and Wounded," July 18, 1864, 8.

78. A. T. Brewer Memoir, CWTIC.

79. *Tioga Agitator* (Pennsylvania), June 29, 1864, 2.

80. William Rome Diary, July 5 and 7, 1861, William O. Rome Papers, GLC3131.09, Gilder Lehrman Institute. See also Schultz, *Women at the Front*, chap. 3.

81. Stearns, *The Lady Nurse*, 257; Mary Kelly to "Dear Friend," April 4, 1862, James R. Kelley Letters, GLC4197, Gilder Lehrman Institute.

82. "Opening of the Brooklyn Sanitary Fair," *New York Times*, February 23, 1864. Wounded soldiers also participated in the marches that opened sanitary fairs, such as the one reported in "The Northwestern Sanitary Fair: The Inauguration Parade Today," *Chicago Tribune*, October 27, 1863.

83. Walt Whitman, *Specimen Days in America* (1882; New York: E. P. Dutton, 1905), 39.

84. Earl J. Hess, "A Terrible Fascination: The Portrayal of Combat in the Civil War Media," in *An Uncommon Time: The Civil War and the Northern Home Front*, ed. Paul A. Cimbala and Randall M. Miller (New York: Fordham University Press, 2002), 1–26; Henry F. Wellington to "Sister Abby," March 15, 1863, Henry Francis Wellington Letters and Diary, Massachusetts Historical Society; James McWhinnie to "Dear Father Brothers & Sisters," February 4, 1864, McWhinnie Papers.

85. Unsigned letter to Frank Moore, dated February 1, 1867, contained in U.S. Sanitary Commission Papers, New York Historical Society. This twenty-seven-page letter looks to be a copy of an original, submitted to Moore (probably by Mary Jane Safford) as the basis for his history of women's war work, which I deal with in "Forgetting the Women: Contests Over Female Patriotism After America's Civil War," *Journal of Women's History* 23, no. 2 (Summer 2011, forthcoming).

86. A broad idea that willpower can aid recovery still influences medical practice, but not to the same degree, or in the same way, as in the nineteenth century, when lack of willpower was often discussed as a sole cause of death. Robert Weldon Whalen, in *Bitter Wounds: German Victims of the Great War, 1914–1939* (Ithaca, N.Y.: Cornell University Press, 1984), 65–66, discusses the way an emphasis on willpower and strong character continued to pervade the medical and popular literature on soldiers' rehabilitation in the wake of World War I, for instance. Yet willpower took on a particular meaning among German physicians at this time, he notes, focusing on a patient's acceptance of a physician's regime—his need to surrender his will in the face of superior medical expertise.

CHAPTER FOUR

1. Reynolds, "Fortnight with the Sanitary," 246–47.

2. Jean Bethke Elshtain, *Women and War* (New York: Basic Books, 1987).

3. Patricia L. Richardson, *Busy Hands: Images of the Family in the Northern Civil War Effort* (New York: Fordham University Press, 2003), supports the general arguments made in this chapter regarding the significance of domesticity to Civil War Northerners and their interest in shaping voluntary efforts in ways that facilitated ties between soldiers and the home front.

4. Fredrickson, *Inner Civil War*, chap. 7; see also Ginzberg, *Women and the Work of Benevolence*, chap. 5; and Bremner, *The Public Good*.

5. Attie, *Patriotic Toil*; Giesberg, *Civil War Sisterhood: The U.S. Sanitary Commission and Women's Politics in Transition* (Boston: Northeastern University Press, 2000).

6. Giesberg, *Civil War Sisterhood*, ix–xi; Attie, *Patriotic Toil*, 3–4.

7. Order issued by R. C. Hale, September 10, 1861, newspaper clipping contained in Minute Book of the Richmond (later Mansfield) Soldiers' Aid Society, 1861–1864, MG-211, Pennsylvania Historical and Museum Commission, Harrisburg. This aid society formed in response to this order, as did dozens of others in the vicinity.

8. Mary Elizabeth Massey, *Women in the Civil War* (Lincoln: University of Nebraska Press, 1994), 32; originally published as *Bonnet Brigades* (New York: Knopf, 1966).

9. See Emerson David Fite, *Social and Industrial Conditions in the North During the Civil War* (1910; Williamstown, Mass.: Corner House Publishers, 1976), chaps. 1 and 4, for a discussion of agricultural and manufacturing output in the Civil War North.

10. According to William Quentin Maxwell, *Lincoln's Fifth Wheel: The Political History of the United States Sanitary Commission* (New York: Longmans, Green and Co., 1956), 35, a basic ration in 1861 consisted of a pound of hard bread, one and a quarter pounds of fresh or salt meat or three-quarters of a pound of bacon. Added to this, for every hundred men the army provided eight gallons of beans, ten pounds of rice or hominy, ten pounds of coffee, fifteen pounds of sugar, four gallons of vinegar, and two pounds of salt. The typical ration was supplemented later in the war with a slight increase in hard bread and the addition of three pounds of potatoes. Many companies also pooled funds to purchase fresh produce, such as vegetables, eggs, and milk, and hospital administrators did the same. By war's end, the Medical Department had created special diet lists, which itemized the type and amount of particular foods that army doctors were supposed to

give to men suffering from specific ailments. Nonetheless, soldiers' diets tended to be nutritionally deficient. And poor hospital management, sudden influxes of patients, or lack of nearby resources meant that physicians continued to rely on volunteers to supply fresh food and other necessities.

11. In the West and East, the USSC ran thirty-nine hospital railway carriages that transported 225,000 soldiers over the course of the war, while tens of thousands more were carried north in USSC-managed hospital ships. Discovering that the government was liable to commandeer trains in the event of military necessity, the USSC also purchased its own engine for use in the West. Other voluntary organizations, such as the Western Sanitary Commission (mentioned below), similarly sponsored their own hospital cars. The government took over the management of hospital cars and boats in the war's last year, although voluntary agencies generally retained agents on board these transports to dispense food and supplies. George A. Otis and D. L. Huntington, *The Medical and Surgical History of the War of the Rebellion*, 2d issue, pt. 3 (Washington, D.C.: Government Printing Office, 1883), 2:957–71, details these arrangements. See also Ralph C. Gordon, "Hospital Trains of the Army of the Cumberland," *Tennessee Historical Quarterly* 51 (1992): 147–56.

12. These events raised millions of dollars, mostly in support of the USSC. Details can be found in J. Matthew Gallman, "Voluntarism in Wartime: Philadelphia's Great Central Fair," in *Toward a Social History of the American Civil War*, ed. Maris A. Vinovskis (Cambridge: Cambridge University Press, 1990), 93–116; J. Christopher Schnell, "Mary Livermore and the Great Northwestern Fair," *Chicago History* 4 (1975): 34–43; Robert W. Schoeberlein, "A Fair to Remember: Maryland Women in Aid of the Union," *Maryland Historical Society* 90 (1995): 467–88; Harriet Mott Stryker-Rodda, "Brooklyn and Long Island Sanitary Fair, 1864," *Journal of Long Island History* 4 (1964): 1–17; and William Y. Thompson, "Sanitary Fairs of the Civil War," *Civil War History* 4 (1958): 51–67.

13. See, for example, "What They Have to Do Who Stay at Home," no. 50, *Documents*, 1:1–10.

14. "Statement of the Object and Methods of the Sanitary Commission, 7 December 1863," no. 69, *Documents*, 2:7 (emphasis in original).

15. The USSC's board eventually included twenty-four members who met quarterly in Washington. To cope with an enormous workload, the organization formed a Standing Committee that gathered in New York five or six days a week. Frederick Law Olmsted held greatest responsibility, filling the position of executive secretary until 1863. This role was then filled by Dr. J. Foster Jenkins, who, in turn, was succeeded by Johnathan S. Blatchford in April 1865. Most of the USSC's work was channeled through associate secretaries and chief sanitary inspectors. Until 1864, there were three associate secretaries: one responsible for work east of the Alleghenies plus New Orleans, another in charge of work in the West, and one designated Chief of Sanitary Inspection. In addition, the USSC appointed a chief sanitary inspector for each large division of the army. On the USSC's organization, see "Statement of the Object and Methods," *Documents*, 2:1–58; and William Y. Thompson, "The U.S. Sanitary Commission," *Civil War*

History 2 (1956): 41–63. The USSC employed around 200 additional workers by 1864, many of whom held salaried positions. Biographical information on the USSC leadership is contained in an appendix to Maxwell, *Lincoln's Fifth Wheel*, 317–50. For similar details on the USSC's women leaders, see Attie, *Patriotic Toil*, chaps 1–2; and Giesberg, *Civil War Sisterhood*, chaps. 2–3.

16. Attie, *Patriotic Toil*, 70. On this point, see Attie, *Patriotic Toil*; and Giesberg, *Civil War Sisterhood*, in particular.

17. William E. Parrish, in "The Western Sanitary Commission," *Civil War History* 36 (1990): 17–35, notes that the WSC raised almost $780,000 and distributed stores valued at $3,500,000. See also J. G. Forman, *The Western Sanitary Commission: A Sketch of Its Origin, History, Labors for the Sick and Wounded of the Western Armies and Aid Given to Freedman and Union Refugees* (St. Louis: R. P. Studley and Co., 1864); W. R. Hodges, *The Western Sanitary Commission and What It Did for the Sick and Wounded of the Union Armies from 1861 to 1865* ([St. Louis]; privately printed, 1906); and Frank B. Goodrich, *The Tribute Book: A Record of the Munificence, Self-Sacrifice and Patriotism of the American People During the War for the Union* (New York: Derby and Miller, 1865), chap. 7. For a discussion of the acrimonious relationship between the WSC and the USSC see Maxwell, *Lincoln's Fifth Wheel*, 97–106.

18. Goodrich, *Tribute Book*, chap. 8.

19. James Moore, *History of the Cooper Shop Volunteer Refreshment Saloon* (Philadelphia: James B. Rodgers, 1866).

20. "Statement of Object and Methods," *Documents*, 2:22–30; and Charles J. Stillé, *History of the United States Sanitary Commission: Being the General Report of Its Work During the War of the Rebellion* (Philadelphia: J. B. Lippincott and Co., 1866), 248–51.

21. Attie, *Patriotic Toil*, chap. 4, deals with these charges. As she notes, these suspicions of USSC fraud and profiteering grew from a longstanding constellation of anxieties concerning the expansion of the market and concentrations of power (144). See also Maxwell, *Lincoln's Fifth Wheel*, 191–93.

22. On the formation of the Christian Commission and its support among women's groups, see Moss, *Annals of the United States Christian Commission*, 63–110, 356–58. Although this organization initially adopted a system of recruiting ministers on a voluntary basis to undertake six-week tours at the front, it later relied on paid field agents. Eventually, the organization employed 5,000 agents, in addition to 157 lady managers of Diet Kitchens, 108 army agents, and 53 agents on the home front. The quote is from Maxwell, *Lincoln's Fifth Wheel*, 192.

23. Maxwell, *Lincoln's Fifth Wheel*, 10; "Plan of Organization for 'The Commission of Inquiry and Advice in Respect of the Sanitary Interests of the United States Forces,'" dated June 21, 1861, reprinted in Stillé, *History of the United States Sanitary Commission*, 533–38. Early USSC publications reiterated that the "chief object" initially contemplated by the organization was that of sanitary inspection and disease prevention. See, for instance, "Statement of Object and Methods," *Documents*, 2:15.

24. While women's groups around the country were busy collecting supplies for the troops, the business of systematizing voluntary contributions formed no part of

the USSC's original design. In fact, the executive did not draw up plans to engage in such work until several months after beginning operations. See Frederick Law Olmsted, "A Report to the Secretary of War of the Operations of the Sanitary Commission and upon the Sanitary Condition of the Volunteer Army," December 9, 1861, no. 40, *Documents*, 1:75.

25. Stillé, *History of the Sanitary Commission*, 251–56. If this initiative was originally undertaken without thought of rival organizations, USSC agents were soon conscious of the need to present themselves in a manner designed to win favor among the Northern public. Advising a subordinate to ensure that field relief agents maintained morally upright and sensitive behavior, Steiner cautioned that a "scrutinizing fa[u]lt-finding eye is upon us all the while." Lewis H. Steiner to "Capt. Isaac Harris," August 20, 1863, Lewis H. Steiner, Letterbook 1863–1864, Box 2, MS1430, Maryland Historical Society, Baltimore (hereafter Steiner Letterbook).

26. Steiner advised his field relief agents to "see every medical officer in the Corps, find out the wants of his Hospital and courteously offer assistance, not obtruding this or interfering with his plans." Lewis H. Steiner to David S. Pope, n.d. [August 1863], Steiner Letterbook.

27. William Howell Reed, ed., *War Papers of Frank B. Fay: With Reminiscences of Services in the Camps and Hospitals of the Army of the Potomac, 1861–1865* ([Boston:] privately printed, 1911), 95.

28. Reed, *Hospital Life*, 72–73; Stillé, *History of the Sanitary Commission*, 274–77. The number of auxiliary relief agents was augmented with civilian volunteers during major battles.

29. "Statement of the Object and Methods," *Documents*, 2:56–57. Bremner (*The Public Good*, 55), for instance, argues that the USSC "discharged its tasks with acumen rather than sentiment"; see also Fredrickson, *Inner Civil War*, 104 and passim.

30. Henshaw, *Our Branch and Its Tributaries*, 98–99. In addition, the USSC employed "travelling missionary agents" to tour the country and hold public meetings about their work, information on which can be found in Box 883, U.S. Sanitary Commission Records, New York Public Library, Rare Books and Manuscripts Division, New York (hereafter USSC Records).

31. [Mary Clark Brayton and Ellen F. Terry], *Our Acre and Its Harvest: Historical Sketch of the Soldiers' Aid Society of Northern Ohio* (Cleveland: Fairbanks, Benedict and Co., 1869), 33, 58–59, 67–68. The USSC also requested family members to forward letters from soldiers in order to inspire their contributors, some of which were later published in Lydia Minturn Post, *Soldiers' Letters from Camp, Battle-Field and Prison* (New York: Bunce and Huntington, published for the U.S. Sanitary Commission, 1865).

32. Henshaw, *Our Branch and Its Tributaries*, 95, 103.

33. Knapp was born in New Hampshire in 1821. He graduated from Harvard Divinity School in the 1840s, before setting up a parish in Brookline, Massachusetts, which he left to join the USSC. After the war, he continued his guardianship over young men, first as principal of the Engleswood Military Academy in New Jersey until 1867, thereafter by founding a home school for boys in Plymouth, Massachusetts. An obitu-

ary, taken from the *Old Colony Memorial* (Walpole, N.H.), can be found in Frederick Newman Knapp Papers, Box 1, Massachusetts Historical Society, Boston (hereafter Knapp Papers).

34. Frederick N. Knapp, "Two Reports Concerning the Aid and Comfort Given by the Sanitary Commission to Sick Soldiers Passing Through Washington," September 23, 1861, no. 35, *Documents*, 1:1–2; Frederick N. Knapp, "Third Report Concerning the Aid and Comfort Given by the Sanitary Commission to Sick Soldiers Passing through Washington," March 21, 1862, no. 39, *Documents*, 1:5. Large numbers of men arrived at the paymaster's too late in the day to submit claims, while many more had irregular documents that might require weeks, even months, of investigation. Slow-moving officials were not solely to blame. Commanding officers sometimes listed as deserters men who had in fact been wounded in battle or taken ill on a march. Once these men had been transferred from one hospital to another, it was often tricky for them to procure records detailing their movements, making it extremely difficult to obtain discharge papers or refute charges of desertion. Likewise, it was common for volunteer doctors who lacked experience with military regulations to incorrectly fill out discharge or transfer papers, thus stranding soldiers in bureaucratic limbo. Volunteers like Knapp—highly literate and well versed in official procedures—were essential in navigating military bureaucracy for these men.

35. To Knapp's mind, these stranded troops were easy prey for the corrupting influences of the city. His official reports were replete with apprehension that soldiers would drink or gamble away their money, or become prey to confidence men, ever ready "like evil birds of prey," to rob the unwary. Knapp, "Third Report," 3. See also Knapp, "Fourth Report Concerning the Aid and Comfort Given by the Sanitary Commission to Sick Soldiers Passing Through Washington," December 15, 1862, no. 59, *Documents*, 1:7–9. Knapp handed out to such men a USSC publication titled *The Soldier's Friend* (Philadelphia: Perkinpine and Higgins, 1865).

36. Knapp, "Third Report," 5. Fearing that some might still fall through the cracks in places where the Commission had established no Lodges or Homes, Knapp drew up a circular in May 1864, which he sent to communities near all of the principal railroad stations in Union-held territory, pleading with civilians to aid disabled soldiers as trains stopped in their areas. Frederick N. Knapp, "Report Concerning the Aid and Comfort Given by the Sanitary Commission to Sick and Invalid Soldiers, for the Quarter Ending June 30, 1865," July 1, 1865, no. 94, *Documents*, 2:17–19.

37. Stillé, *History of the Sanitary Commission*, 290. These homes and lodges cumulatively provided 4.5 million meals and more than a million night's lodgings. The USSC also claimed that on a daily basis its Department of Special Relief catered to 2,300 soldiers. Anon., *The Sanitary Commission of the United States Army: A Succinct Narrative of Its Works and Purposes* (New York: n.p., 1864; repr., New York: Arno Press, 1972), 230; see also Knapp, "Report for the Quarter Ending 30 June 1865," 44–45.

38. The War Department later took up this more detailed method for recording soldiers' deaths, according to *Sanitary Commission of the United States Army*, 105.

39. Details relating to this massive undertaking can be found in the Washington

Hospital Directory Archives, 1862–1866, RG 12, USSC Records. Summaries are contained in Stillé, *History of the Sanitary Commission*, 307–11; and J. S. Newberry, *The U.S. Sanitary Commission in the Valley of the Mississippi, During the War of the Rebellion, 1861–1866* (Cleveland: Fairbanks, Benedict and Co., 1871), 428–45, 503–9.

40. Other voluntary agencies, even small ones, offered similar services, according to [Linus P. Brockett], *The Philanthropic Results of the War in America*, expanded reprint (New York: Sheldon and Co., 1864), 53. The New England Soldiers' Relief Association, for example, provided soldiers with help in obtaining back pay, pensions and discharges.

41. *Report of the Board of Managers of the New York State Soldiers' Depot, and the Fund for the Relief of Sick, Wounded, Furloughed, and Discharged Soldiers* (Albany, N.Y.: Van Benthuysen's Steam Printing House, 1864), 9–11. Public and private funds kept this venture running, with the New York legislature providing an initial grant of $300,000. The annual reports of agencies are appended to ibid., 47–137.

42. *History and Annual Reports of the Citizens' Volunteer Hospital Association* (Philadelphia: Burk and McFetridge, 1889). Like many other wartime ventures, this one kept minimal records, which were mostly destroyed upon disbanding. In the late 1880s, however, sixteen of the former male board members met and decided to print these remaining annual reports.

43. Knapp, "Report for the Quarter Ending 30 June 1865," 4.

44. Knapp, "Third Report," 7. His reports were often written in the form of first-hand testimony, purportedly taken straight from his daily journal, as if to emphasize the way his writing offered unmediated access to his innermost feelings.

45. Ginzberg, *Women and the Work of Benevolence*, 134.

46. "A Soldier's Thoughts of Home," *Hospital Register* (Satterlee Hospital, West Philadelphia), 2, no. 42 (June 11, 1864): 1.

47. Lewis, "Mother's Love," 210. See also Ruth H. Bloch, "The Gendered Meanings of Virtue in Revolutionary America," *Signs* 13 (1987): 37–58; and Richardson, *Busy Hands*, 96–98.

48. On the many manifestations of antebellum anxiety, see the preface to Paludan, *"A People's Contest."*

49. Lewis, "Mother's Love," 211, 220; Mary Ryan, *The Empire of the Mother: American Writing about Domesticity 1830–1860* (New York: Harrington Park Press, 1985), 144.

50. Lewis, "Mother's Love," 211, 221.

51. Forgie, *Patricide in the House Divided*, 195.

52. On the enormous popularity of mesmerism and spiritualism, see Laurence R. Moore, *In Search of White Crows: Spiritualism, Parapsychology, and American Culture* (New York: Oxford University Press, 1997); and Fred Kaplan, "'The Mesmeric Mania': The Early Victorians and Animal Magnetism," *Journal of the History of Ideas* 35, no. 4 (1974): 691–702.

53. Nudelman makes a similar point (*John Brown's Body*, 117).

54. Reed, *Hospital Life*, 73; Reynolds, "Fortnight with the Sanitary," 247.

55. John Hancock Douglas to "My Dear Brother," July 28, 1861, John Hancock

Douglas Collection, Library of Congress, Manuscript Division, Washington D.C.; S. B. Fales quoted in Goodrich, *Tribute Book*, 419.

56. The USSC Standing Committee's Minutes from June through September 1861, contained in USSC Records, Series 32, Box 971, reveal constant discussions of this issue, with Olmsted favoring an allotment system whereby families would be authorized to draw on soldiers' pay. See also Maxwell, *Lincoln's Fifth Wheel*, 46–48.

57. Olmsted, "Report to the Secretary of War," 30–32.

58. "Address," January 13, 1862, reprinted in Moss, *Annals of the Christian Commission*, 111.

59. Quoted in Maxwell, *Lincoln's Fifth Wheel*, 192–93. In fact, the Christian Commission sometimes represented its work as the very antithesis of orderly processes, claiming that its central office kept no record of expenditures, being too busy in the work of actual distribution.

60. "Address," reprinted in Moss, *Annals of the Christian Commission*, 111; Moss, *Annals of the Christian Commission*, 729, 181. The USCC supplied canvas roofs and stoves for the construction of these chapels, which went to any regiment that had agreed to construct the necessary log walls.

61. Material of this nature can be found in the five scrapbooks containing annual reports, circulars, printed documents, and newspaper articles relating to the USCC contained in "Records Relating to the United States Christian Commission, 1861–1866," RG 94, Records of the Adjutant General's Office, National Archives and Records Administration, Washington, D.C.

62. John F. W. Ware, "The Home to the Camp: Addressed to the Soldiers of the Union," Army Series No. 3, *Tracts of the American Unitarian Association* (Boston: American Unitarian Association [1861], repr. 1865), 1.

63. Moss, *Annals of the Christian Commission*, 651.

64. Goodrich, *Tribute Book*, 153.

65. [Brayton and Terry], *Our Acre and Its Harvest*, 63.

66. M. A. Newcomb, *Four Years of Personal Reminiscences of the War* (Chicago: H. S. Mills and Co., 1893), 101.

67. [Brayton and Terry], *Our Acre and Its Harvest*, 61–62; circular headed "To the Ladies of Vermont," January 5, 1863, by Ed E. Phelps, Surg. U.S.V. Surgeon in Charles and Medical Director for Vermont, newspaper clipping contained in New England Women's Auxiliary Association Records.

68. Richardson, *Busy Hands*, 109–15, makes a similar point.

69. [Hoge], "Address Delivered by Mrs. Hoge."

70. Bloor, *Letters from the Army of the Potomac*, 51. See also [Brayton and Terry], *Our Acre and Its Harvest*, 61–62.

71. "Serg't Bancroft" to Rebecca F. Doane, September 19, 1864, Box 2, Knapp Papers.

72. Schultz, *Women at the Front*, chaps. 3–4.

73. Emily Elizabeth Parsons, *Memoir of Emily Elizabeth Parsons* (Boston: Little, Brown, 1880), reprinted as *Civil War Nursing* (New York: Garland Publishing, 1984). This memoir consists of letters sent to family members during the war (23, 89). Nina

Bennett Smith also describes the way women nurses compensated for their lack of formal authority by advancing claims about women's right and duty to extend domestic care to soldiers (see the introduction to Smith's "The Women Who Went to the War: The Union Army Nurse in the Civil War," Ph.D. diss., Northwestern University, 1981).

74. Jane E. Schultz, "The Inhospitable Hospital: Gender and Professionalism in Civil War Medicine," *Signs* 17 (1992): 363–92, notes that women nurses' rejection of medical models of professionalism was not an indiscriminate protest against men in general. Allying themselves with enlisted men, women nurses instead criticized what they viewed as bureaucratic inhumanity and a detached professionalism that treated soldiers as "medical specimens." The aim of their critique was not to replace male authority, she argues, but to individualize patient care. On official resistance to women nurses and the hostile relationships that sometimes developed between them and medical men, see also Leonard, *Yankee Women*, chap. 1; Smith, "Women Who Went to the War," chap. 3; and Ann Douglas Wood, "The War Within a War: Women Nurses in the Union Army," *Civil War History* 18 (1972): 206–7.

75. Quoted in John R. Brumgardt, ed., *The Diary and Letters of Hannah Ropes* (Knoxville: University of Tennessee Press, 1980), 71.

76. Egbert Sinsabaugh to Sarah Ogden, April 6, 1864, and Christopher Keslar to "Respected Friend," February 16, 1864, Sarah Ogden Papers, GLC6559, Gilder Lehrman Institute (hereafter Ogden Papers).

77. See, for example, Ira P. Jones dated 1863 and Allen T. Richards to Sarah Ogden, February 5, 1864, James Chase to Sarah Ogden, January 24, 1863 and John Groaner to "Most noble & Kind Lady," October 15, 1862, Ogden Papers.

78. Stearns, *The Lady Nurse of Ward E*, 221, 227. This memoir consists of wartime diary entries and letters written by the author to her sisters.

79. Schultz, "Inhospitable Hospital," 378–80; Jane E. Schultz, "'Are We Not All Soldiers?': Northern Women in the Civil War Hospital Service," *Prospects* 20 (1995): 45.

80. Reed, *Hospital Life*, 95, 120. On these efforts, see also Richardson, *Busy Hands*, 246–50.

81. Mrs. H. [Anna Morris Holstein], *Three Years in Field Hospitals of the Army of the Potomac*, 30–31; Smith, "The Women Who Went to the War", 58; *Hammond Gazette* (Point Lookout, Md.), March 13, 1863.

82. [Brayton and Terry], *Our Acre and Its Harvest*, 122–24; Newberry, *USSC in the Valley of the Mississippi*, 314–22; Reed, *Hospital Life*, 153.

83. *Armory Square Hospital Gazette* (Washington, D.C.), March 26, April 2 and 16, and May 7, 1864.

84. Moss, *Annals of the Christian Commission*, 663–70. Wittenmyer initially worked as a sanitary agent for the state of Iowa and president of the Keokuk Soldiers' Aid Society, but she resigned these positions in 1863 to work for the Christian Commission after a series of battles with the male-dominated Iowa State Sanitary Commission. See Leonard, *Yankee Women*, chap. 2; and Noah Zaring, "Competition in Benevolence: Civil War Soldiers' Aid in Iowa," *Iowa Heritage Illustrated* 77 (1996): 10–23.

85. Moss, *Annals of the Christian Commission*, 666; Hoge, *Boys in Blue*, 111, 158.

86. "Report of the Board of Managers of the New York State Soldiers' Depot," 25; "Report of Hartford Soldiers' Rest," reprinted in Knapp, "Report for the Quarter Ending June 30, 1865," 24–25.

87. "Report of the Board of Managers of the New York State Soldiers' Depot," 27–28; Knapp, "Fifth Report Concerning the Aid and Comfort Given by the Sanitary Commission to Sick and Invalid Soldiers, October 1, 1863," no. 77, *Documents*, 2:8–9, for instance, discusses his vigilance in turning possible deserters over to military authorities. He also barred from USSC homes any soldier caught drinking and inquired into soldiers' characters before distributing emergency monies to fund their journeys home.

88. Third Annual Report, December 20, 1865, in *History and Annual Reports of the Citizens' Volunteer Hospital Association*.

89. S. G. Cary, "Thirty Third Report of the New England Women's Auxiliary Association," January 16, 1865, New England Women's Auxiliary Association Records, Massachusetts Historical Society, Boston.

90. William Garrett to his sister, September 27, 1862, William Garrett Papers, HCWRC.

91. Attie suggests that the Civil War was "the first modern war in which masses of women participated with expectations that their home front contributions would translate into expanded political rights" (*Patriotic Toil*, 46). Yet as Silber, in *Daughters of the Union*, 125, notes, this conflict hardly acted as a catalyst for feminism. Most of those active in the women's rights movement had staked out their positions prior to the war. And although a number of prominent women volunteers used their wartime experiences as a springboard to professional careers as social workers, they were in a tiny minority. Most female reformers in the 1860s and 1870s continued to view themselves as guardians of a domestic sphere that safeguarded society's most cherished values, rejecting suffrage as a threat to the division of public and private life. Yet activist women in these years also broke with the antebellum tradition of participating in male-led voluntary organizations, instead joining a wide variety of separatist groups dedicated to much more assertive attempts to bring the values of motherhood and domesticity into the public sphere, shifts highlighted in Sarah M. Evans, *Born for Liberty: A History of Women in America* (New York: Simon and Schuster, 1997, chap. 6.

92. The three organizations that held greatest appeal among women in the postwar years—the home and foreign missionary societies of the Protestant churches, the Woman's Christian Temperance Union, and the Young Women's Christian Association—were all explicitly religious, notes Anne Firor Scott in "Women's Voluntary Associations: From Charity to Reform," in *Lady Bountiful Revisited: Women, Philanthropy, and Power*, ed., Kathleen D. McCarthy (New Brunswick, N.J.: Rutgers University Press, 1990), 42.

93. The militancy that temperance women displayed in the postwar years had roots that lie in the 1850s, as detailed by Jed Dannenbaum in "The Origins of Temperance Activism and Militancy Among American Women," *Journal of Social History* 15 (Winter 1981): 235–52.

94. Rebecca Jo Plant, *Mom: The Transformation of Motherhood in Modern America* (Chicago: University of Chicago Press, 2010), deals at length with this transition.

95. "Keep the Home Fires Burning," arranged by British composer Ivor Novello

with words by American poet Lena Guilbert Ford, was popular in both Britain and the United States during World War I, notes Barbara L. Tishler, in "One Hundred Percent Americanism and Music in Boston During World War I," *American Music* 4, no. 2 (Summer 1986): 164–76.

CHAPTER FIVE

1. On antiwar sentiment and political divisions on the Northern home front, see Jennifer L. Weber, *Copperheads: The Rise and Fall of Lincoln's Opponents in the North* (New York: Oxford University Press, 2006); and Baker, *Affairs of Party*. Scholarship detailing the factors that motivated soldiers' enlistment is canvassed in Larry M. Logue and Michael Barton, eds., *The Civil War Soldier: A Historical Reader* (New York: New York University Press, 2002). The most recent studies of the British response to war in America are Duncan Andrew Campbell's, *English Public Opinion and the American Civil War* (Suffolk: Boydell Press, 2003); and Brian Holden Reid, "Power, Sovereignty, and the Great Republic: Anglo-American Diplomatic Relations in the Era of the Civil War," *Diplomacy and Statecraft* 14 (June 2003): 45–76.

2. Charles Eliot Norton, "The Work of the Sanitary Commission," *North American Review* 104 (January 1867): 152; Charles Eliot Norton, "American Political Ideas," *North American Review* 101 (October 1865): 555.

3. On American exceptionalism, see Dorothy Ross, "Historical Consciousness in Nineteenth-Century America," *American Historical Review* 89 (1984): 909–28, as well as her *Origins of American Social Science* (Cambridge: Cambridge University Press, 1991), pt. 1.

4. "The United States Sanitary Commission," *New York Times*, November 12, 1866, 1.

5. Undated clipping from the *New York Times*, Box 1051, USSC Records.

6. *The Nation*, November 8, 1866, clipping contained in Box 1051, USSC Records. See also Edward Everett Hale, "The United States Sanitary Commission," *Atlantic Monthly* 19 (1867): 417–19; and O. B. Frothingham, "Civil War and Social Benefi-cence," *Harper's New Monthly Magazine* 34 (February 1867): 363.

7. N. Porter to H. W. Bellows, February 1, 1867, Box 647, USSC Records.

8. "Proposed List for Foreign Distribution of Mr. C. J. Stillé's Volume of the History of the Sanitary Commission," n.d., Box 647, folder 3, and C. J. Stillé to J. S. Blatchford, November 29, 1866, Box 646, Folder 7, USSC Records.

9. Quoted in Norman B. Ferris, *Desperate Diplomacy: William H. Seward's Foreign Policy, 1861* (Knoxville: University of Tennessee Press, 1976), 4.

10. Quoted in Frank L. Owsley, *King Cotton Diplomacy: Foreign Relations of the Con-federate States of America*, 2d ed., rev. by Harriet C. Owsley (Chicago: University of Chicago Press, 1959), 186; see also McPherson, *Battle Cry of Freedom*, 551. From the outset, the British press was divided in its opinion on the conflict. On this point, see H. C. Allen, "Civil War, Reconstruction, and Great Britain," in *Heard Round the World: The Impact Abroad of the Civil War*, ed. Harold Hyman (New York: Knopf, 1969): 3–96; and Donaldson Jordan and Edwin J. Pratt, *Europe and the American Civil War* (Boston: Houghton Mifflin, 1931), 79–87.

11. "British Opinion on the War," *Harper's Weekly*, August 31, 1861, 546.

12. Jordan and Pratt (*Europe and the American Civil War*, 123) suggest that the American Civil War was the issue most written about in the English press "not even having temporary rivals." The French press also regularly reported on American events, as noted by George M. Blackburn, *French Newspaper Opinion on the American Civil War* (Westwood, Conn.: Greenwood Press, 1997). In contrast, Reid ("Power, Sovereignty, and the Great Republic," 49–50) cautions against accepting the notion that Europeans all stood "with their mouths agape," as preoccupied as were Americans themselves with their conflict. British statesmen had other things to worry about, especially after 1863 as the Polish struggle against Russian domination threatened to ignite a second Anglo-Russian War, he notes. Yet even if he is right, there was nevertheless a widespread belief in the North that Europeans were closely monitoring the war, and sufficient coverage in the French and British press to give credence to this idea.

13. Paludan (*"A People's Contest,"* 264–73) notes American's "obsession" with what the foreigners thought and said about them in this period. He points out that the *New York Times* printed weekly reports of events in France, and every few weeks its editorials discussed French opinion and policy relative to American events. My survey of the *New York Times* indicates an even more prolific coverage on British reactions to the Civil War. Not all Northern newspapers were equally interested in foreign opinion, however. I found far less concentration on British and French responses to the conflict in the *Philadelphia Inquirer*, for instance, and uneven coverage in local newspapers, with some smaller dailies regularly culling material on foreign opinion from sources like *New York Times*, and others doing so only rarely.

14. Howard Jones, *Union in Peril: The Crisis over British Intervention in the Civil War* (Chapel Hill: University of North Carolina Press, 1992), 2–3; Allen, "Civil War, Reconstruction, and Great Britain," 21–22, 128–36.

15. Whereas the Lincoln administration interpreted the conflict as an insurrection led by traitors and thus a domestic issue, the institution of a naval blockade of Southern ports in April 1861 implicitly recognized the existence of war, which necessitated that foreign powers take sides in the conflict or declare their neutrality. Foreign declarations of neutrality automatically granted the Confederacy the status of a belligerent power with rights under international law to purchase arms, contract loans in neutral countries, and commission naval vessels with powers of search and seizure. See Jones, *Union in Peril*, chap. 1; McPherson, *Battle Cry of Freedom*, 387–91.

16. Paludan, *"A People's Contest,"* 265.

17. Basler, ed., *Collected Works of Abraham Lincoln*, 5:53. See also James M. McPherson, "'The Whole Family of Man': Lincoln and the Last Best Hope Abroad," in *The Union, the Confederacy, and the Atlantic Rim*, ed. Robert E. May (West Lafayette, Ind.: Purdue University Press, 1995): 131–58; and David M. Potter, *The Impending Crisis, 1848–1861* (New York: Harper and Row, 1976), chap. 1.

18. On the popularity of this tune, see Richard Grant White, ed. and comp., *Poetry, Lyrical, Narrative, and Satirical of the Civil War* (New York: American News Co., 1866; repr., New York: Arno Press, 1972), 211–13; and James D. Hart, *The Popular Book: A History of America's Literary Taste* (New York: Oxford University Press, 1950), 117, who

identifies it as the North's most popular sheet music of the war. The song was also popular among Confederates, although with suitably altered words.

19. Henry T. Tuckerman, *America and Her Commentators* (New York: Scribner, 1864), 152, iii–iv, 152; "English Abuse," *Spirit of the Fair* (New York), April 15, 1865, 115.

20. "The Nations That Judge Us," *New York Times*, September 28, 1862, 4

21. Quoted in Allen, "Civil War, Reconstruction, and Great Britain," 35. See also Brian Jenkins, *Britain and the War for the Union*, 2 vols. (Montreal: McGill-Queen's University Press, 1974), 1:121.

22. Jones, *Union in Peril*, 272 n. 4.

23. Quoted in Belle Becker Sideman and Lillian Friedman, *Europe Looks at the Civil War* (New York: The Orion Press, 1960), 173–74. Many in Britain worried that Northern militarism would continue to grow, ultimately threatening their remaining colonies in the New World. On this point, see Ferris, *Desperate Diplomacy*, 201; and Jordan and Pratt, *Europe and the American Civil War*, 21–22. Editors in France likewise warned that Northern democracy was fatally flawed and doomed to degenerate into a dictatorship, as noted in Blackburn, *French Newspaper Opinion*, 134. On the Democrats' criticism of the war effort, see Baker, *Affairs of Party*, chap. 4.

24. Edwin De Leon, "The Truth about the Confederate States of America," reprinted in *Secret History of Confederate Diplomacy Abroad*, ed. William C. Davis (Lawrence: University Press of Kansas, 2005), 212–13. On Hotze's work—particularly the way he shifted his mission near war's end from an unsuccessful bid to champion the slave–holding South, to a more successful effort in propagating a racialist message—see Robert Bonner, "Slavery, Confederate Diplomacy and the Racialist Mission of Henry Hotze," *Civil War History* 51 (September 2005): 288–316. See also Owsley, *King Cotton Diplomacy*, 155.

25. Campbell, *English Public Opinion*, stresses the myriad responses in Britain to the Civil War, rejecting the notion that opinion was sharply divided between a working class and their radical supporters who lined up behind the Union, and an elite that favored the Confederacy. On this point, see also Jordan and Pratt, *Europe and the American Civil War*, 162.

26. Hugh Dubrulle, "A Military Legacy of the Civil War: The British Inheritance," *Civil War History* 49, no. 2 (2003): 153–54, 159.

27. McPherson, *Battle Cry of Freedom*, 197; Paludan, *"A People's Contest,"* xviii–xix.

28. Baker, *Affairs of Party*, 154; McPherson, "The Whole Family of Man," 131–32.

29. Fahs, *Imagined Civil War*, 91–92.

30. Robert MacKenzie, *America and Her Army* (London: T. Nelson and Sons, 1865), 9, 13, 30, 57, 59, and passim. Similarly, see "The Men of the North and the Men of the South," *New York Times*, January 2, 1865, 4.

31. Charles J. Stillé, "How a Free People Conduct a Long War: A Chapter from English History" (Philadelphia: Martien, Printer, 1863), reprinted in *Harper's Weekly* 7 (March 1863): 150–51.

32. The following two examples from the *Philadelphia Inquirer*, for instance, deplored English press coverage of Union soldiers as unjustified: "Comparative Intelligence of

English and American Volunteers," April 19, 1862, 4, and "Versatile Intelligence of Our Volunteers," April 22, 1862.

33. Van Gosse, "'As a Nation, the English Are Our Friends': The Emergence of African American Politics in the British Atlantic World, 1772–1861," *American Historical Review* 113 (October 2008): 1003–28.

34. Harriet Beecher Stowe, *A Reply to "The Affectionate and Christian Address of Many Thousands of Women of Great Britain and Ireland, to their Sisters, The Women of the United States"... in behalf of Many Thousands of American Women* (London: Sampson Low, Son, and Co., 1863).

35. Wendy F. Hamand, "'No Voice from England': Mrs. Stowe, Mr. Lincoln, and the British in the Civil War," *New England Quarterly* 61 (March 1988): 3–24; Jones, *Union in Peril*, 176–77.

36. Whitman, *Specimen Days in America*, 94. Jordan and Pratt (*Europe and the American Civil War*, 163) are among numerous scholars who argue that the Emancipation Proclamation gradually increased support for the Union.

37. Examples include Charles Brandon Boynton, *History of the Great Western Sanitary Fair* (Cincinnati: C. F. Vent and Co., 1864); Charles J. Stillé, *Memorial of the Great Central Fair for the U.S. Sanitary Commission ... June 1864* (Philadelphia: U.S. Sanitary Commission, 1864); *History of the North-Western Soldiers' Fair, Held in Chicago ... November 1863* (Chicago: Dunlop, Sewell and Spalding, 1864); *A Record of the Metropolitan Fair in Aid of the United States Sanitary Commission held ... April 1864* (New York: Hurd and Houghton, 1867); Moore, *History of the Cooper Shop Volunteer Refreshment Saloon*; Iowa Sanitary Commission, *Report of the Iowa Sanitary Commission: From the Organization of the Sanitary Work in Iowa to the Close of Its Service at the End of the War* (Dubuque, Iowa: Ballou and Winall, 1866).

38. L. P. Brockett and Mary C. Vaughan, *Woman's Work in the Civil War: A Record of Heroism, Patriotism and Patience* (Philadelphia: Zeigler, McCurdy and Co., 1867); Frank Moore, *Women of the War: Their Heroism and Self-Sacrifice* (Hartford, Conn.: S. S. Scranton and Co., 1866); Goodrich, *Tribute Book*; and [Brockett], *Philanthropic Results of the War in America*; Stillé, *History of the United States Sanitary Commission*; Moss, *Annals of the United States Christian Commission*; Lemuel Moss and Edward Parmelee Smith, *Christian Work on the Battle-field: Being Incidents of the Labors of the United States' "Christian Commission"* (London: Hodder and Stoughton, 1870); Forman, *The Western Sanitary Commission*. In addition, several USSC branches detailed their work, including: Henshaw, *Our Branch and Its Tributaries*; [Brayton and Terry], *Our Acre and Its Harvest*; Newberry, *USSC in the Valley of the Mississippi*.

39. One exception is Moss, *Annals of the Christian Commission*, 64–67, who attributed wartime benevolence to a "religious awakening of unparalleled extent and power" in the prewar years.

40. Brockett, *Philanthropic Results of the War in America*, 11.

41. Goodrich, *Tribute Book*, 26. According to the author's preface, this work was conceived and funded by George Jones, a proprietor of the *New York Times*. Given the range of data included, it was almost certainly initiated well before the war's end.

42. Moore, *History of the Cooper Shop Volunteer Refreshment Saloon*, 14–15. Most of these writers saw voluntarism itself as peculiarly American, proudly contrasting their freedom of assembly and civic-mindedness with the lack thereof in the Old World. As Jason Kaufman, in *For the Common Good? American Civic Life and the Golden Age of Fraternity* (New York: Oxford University Press, 2002), 20–21, notes, these comparisons drew on foreign accounts (particularly Tocqueville's) of American society.

43. These writers do not suggest that black and white Northerners were united in their voluntary efforts. Black women's groups were, in fact, sometimes barred from charitable endeavors organized by white ladies' aid societies. In Philadelphia, for instance, one black women's group—the Ladies of the Sanitary Committee of St. Thomas' Episcopal Church, auxiliary to the USSC—was prohibited from joining the Sanitary Commission Fair organized in that city in 1864 and forced to hold a separate fair, according to "Fair for the Sick and Wounded Soldiers, St. Thomas' Church (Philadelphia, Pa.)," SM#Am 1864 St. Tho Ch., The Library Company of Philadelphia. Likewise, the volumes cited above often pictured freedmen and women as objects of white charity but did not mention black volunteers, nurses, or aid workers, or cite instances of African American charity. The sole exception is Goodrich, *Tribute Book*, 165, which includes one example of a black woman donating a handmade item to a fair.

44. Goodrich, *Tribute Book*, 27.

45. Ibid., 506 (emphasis in original).

46. "Linus Pierpont Brockett," *Appleton's Cyclopaedia of American Biography*, ed. James Grant Wilson and John Fiske, 8 vols. (New York: D. Appleton and Company, 1886), 1: 382; Brockett, *Philanthropic Results of the War in America*, 13, 9.

47. Quote from Henshaw, *Our Branch and Its Tributaries*, 21–22. Attie, *Patriotic Toil*, 18; and Giesberg, *Civil War Sisterhood*, chap. 4.

48. Fredrickson, *Inner Civil War*, 102.

49. [K. P. Wormeley], *The United States Sanitary Commission: A Sketch of Its Purposes and Its Work* (Boston: Little, Brown, 1863), 253, 256.

50. Hale, "The United States Sanitary Commission," 419; Goodrich, *Tribute Book*, 89–90.

51. For example, "Ornithological," *Our Daily Fare*, June 11, 1864, 28; "Anniversary of the Christian Commission," *Philadelphia Inquirer*, February 12, 1866, 4.

52. Poem written to memorialize the Philadelphia Volunteer Refreshment Saloon, contained in undated volume, U.S. Sanitary Commission Papers, Library of Congress, Manuscript Division, Washington, D.C.

53. On Northern portrayals of Southern women goading men into war, see Mitchell, *The Vacant Chair*, chap. 6; and Silber, "Intemperate Men, Spiteful Women, and Jefferson Davis," 283–305.

54. Norton, "The Work of the Sanitary Commission," 150; Brockett and Vaughan, *Woman's Work in the Civil War*, 55; Moore, *Women of the War*, vi.

55. "England and America," *North American Review* 100 (1865): 331–32.

56. Clipping from the *New York Times*, November 12, 1866, Box 1051, USSC Records.

57. The next International Congress held in Geneva in August 1864 succeeded in drafting the Geneva Convention, the major outcome of which bound signatories to respect the neutrality of war wounded along with their medical personnel. John F. Hutchinson, *Champions of Charity: War and the Rise of the Red Cross* (Boulder, Colo.: Westview Press, 1996), 11–20, 45–52. The Lincoln administration, burdened by domestic issues, declined to send an official U.S. delegate. But the U.S. Sanitary Commission appointed an agent, Charles S. P. Bowles, to attend the conference and publicize their work.

58. "International Sanitary Conference," *Sanitary Commission Bulletin*, January 1, 1864, 148–50; "A Foreign Opinion of the Commission," *Sanitary Commission Bulletin*, March 1, 1864, 272.

59. "Help from Abroad," *Sanitary Commission Bulletin*, January 15, 1864, 170–71.

60. General information on the USSC's English Branch can be found in Maxwell, *Lincoln's Fifth Wheel*, 228–29, 232, 270–76; and Edmund Crisp Fisher, *The English Branch of the United States Sanitary Commission: The Motive of Its Establishment, and the Result of Its Work* (London: William Ridgway, 1865). Box 990 of the USSC Records also contains information on the English Branch, including a diary kept by Branch secretary Edwin Crisp Fisher (hereafter English Branch Diary).

61. Maxwell, *Lincoln's Fifth Wheel*, 229.

62. Commission leaders informed Charles Bowles that fundraising was his least important mission. He replied confirming that his primary objective was to demonstrate to Europeans that "the country which can produce such an Association, and by the people of that Country so universally endorsed, is one which is *not* destined to be extinguished either by bankruptcy, or anything else, or a country which worships only the 'Almighty Dollar.'" C. P. Bowles to J. Foster Jenkins, May 6, 1864, Box 636, Folder 13, USSC Records.

63. James H. Cassedy, "Numbering the North's Medical Events: Humanitarianism and Science in Civil War Statistics," *Bulletin of the History of Medicine* 66 (Summer 1992): 225. The USSC released statistical data during the war relating to such issues as soldiers' nativity and rates of disease and mortality in the Union army, although the full data was not compiled until some years later. It was eventually published in Benjamin Apthorp Gould, *Investigations in the Military and Anthropological Statistics of American Soldiers* (New York: Hurd and Houghton, 1869).

64. Gould imagined his findings as part of a larger effort among American and European scientists to measure and classify the "physical and moral characteristics" of various races. Yet he was reluctant to draw conclusions from his data, deeming it "more proper to leave the discussion to experts" in the fields of ethnology and physiology (Gould, *Investigations*, 317, 320). As noted by John S. Haller, "Civil War Anthropometry: The Making of a Racial Ideology," *Civil War History* 16 (1970): 309–24, his work was enormously influential, providing the foundation for almost all subsequent nineteenth-century racialist studies.

65. This agenda is highlighted in Stillé, *History of the Sanitary Commission*, 460.

66. Gould, *Investigations*, 15, 210; E. B. Elliott, *Military Statistics of the United States*

of America (Berlin: R. V. Decker, 1863). In Berlin Elliott presented statistics derived from his initial measurements of several thousand soldiers, relating not only to soldiers' age but also to mortality and sickness in the army, as well as certain physiological characteristics such as height, chest circumference, weight, and muscular strength. Comparing pre-existing data for European soldiers, he concluded, among other findings, that mortality in the Union army was far lower than that which pertained in previous European wars. Elliott also sent out pamphlet versions of his findings relating to the age and nativity of volunteers. A list of addressees for this work can be found in Box 645, Folder 3, USSC Records. See also B. A. Gould to J. S. Blatchford, November 3, 1864, Box 649, and May 4, 1866, Box 645, USSC Records.

67. Edmund Crisp Fisher, "Military Discipline and Volunteer Philanthropy: A Paper Read Before the Social Science Congress Held in the City of York, September 1864" (London: William Ridgway, 1864). His speeches were reported in *Sanitary Reporter* (Western Dept., Louisville, Ky.), November 1, 1864, 91–92. Letters acknowledging receipt of these documents are contained in Box 339, USSC Records, and in English Branch Diary.

68. Circular dated September 20, 1864, to "All Americans Known to be Resident in Great Britain," Box 990, USSC Records (hereafter "All Americans"); newspaper clipping from *The Patriot*, October 27, 1864, English Branch Diary.

69. "All Amerians."

70. Frederick Milne Edge, *A Woman's Example and a Nation's Work: A Tribute to Florence Nightingale* (London: William Ridgway, 1864). Bowles commissioned a similar work by J. N. Proeschel, *L'oeuvre d'un Grand Peuple* (Paris: Dentu, 1864), which appealed to French readers not by highlighting Nightingale's example (mentioned only briefly) but by referencing that of Henri Dunant.

71. Edge, *A Woman's Example*, 11; Maxwell, *Lincoln's Fifth Wheel*, 329.

72. See entries in English Branch Diary for May 6 and 8, 1865.

73. The Union and Confederate governments had periodically exchanged prisoners in the war's first year and a half, but these exchanges largely ceased in 1863 once the Union began enlisting black troops. Refusing to consider black men as legitimate combatants, the Davis administration declared its intent to treat them as fugitive slaves and to punish their white officers as instigators of servile insurrection. The North responded by halting the return of Confederates captives. See William B. Hesseltine, ed., *Civil War Prisons* (Kent, Ohio: Kent State University Press, 1962).

74. *Report of the Joint Committee on the Conduct and Expenditures of the War*, 38th Cong., 1st sess., 1864, H. Rept. 65, 33–39. Quotations from William B. Hesseltine, "The Propaganda Literature of Confederate Prisons," *Journal of Southern History* 1 (February 1935): 56–66. See also Ann Fabian, *The Unvarnished Truth: Personal Narratives in Nineteenth Century America* (Berkeley: University of California Press, 2000), chap. 4.

75. U.S. Sanitary Commission, *Narrative of Privations and Sufferings of United States Officers and Soldiers while Prisoners of War in the Hands of Rebel Authorities* (Boston: Littell's Living Age, 1864).

76. "Further Proofs of Rebel Inhumanity," *Harper's Weekly*, June 18, 1864, 386.

77. Details on these organizations can be found in Jordan and Pratt, *Europe and the American Civil War*, 171–75.

78. On these efforts, see Philip Van Doren Stearn, *When the Guns Roared: World Aspects of the American Civil War* (New York: Doubleday, 1965), 315–16; Jordan and Pratt, *Europe and the American Civil War*, 171. On Adams's response, see "British Impertinence Fitly Rebuked," *New York Times*, December 10, 1864.

79. English Branch Diary, November 29, 1864; Thomas H. Dudley to Edwin Crisp Fisher, December 5, 1864, English Branch Diary.

80. Z. Eastman to Edwin C. Fisher, December 26, 1864, and George G. Fogg to E. C. Fisher, January 23, 1865, English Branch Diary.

81. Reprinted in Moss, *Annals of the Christian Commission*, 60 (emphasis in original).

82. Ibid., 237; "The Final Anniversary of the Christian Commission," *Littell's Living Age* 88 (1866): 650–51.

83. Moss, *Annals of the Christian Commission*, 42–61 and 734. This work was later condensed and reprinted for a British audience under the title *Christian Work on the Battlefield; Being Incidents of the Labours of the United States 'Christian Commission'* (London: Hodder and Stoughton, 1870). See also "Union Volunteer Refreshment Saloon," *The Fair Record of the Union Volunteer Refreshment Saloon* (n.p.: Philadelphia, 1863), 1.

84. *The Sanitary Commission of the United States Army: A Succinct Narrative of Its Works and Purposes* (New York: n.p., 1864; reprint New York: Arno Press, 1972), vi, 252–53; Goodrich, *Tribute Book*, 506; Moss, *Annals of the Christian Commission*, 734–35.

85. Elijah Couillard to "Dear Sister," September 5, [1863], Elijah Couillard Letters, Massachusetts Historical Society.

86. Rev. J. P. Thompson, "The Advancement of Christ's Kingdom by War," *New Englander* 91 (April 1865): 303–19; Moorhead, *American Apocalypse*, x, 1–22, 80–81; Ernest Lee Tuveson, *Redeemer Nation: The Idea of America's Millennial Role* (Chicago: University of Chicago Press, 1968), 187–214. White ("Lincoln's Sermon on the Mount," 208–25) examines Lincoln's growing religiosity over the course of the war. Similarly, David W. Blight, *Frederick Douglass' Civil War: Keeping Faith in Jubilee* (Baton Rouge: Louisiana State University Press, 1989), chap. 5, provides a moving account of Douglass's increasing millennial expectations.

87. For example, Allan Nevins, *Ordeal of the Union*, 4 vols. (New York: Scribner, 1947; repr., New York: Collier Books, 1992); Fredrickson, *Inner Civil War*; Ginzberg, *Women and the Work of Benevolence*. Recent exceptions include Fahs, *Imagined Civil War*, and Gallman, *Mastering Wartime*.

88. Wilfred M. McClay, *The Masterless Self: Self and Society in Modern America* (Chapel Hill: University of North Carolina Press, 1994), 12. While McClay portrays this spectacle as one of highly disciplined troops, "a single well-oiled marching mechanism of fearsome power and efficiency," many commentators at the time took delight in the Grand Review's rowdy and disorderly aspects. See Stuart McConnell, *Glorious Contentment: The Grand Army of the Republic, 1865–1900* (Chapel Hill: University of North Carolina Press, 1992), 1–17.

89. Quoted in John Jay, *Slavery and the War in America: Speeches, Addresses, Letters etc.,* *1860–1865* (n.p., [1866]).

90. On the optimism of the immediate postwar years, see Blight, *Race and Reunion,* 38.

91. A similar point is made in Moorhead, *American Apocalypse,* chap. 3.

92. Milton Badger, *Welcome to the Returned Soldiers: An Address Delivered at Madison,* *Conn., July 4th 1865* (New Haven: Tuttle, Morehouse and Taylor, 1865).

93. Henry W. Bellows to "My Dear Mr. Strong," August 8, 1866, Box 645B, Folder 7, USSC Records.

94. The following two works, among many others, declared America's other exhibitions a dismal failure: James M. Usher, *Paris, Universal Exposition; 1867. With a Full* *Description of Awards Rendered to the United States Department; and Notes Upon the Same* (Boston: n.p., 1866); and M. D. Conway, "The Great Show at Paris," *Harper's Monthly* *Magazine* 35 (July 1867): 242.

95. A detailed description of the USSC's exhibition can be found in the fourth volume of William P. Blake, ed., *Paris Universal Exposition, 1867,* 6 vols. (Washington, D.C.: Government Printing Office, 1870).

96. H. W. Bellows to "My dear Mr. Blatchford," June 14, 1867, Box 648, Folder 12, USSC Records.

97. On plans to display the material collected by the USSC for the Paris exhibition in the Capitol, see Neil Beckwith to "Dear Sir," January 13, 1868, and William H. Seward to Henry W. Bellows, April 10, 1868, Box 649B, Folder 2, USSC Records.

CHAPTER SIX

1. Fanny Fern, "Left-Hand Manuscripts of Disabled Soldiers," reprinted in "Broadside Concerning Contest," William Oland Bourne Papers, Library of Congress, Manuscript Division, Washington D.C. (hereafter Bourne Papers).

2. "Report of the Committee," *The Soldier's Friend* (New York), March 1866, 2.

3. Taking this duty very seriously indeed, at least seven of the forty-five men who wrote for both competitions had already won a prize the first time around and were thus ineligible for further premiums.

4. Julian E. Kuz and Bradley P. Bengtson, in *Orthopaedic Injuries of the Civil War: An* *Atlas of Orthopaedic Injuries and Treatments during the Civil War* (Kennesaw, Ga.: Kennesaw Mountain Press, 1996), 62, note that among roughly 3 million Civil War soldiers on both sides, surgeons performed approximately 50,000 amputations. In comparison, physicians carried out slightly more than 4,000 amputations on 4 million American servicemen who fought in World War I and roughly 16,000 amputations on the 11 million servicemen who fought in World War II, a difference the authors attribute to advances in weaponry, battlefield evacuation, and medical care.

5. Joseph K. Barnes, ed., *The Medical and Surgical History of the War of the Rebellion* (Washington, D.C.: Government Printing Office, 1883), pt. 3, vol. 2, 877, notes that Union surgeons performed 29,980 amputations with 21,753 Union soldiers surviving. Most men lost an arm, being roughly one and a half times more likely to face upper- rather than lower-extremity amputation. It is likely that these figures significantly

underestimate the number of Union amputees. As Barnes notes, the collection of medical statistics was incomplete in the war's first year. His statistics also fail to encompass amputations performed on officers, those executed by family physicians, or those occurring after soldiers were discharged from service for wounds received in battle.

6. Under federal pension legislation adopted in 1862, Union veterans received monthly pensions ranging from $8 to $30 for total disability, graded according to rank, with lesser amounts paid for partial disability. Congress passed a further pension act in June 1866, which stipulated the rates for 14 specific types of disability. Veterans received $15 a month for the loss or total disability of an arm or leg. On changes in Civil War pension legislation, see John William Oliver, "History of Civil War Military Pensions, 1861–1885," *Bulletin of the University of Wisconsin*, no. 844, History Series, no. 1 (1917): 1–121; and Theda Skocpol, *Protecting Soldiers and Mothers: The Political Origins of Social Policy in the United States* (Cambridge: Harvard University Press, 1992).

7. Patrick J. Kelly, *Creating a National Home: Building the Veterans' Welfare State, 1860–1900* (Cambridge: Harvard University Press, 1997), 23.

8. As the Union army prepared to disband in May 1865, the USSC issued a circular to its branches and aid societies suggesting that they transform their societies into "Bureau[s] of Information and Employment" for the disabled. "Circular to the Branches and Aid Societies Tributary to the U.S. Sanitary Commission," May 15, 1865, no. 90, *Documents*, 2:4–6. Some of the largest USSC branches complied with this request. The Cleveland Branch, for instance, opened an employment bureau where potential employers and employees could register their names. Advertising their work through local papers, personal appeals directed at local businessmen, and a blackboard on the pavement outside the aid society rooms, they eventually found employment for 108 of their 258 able-bodied applicants and 98 of their 153 disabled applicants before disbanding in June 1866. In the meantime, they occasionally provided veterans a monthly allowance for rent; distributed tools and materials for sick men to perform work in their homes; and accommodated a handful of amputees in the soldiers' home attached to the aid society while they received training at the local commercial college or city school. This individualized care was not indiscriminate, with the organization's final report noting: "A few, known to be intemperate and unworthy, were refused entry upon application." The Michigan Branch organized a similar effort in Detroit, which found work for several hundred soldiers, while the USSC's central office likewise opened employment bureaus in several urban centers. On these efforts, see Newberry, *USSC in the Valley of the Mississippi*, 515–16; [Brayton and Terry], *Our Acre and Its Harvest*, 253; also Kelly, *Creating a National Home*, 63–67.

9. Newberry, *USSC in the Valley of the Mississippi*, 512. The USSC was also involved in the establishment of the Soldier-Messenger Corps in New York, which employed disabled veterans to deliver packages and letters. Founded in August 1865, this venture was incorporated as a private company the following year by several prominent New York men and expanded to include 500 messengers, although the USSC apparently declined to fund the expansion. See J. Blatchford to "Gentlemen of the Standing Committee of the U.S. Sanitary Commission," February 8, 1866, Box 644, Folder 11, USSC Records.

10. Dixon Wecter, *When Johnny Comes Marching Home* (Boston: Houghton Mifflin, 1944), 186.

11. Obituary for William Oland Bourne, *New York Times*, June 7, 1901, 9; Box 6, Folder 1, Bourne Papers; *The Soldier's Friend*, December 1864, 2. Monthly editions of this newspaper were published in New York between December 1864 and June 1868. After this date, weekly editions were issued until publication ceased in September 1869.

12. "Work for Disabled Soldiers" and "Four Rules for Discharged Soldiers," *The Soldier's Friend*, March 1865, 1.

13. *The Soldier's Friend*, June 1865, 2. It is likely that Bourne got the idea for this competition from Phineas P. Whitehouse, one of his former patients who wrote to him on April 27, 1865. Anticipating that Bourne would publish his letter, he described his strenuous efforts at left-handed writing, urging other amputees to do likewise. Box 1, Folder 2, William Oland Bourne Manuscript Collection, New York Historical Society, New York. Bourne advertised his competition widely. Entrants mentioned responding to advertisements placed in a number of publications, including *Harper's Weekly*, the *Cincinnati Daily Gazette*, and the *Chicago Tribune*.

14. Major General Oliver Otis Howard, for example, refused Bourne's entreaty to join the competition, although he did agree to judge the manuscripts.

15. William Thomas, competition 1, entry 93 (emphasis in original), Bourne Papers. Hereafter I refer to manuscripts from this collection using the entrant's name, followed by the competition and entry number.

16. *The Soldier's Friend*, March 1865, 1. The proposed memorial volume was never published.

17. W. W. H. Davies, 1:268.

18. To Bourne's original offer of $500 in premiums, the USSC and the Committee of Awards added an extra $500. This sum was divided into first, second, third, and fourth prizes of $200, $150, $100, and $50 respectively. The remaining sum was distributed among seven prizes for second-class penmanship, four prizes for ornamental penmanship, and twelve prizes for literary merit. In the second competition, Bourne awarded ten premiums of $50, each bearing the name of a Union general.

19. As the previous note suggests, only the lesser prizes for "literary merit" focused on the contents of amputees' manuscripts. The rest of the awards took into account the writer's potential for clerical employment.

20. Anon., *The Empty Sleeve; or, Soldier's Appeal* (Boston: G. W. Thomas, 1870). Pamphlets similar to this one, which sold for ten cents, circulated widely during and immediately after the war.

21. For instance, a poem published during the war, "The Cripple at the Gate," juxtaposed wealthy Northerners enjoying themselves while an armless soldier on his way home from the front is forced to beg for his livelihood. White, ed. and comp., *Poetry, Lyrical, Narrative, and Satirical of the Civil War*, 132–34.

22. The popular wartime poem "Driving Home the Cows," anonymously authored by Katherine Day Putnam and reprinted in White, *Poetry, Lyrical, Narrative and Satirical*, 220–23, is one example of a bittersweet poem depicting an amputee. More

frequently it was sweethearts, rather than parents, who featured in stories and poems where despair over a soldier's presumed death gives way to gratitude upon his unexpected return, regardless of a missing limb. One such story is "Kitten," *Harper's New Monthly Magazine* 26 (March 1863): 696–99.

23. Quoted in Francis Winthrop Palfrey, *Memoir of William Francis Bartlett* (Boston: Houghton, Osgood and Company, 1878), 51–52.

24. Quoted in Laura C. Halloway, *Howard: The Christian Hero* (New York: Funk and Wagnalls, 1885), 77.

25. Quoted in ibid.,78.

26. Statistics on men entering the Invalid Reserve Corps were drawn from Byron Stinson, "Paying the Debt," *Civil War Times Illustrated* 9 (1970): 20–29. Recruiting invalid soldiers for use in wartime was not new. An Invalid Corps had been established during the Revolutionary period, following earlier European precedents. On the development of the VRC, see Stanley Michael Suplick Jr., "The United States Invalid Corps/Veteran Reserve Corps," Ph.D. diss., University of Minnesota, 1969, chap. 1.

27. The Provost-Marshal-General ordered the posting of handbills advertising the VRC as a "corps of honor" in June 1863. Convalescent soldiers with limbs intact were generally assigned to the first battalion of the VRC, which performed provost and guard duty. *The War of the Rebellion: A Compilation of the Official Records of the Union and Confederate Armies* ser. 3, 3:337. Although soldiers sometimes viewed the VRC as the repository for incompetent officers and malingering convalescents, wounds received in battle excluded amputees from such indictments.

28. Suplick, "The United States Invalid Corps," 126.

29. In his earlier autobiographical account, A. F. Hill described his wound in a much less upbeat manner, sharply criticizing his physicians for their callousness and ineptitude. See *Our Boys: The Personal Experiences of a Soldier in the Army of the Potomac* (Philadelphia: John E. Potter, 1864)

30. A. F. Hill, *John Smith's Funny Adventures on a Crutch* (Philadelphia: John E. Potter and Company, 1869), 36.

31. Phlegmatic amputees were typically white, although postwar images of black soldiers with missing limbs were not uncommon. Usually emphasizing the shared sacrifices of black and white Union soldiers, they implicitly claimed citizenship rights for African American men on this basis. One lithograph, "A Man Knows a Man," for instance, showed a black and white veteran, each with a missing leg, with the caption: "Give me your hand, Comrade! We have each lost a Leg for the good cause; but, thank God, we never lost Heart." *Harper's Weekly*, April 22, 1865, 256.

32. Joseph Egolf, 1:207; Charles Jackson, 1:221; George W. Akers, 1:114; and John L. Brown, 2:66.

33. The most forthright critic was Martin D. Hamilton, 1:243, who called on his one-armed comrades to demand better financial compensation, writing: "I am [for] Boldly . . . striking for higher wages." Referring to his pension as a "wage," he questioned: "whoe has any beter right than we criples do who helped defend this property of the north?"

34. John Koster, 1:124; William Kipling, 1:231.

35. Ultimately, the Committee of Awards disregarded the time that writers had for practice, or their previous occupations or education, arguing that such considerations "were of too delicate a nature and too complicated to warrant a detailed investigation, especially as they were aside from the main question—which of the competitors excelled in business penmanship?" See leaflet headed "Exhibition of Left-Handed Penmanship," Folder 1, Box 1, Bourne Papers.

36. On Bourne's efforts to find work for entrants see, for instance, a letter attached to the manuscript of D. Stilwell, 1:214. The principal's offer is detailed in "Free Scholarships for Left-Armed Men," *The Soldier's Friend*, April 1866, 2 (emphasis in original).

37. Charles Edwin Horne, 1:179.

38. See, for instance, George Dale, 2:30; John Stewart, 1:93; Henry Chaffee, 1:156; Alfred B. Tuttle, 1:247; or John A. Ludford Jr., 1:11.

39. Alfred Tuttle, 1:247.

40. Phineas P. Whitehouse, 2:8.

41. Alfred Randolph, 1:194.

42. Ira Borshears, 1:64.

43. Henry Palmer, 1:73.

44. C. Dallett Hemphill, *Bowing to Necessities: A History of Manners in America, 1620–1860* (New York: Oxford University Press, 1999), 173.

45. Thomas Perrine, 1:50. This manuscript won a prize for ornamental penmanship. In a letter accepting his prize, Perrine explained to Bourne that his poem was fictitious, as no sweetheart had spurned him. According to his pension file, certificate 420,678, Bureau of Pensions, Records of the Veterans Administration, RG 15, National Archives, Washington, D.C., Perrine was attending school before the war broke out, and he took up the study of law thereafter. He married in 1879 and had several children. Hereafter, pension files are cited by the applicant's name and pension certificate number.

46. Seth Koven, "Remembering and Dismemberment: Crippled Children, Wounded Soldiers, and the Great War in Great Britain," *American Historical Review* 99 (1994): 1167–1202; Bourke, *Dismembering the Male*, chap. 1.

47. Erin O'Connor, "'Fractions of Men': Engendering Amputation in Victorian Culture," *Comparative Studies in Society and History* 39 (1997): 744–47; Lisa Herschbach, "Prosthetic Reconstructions: Making the Industry, Re-Making the Body, Modeling the Nation," *History Workshop Journal* 44 (Autumn 1997): 24–25. Historians of the post–World War I prosthetic limb industry have also argued that the reconstruction of the human body based on principles of engineering was a dramatic achievement of this war, symbolically erasing the suffering of the maimed and reconstructing the male body along utilitarian lines. See, for example, Roxane Panchasi, "Reconstructions: Prosthetics and the Rehabilitation of the Male Body in World War I France," *differences: A Journal of Feminist Cultural Studies* 7 (1995): 109–40.

48. Congress passed an Act in July 1862 guaranteeing artificial limbs for maimed Union soldiers. An allowance of $50 for an arm or foot and $75 for a leg was specified, though commissioned officers were ineligible for such benefits until 1868. Laurann Figg

and Jane Farrell-Beck, "Amputation in the Civil War: Physical and Social Dimensions," *Journal of the History of Medicine and Allied Sciences* 48 (1993): 463. According to Wecter (*When Johnny Comes Marching Home*, 214), however, a government report published in 1866 noted orders for only 3,981 legs, 2,240 arms, 9 feet and 55 hands, while an unofficial newspaper estimate several years later gave a similar figure.

49. In my survey of more than a hundred Civil War amputees' pension files, I found only one man who expressed satisfaction with his prosthetic limb. Instead, many of these amputees claimed a commutation fee in lieu of a prosthetic device (as I note later, this was a self-selected group; the majority of amputees are not represented in pension files, having never made application). From 1870 onward, amputees were eligible to claim either the cost of a new prosthesis or a commutation fee of equal value. It is possible that some who took the commutation money continued to use a prosthetic device supplied prior to 1870, but many others doubtless made do without. It should also be noted that although only twenty-two men in my survey specified their postwar occupations to pension officials, none were industrial laborers. The majority worked in offices, as bookkeepers, real estate agents, pension attorneys, postmasters, or salesmen. Prosthetic limb manufacturers clearly recognized this fact, since advertisements for their products regularly pictured artificial arms holding a pen.

50. Figg and Farrell-Beck, "Amputation in the Civil War," 467–68.

51. William Compton, 1:236; Charles Coleman, 1:49; and Lewis Kline, 1:41.

52. Rotundo, *American Manhood*, chap. 1. On the importance of self-discipline among Union soldiers, see Mitchell, *The Vacant Chair*, 46.

53. Louis J. Boos, 1:10; Rufus L. Robinson, 1:71.

54. T. J. Cavanaugh, 1:169.

55. Tamara Plakins Thornton, *Handwriting in America: A Cultural History* (New Haven: Yale University Press, 1996), 43, 50.

56. G. H. Long, 1:16; Lewis Kline, 1:41.

57. George H. Long's pension file, certificate 34,728, does not specify his prewar occupation, although it does note that in the late 1880s he was an insurance salesman. According to Lewis E. Kline's pension file, certificate 654,569, he was a farmer before the war. It is silent on his postwar occupation.

58. Judith Hilkey, *Character Is Capital: Success Manuals in Gilded Age America* (Chapel Hill: University of North Carolina Press, 1997), chap. 1, examines the popularity of advice literature written for men in the 1850s and 1860s, as well as later success manuals.

59. Allen's pension file lists his prewar occupation, while a death certificate dated 1911 notes that he later became a salesman. Pension certificate 817,848.

60. Henry C. Allen, 1:15 (emphasis in original).

61. Phil Faulk, 2:91.

62. Representations of the wound as a "decoration" or "ornament" to the male body drew on a lengthy history. Tattoos have long been popular among certain groups of men in Europe and the United States (especially those in the military), for instance, not least because they symbolized the bearer's ability to withstand pain. Likewise, Robert A Nye,

in *Masculinity and Male Codes of Honor in Modern France* (New York: Oxford University Press, 1993), describes how European men courted the dueling scar as a symbol of manhood prior to World War I. As Harlan Hahn notes, the meanings attributed to physical differences have altered markedly over time, understood through a complex and changing dialectic of fascination, fear, disgust and sensuality—from the eroticization of the disabled in medieval festivals to the sexualization of the tubercular sufferer's emaciated body in the Victorian era. Only with the introduction of mass-produced standards of physical perfection in the modern period, he argues, have the disabled become "the aesthetically neutered objects of benevolence and assistance." See "Can Disability Be Beautiful?" *Social Policy* (Winter 1988): 26–32.

63. Blight, *Race and Reunion*, introduction and passim.

64. McPherson, *For Cause and Comrades*, chap. 8.

65. George W. Dale, 2:30.

66. John Bryson, 2:23 (emphasis in original).

67. Alfred Whitehouse, 2:73 (emphasis in original).

68. Charles Edwin Horne. 1:179; Julius Wood, 1:115.

69. Paula Baker, "The Domestication of Politics: Women and American Political Society, 1780–1920," *American Historical Review* 89 (1994): 630.

70. *The Soldier's Friend*, March 1866, 1.

71. For example, John Foster, 1:242.

72. Lewis Kline, 2:25; James H. Smith, 1:233.

73. David A. Gerber, "Heroes and Misfits: The Troubled Social Reintegration of Disabled Veterans in *The Best Years of Our Lives*," *American Quarterly* 46, no. 4 (December 1994): 545–74; Sonja Michel, "Danger on the Home Front: Motherhood, Sexuality, and Disabled Veterans in American Postwar Films," *Journal of the History of Sexuality* 3, no. 1 (July 1992): 109–28.

74. Koven, "Remembering and Dismemberment," 1167–1202.

75. Phineas P. Whitehouse, 1:136; Henry C. Allen, 1:15; Jonathan McKinstry Allison, 1:67.

76. These speeches were reprinted in *The Soldier's Friend*, June 1866, 2. No evidence suggests that Bourne succeeded in taking the exhibition overseas.

77. John M. Thompson, 2:63: his pension certificate 175,589.

78. D. E. Bates, 1:7. See also Dorus E. Bates' pension certificate 298,560.

79. Franklin H. Durrah, pension certificate 11,149.

80. William H. Glasson, *Federal Military Pensions in the United States* (New York: Oxford University Press, 1911), 138, 157.

81. Skocpol, *Protecting Soldiers and Mothers*, 116–18.

82. Hollaway, *Howard*, 232.

83. Members of the public and the scientific community could read about these expeditions in newspaper articles and reports and in Powell's journals, published as *Exploration of the Colorado River of the West and Its Tributaries; Explored in 1869, 1870, 1871, and 1872* (Washington, D.C.: Government Printing Office, 1875). According to "Down the Colorado," *American Heritage*, 20, no. 6 (October 1969): 52–61, 83, Powell's

writings "created a sensation" in the early 1870s. Powell went on to found the Smithsonian's Bureau of Ethnology, which he directed for several decades.

84. Sam Ross notes that Fairchild was a member of the Garfield Monument Association, the Gettysburg Association, and the Military Parks Association, as well as a leading member of the GAR's Committee on Teaching Lessons of Loyalty, which sent veterans into schools to give children a pro-Union perspective on the war. Also, equating patriotism with "law and order," Fairchild took a particularly harsh stance toward union militants and striking workers. See Ross, *The Empty Sleeve: A Biography of Lucius Fairchild* (Madison: State Historical Society of Wisconsin, 1964), 95, 218.

85. Bruce Catton, *Prefaces to History* (New York: Doubleday and Co., 1970). This incident is detailed in the first essay, dated 1962.

86. Daniel Edgar Sickles achieved prewar notoriety when he shot his wife's lover in cold blood, thereafter becoming the first accused murderer to mount a successful plea of temporary insanity. A New York senator before the war, Sickles would become a controversial general, with debates over his leadership at Gettysburg continuing to this day. He served a minister to Spain after the war before re-entering Congress. Swanberg, *Sickles the Incredible.*

87. Quoted in Thomas Keneally, *American Scoundrel: Murder, Love and Politics in Civil War America* (New York: Doubleday, 2002), 348.

88. Their numbers were enormous: approximately 41,000 British soldiers survived an amputation, as did more than 66,000 German troops, and a slightly smaller number of French ones. Millions of others returned home from this war with debilitating wounds or illnesses. Bourke, *Dismembering the Male*, 33; Whalen, *Bitter Wounds*, 55–56; and Jean-Jacques Becker, *The Great War and the French People*, trans. Arnold Pomerans (New York: Berg Publishers, 1985), 6.

89. Bourke, *Dismembering the Male*, chap 1; Whalen, *Bitter Wounds*, chaps. 3 and 11.

90. On this point, see also Scott Gelber, "A 'Hard Boiled Order': The Re-education of Disabled World War I Veterans in New York City," *Journal of Social History* 39, no. 1 (Fall 2005): 161–80.

91. Marilyn Lake, *The Limits of Hope: Soldier Settlement in Victoria, 1915–1938* (Oxford: Oxford University Press, 1987), 52–53.

92. Gail Bederman discusses the changing importance of the male body to definitions of male gender identity in the late nineteenth century in *Manliness and Civilization: A Cultural History of Gender and Race in the United States, 1880–1917* (Chicago: University of Chicago Press, 1993).

93. Koven, "Remembering and Dismemberment," 1167–1202; Gerber, "Heroes and Misfits," 545–74; Michel, "Danger on the Home Front," 109–28.

94. Victorian culture was not entirely eviscerated by World War I. As Joanna Bourke notes in *Dismembering the Male*, 58, amputees in the immediate aftermath of World War I made statements suggesting that their injuries provided opportunities to demonstrate a self-controlled manhood. But such statements held a great deal less persuasive power by this time, not least because of the many negative depictions of the war wounded that were in circulation after this conflict.

95. Bourne, *Dismembering the Male*, chap. 1.

EPILOGUE

1. Edith W. Harwood, "GAR Campfires," *Palimpsest* 70 (Spring 1989): 14–17. This reminiscence appears to have been written sometime after World War I.

2. Paludan notes that in 1860 there existed approximately 140,433 manufacturing establishments in areas outside what would become the Confederacy, employing an average of 9.34 workers each (*"A People's Contest,"* 172–73).

3. Sean Dennis Cashman, *America in the Gilded Age: From the Death of Lincoln to the Rise of Theodore Roosevelt* (New York: New York University Press, 1993), chap. 1.

4. General surveys of this period include ibid.; Nell Irvin Painter, *Standing at Armageddon: The United States, 1877–1919* (New York: W. W. Norton, 1987); Alan Trachtenberg, *The Incorporation of America: Culture and Society in the Gilded Age* (New York: Hill and Wang, 1982); and Robert Wiebe, *The Search for Order, 1877–1920* (New York: Hill and Wang, 1966).

5. Nina Silber, *The Romance of Reunion: Northerners and the South, 1865–1900* (Chapel Hill: University of North Carolina Press, 1993), 53.

6. Sutherland, *Expansion of Everyday Life*, 233.

7. Silber, *Romance of Reunion*, 6, 49.

8. On the propagation of the Lost Cause myth see Gaines M. Foster, *Ghosts of the Confederacy: Defeat, the Lost Cause, and the Emergence of the New South* (New York: Oxford University Press, 1987), and John David Smith, *An Old Creed for the New South: Proslavery Ideology and Historiography, 1865–1918* (Carbondale: Southern Illinois University Press, 2008), chap. 2.

9. Blight, *Frederick Douglass' Civil War*, chaps. 9–10.

10. Frank Luther Mott, *A History of American Magazines, 1850–1885* (Cambridge: Harvard University Press, 1957), 457–80; see also Fahs, *Imagined Civil War*, 314; and Blight, *Race and Reunion*, 173–87.

11. Several hundred thousand veterans paid dues to the GAR in the early postwar years, although membership dwindled to around 30,000 by the late 1860s, where it remained throughout the following decade. This trend reversed in the 1880s with a large-scale renewal of interest in veterans' organizations. Thereafter GAR membership climbed steadily, reaching a peak of almost 410,000 in 1890. Smaller groups also gained adherents in the last two decades of the century, although none came close to matching the GAR's enormous popularity. After this period, GAR membership began to taper off due to a natural decline among the veteran population. Historians agree that the meteoric expansion of the GAR is largely attributable to the organization's success in lobbying for liberalized pensions for Union veterans. Skocpol, *Protecting Soldiers and Mothers*, offers the most comprehensive analysis of the history and political impact of Civil War pensions.

12. Blight, *Race and Reunion*, 182.

13. Fahs, *Imagined Civil War*, chap. 9. On the growing popularity of stories depicting Northern men marrying Confederate women, see also Silber, *Romance of Reunion*, chap. 2.

14. Holmes, "Soldier's Faith," 181–85.

15. Ahlstrom, *Religious History of the American People*, 733; Arthur Meier Schlesinger,

"The Critical Period in American Religion, 1875–1900," *Proceedings of the Massachusetts Historical Society* 64 (1932–33): 523–47.

16. Ahlstrom, *Religious History of the American People*, 735; Cashman, *America in the Gilded Age*, 74.

17. Ahlstrom, *Religious History of the American People*, 768; Cynthia Eagle Russett, *Darwin in America: The Intellectual Response, 1865–1912* (San Francisco: W. H. Freeman, 1976), 11.

18. Russett, *Darwin in America*, 89.

19. On the late nineteenth-century celebration of male physicality, see Bederman, *Manliness and Civilization*; T. J. Jackson Lears, *No Place of Grace: Antimodernism and the Transformation of American Culture, 1880–1920* (Chicago: University of Chicago Press, 1981), 98–139; Rotundo, *American Manhood*, chap. 10; and Michael S. Kimmel, "Consuming Manhood: The Feminization of American Culture and the Recreation of the Male Body, 1832–1920," *Michigan Quarterly Review* 33 (1994): 7–36.

20. Bederman (*Manliness and Civilization*, 18) notes that the new noun "masculinity" was applied from around 1890 onward to denote these different concepts of male power and identity. Whereas Victorian "manhood" was synonymous with moral attributes like sexual self-restraint, spirituality, strength of character, and principled conduct, this new term was "devoid of moral or emotional meaning," referring to "any characteristics, good or bad, which all men had."

21. Lears (*No Place of Grace*, 98–139) discusses how middle-class Americans embraced martial ideals in response to fears of overcivilization. See also John Pettegrew, "'The Soldier's Faith': Turn-of-the Century Memory of the Civil War and the Emergence of Modern American Nationalism," *Journal of Contemporary History* 31 (1996): 49–73.

22. Frank Wilkenson [*sic*], "Spotsylvania: Reflections," *Civil War Times Illustrated* 22 (April 1983): 19; originally published as Frank Wilkeson, *Recollections of a Private Soldier in the Army of the Potomac* (New York: G. P. Putnam's Sons, 1887).

23. Blight, *Race and Reunion*, chap. 5. See also G. Kurt Piehler, *Remembering War the American Way* (Washington, D.C.: Smithsonian Institution Press, 1995), chap. 2.

24. Compared to the sustained wartime discussion of Northern women's voluntarism, little was written on the subject in 1870s. In the 1880s, however, as male veterans increasingly reminisced about the war, a number of former nurses took advantage of this heightened interest in the conflict to publicize their memoirs. Several compiled wartime diaries, journals, and letters for publication, while approximately ten female authors either featured their war work as part of their memoirs, or devoted manuscripts to this aspect of their lives.

25. Hoge, *The Boys in Blue*; Mary A. Livermore, *My Story of the War: A Woman's Narrative of Four Years Personal Experience as Nurse in the Union Army, and in Relief Work at Home, in Hospitals, Camps, and at the Front, During the War of the Rebellion* (Hartford, Conn., 1887; repr., New York: Da Capo Press, 1995) (page citations refer to reprint edition); Annie Wittenmyer, *Under the Guns: A Woman's Reminiscences of the Civil War* (Boston: E. B. Stillings and Co., 1895); Adelaide W. Smith, *Reminiscences of an Army Nurse During the Civil War* (New York: Greaves Publishing Co., 1911).

26. There are a few exceptions to this trend. Like Newcomb, *Four Years of Personal Reminiscences of the War*, a number of former nurses continued emphasizing the exceptional character of Union sufferers, retaining their wartime identities as motherly advocates of enlisted men. They were typically allied to the GAR, appearing at campfire meetings where they were feted as exceptional women. The WRC worked to promote this status, for instance by distributing booklets on nurses' war experiences at GAR encampment, seeking to have their work recognized as equivalent to soldiering. As Jane E. Schultz notes, these efforts were geared toward gaining pensions for a narrowly defined group of former nurses; see "Race, Gender, and Bureaucracy: Civil War Army Nurses and the Pension Bureau," *Journal of Women's History* 6 (Summer 1994): 45–69. As nurses singled themselves out as appropriate pension recipients, they separated themselves from the mass of women who labored on the home front, undercutting older claims that the mobilization of women as a whole had been decisive in securing the Union's victory.

27. After failing in a national petition drive to alter drinking laws in the late 1870s, WCTU leader Frances Willard urged suffrage as the only effective way for women to protect their homes and promote morality. As acceptance of suffrage grew in the following decade, the WCTU increasingly advanced natural rights arguments in defense of women's enfranchisement, notes Ruth Bordin, in *Women and Temperance: The Quest for Power and Liberty, 1873–1900* (Philadelphia: Temple University Press, 1981), chap. 7. The WRC was not far behind in embracing suffrage and increasing its involvement with the broader women's rights struggle. Initially formed as a national organization in 1883, the WRC began turning away from veterans' aid and toward mobilizing women as an autonomous bloc to shape political discourse and public life in the 1890s, notes Cecelia O'Leary in *To Die For: The Paradox of American Patriotism* (Princeton, N.J.: Princeton University Press, 1999), 97. Its new mission focused around efforts to instill patriotism in the nation's citizenry, particularly among new immigrant groups (agitating for schools to display the national flag and introduce the pledge of allegiance, for instance, or supporting Memorial Day observance, flag desecration laws, the erection of memorial halls and monuments, and a range of patriotic holidays). WRC leaders proposed in 1890 to join the National Council of Women, an umbrella group established in 1888 to unite suffrage and temperance activists that soon included every major women's organization. Despite some initial resistance to this proposition, it passed in 1893.

28. Nancy Cott, *The Grounding of Modern Feminism* (New Haven: Yale University Press, 1987), 29.

29. Quotation from Livermore, *My Story of the War*, 125.

30. For Jane Hoge's description of the same scene, see *Boys in Blue*, 42.

31. Livermore, *My Story of the War*, 187–88.

32. Ibid., 196.

33. Unlike GAR members, who campaigned for the introduction of military drill in schools in the 1890s, both the WRC and the WCTU advocated peace and the use of arbitration in conflict resolution. On the WRC's peace campaigns, see O'Leary, *To Die For*, 96–97; on similar activism among the WCTU see Bordin, *Women and Temperance*, 109–10.

34. Livermore, *My Story of the War*, 191–92, 321–22. In another passage, Livermore does discuss the "Christ-like patience" of the wounded, but her declaration of esteem is undercut by the next line, which depicts men in general as more "impatient in sickness, more exacting, and less manageable than women" (202–5).

35. For example, Linderman, *Embattled Courage*, 30.

36. Livermore delivered an average of 150 speeches a year on suffrage and temperance in a lecture career that began in 1875 and spanned a quarter of a century. She was also active in various suffrage organizations and edited several suffrage newspapers, notes Robert E. Riegel, "Mary Livermore," in *Notable American Women*, ed. Edward T. James (Cambridge: Harvard University Press, 1971), 2: 41.

37. On the way Protestant spokespeople came to advocate physical vitality as a means of religious revitalization around mid-century, see Clifford Putney, *Muscular Christianity: Manhood and Sports in Protestant America, 1880–1920* (Cambridge: Harvard University Press, 2001). By this time, notes Edward A. Purcell Jr., religious spokespeople were fast losing their dominant position in range of fields extending from education to humanitarianism, replaced by new disciplines that rejected metaphysical thinking for scientific naturalism; see Purcell, *The Crisis of Democratic Theory: Scientific Naturalism and the Problem of Value* (Lexington: University Press of Kentucky, 1973), chaps. 1–2.

Index

A

Abbott, Rev. John, 99
abolition (of slavery), 13, 14, 21–22, 26,
31, 123, 124–25, 140. *See also* emancipation (of slaves); slavery
Adams, Charles Francis, Jr., 4, 33–34
Adams, Charles Francis, Sr., 34, 138
African Americans, 60, 64–65, 116, 123,
141, 142, 159, 167, 178–79, 180,
229n43; depictions of, 21, 25, 25, 65,
154, 212n41, 236n31; as soldiers, 60,
64, 82–83, 114, 122, 133, 148, 184;
and suffering, 11–12, 26, 64–65;
women, 11–12. *See also* slaves
Ahlstrom, Sydney, 182
alcohol, 5, 19, 36, 68, 109, 111. *See also*
temperance movement
Allen, Henry, 164, 168
Allison, Jonathan, 168
ambulance corps, 56, 68; calls for, 42, 88
amputees, 144, 145, 146–47, 159–61,
233nn4–5; accounts by, 7, 68, 72,
74–75, 76, 144, 145–46, 150–51,
154–59, 160, 161, 162; depictions of,
73, 79, 160, 236n31; and family, 168,
169; and manhood, 159–61, 173;
patriotism of, 153, 164–65, 167–68,
170, 171–72; stories about, 1, 2, 6, 82,
150, 151–52, 169, 173, 174, 176
anesthesia, 11, 12
Armory Square Hospital, 107
Attie, Jeanie, 86

B

Bancroft, George, 139
Banks, Nathaniel, 169
Bartlett, Col. William, 152–53
Barton, Clara, 56
Bates, Dorus, 169
Bellows, Henry, 94, 142–43
Bibles, 16, 17, 67, 88, 91, 102
Bierce, Ambrose, 4
Boos, Louis, 161
Borshears, Ira, 158

Bourne, William, 144–45, 147–48, 235n13

Bowditch, Henry, 28–30, 31, 32, 35–36, 39–40, 41–43, 47–48, 49–50, 201n8

Bowditch, Nathaniel, 28–29, 31, 32, 33, 38, 39–40, 42; death of, 42, 44–45, 47–48; and faith, 38, 40, 41; and family, 31, 34, 36–37, 39; letters of, 29–30, 38, 39–40; self-doubt, 32, 39–40, 48

Bowditch, Nathaniel (senior), 31

Bowditch, Olivia, 31, 37, 39, 41, 43

Bowditch family, 28, 29, 30, 31–32, 34, 36–37, 44, 47

Brady, Matthew, 81

bravery, 7, 34, 35, 37, 38, 39, 46, 49, 50, 53, 70, 71, 85, 120; and class, 35, 46. *See also* soldiers (Union)

Britain, relations with, 117–18, 119, 120, 123, 132, 137

Brockett, Linus, 128–29, 130–31

Brown, Elon, 75

Bryson, John, 165

Butler, Josiah, 80

C

Canada, 123

casualties, 2, 6, 55, 58, 81–82; aestheticization of, 4–5. *See also* amputees; Civil War: death toll; death; suffering

Catholicism, 18

Catton, Bruce, 171

cavalry, 37–38, 44, 202n24

Cavanaugh, J., 161

chaplains, 1, 51, 68, 91, 93, 147

Chase, John F., 73

Chase, Salmon P., 139

Civil War, 3, 5, 6, 7, 38–39, 41–42, 43, 46–47, 52, 87, 88, 111–12, 113, 123–24, 199n58; criticism of, 3, 4, 114–15, 119–23, 124, 128, 129, 134, 143, 208n6; death toll, 3, 4, 58, 114, 119, 128, 169; and medicine, 55–56,

66–67; memorialization of, 175–88; and modernity, 3, 4, 5, 38, 87, 114, 120, 141; reporting of, 54, 56–57, 58, 81–82; scholarship on, 3–5, 29, 33–34, 52–53, 85–86, 114–15, 120–21, 125, 140–41, 176, 190n7, 225n1

Clark, James Freeman, 29

Clark, Joseph, 45

Coleman, Charles, 160

Colfax, Schuyler, 168–69

compassion. *See* sympathy

conscription, 114; opposition to, 3, 119, 126, 128, 143

Cooper, Anthony Ashley (3rd Earl of Shaftesbury), 14

courage. *See* bravery

Crimean War, 54–55, 135, 209n8

D

Dale, George, 165

Darwin, Charles, 182–83

Davis, Col. W., 148–50

death, 4, 8–9, 11; anonymity of, 6, 61–62, 95; and class, 8, 9, 10; futility of, 47, 49; inspirational, 6, 31, 44, 47–48, 49, 50 (*see also* martyrdom, stories of; suffering: exemplary); meaning of, 43, 52–53; religious aspects, 4–5, 31, 61, 64; stories of, 2, 6, 9, 31, 57, 61–62, 64–65, 67, 69, 158, 176; of women, 8–9. *See also under* officers (Union); soldiers (Union)

De Forest, John W., 4

Democratic Party, 3, 119

Dickinson, Emily, 4

disease, 5, 6, 9, 10–11, 55, 64, 68, 69

Dix, Dorothea, 56

Dix, Otto, 172

doctors, 10, 66, 68, 129, 132; army, 59, 61, 63, 66, 92, 106, 132; Confederate, 63, 68, 82, 162; and suffering, 10–12, 19–20, 69, 174; uncaring, 55, 66, 106; volunteer, 41–42, 137

domesticity, 19, 20–22, 26, 97–112, 156, 157, 183; at front, 85, 93, 96, 101; in hospitals, 105, 106–8; maternal, 97–99; patriarchal, 20–21, 97. *See also* family
Douglass, Frederick, 180
draft laws. *See* conscription
Dubrulle, Hugh, 120–21
Dudley, Thomas, 138
Dunant, Henry, 132
Durrah, Eliza, 170
Durrah, Franklin, 169–70

E
Eastman, Zabina, 138
Edge, Frederick Milne, 135
egalitarianism, 5–6, 115
Egolf, Joseph, 154
Eliot, Charles W., 32
Elliot, Ezekiel B., 133, 134, 230n66
emancipation (of slaves), 113, 123–25, 142, 154, 167
emotions, 15, 16, 22–23, 87, 97, 98, 99, 109. *See also* sympathy
Evarts, William M., 132
Everett, Edward, 48
exceptionalism, 2–3, 7, 115, 180

F
Fahs, Alice, 180–81
Fairchild, Lucius, 171
faith (Christian), 1, 2, 4–5, 7, 12, 17–18, 29, 34, 38, 39, 40–41, 42, 43, 50, 51, 206n61; loss of, 4. *See also under* soldiers (Union); suffering
family, 63–64, 65, 75, 97–99, 122, 195n37; bourgeois, 32, 36–37, 85, 98; and morality, 63–64, 85, 98; working-class, 34–35, 36
Faulk, Phil, 164, 165
Faust, Drew Gilpin, 4
Fay, Frank B., 92–93
Fern, Fanny, 144
Fisher, Edmund Crisp, 134–35, 138

Fogg, George, 138
Fox, Feraline, 44
France, relations with, 117–18, 119, 120, 132
Fredrickson, George, 4, 47, 129
funerals, 8, 9. *See also* graves

G
Garrett, William, 110
Giesberg, Judith, 86
Gifford, Thomas, 109
Gilson, Helen, 64–65
Goodrich, Frank, 126–28, 139
Gould, Benjamin, 133, 134
Grand Army of the Republic, 175, 180, 241n11
Grant, Ulysses S., 128, 161, 168, 178
graves, 9, 10, 63; unmarked, 6, 52, 55, 61–62
grief, 10, 14, 42–43, 44, 158; suppression of, 42–43, 44
Grimbs, James, 109
Grosz, George, 172

H
Hamand, Wendy, 124–25
Hammond Hospital, 106–7
Harwood, Edith, 175, 181
Henshaw, Sarah, 65
Herschbach, Lisa, 159
Hess, Earl, 71
Hill, A. F., 153–54, 172
Hobbes, Thomas, 15
Hoge, Jane, 57–58, 62, 108, 185, 186
Holmes, Oliver Wendell, 4, 181–82, 183
hospitals, 56, 66, 80–81, 106–8; "colored," 64; field, 53, 55; private/volunteer, 88, 90, 90–91, 96
Hotze, Henry, 120
Houghton, Annie, 37
Howard, Oliver Otis, 152–53, 170
humanitarianism, 13–15, 132, 193n19
Hutcheson, Francis, 14

I

Indiana Sanitary Commission, 90
industrialization, 18, 20, 35, 176, 187, 185. *See also* Civil War: and modernity
insanity, 14, 170
Invalid Reserve Corps, 153, 236n36
Iowa Sanitary Commission, 90

J

Jackson, Charles, 154–55
Johnson, Andrew, 141
Junger, Ernst, 172

K

Kelly, Mary, 80
Kipling, William, 155
Kline, Lewis, 160, 162
Knapp, Frederick, 94, 219n33
Koster, John, 155

L

Leon, Edwin de, 120
letters, 2, 4, 6, 28, 33, 34, 36, 37; advice, 32, 35–36, 77–78; condolence, 28, 44–45; from front, 38–39, 45, 90, 93, 102, 104–5, 110, 125; from patients, 53, 66–67, 75, 77–78, 93, 105–6; valedictory, 38, 39
Lewis, Jan, 97–98
Lincoln, Abraham, 18, 26, 38, 114, 115, 117, 123–25, 150
Linderman, Gerald, 4
Livermore, Mary, 185, 186–87, 244n36
Locke, John, 15
Long, G. H., 162
Lorenze, John, 51, 53
Loyal Leagues, 135, 137

M

Mackenzie, Robert, 122, 136
manhood, 5–6, 30, 40, 147, 148, 153, 160, 176, 181, 183, 184, 187, 188, 242n20; bourgeois, 24, 34, 35, 36, 162–64; and bravery, 30, 53, 96, 164; civic, 23–24,
167, 172; and emotion, 96, 187; and self-control, 6, 7, 24, 26, 29, 34, 35, 36, 41, 43, 53, 60, 64, 65, 72–74, 98, 160–61, 172, 187
martyrdom, stories of, 2, 18, 28–29, 30, 46, 47, 49, 50, 52
McClary, James, 58
McClay, Wilfred, 141
McPherson, James, 121
McWinnie, James, 77–78, 81
Medical Department (Union), 55, 87, 88, 216–17
mesmerism, 99
Mexico, 114
Mitchel, Franz, 76
Moore, Frank, 130–32
Moore, James, 126
Moorhead, James, 140
Moss, Lemuel, 139
mourning, 9, 10, 158
Moynier, Gustave, 132

N

New England Soldiers' Relief Association, 90
Newman, William, 76
Nightingale, Florence, 130, 135
Norton, Charles Eliot, 114–15, 131
nurses, 56, 105–7, 223n74; accounts by, 51, 57, 60, 61, 62, 67, 80, 105, 185, 243n26; male, 68; stories of, 2, 64–65, 68, 84, 167, 184–85; volunteer, 56, 80, 88, 89, 90, 93, 105–8

O

officers (Confederate), 62, 82
officers (Union), 55, 66, 170; deaths of, 29, 30, 45, 46, 49; and family, 29, 30, 35, 36; incompetence of, 41–42, 88; qualities of, 29, 30, 34, 39, 41, 46, 72; stories of, 2, 4, 6, 28–29, 30, 44–46, 148–50, 170
Ogden, Sarah, 105–6
Olmsted, Frederick Law, 21–22, 59

P

pain, 8, 10, 11, 12, 57, 67, 69, 156; and
class, 11–12, 19–20, 40, 193n14;
enduring, 13–14, 57, 70, 82; and
gender, 11–12; infliction of, 13, 19,
100; insensitivity to, 13, 193n14; and
medicine, 10–11, 19, 69, 83; moral
value of, 11, 12, 13; and race, 11–12,
14. *See also* suffering

Palmer, Henry, 158

patriotism, 2, 22, 23, 26, 32, 34, 44, 84,
85, 139–40, 176; in stories, 2, 4, 30,
42, 50, 51, 57, 113. *See also under*
soldiers (Union); suffering

penmanship competitions, 7, 144–46,
148, 155–56, 235n13, 235n18

Penn Relief Association, 90

pensions, veteran, 147, 151, 155, 170,
234n6

Pernick, Martin, 12, 13

Perrine, Thomas, 159

Philadelphia Ladies Aid Society, 90

photography, 9, 36, 50, 54, 55, 81, 99,
136, 137, 138, 160

phrenology, 46

physicians. *See* doctors

"pluck," 53, 72, 80, 83, 162–64

Pomroy, Rebecca, 106

Powell, John Wesley, 170–71

prisoners of war, 136–38, 231n73

prosthetic limbs, 159–60, 174,
237nn47–49

Protestantism, 16–17, 40–41, 46, 91, 140,
244n37

providentialism, 82, 113–14, 140, 142,
146, 156, 176, 182–83

punishment: capital, 13; corporal, 13,
20, 21

Putnam, Katherine, 41, 49–50

R

Ramsden, John, 117

Randolf, Alfred, 157–58

Reed, William Howell, 64–65

refreshment saloons, 88, 90, 100, 126,
130. *See also* soldiers' rests

Republican Party, 22, 26, 130, 135, 143,
176–77

Riebsam, Pvt., 80

Robb, Benjamin, 76

Robinson, Rufus, 161

Roebuck, John, 119

Rogers, Sgt., 80

Rollins, George, 75

Rome, William, 80

Roosa, Calvin, 78–80

Rosenberg, Charles, 69

S

Schantz, Mark, 4–5, 9

Schofield, Gen., 141

Schultz, Jane, 106

Sentell, Henry, 66

sentimentalism, 14, 19–20, 25–27, 93,
96, 98, 172, 176, 181, 183, 199n60; in
stories, 2, 4, 9, 18–19, 26, 57, 86–87,
121–22, 126, 156

Shaftesbury, 3rd Earl of (Anthony Ashley Cooper), 14

Sickles, Daniel, 72, 171–72

Silber, Nina, 178–79

slavery, 13, 14, 20–21, 63–64, 118–19,
120, 131, 179–80; as national shame,
18, 140; opposition to, 21, 64, 123–24.
See also abolition (of slavery); emancipation (of slaves)

slaves, 12; depictions of, 14, 19, 65;
emancipated, 90, 116, 124, 142, 148,
179. *See also* African Americans

Smith, Adam, 14, 15

Smith, Adelaide, 185

soldiers (Confederate), 53, 60–61, 62–63,
82, 120, 182

soldiers (Union), 1, 4, 23–24, 34–35, 37,
52–53, 55, 60–61, 93, 115, 121–22,
123, 133–34, 136, 141, 148, 177,
181–82, 183; African American,
60, 64, 82–83, 114, 122, 133, 148,

soldiers (Union) (*continued*)
  184; bravery of, 35, 52, 57, 114, 121;
  compassion of, 62–63; deaths of,
  52–53; drafted, 159; and faith, 4, 5,
  59, 62, 85, 122, 139, 141, 181, 182;
  and family, 37, 51, 55, 57, 59, 85, 93,
  94, 97, 100–101, 102, 122, 176, 181;
  patriotism of, 23, 35, 51, 57, 59, 123,
  168–69; self-control, 22, 72, 168 (*see
  also* "pluck"); selflessness, 59, 181;
  stoicism, 59, 60; suffering of, 22,
  51–52, 53–54, 55, 57–59, 62, 66–67,
  72–73, 106, 208n5. *See also* volunteers,
  military
Soldiers' Depot (NY), 95–96, 108, 109
soldiers' homes (convalescent), 85, 88, 90,
  94, 95
soldiers' rests, 90–91, 108. *See also* refreshment saloons
Souder, Emily, 60
Spence, James, 137–38
Spencer, Herbert, 183
spiritualism, 9, 99
Stanton, Edwin, 136
Stearns, Amanda, 80
Steiner, Lewis H., 92
Stillé, Charles Janeway, 122–23
Stowe, Harriet Beecher, 19, 124, 125
Stowe, Jonathan, 67–70, 75
suffering: and class, 8, 9, 22, 72–73, 151;
  and culture, 8, 9, 22; exemplary, 51–
  52, 53–54, 57–59, 61, 65–66, 68–69,
  74, 76–77, 81, 82–83, 84, 144–46,
  156, 186; and faith, 1, 2, 4, 17, 18, 20,
  30, 40–41, 42, 51, 53, 65, 67, 69–70,
  75, 82, 145, 146, 156, 170, 174, 182;
  idealization of, 3, 5, 7, 18, 25, 27,
  58–59, 176; and manhood, 5–6, 61,
  65, 146, 156, 182; mental, 8, 74; moral
  aspects, 2, 11, 16–17, 19, 40, 53, 61,
  101; and Northern identity, 5–6, 7,
  8, 22, 53–54, 60–61, 82–83, 114;
  and patriotism, 58, 61, 70, 75–76, 82,

115, 146, 152, 174; physical (*see* pain);
  and race, 9, 22, 25, 60, 64–65, 82–83,
  212n41; and self-control, 7, 21, 49, 51,
  53, 60–61, 65, 67, 69, 72, 73–74, 83,
  152, 161, 162–64, 174, 184 (*see also*
  "pluck"); stories of, 2, 3, 5, 6–7, 8, 14,
  18–19, 20, 26–27, 34, 42, 51, 52–53,
  57, 59–60, 64–65, 66–67, 68–69,
  74–75, 82, 84, 93, 176; surveillance of,
  76–80, 82
surgeons. *See* doctors
Sydney, Phillip, 47
sympathy, 8, 13, 14–16, 25–27, 62–63,
  82, 84, 100, 110, 176; and class, 9, 14,
  20, 25–26; and morality, 14–17; and
  race, 9, 26; in South, 63–64; theories
  of, 14–16; and women, 63, 82, 85

T

telegraph, 36, 42, 55, 99
temperance movement, 19, 68, 107, 111,
  122, 185, 243n27
Thomas, Will, 148
Thompson, John, 169
Thompson, J. P., 140
Thornton, Tamara, 162
Toller, Ernst, 172
Tuckerman, Henry, 118–19
Tuttle, Alfred, 156–57
Twain, Mark, 4, 171–72

U

Unitarians, 94
United States Christian Commission,
  91–92, 101–2, 107–8, 125, 139,
  218n22
United States Sanitary Commission, 37,
  59, 80, 85–86, 89–90, 91–95, 101,
  104, 107–8, 116–17, 125, 135, 139,
  142–43, 147, 217n11, 234n8; criticism of, 116–17; English Branch, 132,
  134–36, 138; gender division in, 86,
  89, 92–95, 129; leadership, 86, 89–90,

92, 96–97, 100–101, 129, 132–33, 217n15; philosophy of, 86, 89–90, 94–95, 135; and prisoners of war, 136, 137; scholarship on, 85–86, 92–95, 116, 129–30, 132
urbanization, 18, 178, 185

V

Vaughan, Mary, 130–31
Veteran Reserve Corps, 153, 236n26
veterans, 147, 150, 164, 171, 172–73, 175–76, 180, 181
voluntarism, 7, 85–112, 113, 115, 116, 145, 146; and domesticity, 84, 96–97, 109–10; as emotional connection, 89, 101–5, 110, 139–40; and faith, 89, 90–92, 94, 96, 131, 135, 139; and family, 93; idealization of, 22, 84–112, 123, 125–29, 130–32, 133, 139, 141–43, 167, 184–85; paternalism of, 86, 96, 108–9, 126, 156, 176; scholarship on, 85–86, 89–90, 209n15; among women, 37, 84–85, 86–87, 92, 93, 110, 111, 125, 129, 130–31, 184–86, 224nn91–92
volunteer organizations, 88–96, 102, 104, 114, 116, 135; memorialization of, 113–43. *See also* United States Sanitary Commission; *and specific organizations*
volunteers, civilian, 55, 56–58, 68, 88, 89, 91, 92, 103–5, 113, 126, 167, 181. *See also* chaplains; doctors; nurses
volunteers, military, 52, 55–56, 59, 87–88, 113, 123, 126, 146, 164

W

Washington, George, 54, 121
Western Sanitary Commission, 90, 125
Whalen, Robert, 172
Wharncliffe, Lord, 138
Whitehouse, Alfred, 165
Whitehouse, Phineas, 157, 168, 235n13
Whitman, Walt, 4, 80–81
Williams, Hiram, 74–75
Wittenmyer, Annie, 107, 185
Women's Relief Corps, 175
Woodbridge, Sarah, 108
World War I, 72, 111, 159, 172–73, 191n11
Wormeley, Katherine Prescott, 129–30
wounded, on display, 80–81. *See also* amputees: depiction of